T0330019

TRANSATLANTIC SPECULATIONS

TRANSATLANTIC SPECULATIONS

Globalization and the Panics of 1873

HANNAH CATHERINE DAVIES

Columbia University Press
New York

Columbia University Press
Publishers Since 1893
New York Chichester, West Sussex
cup.columbia.edu

Library of Congress Cataloging-in-Publication Data
Names: Davies, Hannah Catherine, author.
Title: Transatlantic speculations : globalization and the panics of 1873 / Hannah
    Catherine Davies.
Description: New York : Columbia University Press, [2018] | Includes
    bibliographical references and index.
Identifiers: LCCN 2018012327 | ISBN 9780231185561 (cloth : alk. paper) |
    ISBN 9780231546218 (e-book)
Subjects: LCSH: Depressions—1873—United States | Depressions—1873—Europe |
    Speculation—History—19th century. | Journalism, Commercial—19th century.
Classification: LCC HB3717 1873 .D38 2018 | DDC 330.9/034—dc23
LC record available at https://lccn.loc.gov/2018012327

Cover design: Noah Arlow

CONTENTS

ACKNOWLEDGMENTS

First and foremost I would like to thank Sebastian Conrad who, as advisor of the doctoral thesis on which this book is based, encouraged my interest in the history financial markets and crises from the very beginning and, throughout the years, provided suggestions, advice, and criticism as probing as it was constructive. I would also like to thank my second reader, Michaela Hampf, and the other members of my dissertation committee, whose questions and comments guided me in the process of turning the thesis into a book. At various stages, the German National Academic Foundation, the German Academic Exchange Service, and the German Historical Institute, Washington DC, provided funding for my research, which I gratefully acknowledge.

Over the years, I received important feedback from audiences at various conferences, workshops, and colloquiums, including at Humboldt University of Berlin, Hanover University, Harvard University, the Wissenschaftszentrum Berlin, Basel University, and Frankfurt am Main University. I have especially fond memories of the biannual workshops of the Global History Research Area at the Free University of Berlin, where I presented several first drafts. The discussions there were always a model of scholarly engagement, and I greatly benefitted from them. I would also like to thank all those who commented on individual chapters and/or otherwise generously shared their time and knowledge with me, especially Samuël Coghe, Franziska Davies, Boris Gehlen, Lasse Heerten, Kristin Meißner, Simone Müller, Mischa Suter, and, most of all, Simon Rothöhler. In revising my manuscript for publication, I was aided by my excellent editor, Bridget Flannery-McCoy, and by the very valuable suggestions I received from the anonymous reviewers for Columbia University Press.

Finally, I wish to thank my family for their unfailing support and encouragement. This book is dedicated to my father and to the memory of my mother.

INTRODUCTION

I n July 1866, Henry Villard, a first-generation German American, set sail for Europe, having been commissioned by the *New York Tribune* "to report on the impending war between Prussia and Austria."[1] Upon his arrival, he discovered that the fighting was all but over, and, after a brief tour of the war's battlefields, retired to Munich, where he spent the winter. Following stints in Italy and France, from where he reported on the World Exhibition, he returned to the United States in mid-1868. There he was elected secretary of the newly founded Social Science Association, and he began familiarizing himself with the financing of railroads and banks, a timely topic in a period of frenzied railroad construction. In 1870 Villard's friend Friedrich Kapp, the former immigration commissioner of New York State, who had returned to Germany and become a member of the Berlin City Council and the director of a local bank (as was Villard, Kapp was also German born), advised him that German banks were eagerly snapping up American railroad bonds, and that middlemen between them and American brokerage firms stood to make a fortune.[2]

As was the United States, Prussia was also experiencing a boom in railroad construction. Consequently, when he returned to Germany in 1870 to seek medical advice, Villard decided to engage in financial speculations on the future: he took the opportunity to form contacts with members of the Frankfurt business community and eventually arranged to sell bonds of the Wisconsin Central Railroad (whose president, Gardner Colby, he had befriended in America), to the Frankfurt Vereinsbank, and to the banking house of Jacob Stern. However, his speculations turned quickly sour, as American bonds began falling out of favor with German investors.[3] When German stock markets crashed in September in what soon became known as the *Gründerkrach* ("Promoters' Panic"), German demand for American railroad bonds came almost to a standstill. Yet Villard quickly adjusted to the new situation and began working on behalf of German bondholders who feared they had lost their investments in American railroads. For Villard, the financial crisis of 1873 marked the beginning of a highly successful and remunerative business career. When he died in 1900, he was widely considered one of the most influential business figures of his age.[4]

Financial eruptions were numerous in 1873. They were dispersed geographically, stretching from Vienna to Berlin and New York. All three countries—Austria, Germany, and the United States—had experienced a boom in railroad building and a proliferation of corporations. Investors had optimistically flocked to these new enterprises, buying their securities in the hope that they would increase in value and yield high rates of return. Not content with domestic opportunities, German capitalists had even sent their money overseas in search of ever-higher yields. The structure began to unravel in 1872, slowly at first and then quickening. European investors turned their back on American securities early that year, and the American money market tightened in autumn, a stringency that lasted well into 1873. The Berlin bourse began a slow, protracted decline in December. In May, the Viennese stock market crashed, suddenly and forcefully. Finally, in September, New York and Berlin followed suit.

Contemporaries saw connections between these distant yet similar events. Some, such as Villard, had actively forged such links; to others, they were palpable, though elusive; and still others wondered whether they existed at all or were a mere chimera. Although we cannot glean from Villard's letters whether he anticipated the meltdown on the stock markets during that fateful year, we may surmise that he, more than others, closely observed what was happening on financial markets. He had, after all, been aware for many months that the mood among German investors had soured. To others, the crash and its consequences came unexpectedly. The realist writer Gottfried Keller would later describe it thus:

> From beyond the ocean came one of those grim crises and enveloped the entire commercial world, and shook the House of Glor, which seemed to be standing so firm, with such force that it was almost destroyed and withstood only with great distress. . . . Masses of commodities lay devalued on the other side of the seas, every claim was all but lost, and the accumulated wealth disappeared by the hour together with the high-yielding securities in which it was invested, so that in the end only landed property and some inherited ancient land titles remained. But this was to be sacrificed to meet one's own liabilities.[5]

The storm that blew over the House of Glor, an old trading house, came from across the Atlantic, an outside, alien power. Yet Keller also hints at connections, opaque perhaps, and mysterious, but very real in their consequences: transoceanic flows of commodities, chains of paper, virtual symbols of wealth that are drained of their value by an invisible force. Following the panic, this invisible force—"one of those grim crises"—became the object of another kind of speculation: interpretative speculation. Who and what, contemporaries asked, had caused the panic? Were individuals to blame? Was it the legal or monetary system that was at fault? When and why had financial transactions become a force of their own, and how could they be reined in?

Historians, too, have pondered the question of what caused the panics of 1873, and of whether and how they were linked. Most assumed that they were related, yet the exact nature of this relationship has proven elusive. Charles Kindleberger, for example, along with others, argued the New York panic erupted partly as a consequence of European investors turning their backs on American securities. Yet this had begun in early 1872, while the American panic only erupted eighteen months later.[6] More recently, Scott Nelson blamed the Bank of England for raising interest rates in the wake of the Vienna panic in May, thus causing financial distress among banks in New York. But the American money market in the spring of 1873 became less, not more, stringent than it had been during previous months.[7]

While such questions of causality are intriguing and may yield valuable insights, they capture only part of the story and often leave much room for uncertainty, as these arguments show. More importantly, however, they are to some extent ahistorical in that they neglect an important dimension: the way contemporaries—before, during, and after the panic—forged, perceived, and experienced transnational capital flows and financial contagion. Both Henry Villard and the Swiss House of Glor form part of the story of the panics of 1873, and yet their experiences differed markedly. Bankers, merchants, investors, journalists, and policymakers each occupied different locations within the transatlantic economy, and it is to their actions and experiences that we must look if we seek to comprehend the nature and scope of this brief but disruptive and far-ranging event.

Drawing on investment manuals, newspaper articles, advertisements, business correspondence, credit reports, pamphlets, legal treatises, and parliamentary debates, this book maps the "transatlantic speculations" of the 1870s: the financial speculations born of exuberance as well as the interpretative speculations born of crisis. It explores why and how investors were prompted to put their money into far-away enterprises, and how journalists and bankers created and spread financial information (and disinformation) and, through words and actions, made and unmade transatlantic flows and connections. It analyzes the interpretative frameworks people used to make sense of the panic, the ways in which they informed policy responses, and what this in turn reveals about contemporary notions of the world economy and transnational economic relations.

In harnessing these issues, I intend to make a larger argument about the relationship between capitalism, finance, and globalization. In the course of this study, my aim is to show how the peculiarly abstract, virtual, and expansive nature of financial markets produced certain forms of narration and interpretation that rendered financial relations real, concrete, and material. During the nineteenth century, financial markets grew both in scope and in size, increasingly transcending national borders and linking distant places through chains of paper and credit, and drawing in an ever greater number of investors. Contemporaries registered this but at the same time felt that the exact mechanisms of this process appeared strangely elusive. The British journalist and economist Walter Bagehot noted the belief that the money market was "something so impalpable that it could only be spoken of in very abstract words."[8] This seemingly "impalpable" nature of financial markets occasioned a particular kind of hermeneutic exertion: financial activity required constant explanation, an account of what "the play of economic signs" actually referred to. What, contemporaries asked, did price fluctuations and financial markets represent? How were they to be read and interpreted? This preoccupation with the meaning of financial signs has a long pedigree in the history of economic thought.[9] But the interpretation of financial markets was not just a matter of theorists but of economic actors, too, as the panics of 1873 show.

An analysis of the writings and practices that accompanied the speculative bubble and financial crises of the early 1870s, I contend, comprises two basic elements, both neatly captured by the semantics of the term "speculation." "Speculation" can mean both the "action or practice of buying and selling goods, land, stocks and shares, etc., in order to profit by the rise or fall in the market value" and a "conclusion, opinion, view, or series of these, reached by abstract or hypothetical reasoning."[10] The *financial* speculations of this period (i.e., speculation in the former sense) were made by people who, as did Henry Villard, banked on the future to bring growth and formidable returns, a promise that lured more and more investors to try their luck on financial markets. Yet at the same time, the aggregate result of these many individual acts of speculation also appeared as an abstract, inscrutable force, a force that assumed an agency of its own, seemingly eliding human control and intervention, and in 1873, suddenly and disruptively swept across oceans and national borders, destroying values and livelihoods. The *interpretative* speculations that emerged in response to the crisis, I argue, reacted to this expansive nature of finance: they translated the abstract into the personal, the virtual into the material, and the transnational into the national and local.

This mechanism of interpretation, I further argue, also shaped and informed the contemporary experience of transnational connections: precisely because finance required translation and interpretation, perceptions and interpretations of the panics of 1873 were shaped by local and national conditions and experiences. Capitalism, it is often assumed, was and is *the* main agent of globalization, an all-powerful force that, in the words of the *Communist Manifesto*, replaced "the old local and national seclusion and self-sufficiency" with "intercourse in every direction, universal inter-dependence of nations."[11] But as the history of the panics of 1873 reveals, while the interconnectedness of financial markets was acknowledged and pondered during these years, it is also true that subsequent responses and interpretations reveal that the individual panics were, more often than not, considered *national* events. The notion that events of a global scope were interpreted within national frameworks seems familiar enough, but we must think of this not simply as interpreting and nationalizing its *global* aspect but also as an interpretation of *finance*, whose global quality was but one aspect of its expansive nature.

Writing the History of Financial Panics

Although instances of widespread overspeculation were known already in the seventeenth and eighteenth centuries, it was during the nineteenth century that they began recurring with some frequency. This was not least a consequence of an expanding money supply, itself a necessary lubricant of rapidly growing commercial activity. While most economically advanced countries had nominally adopted some sort of specie standard, which was thought to check an unhindered expansion of credit, this could not prevent the development of monetary substitutes. In periods of commercial upswing, new financial instruments such as bills of exchange or clearing-house certificates were used to issue loans well in excess of banks' specie reserves. When credit became overextended, as in 1819, 1837, and 1857, the sudden failure of a well-known firm was often enough to trigger a fear among creditors that their loans would not be paid back, resulting in a scramble for cash and in widespread financial, and then economic, contraction.[12]

What, then, makes financial crises a promising subject of historical inquiry? One reason is that contemporaries perceived them as momentous events in their own time, prompting a wide range of "interpretative speculations," or "panic texts" (Ann Fabian): written explorations of a panic's causes, nature, and consequences, all aiming to attribute meaning to an event which, even as it recurred in different guises throughout the century, continued to challenge contemporary notions of meaning, order, and causality.[13] And it is precisely because crises present a hermeneutic challenge, I propose, that they not only upset but also crystallize and highlight contemporary beliefs, norms, and attitudes that emerge in debates about the nature and meaning of financial markets, individual responsibility, moral economies, and transnational economic relations.[14]

This approach comes with certain implications regarding the methodology, scope, and aims of this book. One is that unlike many studies of financial crises, this study does not intend to identify what the panics of 1873 have in common with other panics, or to what extent they corroborate economic theories of financial crises, a perspective that tends to make such studies "not entirely satisfactory from a historical point of view."[15] Especially economic historians of the cliometric persuasion, to whom we owe a significant part of historical studies of financial crises, are apt to treat them as material that can be used to test models or theories that inform present-day debates. One such long-standing debate concerns the question of what financial crises tell us about the rationality or irrationality of investors, the implicit assumption being that if investors can be shown to have displayed a certain degree of one or the other, the same will apply to our present, a conclusion that might sit uneasily with historians invested in the idea of the uniqueness of historical events.[16] A concern with pressing issues of his time was also what gave rise to the influential study by Oliver M. W. Sprague, who early in the twentieth century used statistics of bank reserves and monetary flows to determine the causes of American financial crises since the early 1860s. His analysis of monetary factors in the making of panics helped make the case for the establishment of the Federal Reserve.[17] Most of these studies rely heavily (though not exclusively) on quantitative data. Charles Kindleberger's by-now classic account, *Manias, Panics, and Crashes*, by contrast, privileged the narrative over the quantitative mode while still espousing the idea of the essential sameness of crises. Written in defiance of the zeitgeist at a time when the last major financial crisis lay in a seemingly distant past, and inspired in part by Hyman Minsky's theory of the credit cycle, Kindleberger set out to show that "the cycle of manias and panics results from the pro-cyclical changes in the supply of credit." His book spanned several centuries and crises in the United States, Asia, Europe, and Latin America.[18] Kindleberger, as did others before and after him, addressed the question of irrationality, assigning it a central place in his explanation of the credit cycle. This book, too, examines these issues. But instead of aiming to provide a timeless theory of crises, corroborating it with quantitative data or recurring structures, I am much more interested in asking how contemporaries constructed and interpreted notions of rationality or theories of the business cycle. This means exploring, for example, how investment manuals depicted rational investment as an essentially masculine activity; or how legal experts and policy-makers perceived the rationality of small-time investors when discussing reforms of shareholder protection regulations. Likewise, I examine nineteenth-century theories of the business cycle to show how contemporaries used them to make sense of developments in financial markets.

Other studies of the 1873 crises have adopted a social or political history approach, often focusing on how, during the years immediately following the crash, the experience of economic hardship gave rise to class conflict and political realignment. Thus Samuel Rezneck, in an article published in the 1950s, explored how rising unemployment and the perception of widespread economic stagnation shaped labor struggles and welfare policies in the United States. Similarly, Hans Rosenberg, in his famous study *Große Depression und Bismarckzeit*, interpreted shifts in German domestic politics and the popularity of anti-Semitic conspiracy theories as a reflection of economic developments such as declining price levels and lower rates of growth. Although Rosenberg did not examine the bubble period of the early 1870s, his approach is similar to mine in that he, too, was interested in contemporaries' experiences and perceptions. Unlike Rosenberg, however, I do not subscribe to the idea that these were simply a reflection of long-term economic trends.[19] More recently, Nicolas Barreyre has argued that the panic of 1873 led to a realignment in American politics by bringing the issue of monetary policy to the fore and simultaneously marginalizing other issues, ultimately bringing about an end to Republican dominance in American politics and thus ending Reconstruction in the South.[20]

While all these studies dealt with the "panic" or "crisis" of 1873 in one way or another, they ascribed different meanings to these terms. In its narrowest definition, to which Kindleberger and Sprague subscribe, the event encompasses a period of about two or three weeks in late September and early October 1873, during which several American banks and brokers failed or suspended, and the New York Stock Exchange (NYSE) temporarily closed its doors.[21] Social and political historians, by contrast, pay scant attention to this *financial* crisis or panic but, instead, focus on the *economic* crisis it triggered, which dragged on for several years. This is arguably due to the fact that economic crises often engender social conflict and, consequently, political upheaval.[22]

My approach combines elements of both the former and the latter. Throughout this study, I will use (interchangeably) the words "panic" and "crisis" or "financial crisis" to denote those periods (in May 1873 in Vienna, and in September/October 1873 in New York and Berlin) when stock markets crashed, prices fell, and investors scrambled for cash. The terms do not, however, encompass the protracted period of contraction and stagnation in trade and industry that followed. To analyze and interpret the panics of 1873, I proceed roughly chronologically, devoting two chapters to the years preceding the panic to describe and analyze some of the factors that caused and enabled it. In the third chapter, I explore in detail the panics themselves and how they played out in Vienna, New York, and

Berlin. In the following three chapters, I examine some of the panic's consequences in the late 1870s and early 1880s. My focus here is exclusively with issues such as currency reform and shareholder protection, which became important topics during this period because they were seen to have caused the initial *financial* crisis. This means bracketing other major issues of the day, such as debates on tariff policy and unemployment, which were indirect consequences, not causes, of the panic in the financial sector.

Another difference between my book and the current literature is that I intend to examine the panic from a comparative and transnational angle. While several authors allude to the fact that financial panics occurred in different places in quick succession in 1873, and briefly indicate what may explain this simultaneity, this aspect has thus far not been examined in a systematic fashion.[23] What is more, although scholars have pointed out possible cross-border mechanisms of contagion or analogous causes, the issue has not been explored on the level of perceptions and experiences.

On the most basic level, examining Germany, Austria, and the United States will be fruitful simply because these countries were the main locales of the financial panics of 1873.[24] Going beyond such practical reasons, however, there are a number of points that suggest that while they share many economic, political, and social characteristics, they are at the same time sufficiently different to be usefully juxtaposed: In the 1860s and 1870s, both Germany and the United States were industrial newcomers and in the process of catching up with Great Britain, still the leading industrial nation in the world at that time. Both were engaged in international commerce on a significant scale. Austria's industry, by contrast, was smaller and its foreign trade less important.[25] All three countries saw a boom in railway construction during this period, which, in the American case, was bound up with the "process of conquering and populating the American hinterlands as the outer edge of an expanding capitalism,"[26] a distinguishing feature that sets it apart from the two European countries. Regarding finance and banking, both Austria and the United States had abandoned the specie standard during the 1860s. Germany, by contrast, remained on a silver standard until 1873. While both Germany and Austria had national central banks, this was not true of the United States. Finally, Germany had recently fought a victorious war of national unification, an experience it shared with the United States but not with Austria. Taken together, these commonalities and differences constitute a fertile ground for teasing out the intricate enmeshment of different scales and planes in an age that was marked both by the consolidation of nation states and national institutions on the one hand, and growing transnational integration on the other.

The panics of 1873 were a symptom and a manifestation of a process which many historians, taking their cue from social scientists, refer to as "globalization."[27] When historians first began exploring its history in the 1990s, Frederick

Cooper argued that a one-sided focus on interconnectedness and linearity, a notion of globalization as "the progressive integration of different parts of the world into a singular whole," risked falling victim to a teleological view of history.[28] Indeed, historians now agree that globalization happened neither evenly nor steadily. Rather, it is widely acknowledged that periods of growing economic integration were followed by periods in which the process of economic integration decelerated or stalled. Thus economic historians used evidence of a convergence in wages and commodity prices in the transatlantic economy to demonstrate the degree of economic integration in the last third of the nineteenth century while also stressing that globalizing forces led to a backlash in the form of, for example, tariffs and growing immigration restrictions, and, in some instances, contributed to a rising economic inequality rather than creating uniformity.[29] Globalization, then, is best understood not as a linear development toward ever-increasing interconnectedness but as a process in which phases of increasing interaction were followed by phases of increasing isolation.[30] Moreover, it did not just entail growing homogeneity and uniformity but could, at the same time, also create differences and hierarchies.[31]

These ambiguities and complexities apply both to the economic and to the cultural aspects of globalization. Some scholars have welcomed the interest in the history of globalization because it promised a renewed emphasis on economic questions after many years in which these were marginalized in favor of a focus on cultural history, discourse, and the constitution of meaning.[32] But seeing these approaches as mutually exclusive comes with pitfalls of its own. Thus, there is a tendency to write about the history of nations and empires, and of economic growth and revolutions without submitting these categories to a critical analysis, questioning their implicit premises, or asking how they were constructed and debated by contemporaries.[33] With this in mind, this book aims to explore how actors made and interpreted transnational economic flows and connections. Instead of simply assuming the existence of a world market as a given, it asks what type of information, narratives, and categories people had at their disposal to make sense of it, and how cultural norms and concepts informed their behavior as actors within this market. When contemporaries used terms such as "world" and "worldwide," these were not, I maintain, simply descriptions and reflections of a process of economic integration happening in front of their eyes but, rather, claims about a world order that were heavily loaded with, and informed by, specific interests and power relations.[34] Perceptions and experiences of globalization were, just as was their material counterpart, a heterogeneous affair, neither growing in a linear fashion nor devoid of ambiguities. In the case of 1873, "global consciousness" during this period was uneven and asymmetrical, more pronounced in some localities than in others while never entirely supplanting a vision of the world and the world market in which nations and national economies remained central players.

In examining these questions, I also intend to elucidate the relationship between global, national, and local factors. There is now something of a consensus that globalization must not be considered a process of diffusion by which a non-Western periphery received and absorbed trends and developments originating in the West. Rather, they were "accepted selectively, reshaped and sometimes recycled with the result that it is now hard to distinguish source from recipient."[35] While my study remains confined to two European countries and the United States, this perspective nevertheless informs my approach in that I consider how national factors influenced contemporaries' responses to, and interpretations of, the 1873 financial crisis. In examining this interrelationship between global and national factors, the panics of 1873 present an especially promising case study, for they happened at a time when globalization, compared to earlier decades, was rapidly gaining in speed in speed and visibility.[36]

For all the emphasis on language and culture, this book does not intend to downplay the importance of hard, material factors of economic and social processes. Rather, it shows how the capital flows and investment decisions that produced the bubble and subsequent panic were embedded culturally, socially, and institutionally in investment discourses, organizational structures of stock exchanges, and concepts of financial information and market integration. While factors such as the money supply, technology and legal frameworks are necessary to explain the panics' preconditions and timing, careful attention to concepts, experiences, and discourse is necessary to understand *how* they unfolded. Hard institutional and economic factors and soft cultural ones were interdependent and shaped one another.[37] In this context, comparisons between the three countries can be useful to better describe and determine this relationship. In some instances, national institutional differences may help explain disparate developments on the level of discourse, while in other instances, the relationship is reversed. This book relies on such comparative approaches both to tease out the relationship between local, national, and transnational factors, as well as that between cultural and material ones. To achieve this, it will not always be necessary to engage in a symmetrical three-way comparison. The focus will, depending on the issues at stake, sometimes lie in one or two locales, and refer to the others as a way of highlighting and defining salient features and developments.[38] Such comparisons, of course, are not without risk. As scholars critical of the method have remarked, a comparative approach tends to assume the existence of the national framework as a given, and to overemphasize national differences at the expense of transfers and exchange. Mindful of such potential dangers, this book does not aim simply to affirm the existence of different (national) traditions or varieties of capitalism, whose validity has, in any case, been increasingly questioned in recent years.[39] Rather, the issues examined here—such as the perception of transnational connections, the role of the press, and the shape and significance of currency debates—are in many ways orthogonal to categories traditionally examined by scholars of the varieties of capitalism debate.

This book, then, zooms in on one particularly momentous period in time to examine how contemporaries made, experienced, and perceived financial flows, and to elucidate their responses when these flows suddenly and forcefully stopped. It opens with the late 1860s, just as the bubble was forming, and ends with the 1880s, a decade in which the forces of globalization were once again in the ascendant.

TRANSATLANTIC SPECULATIONS

CHAPTER 1

SETTING THE STAGE

*Institutions and Cultures of Speculation in the 1860s and
Early 1870s*

During the course of the nineteenth century, stock exchanges
had evolved from small, infrequent gatherings of merchants to
become large, thriving institutions. This evolution had been
neither linear nor steady; stock markets had always been characterized by
alternating periods of frenzied trading and periods in which the speed
of transactions slowed, prices declined, and investors withdrew from the
market. By the early 1870s, securities trading was once again in the ascendant: investors were in a buoyant mood, and companies were hungry for capital, thus producing a self-reinforcing momentum that would come to an
abrupt halt in 1873. The first part of this chapter examines how bourses in the
United States, Austria, and Germany responded to and enabled this development by adapting their regulations in order to accommodate the growing
demand for securities. But this growing appeal was not simply a cause and
consequence of changing economic and institutional structures. Rather, as I
will show in the second half of this chapter, changing discourses of investment helped legitimize securities trading as a productive, demanding, and
complex economic activity. Although these developments could be found in
all three countries, the cultures of finance were by no means uniform, and the
way Germans and Austrians rendered financial markets intelligible differed in
significant ways from American discourses and practices, a fact that was not
lost on contemporaries and would inform their subsequent experience of the
1873 panics.

Burgeoning Economies

The early 1870s were a time of optimism for producers and investors in the Western world. Unlike in previous decades, production was keeping pace with growing populations, allowing more and more people to enjoy higher incomes. The growing accumulation of capital in turn stimulated investment and spurred the development of new techniques and commodities. Steamships and railroads, which had made their first appearance during the first half of the nineteenth century, were now being constructed at a rapid pace, moving goods and people at an ever faster speed and creating new markets and new sources of supply. At the same time, a growing network of telegraphic cables facilitated the transmission of political and financial news and information. The laying of the first transatlantic cable in 1866 and the opening of the Suez Canal in 1869 were two events that prominently demonstrated the growing interconnectedness of the nineteenth-century world. Together, the new technologies spurred on the integration of national and international markets, a process that was aided by a widespread belief in the beneficial effects of free trade. Europe during this period came as close as it ever did during the nineteenth century "to attaining the ideal trading conditions postulated by classical economic theory."[1]

Political events and developments left contemporaries convinced that they were witnessing truly momentous transformations. Germany's victory in the Franco-Prussian War prompted euphoric jubilations, and looking back just two years later, the Berlin Association of Merchants noted that the establishment of peace between the two countries had triggered "an activity so sustained and energetic in all branches that has rarely been experienced."[2] Following a series of reforms in the late 1860s, which had introduced freedom of trade and freedom of movement, a stream of workers seeking employment in the city's industry poured into the German capital, resulting in a rapid population growth. The year 1870 saw an overhaul of German corporation law. Now, in keeping with the contemporary spirit of economic liberalism, promoters of corporations were no longer required to obtain a government license for their enterprise, and new corporations proliferated. When the French government started paying the war indemnity that had been laid down in the 1871 peace treaty in Versailles—it would eventually total five billion francs—the government immediately began retiring its debt. Suddenly flush with yet more capital, investors eagerly snatched up the securities of the newly formed corporations.[3]

While military triumphs could imbibe the public mood with a spirit of optimism and contributed to an already favorable economic environment, the latter was not dependent on the former, as the Austrian case shows. Though Austria succumbed to Prussia's military might in 1866, the war effort also forced the finance minister to expand the money supply, a decision which, despite dire warnings to the contrary, proved beneficial to Austria's economic recovery. By happy coincidence, a series of "wonder harvests" began in 1867, just as the gulden depreciated in response to the government's monetary policy, triggering an export boom that was to last into the early 1870s. This newly acquired wealth soon made its way onto the stock market in Vienna, where it triggered a speculative frenzy, resulting in a first crash in 1869. Investors, however, were not spooked for long, and prices on the Vienna bourse quickly resumed their upward movement.[4]

In the United States, the Union's victory in 1865 ushered in a period of large-scale nation building, as Reconstruction in the South coincided with western expansion and the need to integrate millions of newly arrived European immigrants, a period which, as Mark Twain and Charles Dudley Warner would famously observe at the height of the speculative bubble, "uprooted institutions that were centuries old, changed the politics of a people, . . . and wrought so profoundly upon the entire national character that the influence cannot be measured short of two or three generations."[5] In the United States, too, the government had been forced to suspend specie payments and issue paper money in response to exigencies of the war economy, and here, too, the period that followed was one of rapid economic growth as the pace of industrialization quickened, factories multiplied and mechanized rapidly, and novel technologies spurred productivity gains and the development of new industries. As merchants, manufacturers, and bankers reaped the profits, land values in New York City's fashionable districts soared, and a residential construction boom developed in the nation's economic capital.[6] Looking back on the past decade, a leading American journal wondered in 1870, in the midst of a brief contraction, whether the "era of speculation" was about to end. The violent price fluctuations of the postwar era that had enriched many a speculator, it argued, would soon be a thing of the past, and the country was about to settle into a more stable state of affairs.[7] But the postwar business cycle had yet to run its course; by 1871, expansion was under way once more.[8]

Well into the second half of the nineteenth century, the business cycle had been largely determined by the agricultural sector, and the size and timing of harvests. By the late 1860s, however, with industrialization making rapid headway, cycles of investment in the secondary sector began dominating the rate of growth of the entire economy, at least in the four largest national economies. In Germany and the United States (as well as in Great Britain and France), the relatively largest share of real capital investment was absorbed by railroads, which accounted for 25 and 20 percent of net investments respectively.[9] In Germany, railroads had been the dominant factor of economic growth since the 1850s. By 1850, 5,875 kilometers of railroad tracks had been laid in the area of the German Confederation. By 1870, this number had risen to 18,810. The following three years saw a further increase of more than 5,000 kilometers.[10] In the United

States, in 1860, railroads already traversed a distance of 30,000 miles. Investment in railroads virtually ceased during the Civil War but picked up rapidly in the second half of the decade, not least thanks to western expansion and the construction of the first transcontinental railroads. Between 1868 and 1873, an additional 29,589 miles of railroads were built.[11] On a smaller scale, Austria-Hungary, too, witnessed a similarly rapid growth of its railway network, from 6,125 kilometers in 1866 to 15,597 kilometers seven years later, an increase of 155 percent. As in Germany, the growth of the railway industry spilled over to other sectors, most notably the mining and iron industries.[12]

Unlike in earlier decades, when founders of new companies had relied on their family's capital for investments, the sheer size and scope of railroads meant they had to turn to a relatively novel form of financing, the corporation. In a corporation, the managers of the company were no longer identical with its owners. Instead, shares in the company were sold to a large number of investors, who, in return for their capital, acquired the right to vote in shareholder meetings and the chance to profit from the company's earnings in the form of dividends. Investors took to this new financial instrument because, unlike in a partnership, their financial liability was by and large limited to the size of their original investment. Moreover, company shares were readily tradable and could be converted into cash at short notice, though their price was necessarily volatile, potentially exposing investors to high gains as well as sharp losses.

To help them place their securities with the general public, corporations enlisted the services of investment banks, whose role as financial intermediaries had originated in the 1850s. They purchased blocks of securities and sold them first to special clients and friends, and then, via the stock exchange, to the larger investing public. Occasionally, a significant number of shares remained on the bank's books, making it essentially an institutional coowner, and providing it with long-term influence over the company's direction. Some of these banks were privately owned while others were incorporated. In Germany, the number of such *Kreditbanken* grew rapidly during the early 1870s, from 31 in 1870 to 139 two years later; many not only placed securities for clients but also, themselves, founded corporations. Many of these young banks would not survive the crash, finding themselves squeezed by the declining value of securities on their books and outstanding liabilities.[13] The reputable private banking house Mendelssohn & Co., for example, burned its fingers when it joined forces with an engineer in floating an unsuccessful railway construction company that went into liquidation in 1875. The bank survived but henceforth avoided the business of industrial financing.[14] In New York during the early 1870s, banker George Opdyke first made advances to the New York & Oswego Midland Railroad Company and was subsequently made its president. He spent much of 1872 trying to sell its securities, with mixed success. During the following years, a large number of them remained unrealizable and on the banks' books.[15]

At the Vienna exchange, the number of securities listed increased from 169 to 605 between 1867 and 1873.[16] In Germany, following the overhaul of corporation law in 1870, the number of new corporations officially traded on the Berlin Stock Exchange rose from 32 in 1870 to a high of 275 just two years later.[17] Although the United States had been the first country to become "suffused with corporations," incorporation there proceeded at an altogether steadier pace in the late 1860s and early 1870s.[18] At the NYSE the number of railroad companies listed grew from 32 in 1865 to 71 in 1871.[19] While the total number of new corporations (both listed and unlisted) continued to grow in line with the trajectory of general business, there seems to have been no sudden increase in the rate of incorporation.[20] More so than in Germany and Austria, the bubble on American financial markets of the early 1870s was concentrated in the railroad sector, and especially in bonds, with the number of railroad bonds listed on the NYSE increasing from 39 in 1867 to 91 in 1871 and 141 in 1873.[21]

Rapid economic growth also provided a fertile ground for trade unions. Laborers in all three countries organized, often successfully, to demand shorter working days and higher wages, wishing to partake in the gains of the economic boom visible around them.[22] At the same time, large-scale immigration from the countryside to Berlin resulted in an acute housing shortage, and several hundred families that had been evicted from their homes found themselves forced to live in shantytowns outside the city's gates. Journalists both denounced these as "objects of disgust" and hailed them as "evidence of the heroic German spirit," reflecting a prevalent spirit of unbridled optimism unfazed even at salient manifestations of poverty and distress.[23] In 1872, protests against rising rents erupted in a working class area of Berlin only to be met by a violent crackdown by the city's police.[24] In New York, Irish and Protestant workers clashed in 1871, and urban disorder and riots ensued, leading to the unraveling of "Boss" Tweed's regime, which had created social peace through a "system of public aid and patronage jobs for the city's working class."[25] Occasionally, laborers in their struggles directly alluded to developments on financial markets, arguing that promoters engaged in fraudulent stock market activities were depriving them of the fruits of their labor. From this perspective, low wages were illegitimate especially where dividends for capitalists were high.[26] Mostly, however, the trajectory of financial markets was not the subject of much debate in labor circles. Conversely, social protest and strikes appeared less threatening to authorities and investors than in earlier decades and could not dampen the optimism prevalent on financial markets.[27]

Stock Exchanges in New York, Vienna, and Berlin

Stocks and bonds were traded on exchanges that had served as marketplaces for investors for several decades, evolving from small and infrequent gatherings of merchants in the early nineteenth century to large, bustling hubs of capitalism by the late 1860s. When trading in securities first became institutionalized in the late eighteenth and early nineteenth century, the market had been dominated by government bonds, which were issued en masse as cash-strapped governments struggled to defray war-related expenses. In Vienna, Empress Maria Theresa, in 1761, announced the establishment of a stock exchange, noting that the price of government bonds had dropped because owners wishing to sell them had been forced to do so in the homes of the prospective buyers, who had deceived them as to the securities' value.[28] In the United States, trading in government debt began when the federal government assumed the Revolutionary war debts of the Continental Congress and the states, though it was only in 1817 that New York brokers formally institutionalized and regulated their dealings in stocks by establishing the New York Stock and Exchange Board.[29] In the German lands, regular trading in securities began in 1805 in Berlin and in 1816 in Frankfurt. As in Vienna, the bourse in Berlin was established by a royal decree. The Frankfurt bourse, by contrast, began as a private institution when merchants formed a trading club, commissioned the construction of a trading house, and agreed to formal regulations.[30]

In the following decades, as stocks and bonds of corporations were added to the list of publicly traded securities, the volume of trading increased, and the exchanges adopted new rules and techniques to accommodate the growing demand. In 1854, the Austrian government passed a law freeing the bourse from the most onerous forms of state control, allowing it to become a largely self-administered institution. In the following nine years, the number of certified agents (*Sensale*) doing business at the stock exchange increased rapidly from 13 in 1854 to 33 in 1863. Membership of the Viennese exchange continued to increase steadily throughout the 1860s, growing threefold between 1868 and 1872. As the number of visitors grew, so did the share of those who had no previous experience with securities trading. In 1872, the share of first-time visitors had grown to 38 percent, and more than a third were private investors, a marked shift from just a few years earlier. In 1863, the *Börsekammer*, the body tasked with the self-administration of the exchange, had lost the right to review the credentials of people seeking membership, and a request to the government that membership be curtailed in 1872 was not granted.[31]

During the same period, the Berlin exchange saw a similar upsurge in business, forcing it to leave its old premises and move into a new, grander building in 1863. As did their Austrian counterparts, Prussian authorities, in keeping with the prevalent liberal zeitgeist, mostly believed that government oversight over securities trading was unnecessary. In 1869, the Prussian finance minister noted that he had no reason to believe that the "unfettered and uncontrolled development of the stock exchange" might harm the "solidity" of Prussia's industry. Excessive speculation, he argued, was most effectively corrected through the freedom of trade, and any restriction could only be harmful in its effects.[32] In this atmosphere, the volume of trading at the Berlin exchange continued to grow, as more and more people began frequenting the bourse, prompting the administration to reduce the size of the seating area to accommodate more visitors. At the same time, the number of certified brokers rose from 37 in 1871 to 110 in 1873.[33] The fact that anybody could trade on the floor in exchange for a fee facilitated this process of rapid expansion. In 1872, visitors to the stock exchange became so numerous that the governing body, the *Korporation*, decided that visitors from outside the city would only be admitted if officially invited by one of its members.[34] In New York, too, the volume of trading exploded with the onset of the Civil War, as investors sensed the manifold opportunities of a war economy. For a short time in 1864, New York even became the only city in the world where one could trade twenty-four hours a day. Following a brief contraction in the mid-1860s, the stock market expanded once again, and in 1869, the number of members was set at 1060, significantly higher than the previous limit.[35] Unlike in Vienna and Berlin, then, admission to the trading room was heavily restricted.

At the same time, this growing demand for securities was met with resistance, as authorities as well as the trading community itself tried to curb what they considered the more worrying excesses of the speculative mood. In all three countries, governments attempted to outlaw the practice of futures trading where investors entered into contracts allowing them to buy or sell securities at an agreed-upon price at a future date, a practice that was deemed immoral and fraudulent and was subject to widespread public condemnation. In practice, however, such laws had little effect, and futures trading continued almost unabatedly, with brokers enforcing contracts privately, without reliance on the legal system.[36]

The rigorous rules of admission at the New York Stock and Exchange Board (renamed New York Stock Exchange [NYSE] in 1863) had prompted the emergence of the curb—more or less institutionalized outside trading groups—almost from the beginning. In 1836, the board had forbidden its members from participating in those groups. During the Civil War, the situation became particularly acute, as the intensified pace of business spawned dozens of separate trading groups. The most important one, the Open Board of Stock Brokers, remained in existence until it merged with the exchange in 1869. Unlike the latter, the Open Board, instead of auctioning stocks at specified times twice a day, adopted the practice of continuous trading, making prices more responsive to current demand.[37] The merger temporarily reduced the number of rival trading groups, though in 1872 the NYSE once again "passed stringent resolutions against members guilty of trading on the street after the close of the Exchange."[38] In Vienna, too, several attempts had been made at suppressing the emergence of unofficial trading sites (*Winkelbörsen*). Despite such efforts, they remained persistent features of the Viennese securities market.[39] In Berlin, outside trading groups operated several unofficial exchanges both in front of the bourse and in coffee houses and pubs. The Sunday exchange was closed down by the police in the 1880s on the grounds that the Korporation der Kaufmannschaft was officially the only body authorized to organize a stock exchange.[40]

As the size of and interest in the securities market increased, brokers developed new techniques to accommodate this demand. At the New York Exchange, an investor wishing to buy securities was only required to deposit 10 percent of the price of the stock with his broker and was thus able to leverage his capital many times over, a practice that became widespread during the 1860s, prompting administrators in 1869 to give brokers specializing in the lending of money and securities a separate post in the stock exchange.[41] In Berlin, in the early 1870s, so-called *Rentenbanken*, many of them recently founded, began allowing customers to pay for shares in installments, enabling even investors of relatively modest means to become shareholders. In a similar vein, banks advanced funds against deposits in the form of shares, a practice known as *Lombardgeschäft*. Individual brokers and agents, too, offered to pay for transactions on a buyer's behalf, usually advancing the requisite funds for a day before charging the customer with the full price of the transaction as well as with a fee to cover the loan. Occasionally, this type of service, which was also common in Vienna and known as *Kostgeschäft*, might cover a longer period than the standard twenty-four hours. Consequently, investors were able to buy shares without possessing the necessary capital.[42]

With the volume of trading rapidly increasing, the settling of accounts became more complex and time consuming, and attempts were made at facilitating and streamlining the process through clearing houses. In Berlin, bankers and merchants could open an account with the Kassenverein, which organized the transfer of securities between the different accounts. A clearing house for futures was established in 1869.[43] Similar efforts were made in New York but proved short-lived, not least because brokers feared the publicity of having to provide lists of purchases and sales.[44] In Vienna, following earlier, unsatisfactory attempts at solving the problem, a bank, the Wiener Giro- und Kassenverein, was tasked with administering the clearing process in 1872. This solution soon became accepted, and the larger part of stock exchange transactions was henceforth settled through the Kassenverein's books without cash changing hands.[45]

The most important new development affecting the nature of securities trading in the nineteenth century, however, was the invention of the telegraph. When cables were first made available for public use in the 1840s, the business of spreading and transmitting news quickly reached an unprecedented scale. On both sides of the Atlantic, newly founded news agencies catered to this growing demand by supplying newspapers all over the country with political, commercial, and financial information. In the German lands, Wolff's Telegraphisches Bureau (WTB) dominated the market for financial news. In 1869, it signed an agreement with the Prussian state stipulating that all cables be submitted to officials of the Königliche Staatsministerium for inspection prior to transmission but exempted telegrams containing markets data and commercial news. The contract also instructed the company to transmit "all publications pertaining to commercial interests . . . only in an equitable manner that precludes every form of preferential treatment."[46]

While the WTB had originally started out as a private company and was only partially nationalized when the British news agency Reuters seemed about to oust the WTB from the German market, its Austrian equivalent, the Telegraphen-Korrespondenz-Bureau, was founded in 1859 as the world's first state-run and state-owned news agency. Although initially created mainly as a tool for controlling and influencing public opinion in political matters, the transmission of commercial and financial news also constituted a significant part of its activities.[47] In 1873, Austria's central telegraphy station moved to a newly erected building just a few meters from the stock exchange.[48] In the United States, the market for news was dominated by the Associated Press, a coalition of regional press associations. Closely aligned with the Western Union (WU), a company that by 1866 controlled more than 90 percent of the telegraphy market, the AP's agents collected national and international news and information and sent it to the WU's Commercial News Department. This in turn "supplied subscribers with a synopsis of prices in the major markets three or four times during business hours, and it also distributed special bulletins of important changes that had occurred."[49]

Previously, bankers and merchants had often relied on private messengers and messaging systems which, by operating faster than the public postal services, enabled them to profit from exclusive information advantages. The telegraph, however, undermined this strategy. Now, political and financial information could be transmitted from one city to another in a matter of minutes and almost immediately spread to a large number of people. Although telegraphy was costly, and hence far from universally accessible, the new technology did diminish the profits that could be made by individuals from arbitrage operations. In earlier periods, securities that were listed on more than one exchange had often traded at different prices. With the invention of the telegraph, such regional price differentials were significantly reduced, as a growing number of arbitrageurs specialized in selling securities between markets, thus ensuring that any discrepancies quickly disappeared.[50] When the transatlantic cable was laid in 1866, the price of cross-listed stocks on the London and New York exchanges likewise converged.[51] When the first ticker—a printing machine connected to the telegraphic network that recorded the market values of securities almost in real time—was installed on Wall Street in 1868, brokers and other investors who did not hold seats on the NYSE no longer had to rely on messenger boys to obtain price information. Instead, they could follow developments on the NYSE from their homes and offices.

While these developments point to a popularization of securities trading in this period, it is not possible to determine precisely how many people dabbled in stocks. The NYSE stipulated a minimum transaction value of $10,000, meaning that even with a minimum margin of 10 percent, only the wealthy could afford to buy and sell stocks there. But because this minimum transaction value did not apply to the curb, and because the vast majority of corporations were not listed on the NYSE but placed their securities through other channels, it was possible for small investors to purchase stocks and bonds for much smaller amounts.[52] For the Viennese market, too, there is reason to believe that people of moderate means could and did buy stocks. While the minimum transaction value at the Viennese bourse was 5,000 florins, smaller amounts could be bought and sold outside the official trading room.[53] On the German exchanges, an 1861 law prescribed a relatively low minimum value of 50 taler for *Namensaktien* and 100 taler for *Inhaberaktien*. Otherwise, there was no formal minimum transaction value for traders at the Berlin Stock Exchange.

Normalizing Securities Trading

The rapid growth of securities trading in the late 1860s and early 1870s occurred at a time when the academic and popular discourse on speculation no longer simply condemned it as an immoral and unproductive practice. Earlier economic theorists, beginning in the early eighteenth century, had attacked the practice of securities trading, arguing that it drained capital from productive sectors of the economy and was tantamount to gambling. Moral commentators, too, had decried it for fostering corruption, greed, and inequality, and generally corroding the social order.[54] As the century progressed, however, this negative discourse gradually gave way to one that, while not uniformly positive, increasingly began distinguishing between good and bad forms of securities trading and speculation.

As early as 1828, the American economist Willard Phillips had argued that some forms of speculation stabilized prices, while others made them more volatile.[55] Using a different criterion, the anarchist author Pierre-Joseph

Proudhon also attempted to distinguish between good and bad forms of speculation in his widely read *Manuel du spéculateur à la bourse*. According to Proudhon, speculation, by which he meant all forms of entrepreneurship, was legitimate and productive as long as the profit it yielded was an adequate compensation for the risks involved but illegitimate where it depended on inside information and involved little or no risk on the part of the speculator.[56] Going further than Proudhon, two noted German economists, Gustav Cohn and Otto Michaelis, in the 1860s, each published articles arguing that futures trading both in securities and in commodities was essentially a mechanism for extrapolating future prices from present circumstances. Speculation, Michaelis claimed, meant profiting from price differentials without buying and selling the actual objects of trade. This activity was not, as many had previously claimed, fictitious but was intimately connected to production and commerce and influenced prices just as much as "real" trades did.[57] In a similar vein, Cohn asserted that speculation was not just different from gambling but its opposite: "Gambling organises chance to take from one person what it gives to the other, while speculation by contrast tends to annul chance by calculating its effects in advance."[58] However, unlike Michaelis, whose view of speculation was almost uniformly positive, Cohn, while praising the advantages of speculation in theory, nevertheless at the same time denounced the practice, which he found offensive on both moral and aesthetic levels.[59] The arguments made by Michaelis and Cohn soon began permeating into a broader economic discourse outside the confines of academia. Thus in 1871 *Der Welthandel*, a nonacademic journal catering to merchants and nonspecialists interested in questions of world trade, published an article laying out why speculation in commodities and securities benefitted both consumers and investors.[60]

While American economists would only begin studying the phenomenon in depth toward the end of the century (and would then rely heavily on the works of their German precursors),[61] the problem of speculation nevertheless garnered a great deal of attention in the pages of financial journals and other publications aimed at merchants, industrialists, bankers, and brokers. The idea that speculation was beneficial for its price-smoothing effects did not immediately catch on among American commentators. Aiming to rebut the argument that gold speculation had helped prevent an outflow of gold from the United States, a writer for *Bankers' Magazine* argued in 1872 that speculation in securities and commodities added nothing of value if the speculator's only purpose was to buy in order to sell later at a higher price. Unlike Michaelis and Cohn, he claimed that this type of speculation unsettled prices and was therefore unproductive.[62]

In commercial circles, too, speculation continued to be looked upon with suspicion without, however, being considered as fundamentally damaging to one's reputation. Thus in January 1872, an agent for R. G. Dun, America's largest credit reporting agency, noted that New York banker George Opdyke was reputedly very wealthy, but that his bank's reputation was "not of the best kind" since "there has been a constant suspicion that their operations partook largely of a speculative character."[63] Of a stock broker, David B. Van Emburgh, it was said that he was "considered careful & prudent, though is thought to speculate at times," indicating that while speculation was still seen as antithetical to prudence, it was nevertheless conceivable that both traits could coexist.[64]

The pragmatic, everyday aspect of this process of normalizing and legitimating speculation and securities trading, however, manifested itself above all in contemporary investment manuals. The first such manuals were written in the eighteenth century. In the 1860s and 1870s, they multiplied, testifying to the expansion of securities trading in this period.[65] Most often authored by brokers or journalists, they addressed nonprofessional, small-time investors, explained the basic mechanisms of securities trading, and encouraged them to embrace it as a respectable, if complex and demanding form of economic activity. These strategies of normalization were by no means unambiguous or straightforward. Rather, they reveal a complex and sometimes downright paradoxical view of the workings of financial markets and the role of the buyers and sellers of securities. This contradictory nature was inherent in the very meaning of the word "speculation," more common than the word "investment," and encompassing features that we would nowadays consider to be diametrically opposed to each other.[66]

All authors of investment manuals agreed that risk and uncertainty were crucial elements of speculation. But as one broker took pains to point out, in this respect the difference between speculation and other forms of economic ventures was relative, not absolute: "There is, of course, some degree of risk in every form of investment. The tradesman who opens a store can have no guarantee beforehand that his business will prove a success. He may commence with a capital of $5,000 or $50,000, but it is after all a speculation, which, it is needless to say, often ends in failure."[67] Another broker noted that in the past years, many on Wall Street had seen their fortunes rapidly accumulate, and that "speculating in . . . stocks and other monied securities" was "as straightforward and legitimate as that of buying or selling produce, or merchandise of any kind." This was one strategy of normalizing speculation: asserting that "speculation is honorable" and assimilating the trading of securities to the "production paradigm," according to which economic activity consisted of the production and exchange of commodities.[68]

Another strategy of normalizing speculation was to stress that in a speculative venture, the element of risk could be balanced by countervailing forces. The author of a well-known account of Wall Street described how "speculative ideas" had taken hold of Americans in the aftermath of the Civil War: "The events of ten years have educated us into a certain appreciation of hazards, into a greater degree of foresight, into a habit of action which combines conservatism with an aptitude for risks."[69] In this view, conservatism and an appetite for risk did not have to be mutually exclusive. Adopting a similar perspective, investment manuals sought to address this balance and to show how an individual could best calculate, manage, and if possible, minimize risk when buying securities.

Ideally, many observers agreed, a speculator must minimize risk by determining the exact value of a stock. One American author maintained that this was merely a matter of using "reliable statistics regarding the standing of any incorporated company, and the value of its shares and bonds."[70] One Austrian manual was more skeptical, noting that those "wishing to become rich on the stock exchange must enter it with the same spiritual occupation with which an alchemist enters his laboratory."[71] But perhaps not quite content with the dubious implications of this analogy, he was equally keen to assimilate speculation to the paradigm of the modern empirical sciences. The "science of experience" (*Erfahrungswissenschaft*), he claimed, aimed to induce rules from experience and to use them as a guide for future actions, a method that could be applied both to commercial life and to the stock exchange.[72] In a similar vein, American manuals asserted that the "rise and fall in the price of all active stocks, which is daily taking place, is almost invariably preceded by certain signs well known to the careful observer," and that the "speculator, to be successful, must know what he is about; he must have knowledge, and watch the signs of the times."[73]

At the same time, many authors of manuals also observed that fluctuations on the stock exchange could not simply be subsumed under the paradigms of science and production. Prices, it was admitted, could be distorted through "false reports, forged telegrams, and letters, and other such illegitimate means."[74] "The Nabobs of Wall street," another author noted, "are continually forming new enterprises. They tighten money, lock up gold, and raise or depress the price of stocks at will."[75] The same phenomenon was also known in Vienna, Frankfurt, and Berlin: "These are fundamentally the determining element of the stock exchange, all other men of the exchange willingly follow their lead."[76] Accordingly, brokers often recommended themselves to their readers by advertising their "thorough knowledge . . . of the movements of the powerful combinations of capitalists" or their ability of "anticipating large and heavy speculations."[77]

Potentially, this could have undermined the case for speculative knowledge— and, indeed, the rationale for the entire genre of investment manuals. Authors were therefore careful to stress that a speculator would usually succeed in making a profit as long as he observed certain rules. The most common advice was to buy low and sell high, a rule that clearly did not rely on any indicators of an objective "real" or "intrinsic" value. Instead, it simply took advantage of the fluctuating nature of the stock market. Since prices would never stop fluctuating, an investor could simply wait out a period of low prices. Thus one broker advised his readers to "always go with the tide, instead of against it, no matter what your personal opinion may be."[78] In the world of investment manuals, this, fundamentally, was the speculator's dilemma: intelligent investment strategies, they maintained, could in theory be induced from experience and applied to the present. But almost universally, manuals stopped short of specifying what exactly these strategies were, instead confining their advice to the trivial "buy low, sell dear."

Consequently, the speculator, if he wished to be successful, required more than simply intelligence and good judgment. Bridging the gap between the precarious knowledge of past lessons and the often chaotic present required "shrewdness, coolness, mental alacrity," "discretion and common sense," as well as cool-headedness.[79] In some cases, it could even be imperative that determination and mental strength trump what the speculator might consider his own better judgment: "It requires more pluck than capital to take contracts on a line of stocks regardless of one's judgment as to advance or decline, and the rumors relating thereto, but a man of nerve can do it."[80] "Who makes money?" one manual asked. "Is it the man of great experience? No! Is it the cautious, timid man? No! It is the man of bold and fearless action . . . men of speculative minds, that are not too timid to venture and not crazed by success."[81] Indeed, this emphasis on fearlessness coupled with levelheadedness was a corollary to the rule of anticyclical investments: For going against the tide almost certainly required greater affective exertion than jumping on the bandwagon of an upward price movement. At the same time, readers were warned that determination and courage were not to be equated with sheer recklessness. Rather, as one manual explained, "it is often best to act on your own judgment, using caution or boldness as necessity may require."[82] The ever-present danger, moreover, was that "suspicion, over-confidence, timidity, vacillation" will prevent a successful investment, since "there is not a speculator . . . who is not subject to undercurrents blinding the judgment, coloring all views."[83]

If in these accounts successful speculation fundamentally seemed to hinge on manly qualities of "pluck" and "determination," of "bold and fearless action," this implicitly marginalized the role of "experience" and suggested that the idea of speculation as a rule-bound practice remained a chimera, an abstract idea devoid of any concrete content. Depicting speculation as a "cognitive practice" and subsuming it under the paradigms of production and science normalized and legitimized securities trading. At the same time, speculation appeared as a question of character, driven more by emotions than by mechanical applications of rules of experience. Mastery of the market hinged on certain specifically masculine qualities that could not be subsumed under the paradigm of rational calculation. Stock exchanges, then, were locations in which manhood was asserted and performed while women were categorically excluded.[84] In this respect, investment manuals differed from American antebellum popular literature, which had depicted the stock exchange as a locale of masculine economic anxiety.[85]

Still, the manliness in question was a complex one.[86] Notions of cool and rational calculation sat uneasily with a semantics of audacity. If, after all, intelligent calculation yielded the right results quasi automatically, what need was there for intrepidness on the part of the speculator? Of course, framing successful speculation as a question of bold manliness did not necessarily undermine the tendency toward normalization. Rather, it could enhance the reader's fascination with the stock exchange and endow the activity of securities trading with an appeal that was hard to resist, especially in times of rising prices.

Men of the Exchange

In many respects, then, the three countries witnessed similar developments during the years preceding the panics of 1873. In all three countries, stock exchanges expanded and transformed to accommodate the growing appetite for securities trading. Concurrently, the discourse on speculation, too, changed, becoming more varied and less hostile compared to earlier periods. This should not suggest, however, that cultures and practices of speculation on both sides of the Atlantic were uniform and homogenous. Rather, significant differences, both in terms of practices and in terms of perceptions and discourses, persisted. These differences would later shape and inform the countries' experience of and reaction to the crises to come. One major difference between Germany and Austria on the one hand, and the United States on the other, was the role played by large speculators in the public's perception of the stock exchange.

While many Americans knew Wall Street's major players by name, the same could not be said of the bourses in Vienna and Berlin. In the 1830s, Jacob Little had been the first professional speculator to rise to fame. By the 1860s, four men above all dominated Wall Street: Cornelius Vanderbilt, Daniel Drew, Jay Gould, and James Fisk, all of whom had grown up in poverty and had risen out of obscurity to become the NYSE's foremost operators. Contemporaries "described them as 'bold', and 'magnificent of view', full of 'verve.'"[87] Their concerted large-scale transactions on the stock market enabled them to gain control of railways and to merge different lines to build railway networks of a hitherto unseen size. In other instances, they would organize "corners" to force prices up or down; when a security had reached the desired price, they would suddenly reverse course and buy or sell in large quantities, reaping huge profits at every turn.[88]

In late 1872, an operation that was quickly dubbed the "great Northwestern corner" garnered significant public attention. Earlier that year, Jay Gould had been ousted from the Erie Railroad, a company he had controlled for many

years, leading some to hope that Wall Street had seen the last of his machinations. Gould, however, was in no mood to give up and in October decided to
drive up the price of money by withdrawing large amounts of gold and legal
tender notes from circulation. By October 19, money at call was trading at a
rate of 50 percent. Fearing a panic, the Treasury once again felt compelled to
intervene. The immediate danger was successfully averted, but the *New York
Times* still fumed with disgust at Gould's ability to "find countenance and admiration from influential capitalists and institutions, as well as counsel and others, who feel they will incur no inconvenience or social shame from being
known as their abettors."[89] Gould, not to be deterred, swiftly moved on to the
next scheme and teamed up with an erstwhile foe in the form of Cornelius
Vanderbilt's son-in-law to organize yet another corner, this time in railway
shares, as the *Chronicle* recounted in November.[90] In recent weeks, the article
explained, a "certain class of well-known speculators," commonly known as the
"Vanderbilt party," had been buying large amounts of shares of the Chicago and
Northwestern Railroad, allowing them to seize control of the company and to
connect the Union Pacific, which they already owned, to the rest of the Vanderbilt system of railroads. The company's managers had been unable to resist the
takeover, as they had shorted the stock of their own railroad and, in order to
avoid "ruinous losses" when the corner began, had "made terms with the
Vanderbilt clique." As a result, the Vanderbilt party was now closer than ever
to its goal of building the "greatest railroad monopoly in the United States,"
while "a number of firms and individuals in mercantile and banking circles"
had seen their solvency "seriously compromised by that demoralizing and disastrous event."[91]

The story of the "great Northwestern corner" was essentially that of a conspiracy in which several powerful individuals colluded in secret to defraud
guileless small-time shareholders. Yet though the scheme had been carried out
in secret, Vanderbilt and his allies had not been able to shield their operations
from the public's view for long, as the *Chronicle*'s article showed. By exposing
the "real nature and progress of the speculation," that which had previously
been carried out by stealth was rendered transparent—albeit, inevitably, after
the fact. This indeed was a distinguishing feature of American financial market reports: Their accounts of market machinations were often highly personalized, depicting market movements as at least as much the result of individual
actions as of anonymous market forces. Corners such as the Northwestern one
were, to be sure, the most visible and extreme instances of this personalized
market logic. But even when price movements were less pronounced and of
shorter duration, market observers still looked to the NYSE's most well-known
operators for explanations.[92] More often than not, this logic was accepted as a
given and stated in a neutral, matter-of-fact tone. Occasionally, however, the
power asymmetries underlying the stock market elicited comments in which

the anger was palpable. Quoting an authority on financial matters, the *Stockholder* called it "a fact beyond dispute that the 'bull' speculators of the street control the market completely, and people who stop to reason will only waste time. The money-power controls the situation."[93]

There was no significant difference between the way this aspect of the financial market was depicted in specialist journals such as the *Chronicle*, the *Stockholder*, and *Bankers' Magazine*, and the market reports in newspapers aimed at a more general readership, such as the *Times* and the *Tribune*.[94] Both types of publications frequently described the stock exchange as governed by personal influence in which the average individual investor was largely powerless. But that is not to say that in their accounts cliques and powerful capitalists were *identical* with the market as a whole. Rather, market reporters still subscribed to the notion—and be it only implicitly—that somehow, somewhere, those elusive "natural forces" of the market remained intact. Indeed, it was only against the backdrop of this concept of natural forces that the charge of fraudulence and personal influence gained its potency.

In German and Austrian market reports, by contrast, the likes of Gould and Vanderbilt were largely unknown. Occasionally, journalists noted the existence of cliques capable of manipulating the price of certain speculative securities that fluctuated more than others. But unlike in the United States, these shares were not associated with the names of notorious entrepreneur-speculators. Writing to the *Workingman's Advocate* in 1871, the German socialist politician Wilhelm Liebknecht claimed that it was a "public secret that the exchange of Berlin is habitually used and manipulated by persons notoriously connected with men in the highest official positions" but refrained from naming names.[95] In one instance, the *Berliner Tageblatt* informed its readers that a certain "Impresario James Hirschfeld . . . well known at the stock exchange and in salons" had recently "reappeared" in Berlin.[96] But Hirschfeld's celebrity was not associated with major financial operations, and his name never came up in market reports. The Austrian *Neue Freie Presse* on one occasion mentioned that a "large speculator" by the name of Borchart had been forced to sell, but this suggested that he was responding to pressure rather than engineering a corner.[97]

There was one name that did crop up repeatedly in the financial pages of the 1870s: that of Bethel Henry Strousberg, the wealthy German British railroad entrepreneur. Having successfully built several Prussian railroads in the 1860s, Strousberg's name became notorious in the early 1870s when his grandiose scheme to build a Romanian railway system came tumbling down, threatening thousands of German investors with ruin.[98] Strousberg's public persona resembled that of the notorious American railroad entrepreneurs; his exploits and lifestyle were subject to a great deal of attention in the pages of the daily press, and his business methods seemed dubious to many, as did those of his American counterparts. But Strousberg, who built his roads from scratch, selling his shares on completion, never became a major player on the German stock markets.[99] Indeed, compared to the United States, gaining control of railways by buying up their shares was a less attractive option in Prussia, where private capital owned and operated only half of the country's track, while the Prussian state owned roughly a quarter and in addition operated somewhat less than a quarter of privately owned roads.[100] In the United States, by contrast, railroads, despite sometimes receiving considerable state subsidies, were private enterprises.[101] German banker Carl Fürstenberg would later recall that furtively gaining control of a company through the stock exchange was still largely unknown in Germany during the 1870s and considered "American."[102] These differences in railroad financing and organization help explain why German and Austrian market reports appeared more anonymous and less personalized than their American equivalent.

Crucially, German and Austrian market reports recognized two main actors on the stock exchange: "speculation," also referred to as the "true element of the stock exchange" (*das eigentliche Börsenelement*) on the one hand, and the "private public" (*Privatpublikum*), "private capital" or "investing capital" (*Anlage-Kapital*) on the other. The former comprised professional brokers who made a living dealing in securities while the latter consisted of people investing any private capital they had to spare. A prolonged bull market, observers agreed, was only possible if private investors followed the lead of the *Spekulation*.[103] Although the *Spekulation* and the *Börsenelement* of German market reports operated anonymously, their function was, structurally speaking, very similar to that of the infamous American operators. By contrast, the other group that featured regularly in German financial columns—the *Privatpublikum* or "private capitalists"—only very rarely made an appearance in the accounts of American market reporters.[104] In spite of the proliferation of advice manuals and the persuasive energy they directed at private small-time investors, this group did not, even during the heyday of railway speculation in the early 1870s, appear as an independent, separate group among Wall Street actors. In this respect, the American perception differed starkly from the German one. Indeed, in German financial discourse, the *Privatpublikum* was indicative of a speculative fever that, in the years between 1870 and 1872, was seen to be proliferating both socially, infecting the petite bourgeoisie and even the working classes, and geographically, spreading from the financial centers to their hinterland and the provinces. According to some observers, the *Provinz* was, in fact, identical with the *Privatpublikum*, and therefore, some argued, a bull market was only sustainable as long as provincial investors were sending buying orders to their brokers in Berlin and Frankfurt.[105]

Market reporters based these observations not only on what they witnessed in the trading rooms but also on what they took to be advertised rumors aimed specifically at inexperienced, small-time investors. In September 1872, a reporter for the Viennese *Neue Freie Presse* noted that a recent issue of the *Berliner Börsen-Zeitung*, one of the longest-running and most reputable financial journals, contained no less than thirty-one so-called *Eingesandte*. These unsigned announcements, printed in the paper's advertising sections, told readers "in the most insistent fashion" that by buying certain securities, they would be able to reap "miraculous profits in the very near future." In most cases, the authors of these notices suggested that circumstances of which the public was still unaware would make an advance in the share price all but inevitable. The Viennese journalist interpreted these proliferating rumors as a sign of how far and wide the speculative fever had spread: "These announcements . . . show above all that the wildest speculation has taken on huge dimensions [in Berlin], and . . . that even the lowest strata of society are participating in this speculative game—those strata which one can influence with [such] means."[106]

American newspapers similar to the *Börsen-Zeitung* in importance and respectability contained no such visible signs of a proliferating speculative fever, and American observers of financial markets were less inclined than their German contemporaries to fret about speculating members of the lower classes. Since, as I discussed previously, the available statistics do not permit us to accurately assess the size of the shareholding demographic during this period, it is impossible to determine with certainty whether these differences in discourse were merely that, or whether they reflected an economic reality in which shareholding and securities trading really were more widespread in the German-speaking lands than in the United States.

National Cultures of Speculation?

Such national peculiarities were not altogether lost on contemporaries. Indeed, for all the tendencies toward economic homogenization and integration, many remained convinced that national differences were not confined to the realms of politics and culture but extended even to such supposedly cosmopolitan practices as speculation. The arguments made by contemporaries about national cultures of speculation reveal that capitalism was not simply a homogenizing force, in which cultural differences were eroded, destroyed, or rendered irrelevant by the imperatives of market integration. Rather, contemporaries subsumed the changes wrought by capitalism and globalization under national narratives and categories.

Securities trading was, to be sure, an almost ubiquitous phenomenon. "Amsterdam, Hamburg, Trieste, Smyrna, Marseilles, Madrid, Odessa, all witness the same capacity for high speculation, stock-jobbing, and financial irregularities," James Medbery, an American writer, noted in the late 1860s.[107] But although such practices were rampant in all of the world's large (and smaller) financial centers, observers frequently insisted that it was possible to identify and describe distinct national cultures of speculation. In these debates, stock exchanges became, as the sociologist Alex Preda has argued, national "mystiques," "quasi-inaccessible center[s] of power on which the whole nation depends."[108] Not surprisingly, the flip side to such patriotic adulation was to claim that some speculative cultures were better than others. Here, the difference between "good" and "bad" speculation—which, as I have argued, had become a common trope by the 1860s—was imbued with a cultural aspect that rhetorically rendered one's own nation's practices superior, more restrained and productive, to that of others.

German financial writers were particularly critical of what they considered speculative excesses in Paris and Vienna. Remarkably, London's money market was not condemned with the same vehemence, perhaps reflecting a view in which London, the cradle of modern financial capitalism, had by now left behind its most excessive phase and become home to a more staid and respectable form of securities trading. Paris's bad reputation, on the other hand, was all the more pronounced if German writers were to be believed. The French railroad speculation of the 1850s, many Germans were convinced, had been far worse than their own infatuation with railroad shares in that decade. "The Paris stock exchange," Hermann Hirschbach, author of a treatise on speculation, claimed, was a "mere gambling exchange whose movements only insiders may guess."[109] According to Gustav Cohn, while speculators in general were a people of spiritual poverty and unrestrained passions, these traits were especially pronounced among Parisian stock-jobbers, and Berlin was lucky to have thus far avoided the fate of the French capital, where all classes speculated.[110] In early 1871, following France's surrender in the Franco-Prussian War, the *Aktionär* reported on an anti-German backlash at the Paris exchange where French traders were fearing a German takeover of business. According to the reporter, this was a childish accusation since the fact that the Parisian market in foreign securities was largely organized by Germans was simply due to their superior skills.[111] At their most extreme, such denunciations of French practices were couched in openly anti-Semitic terms, such as when the conservative *Preußische Volksblatt* described the operations of Mirès, the Pereire brothers, Fould, and the Rothschilds as evidence of a Jewish conspiracy to rule France.[112]

But Vienna, too, was considered one of the European epicenters of speculation, and in the early 1870s may even have surpassed Paris, still reeling following military defeat, as the favorite *Feindbild* of German financial writers. To some extent at least, this was the result of a real upsurge in securities trading at the Vienna bourse, whose volume, at its height, surpassed that of other European financial centers.[113] According to Hermann Hirschbach, Viennese investors had erupted in a speculative frenzy in the 1850s, when shares of the Austrian Crédit Mobilier bank for a while became the most sought-after security, leaving speculators of all classes ruined.[114] This kind of excess, another writer maintained, was fed by Austrian financial publications, which, as were their French counterparts, were generally more corrupt than equivalent German papers.[115] Not surprisingly, then, where a figure such as Strousberg painfully reminded the German public that it, too, was not immune to the lure of speculation, he was cast as a foreign intruder whose exploits were at odds with Prussian traditions and who would have found a more congenial environment in Paris or Vienna.[116]

But when James Fisk, perhaps the most infamous of the notorious quartet of American railroad speculators, was shot in his hotel room in early 1872, it seemed to many German financial writers that however fraudulent the practices of French, British, and Belgian "railroad swindlers" had been, they nevertheless paled in comparison to the sheer size and scope of Fisk's nefarious dealings. It was impossible to imagine a man whose qualities and fate were more at odds with European qualities than those of James Fisk, one obituarist claimed, and nowhere in the world but in Manhattan were social conditions so conducive to the success of such a character, so tolerant of his dealings. Fisk was a criminal who had made his fortune through theft but Americans admired him nonetheless, and his spirit was sure to live on even after his death.[117] This, another writer concluded, reflected certain general traits of American society:

> The lack of every barrier of status, the unconditional liberty enjoyed by everyone to make one's fortune, the sheer unlimited possibilities of making money open to men without a conscience, and finally the fact that those distinctions which provide the selfishly ambitious with other goals than mere wealth are lacking in this country, all these things came together to facilitate the unimaginable thriving of a creature like Jim Fisk.[118]

Such descriptions tied in with longstanding views of the United States as the country of "utilitarianism, . . . profit orientation, superficiality, and coldness" that were characteristic of much of German discourse on the United States during the nineteenth century.[119] Yet if such denunciations were harsher than those of French or Austrian practices, one can also detect a certain reluctant admiration in this depiction of American society. Fisk's exploits were, to be sure, deeply immoral by European standards, but they were also indicative of the value Americans placed on individual liberty and of the rapid development of the American economy. Moreover, one reporter reasoned, the fact that men such as Fisk dominated such a large share of stock exchange operations was not altogether bad since rapid price movements were less likely to affect the *Publikum*. In Germany, by contrast, "the reverberations of stock exchange events are much more significant," since almost every business man had some sort of connection to the stock exchange.[120]

Americans, for their part, were by and large much less preoccupied with European practices of securities trading than vice versa, although they did recognize that the ways of Wall Street were far from universal. In September 1873, just before the railroad bubble was about to burst, the *Stockholder* noted that "some of the bad fashions of Wall street have been carried over to London," citing an English article according to which "the worst forms of Wall-street speculation are now fostered and encouraged by members of the house," and that prices were affected no longer "by the action of outside or nervous investors, but by the transactions of organized cliques engaged in the interesting game, which has found so much favor in New York, of 'cornering bears.'"[121] Earlier that year, another observer had noted that speculation was now "as fierce in Hamburg, Frankfort, Berlin, and Vienna as in New-York. . . . In stocks and all the representatives of value, the gambling on German exchanges is as wild as anything ever seen in New-York."[122] This new Germany, the author concluded, was an "American-like Germany." To some it even seemed as though Vienna had surpassed New York where speculation, bad as it was, was nowhere near as universal as it had recently become in the Austrian capital.[123]

Such sentiments, voiced by Austrian, German, and American observers, point to a peculiar paradox in the writing on finance: Contemporaries believed that stock exchanges were agents of integration, institutions of an expansive and steadily growing capitalist order that linked peoples and countries to a hitherto unknown degree. At the same time, however, this cosmopolitan nature of stock exchanges coexisted with a competing narrative according to which stock exchanges were decidedly *national* institutions, embodying national characteristics and practices.

Conclusion

In this chapter, I have traced the manifold economic, institutional, and discursive conditions that gave rise to, and informed contemporary interpretations of, the stock market bubble of the early 1870s. A buoyant economy spurred investors to place their capital with newly incorporated companies, a process that was aided by stock exchanges, which, established in the early decades of the nineteenth century, devised institutional innovations to accommodate the requirements of a growing number of investors and corporations. Another important factor in this process was the discursive legitimation and normalization of securities trading, evident both in the theoretical writings of economists and in investment manuals authored by stockbrokers. In these manuals, financial investment was depicted as something that individuals engage in, using both rational faculties of calculation and emotional faculties of willpower and intuition. Stock market reports, too, employed a language of causality and agency in depicting price developments, identifying stock market actors in order to render intelligible day-to-day market movements. In thus translating finance into a set of relations between actors, American market reporters employed a strategy of personalization that focused on a few well-known market operators. German and Austrian reporters, by contrast, employed an anonymous language to designate groups of operators. As a result of these differing strategies, financial markets in German and Austrian discourse appeared considerably less transparent. Such differences notwithstanding, however, my analysis of these texts shows how market observers sought to interpret finance by translating abstract changes in prices that were expressed through numbers into acts performed by individuals and groups, thus assimilating the abstract notion of the market to everyday categories of experience.

A structurally similar mechanism was the "nationalization" of financial markets and stock exchanges described in the final section of this chapter. Although contemporaries were aware of, and commented on the transnational reach of stock exchanges, which connected market participants between far-flung places, they also sought to depict them as institutions embodying national traits and peculiarities. Thus, the abstract power of finance that, as expressed in market movements, might appear as transcending both the nation and the individual was translated into categories and narratives—of individual agency and national traditions—that rendered financial markets as something familiar and intelligible. Prior to the panics, these differing descriptions did not compete with each other; if a stock exchange was depicted as an agent of worldwide integration at one moment, and as an embodiment of national peculiarities at the next, this did not signify opposite ends of an ideological or discursive spectrum. Rather, differing depictions often coexisted, and were not considered mutually exclusive.

CHAPTER 2

THE VIRTUAL WORLD OF FINANCIAL INFORMATION AND THE MAKING OF A BUBBLE

During the early 1870s, promises of large future gains suddenly appeared plausible to thousands of investors, many of whom dabbled in stocks and bonds for the first time. The media were instrumental in creating and nourishing this atmosphere of exuberance. Buying a financial instrument was quite unlike buying a tangible commodity, something whose utility was present and obvious at the time of purchase. Shares and bonds, by contrast, were promises of future returns, and potential buyers had to be persuaded that these were realistic.[1] But what could function as a substitute for the material quality of a real, tangible commodity? How did investors translate this virtual, not-yet-materialized quality of a financial instrument (the promise of a future return) into something intelligible, something that might anchor their investment decision? The financial pages of newspapers claimed to furnish their readers with information about the quality of corporate securities, both in numerical and narrative form, printing day after day seemingly endless amounts of columns and spreadsheets. This information, they implied, could be used by the reader to ascertain the quality of stocks and bonds. But this mode of presentation, I argue in this chapter, was more likely to leave readers befuddled than well equipped to create a portfolio of financial assets. This was felt even more acutely where American railroad bonds were concerned, since even many journalists considered the sheer physical distance between an investor and the object of investment an impediment to the flow of financial information. To counter this, journalists emphasized the importance of trustworthiness on the part of bankers and promoters. Investors, they suggested, should place their trust in a *person*, more real and concrete than anything that spreadsheets full of numbers might convey. Thus finance was rendered intelligible: a transaction between people rather than an abstract calculation with an uncertain outcome.

Growth of the Financial Press

During the Civil War, Jay Cooke had been the first American banker to harness the power of the press in order to sell war bonds not just to the usual class of elite investors but also to tens of thousands of small capitalists. To reach them, Cooke placed advertisements and articles with information about the loan in newspapers all over country, thus creating, for the first time, a national market for securities. In this, he was aided by technological developments in printing, which led to an increase in the number of newspapers, as well as by the rise of the Associated Press which streamlined and improved the collection and distribution of news.[2] Cooke's strategy quickly caught on; by the early 1870s, many bankers had come to rely heavily on the press to sell their bonds.

Investors who desired information about securities and the companies that issued them could either turn to the financial columns of the daily press or consult specialist publications, depending on the type and breadth of information they required. The *New York Herald*, founded by James Gordon Bennett Sr. in 1835, had been the first daily paper to regularly report on developments on the stock exchange and money market; other daily newspapers quickly followed suit.[3] These financial pages generally provided an overview of prices, interest rates, and dividends, and often also included short items on individual corporations, especially railroads.

Those investors requiring more extensive, detailed information could turn to weekly and monthly publications devoted exclusively to business and financial affairs. Of these, the *Commercial and Financial Chronicle* was the most prominent. Established by William Buck Dana in 1862 in New York City, it was the first American business weekly and aimed to provide comprehensive information to "the economist, the merchant, the banker, the manufacturer, the agriculturalist, the shipper, the insurer and the speculator," as Dana explained in an editorial. In 1870, the *Chronicle* merged with *Hunts' Merchant Magazine*, one of the most important business monthlies of the antebellum era. In 1872, the journal counted between 3,100 and 4,100 subscribers.[4] Another postbellum newcomer, and the first weekly devoted exclusively to the interests of owners of corporate securities, was the aptly named journal *The Stockholder*. Founded in 1862, it claimed to act as an "impartial adviser" to investors and ran long articles on individual companies as well as market reports.[5] The *American Railroad Journal*, a pioneer of financial journalism and the first publication to devote itself to railroad finance in the 1850s, survived into the postwar era but lost its leadership to the *Chronicle* in the 1860s.[6] *Bankers' Magazine*, another important business publication of the antebellum era, continued to circulate and provided its readers, chiefly within the banking community, with monthly market reports as well as more theoretical treatises on economic questions.

In Germany, too, the 1850s and 1860s were a period of growth for the financial press. The weekly *Aktionär* was established in Frankfurt in 1854 during a time of rapidly growing demand for financial and business information. Its correspondents covered stock exchanges, public finances, as well as commerce and industry.[7] The two most important daily publications, the *Frankfurter Zeitung* and the *Berliner Börsen-Zeitung*, were also children of the mid-1850s, and though the appetite for financial information, especially railroad securities, was briefly dampened during the crisis of 1857, the two publications continued to thrive in the following decade. Beginning in 1859, the *Frankfurter Zeitung* published two issues a day and covered both business and political news,[8] both features it shared with its Berlin rival, the *Börsen-Zeitung*. Others quickly sought to emulate their success, as the editors of the *Börsen-Zeitung*, looking back on the first ten years of business, noted in 1865: now, they observed, "every larger political newspaper includes a permanent section for stock exchange reports, and even the tiniest local paper has recognized the need of the public to be continuously supplied with information about the situation on the larger market."[9] The previous year had seen the first publication of the bimonthly *Zeitschrift für Kapital und Rente*, which was specifically devoted to the interests of investors. In 1868, Georg Davidsohn, a former editor of the *Börsen-Zeitung*, published the first issue of a rival undertaking, the *Berliner Börsen-Courier*.[10]

But this was just the beginning. In the early 1870s, the number of financial publications surged, as evidenced by numerous advertisements in the established papers. In 1872, the *Börsen-Zeitung* featured advertisements by the *Börsen-Courier*, the *Neue Börsen-Zeitung*, *Salings Börsenblatt*, and the *Berliner Actionair*.[11] Clearly, the early 1870s were a period of rapidly growing demand for financial information, something which the publisher Rudolf Mosse recognized when he launched a new Berlin daily, the *Berliner Tageblatt*. Explicitly aimed not merely at the wealthy elite but also at a broad range of readers, it included stock market reports as a daily feature.[12] This growing demand was not only visible in the number of new publications but also in the growth of the more established papers: the *Börsen-Zeitung*—which a contemporary described as the "most important and truly influential stock market paper"[13]—numbered between 28 and 30 pages in 1872, a growth of about 25 percent compared to the late 1860s, and boasted somewhere between 12,000 and 14,000 subscribers.[14]

In Austria, the first periodical devoted exclusively to business matters was the semiofficial *Austria: Tagblatt für Handel, Gewerbe und Communicationsmittel*, established in 1849. But it was only during the 1860s that the business press really took off, with the number of publications surging from 12 in 1861 to 42 in

1869 and 91 in 1872, the majority of which were published in Vienna. According to a contemporary statistic, a total of around 40,000 people subscribed to at least one of these publications in 1872, a demand that was stoked by—and in turn reinforced—the speculative bubble of that period.[15] Their business model depended heavily on allocations by banks and companies, though it was unclear who was beholden to whom: companies could pay newspapers both to promote their shares and publish advertisements (in many cases, they far outnumbered a paper's editorial content), and to refrain from publishing damaging information that might have prompted a drop in their share price.[16] Not surprisingly, their existence proved to be short-lived, and following the crash, twenty of them would perish in 1873 alone. In addition, many political newspapers also included a section devoted to business and financial matters. According to one contemporary observer, "We find nowadays hardly a political paper of even just local significance that does not have an economic section."[17] The Vienna newspaper *Die Presse* had pioneered this practice when, in 1856, it introduced its business and financial pages entitled *Der kleine Capitalist*. Headed by the energetic Max Friedländer (who left the *Presse* to found its rival *Neue Freie Presse* in 1864, soon to become Vienna's best known and most influential newspaper), its business and financial pages quickly became essential reading for bankers and businessmen. The liberal press, spearheaded by the *Neue Freie Presse* and dominating public opinion during the early 1870s, generally spoke favorably of the stock exchange, only occasionally criticizing instances of speculative excess. The less numerous and less influential Catholic papers, by contrast, took a much more critical stance, and featured fewer advertisements.[18] Somewhere in between came the official and semiofficial press, of which the *Oesterreichische Oekonomist*, founded in 1869, was expressly designed to dampen the exuberance of the bubble years.[19]

Compared to the United States, neither Germany nor Austria had seen the likes of Jay Cooke, an entrepreneur who, within a short period of time, revolutionized the use of the financial press to create a national market for a financial instrument on a previously unseen scale, a development that was not driven by a speculative fever but by the pressing need to finance the Civil War. Conversely, there seems to have been no similar surge in American financial publications in the early 1870s, indicating that the American experience and nature of the investment bubble of that period differed from the German and Austrian cases.

Calculating Returns

To readers, the financial publications presented themselves as an impartial arbiter aiming to provide the information necessary for making an informed investment decision.[20] More often than not, however, editors did not merely reproduce information but selected, arranged, and presented it in a way that was more geared toward the interests of corporations than to those of investors. The problem was especially acute during the 1870s and 1880s when American railroad men planted stories and bought journalists with free passes or loans. In return, their railroads received favorable coverage and investors were duped into buying questionable securities.[21] In Germany, Bethel Henry Strousberg, in 1866, established a Berlin newspaper, *Die Post*, whose articles more or less openly propagated Strousberg's business interests. Other newspapers, too, were bought or founded by bankers and banking houses, and many journalists at other newspapers were also likely to have been on companies' payrolls.[22] In Austria, this nexus was even more pronounced. Since the state levied considerable taxes from newspapers, publishing them was an expensive and not especially remunerative business. For this reason, both the *Neue Freie Presse* and *Die Presse* were eventually bought out by banks (as were many other newspapers). Others, such as the *Montags Revue*, had been corporate creations from the very beginning.[23] The owner of the financial weekly *Warrens Wochenschrift*, Eduard Warrens, was himself a well-known speculator who regularly won and lost large sums on the stock exchange, and while his publication could therefore hardly be considered independent when it came to financial matters, it was nevertheless influential, as one Berlin journalist noted on the occasion of Warrens' death.[24] Even those papers that were nominally independent had intimate ties with corporations that, during the late 1860s and early 1870s, regularly transferred shares at par value to a journalist's account for which he then paid by selling them when the company went public, usually pocketing a considerable premium.[25]

But even where financial journals aimed to present their readers with accurate information, thus creating a "virtual world of financial information" (Richard White), this did not automatically translate into an informed investment decision. Of course, financial journals claimed to provide investors with the information necessary to make an informed decision about which securities to buy, and prided themselves in their objectivity. The *Börsen-Zeitung* had explained this rationale in a prospectus, a year after publishing its first issue. Their paper would, the editors claimed, "assess the value of the facts [reported] and explain the significance of the figures [collected], and thus be able to provide a *healthy and accurate orientation for speculation*, but always only after giving the interested reader the means to form his own opinion."[26] Other financial publications made similar claims.[27] The *Stockholder* in its first issue promised readers to be an "impartial adviser . . . and, in case of need, a fearless expounder of their grievances;" and the *Chronicle* claimed to offer an "unbiased view of current events" as well as the "fullest and most accurate information as to the multitude of financial schemes which are so eagerly asking for money."[28]

But what exactly did this entail? I have shown in the previous chapter that contemporary investment manuals depicted the buying and selling of securities as a practice that had both an intellectual, calculating, and an emotional, intuitive, component. The financial columns of journals and newspapers, claiming objectivity and impartiality, were mostly concerned with the calculating element of investing. The most important feature in this respect was the stock and bond table or *Kurszettel*. The *Börsen-Zeitung* boasted to its readers that its table was the "largest and most complete." In 1855, its first year, it had comprised seventy-seven railroad securities, twenty-six Prussian government securities, twenty-six foreign securities, and twenty-six others. Seventeen years later, in June 1872, the items had risen to a total of 835, including just under 200 German railroad securities, 92 foreign railroad securities, 139 bank shares, and 93 industrial securities. In addition to their current price, the paper noted the dividends a stock had yielded during the past two years—or, in the case of fixed income securities, their size, their rate of interest, and date of interest payments—whether and to what extent the interest payments were guaranteed, the currency in which a security was traded, and the percentage of paid-up capital. Taken together, readers were told, the numbers were sufficient to enable them to form an impression of a company's "true conditions."[29] This comprehensiveness compared favorably with other stock and bond tables. The *Neue Freie Presse*, whose financial and business pages were the most renowned and widely read in Austria, confined itself to listing the current prices of a security and did not generally provide additional information of the kind the *Börsen-Zeitung* did.

In addition, almost every issue of the *Börsen-Zeitung* included numerous company reports and accounts, which were supplied by the companies themselves. Editors combined these reports and data from several companies into a spreadsheet, thus enabling readers to compare the results of different companies. Regarding a supplement on the "mining and smelting companies in Germany," readers were told that it comprised "all the data desirable for the assessment of the profitability of capital invested in the coal, iron and steel industry." The data had been compiled with the "utmost precision possible," since companies no longer shied away from publicity and had readily supplied all the relevant numbers.[30] The same year, the paper published an overview of German and Austrian private railroads, again in tabular form. This, readers were told, would enable them to make "manifold comparisons." The writer suggested that investors should pay attention to the size of dividends but refrained from explaining the relevance of the other data.

In some instances, financial writers acknowledged that a mere tabular arrangement of numbers could seem confusing. When the *Chronicle* introduced a new table of stocks and bonds in October 1871, it proudly claimed that it was new not only "in the sense of having been compiled from the most recent information" but also "quite new in shape and style, embracing numerous details of information which have never previously been contained in the usual tabular lists of stocks and bonds." More importantly, however, it had been decided to introduce a new column with "remarks" that would summarize "in concise form . . . the latest and most important facts concerning the financial affairs of a state, city, or railroad company, giving in many cases a clearer idea of the value of its stocks or bonds than any precise formula in tabular shape could possibly convey." In addition, the paper would, in connection with the tables, publish an introductory article every month "in relation to investments in the various securities included in the list."[31] These statements implied that words could do what numbers could not, or not to the same extent: convey meaning in a way that was intelligible to investors.

In thus adjusting and expanding its presentation of financial information, the journal had in mind a particular class of investors. Its weekly "complete report of the financial markets . . . adapted to the wants of bankers, brokers and all parties operating frequently in Wall Street," the editors had concluded, did not adequately cater to the needs of the "occasional investors, both in and out of New York, who purchase from time to time such stocks or bonds as they wish to hold for investment." Since these investors desired "more popular information," they would from now on be presented with "such facts and opinions each month as may be of use to persons desiring to invest money, either in large or small amounts, in safe securities paying a good rate of interest." The first installment of "facts and opinions" that followed consisted of a basic overview of different classes of securities. U.S. government securities were too expensive to yield an attractive dividend, and the value of state and city bonds depended heavily on local causes and conditions, the author explained. While railroad stocks were "liable to continual fluctuation," railroad bonds, preferably secured by a mortgage, were "by far the most popular investment." But, having promised "facts and opinions," the writer then went on to profess that "it is not our province to recommend to investors certain bonds by name as the safest and best paying securities in which to place their funds," thus admitting that the paper had, in fact, no intention of offering "opinions," and instead, it again pointed readers to the "facts" to be found in the tables on the previous pages.[32]

Referring to "facts" implied a language of scientific objectivity, of self-evidence, and suggested an investment strategy akin to a mathematical calculation. But what exactly constituted a fact when it came to investing? Were the "facts"—the numbers that corporations furnished—really as self-evident as this writer suggested? Others thought not. Thus a reporter for the money market column of the *Independent* told readers in very unambiguous terms that "in financial affairs it is almost impossible to obtain accurate information from any quarter whatever . . . figures can so very easily be made to lie . . . in the reports of all incorporated companies, municipalities, states." For this reason, he explained, the paper confined itself to "publishing the official facts . . . as accurately as our opportunities for information enable us to do. . . . As to advice, we only give it when it is specially demanded, and very seldom then."[33] Here, then, the language of "facts" was still used but qualified so heavily that the term was little more than an empty shell.

Financial journals had good reason to be cautious in dispensing advice as corporations had significant leeway in deciding if and how much information to publish about their affairs. The editors of the *Neue Freie Presse*, who published monthly overviews of the earnings of Austrian railroads, on one occasion complained that some had failed to furnish them with the latest numbers.[34] In Germany, laws governing the disclosure requirements of corporations were couched in vague, general terms, and were full of loopholes. Corporations were required by law to publish balance sheets but not statements of income. Comparing different balance sheets was difficult as the law did not stipulate a common standard, and corporations were inconsistent when it came to valuing individual assets and liabilities.[35] The tables and spreadsheets that were published in newspapers could not adjust for such inconsistencies, and journalists only alluded to the pitfalls of accounting in very general terms, if at all. In the United States, too, corporations were reluctant to publish detailed and accurate information about their businesses. Some states mandated some form of disclosure; others did not. The state of Massachusetts, for example, required corporations to publish annual "statements of certificate," but only in 1875 did they take the form of a preprinted balance sheet.[36] Companies wishing their shares to be listed on the New York Stock Exchange were, in theory, required to meet certain disclosure standards. In practice, however, these were easily evaded.[37] Annual stockholder reports were woefully inadequate to their task and left investors in the dark regarding the true state of a company's finances.[38]

The tables and spreadsheets in financial publications glossed over these difficulties; they provided little context and suggested comparability even where this was very much open to debate. As such, they spoke to a "sensitivity to quantified material," which was characteristic of those nineteenth century societies that had, for several decades, been experiencing rapid economic growth and a concomitant growing interest in all things statistical.[39] In the United States, there developed, during the early nineteenth century, a mindset according to which "knowledge was composed of facts and counting led to the most reliable and objective form of fact there was, the hard number," an observation that similarly applies to many European countries during this period.[40] This mindset was very much evident in contemporary stock and bond tables. At the same time, however, misgivings about the meaning of numbers were palpable.

Another way in which mere numbers could seem inadequate was when readers suggested that their quantitative and accounting skills were not sufficient to make sense of them. The *Chronicle*, whose editors prided themselves in counting not only merchants, bankers, and brokers but also "occasional investors" among their readership, noted that, more than a year after it had first introduced what was claimed to be an improved and expanded version of its stock and bond tables, some readers had written to the editors to complain that they were finding the new tables difficult to comprehend. One old subscriber had even asked if any such tables were included in the journal while another had wondered why he could not find information about where interests were payable even though this had been included in the journal's tables for well over a year at the point of writing. The "suggestions of these subscribers," the editors concluded in a discernibly irritated tone, "show that they do not sufficiently appreciate the value of THE CHRONICLE nor the extent of the information furnished in its columns."[41] Despite these misgivings, however, they did not revise the tables' format and wording.

Aside from stock and bond tables, almost all financial publications contained several columns of reports and short notices about individual companies. In some cases, these were little more than elaborate versions of the information contained in stock and bond tables, but even where they went beyond these, and detailed a company's business strategy, its promoters and directors, its localities and the most important developments of the past year, they were not easy to decipher. The main problem was the sheer number of articles. The *Chronicle* usually contained between eight and twelve notes on different railways, and the *Börsen-Zeitung* included up to twenty. A reader who already owned a portfolio of securities could scan the pages for information about companies that were relevant to him. But to those readers in search of new investment possibilities, the presentation and nature of such narrative information must have seemed perplexing, even more so since most articles were couched in either uniformly positive or blandly neutral terms, while explicitly negative articles were rare. Narrative reports could be just as difficult to interpret as stock and bond tables.

Perhaps cognizant of such difficulties, the *Berliner Tageblatt*, a newspaper established in 1872, whose aim was to cater to a nonspecialist group of readers, took a different tack. It, too, contained stock and bond tables (though considerably shorter than those of the *Börsen-Zeitung*), as well as daily reports on the Berlin Stock Exchange. In addition to these standard features, however, it also discussed investment matters in a nonfinancial section. In the "Editor's Letterbox," subscribers were invited to ask all kinds of questions pertaining to matters as varied as inheritance law, the procurement of certain types of food, and regularly, capital investment. These would always take the same form: a correspondent, identified only by his initials, would inquire about two or three securities, which were also only identified by numbers or letters so that readers would not be able to know which securities the writer referred to. To them, the advice dispensed was useless; it could only be deciphered by the writer of the specific inquiry. In replying to questions on financial matters, the editors usually adopted a confident, even authoritative tone. Their advice was straightforward and easy to follow; the reader was generally told in unambiguous terms whether to buy, sell, or hold a security, along the following lines: "We believe that O. B. has upward potential, and that St. J. is not solid and its present price is artificial."[42] Occasionally, editors explained their advice by pointing to certain facts about the companies in question, especially when the recommendation was negative. Thus readers would be informed that a company was unprofitable because its debts were too high, because it had yet to start business, because (in the case of railroads) it could not expect much traffic, because promoters had enriched themselves, or because it had disclosed too little information to be evaluated properly.[43]

One observer wondered whether such inquiries were actually authentic, especially where new publications such as the *Tageblatt* were concerned.[44] Yet this hardly mattered. Even if the inquiries were a mere ploy to woo new subscribers, the message was nevertheless clear: for all the emphasis on contemporary investment discourse on facts, numbers, and calculation, the active selection of a security was much easier, and seemingly less arbitrary, when one had access to personalized, unambiguous advice. Nothing could cut through the confusing thicket of figures as well as could a clear order to buy, hold, or sell.

Character and Trust

The "virtual world of financial information," then, was likely to leave readers befuddled more than well informed, and the situation of the investor was characterized by considerable uncertainty. Not surprisingly, investors who entertained personal relationships with bankers and promoters often relied on their advice when making investment decisions. "I am happy to pay a great deal for your Lloyd," one investor wrote to the founder of the North German Lloyd. Such an investment, he believed, was "more honorable" than an investment in banking shares, despite the latter's greater profitability.[45] In nineteenth-century securities markets, personal networks, and issues of character, trustworthiness, and respectability shaped discourses and practices of investing.[46]

Personal networks were used to collect specific information, which was deemed more reliable than anything that was publicly available. Thus the well-connected financier Henry Villard wrote to a correspondent, asking him "for information regarding the solvency of the New York and Oswego Midland R.

R. Company, supposing from your familiarity with affairs in the State of New York generally that you will be able to give me an opinion as to the prospects of the roads." Since the bonds were trading below par, Villard felt he could not trust what was in the public domain and hoped such privately exchanged information would enable him to make a bargain.[47] In turn, he was prepared to share what he knew, boasting on one occasion to a friend that "the organization of the Boston Union Telegraph Company is perfectly familiar to me. In fact, I know the whole history of the concern and am personally acquainted with the principal managers."[48] When an investment he had cautioned against turned sour, Villard reminded his friend that he had "predicted the very unfavorable results," and that his superior judgment in the matter stemmed from his access to "all the confidential reports of the confidential agents that watched the progress of the enterprise on the spot for the banks and bankers . . . that took the bonds as I informed you."[49]

For the wealthy elite in the early 1870s, the matter was even more straightforward. To many of its members, precise information seemed dispensable as investment decisions were largely or entirely delegated to a banker. Moses Taylor, a New York banker whose reputation was well established in American financial circles, catered to wealthy clients who wished to invest their money in securities but did not feel confident enough to take matters into their own hands.[50] In soliciting Taylor's advice, his clients deferred to his "best judgment" in financial matters, either inviting his opinion on a particular investment, or expressly instructing him to buy whatever he thought best, with a minimum of guidance.[51] One client told Taylor to buy bonds of two specified railroads "unless the great rise in the price of gold, or any other reason of which I am not cognizable, should induce you to dislike those investments. In that case put the money in any security you think best. . . . I do not expect any explanations as to your choice."[52] Where Taylor's clients mentioned specific securities, this may well have been in response to articles and advertisements they had seen or read in a daily newspaper or financial journal (their correspondence does not indicate whether or not this was the case). Here, too, however, they ultimately deferred to Taylor's expertise in financial matters. Ironically, Taylor himself was reluctant to impart investment advice to his clients, for he knew from experience of the fickleness of financial markets and believed it was best to let investors decide for themselves.[53] Equally reluctant to snub his clients when approached, however, he obliged, and they thanked him by respectfully declining to reproach him even where investments turned sour.[54]

But such personal advice based on a relationship of trust was not available to the average investor, and much less to those investors who, during the growing bubble of the early 1870s, dabbled in securities trading for the first time. They, too, however, were advised to pay attention to the names and reputations of the men tasked with selling a corporation's securities, as well as to those of the members of the board of directors. One financial publication even suggested that where banks were concerned, "a consideration of the personalities of the promoters and directors" was more important than familiarizing oneself with a bank's statutes.[55] Banks, of course, were a special case. Unlike railways and industrial companies, they did not produce anything material, and their economic function and business could appear opaque, making notions of respectability and trustworthiness on the part of those responsible seem all the more important.

But potential investors in railways and industrial companies, too, were advised to pay close attention to the reputation of their directors and promoters. "The Houston and Texas Central," the *Chronicle* informed its readers, "is one of the leading Southern railroad enterprises, inviting the attention of capitalists in our market, and is particularly prominent from the high character and financial standing of the New York men who are engaged in it."[56] Subscribing to the same logic, the *Stockholder* fawningly described DeWitt Littlejohn, the "originator, organizer and promoter" of the Midland Railway, as having "the brightest integrity, indisputable capacity, the clearest practical business ability," features which, it assured its readers, kept him "above the level of the merely able and conspicuous men of his time," and made his railroad a worthwhile investment.[57] Occasionally, journalists cautioned that well-known names did not in themselves guarantee a well-run business; overall, however, praise for supposedly reputable members of the business community was very common, and rarely qualified.

"High character and financial standing," as the *Chronicle* put it, had of course always been central to commercial transactions; no self-interested businessman wished to deal with deadbeats and crooks. The 1840s had seen the establishment of Lewis Tappan's credit reporting agency, later to become R. G. Dun & Co., which specialized in gathering and selling information about the creditworthiness of American merchants. With the "market revolution" (Charles Sellars) in full swing, personal networks could no longer fulfill this function, and Tappan stepped in to enable Americans to spread their business connections over an ever-expanding territory, engaging in transactions with men and women they had never personally encountered. The information sold by R. G. Dun focused on capital, character and capacity.[58] If a people were known to be honorable, hard working, and modest (and ideally, white Protestants), and had a history of paying their debts, they were considered creditworthy, even where, as was the rule during the first few decades, hard financial data about their business was lacking.[59] In Germany and Austria there existed no credit reporting agencies of a similar scale and importance. Instead, credit cooperatives, chambers of commerce, and other private institutions relied on their members to disseminate information about the character and reputation of merchants, bankers, and industrialists.[60] Bankers also maintained private networks of correspondence and exchange, which they used to systematically gather information about the personal qualities of businessmen, regularly requesting information about a man's "morality" and "character." As were the American credit reporting agencies, they, too, were more interested in human and ethical qualities than in hard numerical data; assessing a person became a substitute for assessing a business transaction.[61]

The financial press, in remarking on such issues of character, subscribed to the principles of credit reports and bankers' networks and sought to emulate their language. Inevitably, however, the pronouncements of journalists on such matters could not possess the same authority as those of specialized agencies. Although a journalist might occasionally refer to a banker's or promoter's past successful endeavors, most statements on character questions were usually lacking in detail and nuance, little more than summary pronouncements on what a journalist believed to be true, based on general hear-say. Compared to the books of credit reporting agencies, moreover, they were mostly positive; explicit warnings of dubious promoters and bankers were a relatively rare occurrence during the early 1870s.

Overcoming Distance

In June 1873, Moses Taylor received a letter from a client instructing him to "invest *Eight Thousand four hundred + eighty seven dollars* forty cents U.S. Currency in first class 1st mortgage R[ail].R[oad]. bonds gaining 7 to 8 percent, Securities that you consider perfectly safe. . . . I don't like those R. R. too far out West."[62] Taylor's correspondent did not explain what prompted his dislike, but Taylor likely understood. The railroads traversing the American West were enormous, relatively new enterprises and posed greater challenges to the ingenuity of engineers and financiers than the more established roads of the Northeast. Americans viewed the "Frontier" in the West as a mythic, awe-inspiring region, a huge reserve of land whose development required vast amounts of capital and labor, making it too risky an investment for conservative capitalists.[63]

For all the emphasis on figures, spreadsheets, and the character of promoters, the question of distance remained a pressing issue for investors and financial intermediaries during the early 1870s.[64] Early roads, both in Europe and the United States, had been held by local investors who had an interest in improving the infrastructure of their communities. Western railroads, and especially the transcontinentals, were different. They were built through vast spaces in which few European settlers had set foot, and were meant to create the towns and farms that would one day supply them with traffic. For this reason, and because of the sheer size of the enterprise, these railroads had to rely on distant investors who would never set eyes on the road in which they put their capital. For potential investors, this meant taking a leap of faith: not being able to rely on local knowledge and local networks of information, they instead responded to various incentives designed to compensate for the considerable risk associated with tying their financial fortune to such large and distant enterprises.

The most popular method of reducing risk was the lien. Instead of becoming an owner of a railroad by buying its stock, investors lent it money in return for the promise of fixed interest payments and a claim to a share of the corporation's land. This financial instrument—mortgage-backed debt—was made possible by the land grants that the American federal government extended to the transcontinental railroads. The transcontinentals "were more than business propositions. They were, like the Civil War, exercises in nation building."[65] From this perspective, providing the railroads with government aid was a legitimate exercise of political power, and throughout the 1860s, transcontinentals received government subsidies in the form of land grants (often land actually owned by Native Americans), loans, and financial guarantees. For potential investors, these subsidies lowered or minimized the risk of default—at least in theory. In a market hampered by problems of asymmetric information, government aid thus provided a source of trust, and made the railroad bond the preferred financial instrument of western and transcontinental railroads.[66]

Investors in the American Northeast and beyond nevertheless regarded the bonds of western railroads with a certain amount of suspicion. Advertising western bonds to one of his correspondents, New York banker George Opdyke noted in a similar vein that "there are a great many Bonds from the West offering on the market & hence anything in this line seeking purchases should challenge the greatest scrutiny." But, he assured his correspondent, "We are careful to handle nothing in which we do not conscientiously believe as reliable and desirable. The Bonds in question we have through the best parties in the West and believe them to be all that is claimed for them."[67] The banker's reputation and expertise, he suggested, vouched for the soundness of the bonds. Still, Opdyke's protestations were not sufficient to quell his client's concerns, as he himself recognized. Even those western railroads in which he had "great confidence" generally yielded higher returns than eastern ones, he remarked to another correspondent. This interest rate differential, he implied, signified a higher risk of default but one Opdyke considered commensurate with the expected return.[68]

Despite such efforts, the American capital market during the late 1860s and early 1870s could not absorb the masses of new railroad bonds. As in earlier periods, therefore, American financiers looked abroad in search for new buyers; experience had taught them that European investors were less reluctant than American ones when it came to putting their capital into "enterprises far removed from their usual experience."[69] American railroad securities had been a feature of German capital markets since the 1850s, sustained by the close personal ties between German American merchants and bankers on both sides of the Atlantic. Beginning in 1866, the Frankfurt Stock Exchange saw a boom of new offerings of American stocks and bonds, in many cases yielding attractive returns for German investors. According to one estimate, Europeans in 1869 had invested 243 million dollars in American railroad stocks and bonds. Although official statistics of German foreign investments do not exist for this period, we may assume that a significant portion of this total was held by Germans.[70]

In a letter to James Lanier, who played a leading role in channeling transatlantic capital flows during this period, Henry Villard noted that the "public at large looks upon all American securities as speculation and as such it wants them cheap and is accustomed to getting them cheap. Cheapness, indeed, is quite important a consideration with the mass of buyers as safety. This may seem strange, but is nonetheless strictly true."[71] A German financial writer took a similarly dim view of German investors in American railroads: "The capitalist in *Flachselfingen* examines the large prospectuses of the American Pacific Road with a knowing expression on his face, follows the road's construction through the endless Native American territories, through the wilderness of *rocky mountains*, examines the chances of the immeasurable rates of return . . . and—buys these valuable securities."[72] The fictive provincial German town of "Flachselfingen" only served to highlight what the writer considered to be an insuperable geographical barrier: a German provincial investor, he suggested, could not possibly possess enough information about the object of investment to allow him to make an informed assessment of the railroad's financial prospects.

Eighteen months earlier, the Prussian minister of commerce had written to the Berlin Board of Trade informing its directors that he had received an anonymous letter from New York warning him that the German market was being exploited by American sellers of dubious securities. Listing several such securities by name, the anonymous writer had suggested that domestic capitalists steer clear of such "fraudulent enterprises."[73] In response, the directors had reported that they had relayed the warning to the public, both at the Berlin Stock Exchange and in newspapers, and had decided to ban the securities of the Rockford and Rock Island Road from being listed at the Berlin exchange but otherwise declined to take any further measures "since this would rightfully be considered an encroachment of the freedom of trade."[74]

Johannes Roesing, the consul of the North German Confederation, had also weighed in on the matter in a letter to the minister of commerce in May, noting that many of the bonds considered dubious were not listed on the NYSE. While American investors confined themselves first to mortgage bonds yielding between 7 and 8 percent interest, he observed, they were happy to leave the riskier securities to foreigners. According to Roesing, not all houses engaged in marketing these securities were fraudulent; one "Jewish consortium," however, was particularly active in getting the German public engaged in "certain speculations," and had managed to influence the editor of the *New Yorker Handelszeitung*, a weekly New York paper that was held in greater esteem in Germany than in New York. But, he concluded, it would be wrong to suggest that the companies in question were out to actively defraud the German public. Rather, if Germans who lacked the means to accurately assess American conditions nevertheless chose to engage in dangerous speculations, they were guilty of considerable foolhardiness since "the high rates of interest . . . ought to enable everybody to recognize that they are running a considerable risk."[75] As did the Berlin Board of Trade, then, Roesing believed that investors themselves were ultimately responsible for the risk they ran, and that the transatlantic market for securities was sufficiently transparent to reflect a significant probability of default in the form of high rates of interest. But his racially tinged indictment of Jewish bankers as well as his comments about the *New Yorker Handelszeitung* also suggest that he did not believe financial intermediaries to be entirely blameless.

Roesing's assessment raises a larger question about the role played by financial intermediaries—both by the press and by bankers—in creating and channeling the transatlantic capital flows of the late 1860s and early 1870s. When it came to American railways, journalists displayed an awareness of physical distance that was very pronounced at times and indicated a significant skepticism regarding the degree of transatlantic integration during this period. The Frankfurt weekly *Der Aktionär* regularly commented on the market for American securities and oscillated between careful optimism, and increasingly, despair. In the early months of 1870, as the sale of American securities was gaining steam, the journal's Frankfurt reporter voiced his hope that "the banks who occupy themselves with importing this commodity [securities] to Europe, are fully conscious of their responsibility . . . and that the data with which they furnish the public and the press . . . (since neither capitalists nor journalists can travel to California or Georgia to examine the situation) will prove to be accurate and reliable." Unlike in earlier years, the correspondent noted, it was much easier to control and keep track of developments across the ocean since banks had expanded their network of agents, and thanks to the telegraph, information could now be transmitted much faster.[76]

As the year wore on, however, the journal's correspondents became increasingly critical in their assessments of the prospects of American railroads.[77] In May, the American banker Jay Cooke arrived in Europe to promote bonds of the Northern Pacific Railroad. Of the transcontinental railroads that were chartered in the 1860s, the Northern Pacific was the last to garner Congressional approval. Jay Cooke, the great financier of the Civil War, had seen the market for government bonds slowly dwindle toward the end of the decade, and, in search of new business opportunities, agreed to finance the road, which at the time had not even begun construction. Cooke had sent out a surveying party and orchestrated a large public relations campaign in which journalists filed dispatches from the surveying trail to their newspapers depicting the railroad as a promising enterprise. The result, however, had been underwhelming—the banking establishment was not won over, and Cooke had realized he would have to look abroad for investors. In Europe, too, he banked on the press to help him sell bonds, and managed to bring thirty of them on board in Germany alone. All in all, his German agents were provided with $100,000 for publicity.[78] The publicity in May and June 1870, however, came to naught when the Franco-Prussian War broke out, effectively scuttling Cooke's campaign. When peace was restored the following year, Cooke's agents managed to persuade a consortium of banks, led by the Union Bank of Vienna, to sign a contract for the sale of bonds. But his hopes were once again dashed when an expedition along the Northern Pacific's projected route by five commissioners on behalf of the consortium returned with an unfavorable impression. The bankers revoked the contract, and Cooke realized that he would have to win the backing of American investors if the enterprise was to succeed.[79] By then, German journalists were questioning the wisdom of German investors who seemed to be snapping up American securities without giving the matter the requisite scrutiny. One noted that Europe was teeming with the presidents of American railways seeking to advertise their companies to investors. The writer cautioned, perhaps mindful of Cooke's failed campaign, that not all that glistened was gold, and the company prospectuses tended to sugarcoat the railroads' conditions, which in reality looked much less auspicious.[80] Such warnings were soon vindicated: three American railroads defaulted that very year, twelve more would default the following year, and in 1873, another thirty-five railroads would fail to pay their bond holders.[81]

The flow of information from the United States across the Atlantic Ocean was indeed fraught with difficulties. Many German papers subscribed to the *New Yorker Handelszeitung* and reprinted or summarized its articles; the simple fact that it was written in German by German Americans made it a privileged source of news for the *Aktionär*, the *Börsen-Zeitung*, and others, presumably not just for practical linguistic reasons but because the shared national heritage in itself made the paper appear more trustworthy than its American counterparts (whose accounts, according to one writer, were likely to be "rather biased").[82]

The *Aktionär* did not restrict itself to reprinting the *Handelszeitung*'s articles but paid a correspondent to report directly from New York and published his reports in a special column entitled "American Mail." In June 1870, the correspondent told his Frankfurt editors that if they were prepared to wait a little longer "because of the work and research [such a task] required," he would soon furnish them with a "reliable spreadsheet from which your readers will very easily gather the location, administration, shares, future, and utilities of all roads currently being built or projected."[83] The correspondent's optimism suggested German investors could approach American railroads much like they would German ones, as a matter of interpreting numbers. But this implied that the information was indeed accurate and reliable. Was a lone American correspondent able to vouch for this? Henry Schuler, who, according to the credit reporting agency R. G. Dun & Co., worked as "the correspondent of some newspaper in Germany" and wrote its "financial articles" was "believed to have little or no means [and] is perhaps earning a living in a moderate way," supplementing his income from journalism with a brokerage business. In fact, Schuler (also known by his German name Heinrich Schüler) worked for the reputable *Frankfurter Zeitung*. Nevertheless, his existence appears to have been a modest one, making it unlikely that he was sufficiently well connected to have been privy to the financial information circulating in New York's banking community.[84]

Accurate information about American railroads, then, was in short supply, and German journalists often explicitly acknowledged as much.[85] Commenting on the newly introduced bonds of the St. Louis and South Eastern Railroad in 1871, the *Aktionär* noted that "New York reports, on whom we must always rely in such instances, since we cannot judge on the basis of an autopsy, describe the bonds as credible."[86] Ultimately, this meant that potential investors were left to their own devices. In some instances, journals would recommend that readers purchase a map depicting the American railway network or a book about the geography of California, noting that it contained important data of relevance both to potential emigrants and investors.[87] If such recommendations suggested the possibility that investors might, after all, overcome the problem of distance by pouring over books, this approach was not much help where individual roads were concerned. Here, investors could choose to believe the content of prospectuses, but journalists made it quite clear that this amounted to a leap of faith. Capital might easily flow across the Atlantic, but information did not.

Do such warnings indicate a critical self-awareness on the part of the media in these years, or do they reflect a bias against American securities that did not extend to German ones? By and large, German journalists refrained from passing critical comments on newly incorporated German companies; only rarely did they invoke the problem of physical distance when discussing investments in Germany.[88] Whether he was based in Frankfurt or Berlin, a correspondent for a German paper did not point out that he had not traveled to the Ruhr district, to Silesia or to Dresden before commenting on the securities of companies based in those regions. Where a company prospectus was judged inaccurate, the problem was not physical distance but a lack of forthrightness on the part of promoters and directors. The German market, it was assumed, was sufficiently integrated to render physical distance irrelevant. In this respect, the German perception differed markedly from how American investors viewed their economy. For, as the quotations at the beginning of this section show, Americans, too, believed that western railroads were a particularly risky object of investment. In some ways, their perspective corresponded to the way German journalists viewed the United States: as a distant, prosperous country with great economic potential, yet too far removed to allow a judicious assessment of exactly what an investor might expect.

Why, then, did German journalists emphasize physical distance the way they did? European travelers to the United States had always marveled at the country's sheer size and vastness. Indeed, the idea of America as a continent of abundant space and freely available land was almost as old as the European discovery of the continent itself. Such images persisted even as Europeans registered America's rapid economic growth following the Civil War. Increasingly, from the 1860s onward, the European discourse on the United States encompassed both images of economic and technological development as well as images of the West as a region of untamed wilderness and abundant natural resources, even as it rapidly filled up with settlers and, increasingly, European tourists.[89] The same set of images pervaded the advertisements that banks published in German newspapers to promote American railroad bonds. Almost all contained detailed descriptions of American geography and nature, evoking greatness and vastness, while at the same time emphasizing the coal fields, doggers, saltworks, and cornfields that would supply the railroads with traffic. Where a road traversed a region that was already densely settled and part of a developed infrastructure, advertisements emphasized the increased speed and efficiency that would result when the new railroad was connected to already existing ones, and no advertisement failed to mention the prospect of a growing population that would supply railroads with passenger traffic. Most advertisements depicted the new railroad as a promising addition to an already prospering economy. In this respect, they were not dissimilar from prospectuses of German railways. Railroads running through the sparsely populated Midwest, by contrast, were depicted as an essential agent of economic development that would make the region an attractive destination for newly arrived settlers. Here, the dominant image was one of vastness, emptiness, and natural abundance. This did not, however, contradict the images of economic growth; the West, from this perspective, was simply a territory waiting to be tapped by enterprising settlers and set on the same course of rapid economic development that the East was already enjoying. The Springfield and Illinois South Eastern Railway, according to one such notice, would traverse "one of the most blessed regions of the state of Illinois, known for its fertility" and would open up rich districts to commerce, "some of which have up until now lacked any kind of communication."[90] Potential investors in the St. Louis and South Eastern Railways were promised that the railroad's value would increase in tandem with the region's development.[91]

In spite of such grandiose claims and elaborate descriptions, however, many journalists remained skeptical as to the profitability of investments in American railways. In August 1872, the *Aktionär* wrote almost despairingly that no other security testified to the "truth of the principle that the bond loan is fundamentally just a personal loan" as did the American bond. Although bonds were nominally secured through real estate, the investor in fact chose to put his trust in the integrity of a person. Most of the time, the investor lacked "even the most general knowledge of the bonded objects; he only sent his money across the ocean in the good faith that the businesses which brought the securities to the European market, are trustworthy."[92] According to this writer, then, choosing to invest in American bonds meant overcoming physical distance by taking a leap of faith, and putting one's trust in the good name and reputation of a banker, much as did the investor who, faced with a confusing array of figures, studied the names of a company's directors and promoters to identify one in whose shares he or she could have confidence.

The banking houses tasked with selling American securities were acutely aware of this. Jay Cooke, in an attempt to assuage the concerns of German investors spooked by the Berlin bourse's warning in the spring of 1871, had publicly touted his credentials as a banker with more than thirty years of experience, and noted that he had "made it a matter of conscience to examine carefully into every railroad project presented to us."[93] Another, lesser-known banker wrote in a similar vein that "only a few specific state and Railroad Bonds have ever proven discreditable because unfortunately managed by *bad men.* . . . It is always best to know the *men* who initiate and manage these securities."[94] In the virtual world of financial information, both numerical information and physical distance could be disregarded as long as one was prepared to trust a person—or, more accurately, to trust a name whose aura was itself the product of the discourse of financial journalism. Henry Villard acknowledged this in a letter to a correspondent, noting that "a good deal of importance is attached to the connection of big names with similar enterprises, inasmuch as they produce a great effect on the public."[95] Names became "big names" by a logic of repetition and seriality: attaching themselves to enterprise after enterprise was what endowed them with authority, respectability, and trustworthiness. Investors, then, could not escape the virtual world of financial information; names, too, were immaterial, a product of words and images that were suggestive of the old way of commerce but could not replicate its principle of face-to-face interaction.

For all the emphasis on discourse, we must not forget that underneath the layers of numbers and images lay something very material: the conquering of men and nature through labor and warfare. In Richard White's words, "money, railroads, nation building, and empire were not easily separated."[96] This nexus was obscured, or at most hinted at, in the pages of financial journals. Often, these conjured an image of the American West as a territory that was vast, fertile—and empty. While exaggerations and unfounded claims were, of course, par for the course in the marketing of financial instruments, describing the territory as uninhabited was especially misleading. For a significant part of the projected Northern Pacific route was, in fact, inhabited by Native Americans, a fact of which Cooke himself was acutely conscious, and which he discussed with William S. Hancock, an army general with intimate knowledge of the region. "In regard of Indian expenditures," Hancock informed Cooke in January 1870, before the start of the European bond campaign, "it is not seen that the construction of a railway into their country upon the line proposed will in any way tend immediately to diminish them; it will most probably provoke their hostility, especially that of the Sioux, and lead to a war ending in their possible destruction."[97]

This was, from Cooke's perspective, not simply an inconvenience to be kept from the European public so as not to dampen their appetite for bonds. Rather, Cooke, quite the pragmatist, ignored the matter when addressing potential investors but was happy to highlight it when seeking political support for his enterprise. The Northern Pacific depended on government subsidies, and Cooke and his partners, in lobbying members of Congress, stressed that the Northern Pacific would, in the words of its engineer, W. Milnor Roberts, "forever settle the question of white supremacy over an area of country covering at least 450,000 square miles."[98] Such imperial ambitions resonated with politicians who believed in westward expansion as America's manifest destiny but would not necessarily have elicited similar responses from European investors. While Europeans were keen readers of sentimental novels depicting the plight of Native Americans, and their displacement and extermination at the hands of the American government was a much discussed topic in European societies (a debate in which Germans often sided with the latter, believing that white settlers had a God-given right to the Native Americans' land), such questions not surprisingly disappeared from view as soon as money was at stake.[99] No matter how one felt about Native Americans, the topic was best avoided in official railroad prospectuses lest potential investors worry that their capital be used to perpetuate the very policies they condemned as armchair moralists, or that the presence of Native Americans would make the entire project seem a less than safe investment.

The Northern Pacific and other railroads also partook of other, very material global processes involving the large-scale movement of people. In promoting the road, it was made clear to the public that its construction would go hand in hand with the settlement of the Northwest by Europeans, especially Germans, since Germany, at the time, was once again seeing large-scale transatlantic migration.[100] Ideally, in Cooke's vision, the flow of people would have followed the flow of capital; both were essential to the project's viability. Wealthy investors would enable and finance the movement of their poorer compatriots, which in turn would marginalize, and eventually destroy, the livelihoods of Native Americans. Taken together, this nexus, never spelled out in detail, was typical of the manifold social and ethnic hierarchies that globalization engendered.

Such hierarchies sustained railroad investments in other ways too. Employees of local northern railroads were disproportionately likely to be white, while in the postbellum South, black railroad workers were denied the skilled positions they had occupied under slavery.[101] Where working conditions were more hostile, as in the case of transcontinentals, the opposite situation prevailed. Thus when the transcontinental Central Pacific had found itself short of funds and with few prospects of raising money in the 1860s, its managers had decided to employ Chinese laborers whose wages were lower than those of white workers.[102] Alluding to this, Milnor Roberts had, in his preliminary report to Jay Cooke, made the point that his estimate of the overall cost made no allowance that labor costs might be lowered by the employment of Chinese workers.[103] Although this was, in 1870, a mere possibility as far as the Northern Pacific was concerned, it, too, pointed to a transatlantic economy more violent than the enticing vision of interconnectedness peddled to European investors.

Narrating Growth

In 1871 and 1872, financial intermediaries constructed a discourse of financial information and investment that shaped and, in part, created the speculative bubble that would burst in 1873. But if the wealth of information was overwhelming, and the prospective returns of an investment difficult to calculate, how then were investors persuaded that the purchase of securities would bring them prosperity? John Maynard Keynes famously argued that in modern anonymous securities markets, where investors have no special knowledge of the businesses in which they might invest, the dominant tendency becomes not to focus on the long-term profits of an investment but to anticipate the psychology of the market. An investor, in other words, must anticipate how other market participants *perceive* the value of an investment. This strategy, coupled with a tendency in humans to base their actions not on "a weighted average of quantitative benefits multiplied by quantitative possibilities" but, rather, on "animal spirits—a spontaneous urge to action," results in a situation where numbers and calculations seem dispensable, and investors become content with anticipating the overall trajectory of future returns.[104] In a rising market, investments are thus made because many investors believe, as well as believe others to believe, that prices will continue to rise, thus nourishing a self-fulfilling prophecy.

What, then, made contemporaries in the early 1870s think that prices on securities markets would continue to rise? The nineteenth-century observers had very few of those economic indicators at their disposal, which in our age have become naturalized to the point of apparent self-evidence; no attempt was made to calculate a country's gross domestic product. Financial markets, too, were not subjected to calculations that would have allowed them to plot their development over time. The now-ubiquitous use of visualizations in the form of plots and curves was unknown. The Dow Jones Index was first designed in the 1880s, and economic graphs only became a regular feature in economic textbooks in the early twentieth century. Before then, the tabular form of representation had dominated not only the pages of financial journals but also academic treatises on economic questions (the natural sciences, by contrast, had long discovered the advantages of visualization).[105] Economic actors of the 1870s, then, had to rely on other means to interpret developments on financial markets, in production and trade. Aiming to make sense of what was happening under their eyes, they relied on narrative representations of economic activity to extrapolate future developments.

In March 1870, just a few months before the beginning of the Franco-Prussian War that would bring the long anticipated unification of the German lands, an observer in Frankfurt noted that "the business of incorporating companies is gaining more and more steam in this city."[106] The shares of two new corporations, another observer wrote in April, had been immediately oversubscribed. He was not sure whether this development was wholly welcome, and suggested that the promoters had only allowed subscriptions of 105 shares or more, thus excluding those more modest and honest investors who were not interested in quick and artificial gains.[107] Such skepticism notwithstanding, the message was clear: promoters were optimistic, and investors were responding to their call. The military campaigns of the following months dampened the prevailing optimism, but France's surrender and the signing of the peace treaty quickly revived it.[108] By March 1872, the Frankfurt *Aktionär* took stock of the economic developments of the past year: "Enterprise and the association of capital have, since the glorious end of the war with France, achieved impressive things. . . . Germany has not seen a similar period of material development. . . . We have surpassed France and are on a par with England and America." Germany's economic rise, he concluded, was motivated by the "course of world history." It was not fraudulent but real.[109] Others, too, searched for indicators that might justify the rising prices of securities, and found them in the growth of production. The iron and mining industries, the *Börsen-Zeitung* observed, had recently seen a great upturn, spurred on not least by the profits they had made during the war. Prices for raw materials were rising, and mining companies in the Ruhr district were as prosperous as never before. Railroads were seeing an upsurge in the transportation of goods that surpassed even the growth of passenger traffic.[110]

Germany's military victory over France and the peace treaty that followed inspired optimism not just in Germans but also in Austrians. "The peace agreement," one Austrian journalist noted when looking back on 1871, "has induced a worldwide change." This process of global dimensions had indirectly affected Austria's economic organism, he explained. The financial development of both Germany and Austria had been most fortunate, even during times of crisis, such as the recent war: "The rule is a progressive growth of values, a significant increase in production and—even more significant than this—a general increase of the productive power."[111] Already in August the same publication had noted that Austrians had ample reason for optimism for the Austrian railroad network was expanding at a rapid pace, and there was, the article's author claimed, "probably no other means of elevating the material wealth of the population and the finances of a state as efficiently as railroads can." The recent progress in this respect was cause for the "greatest expectations."[112]

Likewise, in the United States, it was above all the growth of railroads that suggested to contemporaries that their country was facing a bright and prosperous future. "To a young country such as ours," the *Railroad Journal* noted in May 1871, "there is probably no agency more essential than railroads, and none, perhaps of late years has played more important part in the development of the country."[113] The *Chronicle* was similarly optimistic: "Our railroad system," it claimed in October, "has grown up from small, ill-connected beginnings, during a long course of years, and is rapidly undergoing a series of changes in transition to a more compact, unified, economical and harmonious policy."[114] What motivated these sanguine assessments was a vision of the United States as a young country whose vast economic potential and seemingly unlimited resources had yet to be fully realized.[115]

What the German journalist had termed the "course of world history" implied a linear, progressive vision of historical and economic development. The American idea of the course and future of their country's development carried similar overtones[116] that in both cases also appealed to readers' nationalism and patriotism. To them, these pronouncements suggested that they could and should partake in this development by investing in the corporations that supported it. The effect on the financial market was palpable, as a writer for *Bankers' Magazine* noted in July 1872: "The most engrossing topic in Wall street is the pressing demand for money in behalf of the numerous and heavy railroad undertakings in the West. . . . No roads are undertaken without first feeling the financial pulse of Wall street; and if no political or commercial disturbances are prevailing or threatened, capital responds promptly to the call."[117] "The general public is thoroughly dazed and bejuggled," the *Nation* wrote in August. Though warning of a possible future downturn, it argued that it could not yet be imminent, as the fire in Chicago some months earlier had failed to cause a panic.[118]

There were other signs of growth, not couched in a grandiose language of development but still indicating how wide optimism and exuberance had spread. The intense activity on German and Austrian stock exchanges spawned a new type of bank, the *Maklerbank*. Initially a Berlin phenomenon, the institution quickly spread to other cities, and came under particular scrutiny in 1872, when some commentators began wondering whether the proliferation of *Maklerbanken* were evidence that speculation was getting out of hand. In their operations, these banks focused exclusively on securities trading, collecting money from investors and channeling it to promoters, thus expanding the pool of investors and allowing even those with relatively little means to speculate in futures.[119] The *Börsen-Zeitung* at first embraced them, noting that their "legitimacy derived from the great expansion of the securities business on our bourse." The director of one of the new banks, Hugo Pringsheim, it was noted, was "a personality widely esteemed in stock exchange circles, and his acuity in business matters is widely recognized."[120] Within a short period of time, however, the paper's editors reversed their assessment, noting in mid-January, when it seemed as though a new *Maklerbank* was being established every couple of days, that "the productivity which the stock exchange is currently developing in this respect . . . is hardly beneficial to the general public, even though nothing critical can be said of the personalities heading these new companies."[121]

To learn of the proliferation of *Maklerbanken*, and to understand their function vis-à-vis the stock exchange, a reader had to identify and read the articles inconspicuously tucked away in one of the columns of their daily paper. There were, however, other, more visible manifestations of the rapid expansion of financial markets; even a cursory flick through the pages of a newspaper revealed where corporations advertised their public offering. These advertisements, typically, occupied an entire page, and their layout and physical appearance followed a standard template. The company's name was printed in huge bold letters, followed by information about where and how to subscribe to its shares. Several paragraphs of small print detailed its business model and described, in optimistic terms, its expected future profits. The number of pages devoted to such notices grew so rapidly that even a casual reader was unlikely to miss it, with the number of advertisements, in one paper, increasing from four per week in April 1871 to fifteen per week just one year later.[122] In Austrian papers, too, the space devoted to advertisements grew during this time, from ten pages in the *Neue Freie Presse* on January 1, 1870 to 11.5 a year later and 13 in November 1872.[123]

Another, different kind of advertisement, the *Eingesandte*, similarly proliferated during this time. These short, anonymous messages invited readers to buy the shares of a certain company that, it was predicted, were undervalued. In September 1872, one issue of the *Börsen-Zeitung* printed thirty-one such messages. Readers were told that, if they bought shares now, they would make a handsome profit when the inevitable price increase materialized. The underlying logic was performative, that of a self-fulfilling prophesy: no matter how spurious the reason why a share was undervalued seemed, its price would inevitably go up as long as a sufficient number of investors believed the rumor to be true. This, too, was evidence of a speculative fever in which short-term profits had become the major rationale of securities trading, a logic that appealed above all to small investors with little experience of the stock exchange, as one journalist noted, a further indication of how far the speculative fever had spread.[124]

Symptoms of this could also be found in the Viennese press. In the first half of 1872, a man by the name of Johann Baptist Placht began advertising his business in all the major papers, quickly garnering widespread attention. The first messages were small (typically of the size of one-sixteenth of a page) and unobtrusive, inviting readers to place orders for securities with his house, which he promised to execute at the cheapest rates.[125] By June, Placht's advertisements had grown in size and now typically occupied a whole or half a page. His business model, too, had changed: he now invited clients to deposit a minimum of 500 florins, callable every month at five days notice, with his *Börsen-Comptoir*, which he promised to invest at high rates of interest with "no risk whatsoever," claiming that he had been able to make a 15 percent profit in one month for previous clients.[126] By November, he was promising monthly returns of 20 percent.[127]

American media did not, by and large, display similar visual manifestations of a widespread exuberance. Financial publications and general newspapers relied on advertisements for income, and American bankers used them to promote securities, especially railroad bonds. Unlike their German and Austrian counterparts, however, these notices were not especially conspicuous; even the largest among them occupied only a part of a column and never stretched over whole or even just half a page. Still, a careful observer would have noticed that the advertising space devoted to railroad bonds grew significantly between 1871 and 1872. In June 1871, the New York weekly *Independent* carried, on average, five advertisements for railroad bonds per issue; by June the following year, this number had more than doubled, rising to an average of nine per issue.[128]

The widespread narratives of economic growth, and the proliferation of flashy advertisements lured ever more people to jump onto the bandwagon, seduced by the possibility of quickly won spectacular profits. In this atmosphere, even those of a skeptical disposition might have been persuaded to take the chance to join the fray, hoping to cash in, in the nick of time.

Conclusion

Newspapers and journalists on both sides of the Atlantic shaped the discourse of investing during the early 1870s. Journalists presented their readers with financial information in the form of tables and spreadsheets as well as almost uniformly positive narrative reports. In this, they subscribed to the notion championed in contemporary investment manuals examined in the previous chapter: finance and investing required an active, calculating attitude. But the overwhelming amount of information was more likely to induce indecision than active decision making on the part of the investor. Where American railroad bonds were concerned, the problem was exacerbated by the acutely felt distance between the investor and the object of investment, a distance that was much less likely to be commented on where German companies where concerned. In both cases, journalists, following a logic of personification, frequently stressed that investors must rely on honorable bankers to anchor their investment decisions. Unlike the seemingly endless numbers and words of financial pages, virtual signifiers with no clear meaning, the name of a banker appeared concrete and real, and once again made finance seem intelligible, a transaction between real persons based on traditional notions of trust—though this aura of trustworthiness, too, was largely a product of words. The role of the media in fostering the speculative bubble, then, was not one of straightforward influence with a predictable result. Journalists emphasized rationality and trustworthiness while at the same time constructing a narrative of rapid economic growth. The overall effect was to create an atmosphere of optimism and exuberance in which individually reasoned investment decisions mattered less than the very act of investing itself. The signs of speculative excess that were already emerging in 1872 did little to dampen this mood. Rather, they may well have simply heightened the sense of urgency on the part of investors, signaling that there was, perhaps, not much time left to buy and sell before prices came tumbling down.

CHAPTER 3

PREDICTING AND EXPERIENCING THE PANICS OF 1873

In 1872 and 1873, warnings of a "sudden downturn," a "grand reckoning," were regularly being sounded in the pages of the financial press, as more and more observers began feeling that the current level of economic activity could not be sustained much longer. Financial markets, it seemed, had taken on a life of their own, divorced from individual human action, and threatening to unleash their destructive powers. Capitalist societies on both sides of the Atlantic had witnessed several panicked contractions in the past, some of them severe, and the recent panic of 1857 in particular was still fresh in people's memory. Indeed, many had come to believe that periodically recurring crises were an inevitable component of capitalism. "Interpreting aright the signs," as one commentator put it, was, even in normal times, the very essence of commercial activity; but where, as in 1873, the economy seemed in danger of overheating, it became more important than ever. Consequently, predictions of if, when, and why a panic might strike abounded. Against the mysterious and destructive power of a looming panic, commentators aimed to affirm a measure of predictability and intelligibility by discussing its possibility, shape, and timing. Many contemporaries in the run-up to the panic displayed a clear awareness of past economic crises and frequently considered the possibility of whether a new one might be imminent. Mostly, however, they tended to conceive a potential new crisis as a national, rather than transnational event. This discursive "nationalization" of financial markets was a means of rendering financial markets intelligible by gainsaying their expansive nature. When Jay Cooke & Co. failed in September, Germans and

Austrians at first dismissed the idea that the American panic might spill over to the European continent but, as days and weeks went by, they increasingly began interpreting events in their countries in the light of American developments. In this latter phase, these observers betrayed an acute awareness of transnational economic connections, even where they sought to downplay them. This transnational consciousness, however, was asymmetrical: it was pronounced in Europe but much less so in the United States.

Business Cycle Theories and Transnational Connections

Many observers felt, in 1872 and 1873, that speculative activity on the stock exchange was becoming ever more excessive. The speculative mindset, it seemed, was permeating every sphere of life, and the thirst for quick profits knew no limits. Commenting on the German market for securities in February 1873, banker Gerson von Bleichröder remarked that "in Germany, one is no longer content with low rates of interest, the price of all of life's needs having risen, while at the same time the demands in all walks of society are higher. Private investors, wishing to enjoy a better life, now prefer mining securities and other industrial items or speculative securities, regardless of whether they can still sleep at night."[1] A year earlier, the *Berliner Tageblatt* reported on the "addiction to wealth without work" and related the story of a milkman from the provinces who, wishing to invest his inheritance safely, had been lured to an "elegant room" in Berlin by a genteel-looking couple, who then proceeded to sell him shares of little value.[2]

Such phenomena were hardly new. Max Wirth, whose *Geschichte der Handelskrisen* had first been published in 1858, quoted from an "old scripture" by a contemporary in his account of the Dutch tulip mania: "Noblemen, merchants, craftsmen, shippers, peasants, gate carriers, chimney sweeps, workmen, maids, women trading in junk [*Trödelweiber*] were afflicted with the same addiction."[3] These well-worn images evoked events of an earlier age that, in the end, had brought ruin to all those small-time speculators, who were now once again populating the scene. What could seem more plausible, therefore, than drawing a parallel between the history of earlier panics and present-day developments, concluding that a financial disaster was in the making?

In the United States, the notion of periodically recurring economic crises had first been put forward in the 1820s. Classical political economists, however, whose models were premised on the concept of an economic equilibrium, had shown little interest in such disruptions. It was only after the dramatic commercial disruptions of 1825, 1837, 1848, and 1857 that the theory of continuously recurring crises gained currency. In 1862, the French doctor and statistician Clément Juglar published a study in which he used the method of time series analysis to argue that crises recurred with a certain regularity and shared various causes and features.[4] In 1865, the German economist Wilhelm Roscher denied that crises erupted on a regular basis. In this, however, he differed from the majority of his German colleagues who, influenced by Mill's *Principles of Political Economy*, recognized the existence not just of crises but of an entire business cycle—as did Juglar—in which crises constituted a necessary corrective to manic overspeculation and temporary gluts.[5] In the United States, the concept of overproduction as the cause of commercial crises was less popular. Instead, Americans were more likely to believe that panics were caused by a flawed monetary system.[6]

Many crisis theorists recognized the significance of transnational economic and financial connections. According to the German economist and journalist Max Wirth, these had been manifest since the early nineteenth century: "Since the beginning of the nineteenth century the commercial relations between England and North America in particular have become so close and significant, the mutual trade [*Verkehr*] interacts so precisely, that not only the stagnations in trade in one country are vividly experienced in the other but that the causes of true crises emanate from one realm as much as from the other, and that one experiences the hits affecting the other almost to the same degree."[7] Juglar, who (unlike Wirth) relied on statistical material to corroborate his claims, had observed something quite similar: "The more we observe commercial crises since we possess official information about the situation from the banks in France, in England, and in the United States . . . the more we are convinced that their trajectory, their accidents are becoming more and more concurrent, and that as soon as an embarrassment makes itself felt on one or the other side of the Atlantic, it is rare that the opposite side does not respond."[8]

Juglar believed that crises could only occur in countries in which industry and trade were highly developed. Where there was little division of labor and little trade with foreign countries, he claimed, domestic trade was more secure and less prone to the disruptions caused by a credit economy. In the United States, Henry Carey argued in a similar vein that crises and depressions were the result of a mismatch between supply and demand, and such a mismatch was more likely to occur in a large, anonymous market. For this reason, countries engaged in international trade were prone to panics and economic depressions. In a variation on this theme, Carey's student William Elder described periodically recurring cataclysms as the result of excessive speculation in foreign goods, which condemned domestic capital and industriousness to idleness.[9]

But such an awareness did not necessarily translate into a clear concept of contagion. Rather, these works explicitly or implicitly relied on an understanding of the world economy as an ensemble of national entities interacting with each other. Thus both Wirth and Juglar in their accounts posited nations as the main actors of their narrative and, while acknowledging the connections between them, treated each country individually and consecutively.[10] This view was prevalent throughout the second half of the nineteenth century when the idea of a "world economy" first gained traction among German economic writers and theorists.[11] Writers on the business cycle, although they did not use the term "world economy," implicitly subscribed to this notion.

German Premonitions

Wirth, Juglar, and Carey were theorists, not men engaged in commercial activity. Yet their ideas—whether through active reception or by virtue of shared observations and experiences—resembled those of bankers, merchants, and financial journalists who, believing that crises had come to be a regular feature of economic activity, in 1872 and 1873 wondered whether a new one might be on the horizon. In Germany, some had considered the pace of economic activity unsustainable as early as 1870. In the second half of 1872, warnings of an impending financial disaster rapidly multiplied.[12] One financial writer recalled the panic of 1857 and wondered what would become of the "countless railroad and industrial securities of all kinds . . . if a huge crisis, like the one seen in America in 1857, were to engulf Europe?"[13] In October 1872, the *Aktionär* published a translation of an article that had previously appeared in the *Nation*.[14] The article criticized the current "feverish" taste for railroads securities and maintained that the number of new railroads far exceeded demand. It concluded that while a financial crisis was not imminent, there was nevertheless reason to believe that a financial storm was brewing, to erupt sometime during the few next years. The *Aktionär*'s Frankfurt correspondent similarly evoked the possibility of a renewed crisis, noting that all of Europe's bourses were experiencing a "feeling of uneasiness," but he did not consider the possibility that the expected American crisis might be the trigger of such an event.[15] Neither writer imagined the coming crisis as a transatlantic one. If it were to happen, they suggested, it would be a German, or at most a European event. The interconnectedness of European financial markets was vividly demonstrated when the French government, in 1872, began transferring installments of the French war indemnity from Paris via London to Germany, a process that was closely followed by financial observers. Some noted that the sudden plethora of money had helped fuel a speculative bubble, others emphasized that as long as a part of the sum remained outstanding, a panic born of stringency was not to be expected.[16]

While the United States did not seem a likely source of instability, German observers subjected the Viennese stock exchange to much closer scrutiny. The financial connections between Vienna and Berlin as well as Vienna and

Frankfurt were strong. Some Austrian shares were cross-listed on German exchanges and enjoyed great popularity among speculative investors, on some days dominating the mood of the entire market. Price differentials between these exchanges were accordingly small. In terms of price formation, Berlin enjoyed the upper hand: up to 80 percent of new price information regarding two Austrian railway companies originated in Berlin and spread not only to Vienna but also to Paris and London.[17] To contemporary observers of the stock exchange, however, the relationship between the two bourses did not appear wholly one-sided. Rather, people feared that a crisis would not originate in Berlin but in Vienna and only then spread to German markets.

Toward the end of 1872, these fears began to materialize. In early October, things at first had seemed promising: the *Börsen-Zeitung* announced an upward movement on the Berlin exchange and traced this development to positive developments on foreign bourses. The recent concerns about a crisis in Vienna and its negative effects on the atmosphere in Berlin, the writer argued, could, for now, be put to rest.[18] Most observers, however, agreed that conditions in Vienna were still unhealthy and thus aimed to immunize the Berlin market from any negative reverberations. In a letter to N. M. Rothschild in London, Gerson von Bleichröder noted that the bulls at the Berlin Stock Exchange were concerned that the speculative fever in Vienna might negatively affect the situation on their home market; Bleichröder himself believed that, "for the time being," no crisis was imminent, and that the feverish excess would correct itself.[19] The Berlin stock market, however, embarked on a protracted decline that lasted into the early months of 1873. "Our market," the *Berliner Tageblatt* now wrote, "is following events in Vienna, which now once again have become somewhat distressing, with as much attention as is warranted in view of the existing solidarity of our bourse with that in Vienna." The fact that the "money calamity" in Vienna had thus far not led to significant declines only reinforced "the solidity or rather the healthy position of our exchange."[20] In this instance, as in others, the causal connections between price movements in both cities was simultaneously recognized and downplayed.

Eager to explore the causes of the sudden downturn, one German journalist looked to the French indemnity and argued that the expectations of a plethora of money, coupled with the continued delay of its actual arrival, had caused scarcity on "all money markets of the world," and wondered whether a "general crisis" was on the horizon.[21] The mood turned gloomier still when the liberal parliamentarian Eduard Lasker, in a series of widely noticed parliamentary debates, publicly accused Prussian state officials of colluding with dubious railroad entrepreneurs for personal gain.[22] Still, as late as April, Gerson von Bleichröder remained optimistic on account of the next installment of the French indemnity: "I cannot describe our market but as somewhat flooded with speculative securities," he wrote, "but I have no doubt that this state of affairs will even out over the next couple of months, namely because the next installment of the French war contribution will produce an over-supply of money which will prevent a significant decline in the stock market."[23] He concluded that a crisis in Berlin was "inconceivable."

Crash in Vienna

In Vienna, meanwhile, the writing was already on the wall. For many months, Austrian observers had looked to other European, especially German, markets for cues, convinced that the Viennese stock exchange was more or less dependent on the influence of foreign bourses.[24] Even the most generous dividends could not guarantee the value of the most solid securities, one observer noted, if Berlin or Frankfurt were in a "frowning mood."[25] By March 1873, however, it was becoming increasingly clear that local, not European, developments were on everybody's mind. At the end of the month, the securities listed on the Viennese stock exchange registered an all-time high, and then began a steady decline. Ominous warning signs were multiplying. While some of the large Austrian banks announced disappointingly meager dividends, several of the smaller banks at first glance appeared to show greater largesse. On closer inspection, however, it turned out that these seemingly generous dividends were not the result of impressive earnings but would be paid out of the companies' capital. Many observers now began wondering whether the account books of the young *Maklerbanken* had been cooked all along.[26]

Suspicion and distrust were ripe, but still investors pinned their hopes on the opening of the world exhibition, scheduled for the beginning of May. The fifth world exhibition had triggered a construction boom in the Viennese capital, and authorities expected as many as twenty million visitors.[27] When the expected influx of visitors failed to materialize, however, it quickly became clear that the event would not provide the stimulus necessary to sustain the stock market, and share prices were sent tumbling. May 9 became Vienna's "Black Friday," when one of the city's best-known brokers failed, with several smaller ones following in his wake. To avert further failures, the *Börsenkammer* announced a moratorium until May 15. Until then, all securities would be valued at a fixed *Compensationscours*, and a fund was established to loan money against collateral to those wishing to settle their balances. On May 11, a group of bankers and traders called on the finance minister to announce government measures to avert further disasters while an association of Viennese merchants warned the minister of commerce that a commercial crisis was imminent. In light of such dire warnings, the Austrian council of ministers, heeding the advice of the deputy governor of the National Bank and of several people affiliated with the stock exchange, decided to suspend the bank act, hoping that an increase in the money supply would provide relief. The decision was officially announced on May 13 but did not have the desired effect.[28] When, on May 15, the *Börsekammer* refused to grant a further extension for outstanding settlements, brokers and speculators went down en masse.

Commenting on the events in Vienna, the *Börsen-Zeitung* noted that the effects on the Berlin market were "relatively small due to the fact that a bearish tendency has been dominating for weeks and that the reaction, which has now manifested itself in Vienna in the stormiest manner, is here proceeding at a slow and calm pace."[29] When stocks in Berlin declined sharply only a few days later, readers were reminded that the situation was not comparable to that in Vienna. One must not, a journalist cautioned, "judge our bourse by the same standard as Vienna's . . . that large amount of merely fictitious values without any real basis that were created in Vienna are lacking here."[30] By calling for the application of different standards, these writers downplayed the possibility of contagion and implicitly treated both bourses as isolated, independent entities.

This does not mean, however, that observers who held such views were engaged in wishful thinking. Rather, a close examination of price movements on the Berlin and Vienna bourses in May 1873 reveals a considerable degree of independence. Instead of closely tracking developments in Vienna, it appears that investors in Berlin decided to ignore the volatile situation in Vienna as best they could and make their own independent judgments regarding the buying and selling of securities.[31]

The Berlin reporter of the *Aktionär* was nevertheless somewhat more skeptical in assessing the Vienna crash's international impact. Given the intimate relationship between both cities and the "connectivity of the stock market trade that is common today," he wrote, the German bourses would inevitably suffer. Nevertheless, the "evil tidings" from Vienna had not resulted in mayhem.[32] Reporting to London, Werner Siemens observed that Berliners were hoping to avoid an outright crash but that prices were nevertheless declining steadily.[33] In August, however, the tone was once again optimistic: "No sound person familiar with the stock market still expects a sudden crash or other . . . eventualities," it was now claimed. A disaster on the Berlin bourse was practically impossible.[34] Even a careful observer such as Bleichröder was not, in the aftermath of the Vienna crash, inclined to revise his earlier prognosis that a "crisis in Berlin was inconceivable." In August, he wrote to London that market conditions in Berlin and Vienna were improving daily and that one had reason to hope that a "regular bull market" would begin in autumn.[35]

Not everyone was similarly sanguine. In an article entitled "Perspectives of World Trade," the *Deutsch-Amerikanische Oeconomist* worried that, if a rich harvest were to reduce European demand for American wheat, a commercial crisis might ensue in the United States, whose economy had already been weakened by lackluster European demand for American railroad securities. Such a crisis would in turn have severe consequences for conditions in Germany. Responding to these observations, the *Oesterreichische Oekonomist* went even further, arguing that a commercial crisis was already brewing in Europe and the United States and was slowly making its way to the surface. Sooner or later, it was sure to erupt with full force and all that remained to be seen was which country would trigger the outbreak. Given the degree of worldwide economic integration, the author concluded, contagion was inevitable: every disruption in every single country was in danger of becoming a general, all-encompassing one.[36] This dire warning, however, was the exception rather than the rule; most observers were still reluctant to imagine a major transatlantic crisis.

American Qualms

Americans, meanwhile, focused their attention on London, the hub of world trade and finance. London-based merchants and agents organized large parts of the movement of international shipping, and London banks, relying on the City's money market and stock exchange, catered to the international trading community by acting as intermediaries between sovereigns, entrepreneurs, and capitalists. Since the London money market was the most liquid, banks from all over the world kept funds in the City.[37] The state of the London money market and stock exchange was hence of crucial importance to world trade, and American and British stock markets displayed a high degree of price convergence. Every major American commercial and financial publication regularly reported on developments on the London Stock Exchange and discussed the significance of the policies of the Bank of England (BOE) as well as specie flows between the two countries. This preoccupation with British affairs was not purely economic in nature. Relations between the two countries had become strained when diplomatic efforts to resolve a dispute stemming from the Civil War failed repeatedly, with stock markets reacting violently to what they saw as a possible harbinger of an armed conflict. Fearing the economic and financial implications of such a turn of events, Anglo-American bankers became key figures in the negotiations that eventually resulted in a peaceful solution.[38]

Compared to London's political and financial clout, the European bourses seemed less significant, and reports from the German exchanges were shorter and appeared less frequently than those from London. American observers noted the potentially disruptive effects of the French indemnity mainly because it was channeled through London and risked upsetting the London money market. Worried that the first installment of the French indemnity would drain gold from the BOE's vaults, creating mayhem on the London stock market, which had recently been flooded by speculative "bubble companies," the *Times* wondered in late 1871 whether the American economy would be able to with-stand a European financial storm, concluding that the "'watered' railways, the non-dividend paying corporations of 'the future,' the hundred delusive schemes born of inflation . . . must ere long go to the wall."[39] But as months passed with-out any serious disruption, observers dismissed such warnings of an interna-tional financial crisis, confidently asserting that America had little to fear from such transnational capital flows.[40]

Similarly, when during 1872 it became clear that American railroad securi-ties were rapidly falling out of favor with German investors, most commenta-tors did not regard this as a potential source of danger to the stability of the American financial system. By the end of the year, the *Chronicle*, having received "an unusual number of inquiries, especially from Holland and Germany, show-ing considerable anxiety as to the nature and stability of the financial basis on which our railroad system is built," felt compelled to remind European inves-tors of the "universal law, controlling all investment" that high interest rates signaled a high risk of default.[41] In January, the *Chronicle* remarked that while the current lack of demand for American railroads in Germany was not in America's national interest, it would surely be short-lived, and the "important connections between the finances of Germany and of this country, which are now so rapidly multiplying," would continue "to play an important part in the future industrial growth and financial progress of the two nations."[42]

When the Vienna Stock Exchange crashed in May, Americans took note, unsure at first as to how much their country's affairs would be affected. "The news from the Continent is not reassuring," the *Tribune* noted at first, "and though affairs abroad should not in the natural order of affairs be provocative of so much distrust . . . its effects are certainly disquieting."[43] If the *Tribune*'s correspondent believed that foreign events normally did not warrant much attention, others took a different tack: "It is always possible to make something like a trustworthy forecast . . . when we base our calculations on the financial condition of our own country," the *Independent* wrote in its report on the American money market, "but, since we are so intimately connected with all other commercial countries, it is difficult to make any calculations as to the future of money." The "wholly unlooked-for trouble in Vienna" had rendered his earlier sanguine predictions for the spring and summer all but invalid.[44] The national financial market, he implied, was an orderly, predictable organ-ism, and it was only through its connections with transnational capital flows that it became opaque.

In a letter to N. M. Rothschild in London, August Belmont, the American agent of the famous banking house, had initially expressed apprehension at the news from Vienna but, two days later, noted that though his fears were "not allayed, our markets are not further affected by the troubles on the continent, excepting the exchanges which are steadily moving upwards."[45] By early June, optimism had returned, and New York merchant Edward Tailer pasted a newspaper report on the Vienna panic into his diary, which noted that the "causes of the prices are purely local, and no better proof is needed than the fact that, while local values fell 200 per cent yesterday, foreign values were subjected to a fall scarcely above that seen in other cities." Unlike on other occasions, Tailer himself did not further comment on the article, perhaps not considering the Austrian events relevant to his own affairs.[46] At around the same time, Belmont observed that the "advance in the Bank rate yesterday to 7% was quite unexpected and caused a renewed advance in gold + more firmness in short exchanges."[47]

The BOE had raised its rate prior to the Vienna panic, prompting Belmont to speculate that it intended to thereby provide "a check to the system of raising money by borrowing sterling bills."[48] Whatever its reasons, following the Vienna panic, the bank raised its rate several times more in quick succession; in June, it finally peaked at 7 percent.[49] It has been argued that this increase in the rate of discount constituted a direct transmission mechanism that spread the crisis in Vienna across the Atlantic to New York. According to this interpretation, the BOE raised interest rates in response to the events in Vienna, leading to a tightening of credit in New York and eventually triggering the September panic.[50] But money became easier, not tighter, following the Vienna panic, a fact that Belmont noted in his letters on several occasions.[51] In any case, the bank soon reversed course; in September, just before the fall of Jay Cooke, the rate stood at 3 percent, lower than it had been on the eve of the crash in Vienna.[52]

The *New York Times*, by contrast, did suggest that the Austrian experience contained important lessons for Americans, not because America must fear direct contagion but because the situation in Vienna was in many respects analogous to the one at home. Like the greenback, Austrian paper money was not backed by specie reserves and this fact had, according to the *Times*, combined with a general prosperity and the Viennese world exhibition to produce a feverish speculative mindset that was in many ways reminiscent of New York: "In place of the Germany of our childhood, where culture ruled, and wealth was of little account, . . . is a new nineteenth-century, American-like Germany. . . . In stocks and all the representatives of value, the gambling on German exchanges is as wild as anything ever seen in New-York." These numerous parallels, the articles continued, ought to teach Americans a lesson: "The wonderful 'paper currency' which was supposed to preclude panics, is found to produce the worst one known in modern times, at the same time that it had demoralized and debauched the whole community. Our own is tending precisely in the same direction."[53] The merits of a gold currency were expounded in a further article that concluded that unless the United States quickly returned to specie payments, the country would soon suffer a disastrous panic. But such a panic, it was implied, would be the result of national, endogenous factors, not of transatlantic contagion.

For many observers, the situation at home provided ample reason for concern. Many assumed, as did the *Times*, that the suspension of the gold standard during the Civil War and the concomitant increase in paper money had destabilized the country's economic and financial system by making it more vulnerable to speculative excess.[54] Another source of concern was the capital flows between New York and the Midwest. These were largely governed by agricultural rhythms. In spring and summer, the West's agrarian producers deposited their money with New York bankers. Because these deposits could be recalled at any time, the bankers used them to provide brokers and speculators with short-term credit, which regularly resulted in a boom on the stock market. Come autumn, country banks recalled their deposits to enable farmers to pay harvest-related expenses. This in turn led to stringency in the New York money market. Every so often, the atmosphere in these months became so tense that a panic seemed likely.[55]

In the first half of 1873, the situation appeared unusual. The Treasury had helped stave off a panic in autumn by releasing greenbacks into circulation, but the stringency had not subsided.[56] Observers were unsure whether to interpret this as a sign of approaching disaster or as a temporary abnormality. "I do not think that the stringency in money can continue many days," J. P. Morgan told his father in April, adding "I do not look for the usual summer money market, such as we have been accustomed to have for the last few years."[57] Others addressed head-on the question of a possible panic and wondered whether New York bankers should brace themselves for this possibility. During the first half of 1873, William Buck Dana, editor of the *Commercial and Financial Chronicle*, authored several editorials in which he addressed such fears. While conceding that the recurring financial convulsions of the past seemed to have a certain pattern to them, he nevertheless insisted that bankers had become wiser in recent years. The fact that the possibility of a panic was discussed in financial circles in itself spoke of a "conservative caution" on the part of bankers and investors. In May, Dana's paper told its readers: "The symptoms of such abuses and dangers [of overspeculation] have for a quarter of a century been familiar. They have been dreaded and watched by men whose observation was sharpened by their knowledge that their all depends on the interpreting aright the signs of the threatening storm, and taking precaution in time." But Dana assured his readers that institutional and political factors made a panic unlikely. Theoretically, one article argued, a premature return to the gold standard might have catastrophic consequences, but such a move was not to be expected in the near future. Moreover, the banks had such large cash reserves that an increasing demand for money in autumn would not be a source of embarrassment. Nevertheless, the *Chronicle* told its readers in May that even the "best authorities" were expecting trouble in autumn.[58]

Although Dana's editorials were mostly optimistic, he repeatedly considered the possibility of a panic, lending visibility to the pessimism that was increasingly permeating financial circles. Other publications were much less prepared to voice such concerns. In early summer, the optimists had seemingly been proved right: exports and imports were coming into balance, less gold was leaving the country, and some were expecting a lower demand for money than usual in autumn.[59] Some still remained skeptical: "the ordinary course of events will doubtless prevail," *Bankers' Magazine* wrote in anticipation of autumn events. "Sharp and sudden calls will derange not merely stock speculation, but legitimate business throughout the country."[60]

While the public discourse was ambivalent, many bankers and businessmen, privately, had ample reason for outright pessimism. Following his first aborted attempt at wooing European investors, Jay Cooke in 1871 had begun a campaign to sell Northern Pacific bonds to the American public. By 1872 Cooke was relying on 140 newspapers a month, on average, to advertise his bonds. In addition, his bank published and distributed pamphlets, speeches and maps detailing the railroad's advantages. The results, however, were disappointing; although agents were, officially, not allowed to sell bonds at a discount, demand was so low that Cooke saw himself forced to buy back bonds to stabilize prices.[61] The railroad faced other difficulties too. There was mismanagement and corruption, which hampered construction. This in turn delayed the settling of the land. Cooke began organizing a campaign to attract prospective American and European settlers to the Northwest. Yet the first large group of settlers would not arrive before 1873.[62]

The previous year, Cooke's bank had almost failed amid an unusually pronounced monetary stringency, only managing a narrow escape when William Richardson, assistant secretary of the treasury, at Cooke's request, began buying bonds and releasing greenbacks into circulation. At around the same time, William Ralston, governor of the Bank of California, received a letter warning him of the diminished demand for American securities abroad and an imminent outflow of gold. "To meet this demand we probably have less than any time within the last 25 years," James Lees, Ralston's correspondent, wrote, "so that the whole thing looks very serious to me indeed." Collis P. Huntington, whose business seemed in serious trouble in early 1873, complained that a "nervous unrest" had not left him for several weeks and feared that he would soon be unfit for business.[63] A few months later, members of Cooke's Northern Pacific survey, dispatched to prepare the lands for construction and settlements, were attacked, and two escorting officers died. The fighting continued between April and August 1873 and was widely reported by newspapers. Cooke, who had sought to downplay the Native American question in his public relations campaign now no longer controlled the narrative, and reviving demand for railroad bonds proved an impossible task.[64] Jay Cooke, for his part, seemed to realize that his political connections would not save him from disaster again. Any hopes that his ailing railroad might receive federal aid through an act of Congress were dashed when Congress's investigation into the Crédit Mobilier scandal brought revelations of widespread corruption in the building of transcontinental railroads, contributing to the further loss of trust in railroad bonds. In spring, Cooke found himself forced to sell the remaining Northern Pacific bonds at reduced prices.[65]

Pivotal actors in the American economy thus had strong premonitions of a significant economic downturn, and the dark premonitions of people such as Cooke, Huntington, and Lees stood in marked contrast to the pages of the business press. It seems plausible to assume that the latter, recognizing that the economy was based on psychology and ideas as much as on hard facts, tried to sustain confidence as best as it could, even in the face of mounting distrust.

Panic in Wall Street

Jay Cooke & Co. announced the suspension of payments on Thursday, September 18, 1873. Cooke had not been the first New York company to fail that month. The New York Warehouse and Security Company and the bank of Kenyon, Cox & Co. had suspended payments on September 8 and 13, respectively, and although the notorious Daniel Drew was a partner at Kenyon, the event had failed to make a significant impression on the markets.[66] But the suspension of Jay Cooke's old and reputable bank forcefully brought home the full extent of the previous years' railroad mania. Cooke had been unable to place sufficient amounts of Northern Pacific bonds with domestic and foreign investors and, since he also acted as the bondholders' trustee, eventually found himself forced to cover the shortfall by advancing to the company significant funds that he took from his bank's depositors. As was their wont, they began withdrawing funds with the beginning of the autumn harvest, eventually forcing Cooke to suspend payments and triggering the bank's failure.

The panic that was soon to engulf the entire country and spread across the Atlantic began as a local event on Wall Street and its environs:

> The first intimation which came into the Stock Exchange of any change in the programme was contained in a brief notice, which said authoritatively that Jay Cooke & Co. had suspended payment. To say that the street became excited would only give a feeble view of the expressions of feeling. The brokers stood perfectly thunderstruck for a moment, and then there was a general run to notify the different houses in Wall street of the failure.[67]

Quickly, the news spread from bank to bank and from street to street. As soon as Pierpont Morgan of the large and reputable banking house Drexel, Morgan learned of Cooke's troubles, he decided to call in all its loans.[68] On September 19, the large and well-known house of Fisk & Hatch announced suspension. "Panic grows in Wall Street," George Templeton Strong wrote, recording the day's events in his dairy, ". . . and indications are graver than at any crisis since 1857. . . . Many notable speculators have suspended, among them Fisk & Hatch, reputed impregnably strong. . . . All this may be a mere flurry, or may be much more."[69]

But from the very beginning, it was clear that this panic on Wall Street would amount to more than just excitement and commotion in Manhattan's South. New York City banks had intimate ties not only with country banks but, since the introduction of the 1864 amendment to the National Banking Act, were also allowed to keep in other commercial centers half of the required reserves of banks, on which they also paid interest. A crisis in New York could hence easily trigger a withdrawal of deposits by outside banks. Many New York institutions maintained extensive national correspondence networks and/or had affiliate banks in other cities, which could also serve as channels of transmission to the interior.[70] For these reasons, a fully fledged banking crisis in the nation's commercial and financial center was almost certain to have national reverberations. Sensing this danger, President Grant and Secretary of the Treasury William Richardson, who had already begun buying bonds in the immediate wake of the panic, arrived in New York on September 20 to examine the situation. Their visit was a clear signal that the administration considered the past days' events to be of national significance. But when, in a conspicuously arranged meeting with leading members of the city's financial community at Fifth Avenue Hotel, Grant and Richardson were beseeched to undertake further measures, they refused, making it clear that New York's financial community would be left to its own devices.[71] In the administration's eyes, it seemed, the panic was a national event but not one warranting government intervention.

But New York bankers had a potent weapon in their arsenal: The New York Clearing House Association comprised the city's most important banks and, as such, had sufficient clout to coordinate its members' actions in a way that would make a structural difference to the market as a whole. At the time, seven large banks held between 70 and 80 percent of deposits, and their reserves had been successively declining for several months. Fearing that a large-scale bank run might eventually culminate in a collapse of the entire financial system, the Clearing House's committee decided on September 20 to issue certificates that would allow temporarily illiquid banks to settle interbank accounts. In doing so, they availed themselves of an instrument that had first been devised in the aftermath of the panic of 1857 to counter shocks to the system.[72] The committee also agreed on the equalization of its members' reserves and granted itself the right to redistribute the currency reserves of individual banks. Finally, "in the presence of universal disaster and the menace of a general destruction of all values," as the *Stockholder* described it, it was announced that the NYSE would close its doors.[73] A partial suspension of payments was announced on September 24. By pooling the banks' reserves and issuing certificates, the clearing house had effectively acted as a lender of last resort: it had provided the market with sufficient liquidity at a time when acute stringency was threatening to trigger large-scale bank runs.[74]

On an individual level, too, it quickly became clear that local events had the potential to spread beyond the city's borders. Following Cooke's suspension, banker George Opdyke had assessed the situation and, in a letter to a correspondent, concluded that the panic would quickly blow over.[75] By then, however, he himself had become the victim of a potentially devastating development. On September 17, papers had begun reporting a rumor that Opdyke's bank was in difficulties. Opdyke, realizing the potential of a self-fulfilling prophecy, sought to reestablish confidence in his business by making a lengthy statement to the city's financial community, telling the *Times* that his house was sound and affirming "in the most positive terms that the house or its creditors had nothing to fear. All they required was a little time to tide over the present difficulty."[76] Not all papers, however, were equally assiduous in distinguishing hearsay from fact. Alluding to the continued circulation of rumors about Opdyke in some of the city's papers, the *New York Journal of Commerce* on September 25 stressed that these could not be considered credible until reported as a fact in print.[77] Opdyke, for his part, understood that a note in a New York paper might do little to reassure his far-flung business partners who would sooner or later learn of the rumors. His public protestations had to be matched by continued public demonstrations and private reassurances of solvency. Accordingly, he spent the next several days informing correspondents from all over the country that his bank was meeting all demands and would continue to do so in the future.[78] In doing so, recognizing that his situation had potential national ramifications, he did everything to make sure that these would not become acute. By the end of the month, Opdyke finally felt vindicated: "The papers seemed determined to make us 'stop payment,'" he wrote, "but we did not falter for a moment nor doubt our perfect ability to weather the storm."[79] Having managed to squash all doubts, he was able to use his newly proven solidity to woo potential customers: "The past two weeks have tested our strength pretty effectually and we feel we can apply for accounts with a good deal of confidence."[80] For Opdyke, the experience of the panic had not precluded positive action. He realized he was entering a phase of rapid change that to the shrewd and decisive did not just spell danger but also offered rare opportunities. August Belmont displayed a similar mindset, writing to N. M. Rothschild and Sons to urge them to shed their usual caution in the face of an unusually promising set of circumstances: "There is no doubt that a great deal of money can be made at the present panicky prices which are sure to go up again after the excitement is over."[81] Belmont's words displayed more than a simple appetite for profit. Rather, they were evidence of a performance of masculinity according to which manliness in financial markets required both audacity and rational calculation, especially in times of crisis.[82] In a similar vein, investment bankers Isaac and William Seligman in London and Paris berated their American partners for not having take advantage of the unusually large profit opportunities in the exchange business at the height of the panic.[83]

Meanwhile, the clearing house's intervention seemed to have calmed markets. Moses Taylor, who as committee chairman had been directly involved in its decisions, noted on September 23 that the situation was slowly improving. The *Journal of Commerce* summarized the day's events with an optimistic headline: "The Panic Subsiding." To Strong, the crowd on Wall Street on September 22 seemed "still abnormal but less feverish than it was last week." But only two days later, he reversed his positive assessment: "Relapse in Wall Street," he now wrote. "The street was not excited but faint, sick, prostrate, and resigned to the approach of some great indefinite calamity." On September 25, Moses Taylor, too, noted that the excitement seemed far from over, and Simon F. Mackie wrote, "The panic of last week has somewhat subsided but everyone is looked upon with suspicion and it is utterly impossible to say whether it is over or no."[84] Looking back on the week, the *Railroad Journal*, in its September 27 edition, described it as one of the "most unfortunate in the history of financial affairs." By the end of the month, things were finally looking up. The stock exchange reopened its doors and Moses Taylor notified his correspondents that the financial situation seemed to be improving.[85]

Elsewhere, however, the panic's effects were only beginning to make themselves felt. Once New York banks had suspended cash payments, banks in other parts of the country quickly decided they had no choice but to follow suit. In Chicago, the local clearing house took the "unprecedented step" of explicitly recommending that members follow this course of action as they saw fit. Those who refrained from suspending payments in many cases experienced bank runs and had to recall their New York funds. Five banks were temporarily forced to shut their doors, spreading fear and uncertainty throughout the Midwest. At the same time, the panic was making its way down the Eastern seaboard, triggering financial disruptions in Philadelphia and Washington, D.C., as well as in Virginia, Georgia, and South Carolina.[86] In Ohio, the *Daily Cleveland Herald* reported a "feeling of uneasiness" caused by the "panic in the East" but reassured its readers that while local banks were experiencing "quite a run . . . the amounts deposited have been as great as ever."[87] When a local broker in Little Rock was informed by cable that banks in St. Louis had suspended and was advised to draw drafts payable through the St. Louis clearing house, "the excitement among the merchants . . . was noticed by all." The following day, the *Daily Arkansas Gazette* reported that several banks in Louisville had also closed their doors.[88] Taken together, these events vividly demonstrated the integration of the American banking system.

Panic Spreads to Europe

Meanwhile, people in Europe, too, were beginning to experience the panic's effects. Thanks to the transatlantic cable, news of Jay Cooke's failure had quickly spread across the Atlantic. Americans in Paris reacted immediately:

> When the news first came that Jay Cooke & Co. had suspended payments, and that other houses might follow, there was general consternation. . . . Every one thought he was 'hard hit,' and each was rushing home for his letters of credit in order to present them to the agents here. Within an hour a hundred or more of such letters were presented, the reply being that no more money could be paid upon them until further information had been received from America.[89]

But, the correspondent noted, while wealthy Americans whose bills had been issued by one of Cooke's American branches (the bank's London branch did not suspend payments) had the means and connections to procure funds from friends and business partners, it was "the people of moderate fortunes who suffer," as dispatches from "all parts of the Continent" were showing: "Several ladies in Dresden claim to have been left utterly destitute."[90] One such woman of moderate means, desperate for help and lacking any illustrious connections, Mrs. C. N. Moore from Stuttgart, turned to the American ambassador: "I received last week . . . a letter of credit from them [Jay Cooke & Co.] given 26th of August. I have not been able to draw one dollar on it and I am needing the money very badly." She implored Bancroft to advance her the money Jay Cooke owed her.[91]

Americans in Europe were not to remain the panic's only victims. On September 19, the *Börsen-Zeitung* published a telegram from Reuters' London office in its evening edition, noting that the bank had suspended payments. At this point, the correspondent explained, the only thing that could be said for certain was that its troubles stemmed from its involvement with the Northern Pacific Road. During the following days, news from New York proliferated as more telegrams began pouring in. From these often confusing, sometimes contradictory morsels of news, people in Vienna and Berlin tried to assess the effects the American events would have on European markets.[92] On September 20, the Berlin Stock Exchange was in the throes of a "complete panic,"[93] and investors and speculators feared the worst: "It was said that namely London, as well as Hamburg and Frankfurt would be affected by this suspension of payments to a great extent, and that further bad news was to be expected from those quarters."[94] A "frightening panic" of the kind last seen in May erupted in Vienna, and many felt reminded of 1857, when an American panic had quickly spread across the Atlantic Ocean, leading to an economic downturn so severe that it was still fresh in many people's minds.[95]

Reporters for the major newspapers, however, either fearing the pernicious potential of a self-fulfilling prophecy or speaking from genuine conviction, would have none of it. A replay of 1857 was impossible, one wrote, since Europe was no unsuspecting victim of American overspeculation but had already experienced its very own financial crisis in May.[96] Even those who, just months before, had warned of the dangers of a transatlantic crisis insisted that fears of contagion were unwarranted, and that the American *Krach* was of purely "local and temporary significance" and would quickly blow over.[97] After all, none of the failed American banks had strong connections to European banks and their downfall was thus unlikely to affect transatlantic trade. Since European investors had wisely been shunning railroad bonds for well over a year now, the "pecuniary" ramifications were certain to be negligible.[98]

Reports from London, moreover, indicated that English markets were not about to experience a similar panic. Following the news of Cooke's failure, the BOE immediately raised its rate of discount to counteract the increased demand for gold that the American crisis was certain to produce.[99] At the same time, Americans, desperate to increase their liquidity in the face of immense stringency, were trying to sell their bills on London, leading to a fall in price and causing "commotion among the London Exchange dealers" and withdrawals from the BOE.[100] Such minor disruptions aside, however, the London market seemed remarkably stable. Noting this fact, Germans and Austrians pointed out that since London was the hub of all transatlantic financial and commercial relations, the American crisis could hardly spread to the Continent as long as the British capital displayed such steadfastness. In fact, as one observer noted, so healthy was the condition of London's money market that it had managed to withstand even the heavy shocks that had emanated from the continent during the past months. Surely it would now shield Europe from any malign American influences?[101]

The arguments made by German and Austrian observers were not without merit: Cooke's campaign to woo European investors had indeed been a failure, and Germans (not to mention Austrians) did not have large amounts of capital tied up with Cooke or with any of the other banks that were experiencing trouble. Given London's preeminence, one could easily conclude that a transmission that affected Berlin and Vienna but not London was unlikely, and that the sharp reaction on continental stock markets was puzzling. It is possible that journalists spoke from genuine conviction when dismissing the possibility of a European crisis. But at the same time, the journalists' eager protestations were likely just as much an attempt to shape the future as to describe the present. Knowing that in a panic everything depended on expectations, molding these could seem as a way of staving off the very event that they might produce. Negations of transnational connections, then, were also an expression of a fear of entanglement, and the very act of denying it only affirmed its existence.

Indeed, even as German and Austrian observers downplayed the potential impact of Cooke's failure on European markets, many people were winding down investments in order to cut their losses and increase their liquidity, thus displaying clear signs of a fully fledged financial panic; through their panicked actions, they belied and undermined the financial journalists' placatory words. As early as September 23, papers began reporting rumors about the distressed state of certain Berlin banks, noting a plunge in bank shares. Attention quickly focused on the Quistorp'sche Vereinsbank, which, it turned out, had already been experiencing difficulties for some time and had, according to some reports, been thrown a lifeline by the Prussian Bank following the crash in May. This decision was said to have originated with one of the bank's directors who was himself heavily invested in Quistorp's many projects.[102] Now, the bank was in desperate need for more, and, with the Prussian Bank declining to up its ante, it was left to some of Berlin's most well-known companies to come up with a solution.[103] Several days of negotiations ensued during which uncertainty regarding the bank's future weighed heavily on stock market sentiment in Berlin and Vienna. By October 8, it seemed as though the Quistorp question had effectively sidelined any attention Berlin had been paying to American events and was now the sole decisive influence on the mood in financial circles.[104] Once it became clear that the bank did not have sufficient assets to cover a new loan, the Quistorp'sche Vereinsbank suspended payments; on October 15, it was announced that the company's creditors had agreed on a moratorium on all liabilities until the end of the following year.[105]

As had Jay Cooke's failure, Quistorp's end forcefully brought home the full extent of past speculative excesses. In many respects, however, Quistorp was an unlikely counterpart to the once highly respected financier of the Civil War era. According to one reporter, Heinrich Quistorp was neither ruthless nor a financial genius:

> At the stock exchange, he never enjoyed any credit, not even when his companies were at their most prosperous; and neither did he require it. His people were small rentiers, the newly rich, aspiring bourgeoisie, the small property owner . . . and finally the somewhat better-off laborer . . . and he made an impression on the general public with his name, his modest demeanor, and with the fact that his projects responded to actual needs and basically served the public good.

Originally from Stettin, he continued, Quistorp had emigrated to the United States and, after his American endeavors had yielded but a very moderate fortune, returned to Berlin to speculate in real estate, attracting "masses" of small-time investors.[106] This, the author suggested, and not the financial interests of one of its directors, had prompted the Prussian Bank to advance money to the troubled *Vereinsbank* after the panic in May.[107] Whether these conjectures were true or not, the author neatly captured what he believed to be the specifically German flavor of this distant, if indirect effect of the New York panic: Here was an entrepreneur who sought to promote equitable relations between capital and labor by marrying personal gain with a desire to improve the living conditions of the working class. Accordingly, his investments had not been in American railways but in Berlin real estate. His modest, even hapless persona epitomized what Germans felt distinguished their way of doing business from American-style capitalism, where everything seemed grander, faster, and more ruthless.[108] In Germany, nevertheless, Quistorp led the way. Soon, failures were being announced all over the country, from Rostock and Erfurt to Stuttgart, and even newly annexed Alsace began feeling the effects of the crisis.[109]

Vienna, meanwhile, oscillated between an almost obsessive preoccupation with American and European developments, and a continued susceptibility to the aftereffects of its very own panic in May. "For there, across the great ocean," one observer mused in early October, "lies that tangled ball from which everything that is still moving us in Europe has been unraveling, and it will probably be moving us for some time to come."[110] In this respect, one could regard the American events as having had a salutary effect on Viennese financial circles: Having for years ignored and mocked "all warnings and all theories of the international context of the money markets, of the relationship between one's own power and the scope of foreign credit," men of the stock exchange could now be seen incessantly scouring the press for news from abroad, pondering its effects on domestic markets. At the same time, one observer claimed, this susceptibility was itself an effect of local conditions: If the recent statements of an Austrian construction company had not already depressed the mood on the exchange, international news would certainly have been less relevant.[111]

The sensitivity to foreign news during these weeks was a fleeting one, pronounced on some days and absent on others. In early October, foreign cables were awaited more eagerly than ever, and the stock exchange seemed to have resigned itself to the idea that any relief to present depressed conditions could only come from outside.[112] But by the middle of the month, attention had been redirected inward, and observers voiced their amazement that rumors about the misfortunes of a single local company could dominate the stock market's trajectory. International markets now seemed completely irrelevant and had, as far as Vienna was concerned, practically ceased to exist.[113] At the same time, Austrian observers wondered whether the lessons of the American panic were applicable to Europe. The *Oekonomist*, which had so presciently foreseen a transatlantic crisis in July, was now in no mood to entertain the notion that Europe might learn from recent American experiences, since, it argued, economic conditions in Austria were quite different from those in the United States.[114] Others, though, were less reticent. Triumphantly, the liberal *Neue Freie Presse* claimed that the American panic presented a considerable source of embarrassment to the "feudal party," which, in the aftermath of the crash in May, had blamed Austria's "centralism" and, in accordance with its political principles, called for strengthening local organization and control. Now that even the United States with its federal constitution had experienced a panic, the feudal party's theory had seemingly been refuted: "The sad, far-reaching events in New York . . . provide a refutation which could hardly be more effective." While Austria had never before experienced a panic of such proportions, the author pointed out, in America such events were neither new nor rare: "That country whose entire activity in all spheres of political and economic life is of colossal dimensions, which knows over-speculation and swindle in all its forms . . . that country is sporadically the main location of crises of unknown dimensions."[115] Austria would therefore do well to heed the lessons of this and past American panics: if Austrians had acted as decisively as the American government and banking community had, the worst effects might have been averted.

As the panic wore on, however, such arguments seemed less persuasive; government action, it now became clear, was no panacea. And could the Austrian government really be faulted for its passivity, the *Neue Freie Presse* asked? It had, after all, suspended the bank act, and anything beyond that might have further impaired its already stretched fiscal position. Still, the author went on, at least American banks had banded together to support the weaker institutions, and the federal government was giving the crisis its full attention. Seen in the light of American events, one could not complain "if the stock exchange thinks that every act of help reported by the cable plainly shows the difference between America and Austria and expresses this difference through a further decline in the stock market."[116] Before long, the Austrian government had reversed its earlier stance of nonintervention. The first rumors that the state would invest in infrastructure to support the ailing economy had started circulating in early October. In November, the finance minister finally announced that in view of the continuing economic downturn, the government would provide merchants and manufacturers with short-term loans, and promote the construction of new railroads. These measures presented a far greater commitment than Richardson's bond-buying schemes, which had been purely monetary in nature. Most contemporary observers accordingly attributed this volte-face not to American models but to the troubles of local Viennese companies in which high-ranking members of Austria's nobility had a significant stake.[117] Nevertheless, it still seems plausible to assume that since the news of the American government's actions had led even the more liberal elements of the Austrian public to reassess their previously critical stance vis-à-vis government intervention, this transatlantic comparison helped ease the political transition toward a more interventionist approach.

Back in America, meanwhile, news about events in continental Europe had begun to arrive. In early October, Americans had first been notified by cable of "financial troubles" in Germany. Two weeks later, they learned of the first failures. In an article entitled "Probable effects of the panic in Europe," the *New York Journal of Commerce* informed its readers on October 4 that German bourses were experiencing uneasiness and pointed to the large amount of American bonds that had been floated there.[118] At the end of the month, August Belmont noted that European events were negatively affecting the American market: "The advices from your side of a probable further advance in the Bank rate, troubles in Vienna + unsettled state of things in other continental financial markets . . . tend to retard a restoration to confidence."[119]

While business correspondence suggests that bankers were aware of continental reactions to the American panic, newspaper accounts mostly painted a different picture. "It does not appear that the financial crash in America affected seriously the Berlin market," the *Chicago Tribune* reported. Since German investors had largely shunned American railroad bonds, the author explained, the bursting of the American railroad bubble had not affected them. Rather, Germans were experiencing a speculative phase of their own which, propelled by the French war indemnity, had yet to run its course. This German crisis, the author indicated, was as unlike the American one "as a slow fever is unlike a stroke of apoplexy." Since Germans were a "slow people," who invested their money "with caution," the present crisis would take many months to play out.[120] Here, national stereotypes precluded the analysis of both crises as one. In other cases, too, the causal relationship between both events went unnoticed. Thus one correspondent did note the parallels between the panics without, however, implying that they were causally related: "Berlin has recently had its financial crisis, and as ours was precipitated by the failure of Jay Cooke & Co. . . . . so theirs was brought on by the collapse of a speculator as daring and successful."[121]

Mostly, the German and Austrian panics of that autumn went unnoticed by the American public, which, after all, had not invested in foreign companies. Where Americans did write about European financial events, they focused on American victims; the crises in Vienna and Berlin were not interpreted as causally related to their own panic. The imagined transatlantic economic space during these months, then, was a heterogeneous one, in which awareness of a shared experience was pronounced in one direction but largely absent in the other.

Trade and Industry Suffer

Once it became clear that the financial unrest would not remain confined to New York, observers began discussing the possibility that the panic would spread to commerce and industry. According to the dominant understanding of the economic sphere as an organic set of relations between different groups (bankers, merchants, industrialists, farmers, and workers), the possibility of an encompassing commercial crisis could not be easily dismissed.[122] At first, such fears presented themselves as a mantra-like claim that mercantile circles were likely to be spared. "The merchants, having had their business on an unusually solid foundation, were far less adversely affected than might have been anticipated," one observer wrote, and the *Chronicle* repeatedly stressed that the present crisis was a "capital panic," not a dangerous "credit panic": "[Credit panics] destroy and break down all the foundations of credit and confidence on which the activity of business and the recuperative energies of finance fundamentally depend. . . . Our present financial flurry has no symptoms of this malignant character in it."[123]

But others recognized that in a credit-based economy contagion was difficult to avoid. As soon as money and credit became scarce, transaction costs rose for buyers and sellers of real goods which inevitably affected the entire system.[124] As early as September 20, Thomas Ewing informed a correspondent that the events in New York were forcing him to suspend his plans for land purchases, and on September 27, Alexander Brown, a banker, advised the vice president of the Annapolis & Elk Ridge Railroad to stop all construction activities as other railroads had already done.[125] Despite the Treasury's intervention, money remained scarce. In early October, George Opdyke informed correspondents that in view of the prevailing stringency he was not in a position to allow overdrafts. "It is not a question of security but scarcity of money at this point. Over fifty millions of money have been withdrawn from New York within the past two weeks."[126]

The export business, too, was vulnerable, as noted by August Belmont, who worried that with the "utter demoralization of the foreign exchanges . . . it is to be feared that the general commercial interests of the country will not escape the disastrous results already apparent in financial circles."[127] Another banker notified a correspondent that he had ceased advancing money on shipments of produce to England.[128] What seemed prudent from an individual standpoint had deleterious consequences in the aggregate. In October, Belmont reported that while "the general feeling in financial circles" had improved, there was "still some uneasiness regarding the effects of the panic in commercial matters."[129] When in late October a well-known manufacturing house, A. W. Sprague of Rhode Island, failed, even optimistic observers could no longer ignore the increasingly glum mood among merchants and manufacturers. The *Stockholder* now wrote that the "waves of disaster" had "circled wider" and had touched "the whole production community, even the farmers, who, like other classes, are more or less in debt."[130] Beginning in November, Edward Tailer, the diarist, began giving his entries the title of "The Crisis," indicating his belief that updates on this topic would become a regular feature. In December, he embarked on a tour of several American cities, and reported from Mobile, Alabama, that all his acquaintances there were complaining "of the panic and dull times." Back in New York, he noticed that the panic had "caused several Broadway stores to be unoccupied."[131]

In early 1874, the New York department store magnate Alexander Turney Stewart began receiving letters from all over the country from people asking him for financial assistance. Such requests were not new; Stewart and other famously wealthy members of the business community received several such letters every week.[132] What had changed, however, was that several writers now explicitly mentioned the panic not only as a reason for their present distressed state but also for their decision to write to a distant stranger. Mrs H. C. Conant, a shopkeeper from Appleton, Wisconsin, asked Stewart for $150 to pay off her creditors. "The panic has been severely felt here," she explained, "about the time we got our shop ready to fill up this stringency in money matters came on and we were consequently much delayed." As did a farmer from Columbus, Mississippi, she also claimed the panic had put such a degree of financial pressure on the entire community that they could no longer turn to neighbors for help but had to ask an outsider for loans.[133] The writers thereby continued and reinforced a process that had been underway for many decades: the integration of a national market economy.[134] In this case, however, integration was spurred on not during a time of economic growth but of stagnation.

Conclusion

When Jay Cooke's bank failed in September 1873, commentators on both sides of the Atlantic had been debating the possibility of a panic for several months. European demand for American railroad securities had been falling since the first half of 1872, a fact that did not go unnoticed in American financial circles but did not prompt fears of an imminent crisis. In New York, although the usual autumn stringency had still not subsided by the beginning of 1873, the stock market for many months saw neither a panic nor was there a significant failure.

In Berlin, the stock market had been on a downward trajectory since December 1872. There, too, this did not at first translate into a major crisis. In Vienna, things happened faster, and a major panic erupted—the first of that year— immediately after the Vienna exchange had registered an all time high. For a while, the decline on German stock markets accelerated, though by summer, they seemed to have regained some of their composure. In New York meanwhile, most people seemed confident that the Viennese panic would not spread across the ocean. While, during these months, there was a pronounced awareness of transnational economic connections, people on both sides of the Atlantic were reluctant to imagine the outbreak of a transatlantic crisis. Observers frequently discussed the possibility of a *national* panic but rarely considered the likelihood of *transnational* contagion; by imagining a panic as originating from within their country's borders, financial markets were discursively endowed with a national structure, making them easier to conceptualize and contain. Well before the advent of "the economy" as a theoretical concept denoting an "emphatically national" circular flow of production and consumption, then, popular economic discourse in the 1870s imagined national borders an obstacle to the expansive nature of markets.[135]

When Cooke & Co. failed in September, the national ramifications were obvious to most Americans—to the national government, to the New York Clearing House Association, as well as to the public. At the same time, on the other side of the Atlantic, Germans and Austrians initially tried to dismiss the significance of Cooke's failure, hoping that the London money market, which seemed to be displaying remarkable resilience, would shield the European continent from America's troubles. Even the editors of the *Oesterreichische Oekonomist*, who in June had so presciently warned of an imminent transatlantic crisis, now reversed course and claimed that this was highly unlikely.[136] But even as observers protested their certainty that the American panic would not spill across the Atlantic, they nervously awaited the latest news from New York. Already, the strategy of conceptualizing financial markets as a grid of national structures was eroding. As days and weeks went by, and contagion became an undeniable fact, people began interpreting developments in Berlin and Vienna as reactions to American news, while at the same time noting that national and local factors retained significant influence. Americans, meanwhile, remained largely oblivious to the European ramifications of the New York panic. Where journalists did report on them, they did not suggest they were causally connected. In these days, the awareness of transnational economic entanglement was a one-sided one, more pronounced in Europe than in the United States.

What this chapter has revealed, then, is a double movement that characterizes the panics of 1873: Even where people downplayed the likelihood or effects of contagion, they, at the same time, unwittingly demonstrated that transnational economic integration had become a force to reckon with, affirming its significance even where they sought to deny it. At the same time, while the panic induced a state of paralysis and fear among many, not all considered themselves victims of an overwhelming force. Experienced speculators and investors as well as entrepreneurs big and small seized the opportunity to turn a profit, and so, too, Alexander Stewart's destitute correspondents from rural America attempted to avail themselves of the possibilities of a national credit economy, thus unwittingly acting as agents of the nineteenth century's capitalist revolution.

CHAPTER 4

FLOWS OF PAPER, FLOWS OF GOLD

Theorizing the Panics

The panics of 1873—in Vienna, New York, and Berlin—followed on each other's heels, shaking to their core, within a period of just a few months, the financial markets of some of the world's most advanced commercial nations. As the panic waned and economic depression set in, people began exploring the causes of, and possible responses to, the crisis. One issue that loomed large in these debates was the question of monetary standards, and the relationship between a monetary economy and the development of speculative bubbles. According to an influential interpretation, the panic had been caused by an oversupply of money, and the adoption of gold as a national and international medium of exchange would prevent similar excesses in future. Under such a system, advocates of a gold currency argued, the volume of currency could never exceed the supply of gold, as banks would only issue paper money in proportion to their holdings of the precious metal, thus precluding the possibility of inflation. Gold, it was believed, was a superior medium to inconvertible paper money by virtue of its physical qualities: Its introduction would replace the artificial and seemingly unlimited paper medium with something real and tangible, something that possessed an intrinsic value. But its stabilizing function, according to gold advocates, also hinged on the fact that it would circulate not only nationally but also globally between nations engaged in international trade, thus guaranteeing an efficient mechanism of distribution that would preclude both excess and scarcity. At the same time, however, such notions of the supposedly superior qualities of gold ignored important factors. Gold advocates neither considered the possibility that the world's supply of gold might be insufficient to meet the demands of world trade, nor did they entertain the idea that the transmission of financial crises might become more likely under an international gold standard.

Next to the currency question, economic writers also debated the role of capital flows in the creation of financial crises. In these debates, too, transnational integration was widely considered to be beneficial. At the same time, the nation as an organizing category still loomed large in narrative and theoretical accounts of the crises. Writers compared the crisis of their own country to other crises both past and present without, however, jettisoning the view of financial panics as primarily national events.

Money Questions and the Gold Standard

Both during and immediately after the panics, governments were faced with calls to respond to the growing economic calamity. The question of what constituted the limits of legitimate government intervention was, however, a thorny one, and policy-makers had no national structures of economic intervention to work with.[1] In the United States, the Treasury had confined itself to releasing greenbacks into circulation, thus adding to the money supply. In Germany, the authorities had debated efforts to come to the support of Heinrich Quistorp and his enterprises. Ultimately, though, the state had not saved Quistorp from bankruptcy. At the height of the crisis, Kaiser Wilhelm I had written to the minister of commerce to inquire whether financial aid should be provided to Quistorp's bank, arguing that assistance was desirable as a bankruptcy would affect "masses" of innocent people.[2] Commenting on these efforts, the *Neue Social-Demokrat* angrily declared that they amounted to nothing more than illegitimate public aid to "Prussian speculators."[3] The Liberal Austrian government went further than both its American and German counterparts: in November 1873 it voted to aid the ailing economy by providing loans and building railroads. But, as in Germany, the question of state help was contested. Opponents argued that it constituted little more than a thinly veiled bailout for reckless members of the ruling Liberal elite. Whatever the government's motivation, the measure remained an exception, as most influential Austrian Liberals continued to profess that government aid to troubled companies was undesirable. Instead, they should be left to wither away in accordance with the supposedly natural laws of commerce.[4]

Paradigms of the natural sciences provided liberal politicians, theoreticians, and businessmen with analogies that shaped their understanding of economic events and allowed them to rationalize disorder and confusion. They believed that the laws governing the social affairs of men, including the creation and distribution of wealth, were natural laws, part of a rational and well-ordered mechanistic universe.[5] From this perspective, what had appeared to observers at the height of the panic as a "storm" or "hurricane" was not an instance of chaos and disorder but a salutary process of self-cleansing, a healthy corrective to past excesses.[6] Consequently, government intervention could only delay but not circumvent this process. "Keeping at bay violent and unpredictable disturbances and interventions into economic life is the most effective preemptive help which the government is capable of exercising in order to avert crises of production," the German theorist Erwin Nasse wrote, echoing widely held liberal convictions.[7] The flip side of this liberal belief, as the aftermath of the panics would show, was an equally strong faith in the benefits of a monetary system—a gold-backed currency—which, its proponents believed, functioned according to natural laws of trade, thus obviating the need for a government-managed monetary policy.

In the United States, the panic of 1873 reignited the American debate over the "money question," which, following the Civil War, "absorbed more of the country's intellectual and political energy than any other public question except Reconstruction," ultimately, albeit circuitously, leading to the reestablishment of the gold standard that had been suspended as part of the Union's war effort in the early 1860s.[8] The debate revolved around the question of whether (and, if so, how) to withdraw from circulation greenbacks, the inconvertible paper issued to defray the costs of the war, or to expand their supply, thus increasing the volume of money. In this debate, American bankers, while not unanimously in favor of contraction, mostly belonged to the former—the hard-money—camp, partly because a return to specie payments and deflation was conducive to their business interests but also because they believed that paper money constituted an offense to what they considered the natural laws of commerce, as well as to their sense of propriety. Those favoring expansion—the soft-money men—came in various guises and included manufacturers as well as laborers and some members of the banking community. Money, they believed, had no intrinsic value but was a function of government authority, and inflation was beneficial not only for themselves but for society at large. A government-managed expansion of the money supply would not only prevent banking monopolies from forming but would also ensure a more equitable distribution of wealth.[9]

When Secretary of the Treasury Hugh McCulloch embarked on a policy of contraction in 1865, the ensuing severe deflation prompted even hard-money men to successfully call for the policy's suspension. Jay Cooke, who had previously lobbied for contraction in the late 1860s, became an advocate for easy money, which, he realized, would make for a more favorable environment for his risky business projects.[10] In 1869, the Public Credit Act, which committed the Treasury to pay its obligations in gold (unless otherwise specified), restored a volatile equilibrium that was to last until September 1873.[11] Following the panic on Wall Street, hard- and soft-money men alike were quick to pounce on what they regarded as fundamental flaws of the current monetary system, and hopes that the country would quickly return to gold were dashed.[12] When Congress convened in December that year, hard-money men argued that the panic was the result of an artificial inflation of values brought about by an inconvertible currency, while their adversaries maintained that, on the contrary, the true cause was a scarcity, not an excess, of money. Consequently, it was necessary to expand rather than contract the supply of greenbacks.[13]

Advocates of soft money pointed to historical experience to prove their point. The "untimely resumption of specie-payments by the Bank of England in 1819–21" as well as other historical instances of currency expansion in Europe and America, one author argued, disproved the notion that contraction was necessarily beneficial. Moreover, the "vast credit system which is at once the glory and misfortune of our modern civilization and the source of all speculation and panic, will prevail as widely under a metallic currency as under one purely of paper."[14] According to this interpretation, the volume of the currency was key to an adequate functioning of the money market. The economist Henry Carey, the most prominent advocate of easy money in the post-Civil War era, maintained that a loss of specie through foreign trade would slow the circulation of money, and the ensuing deflation would benefit creditors but hurt debtors. Therefore, the government should issue as much paper money as necessary to ensure a steady mild inflation and an adequate circulation of money, both of which would stimulate investment and economic growth.[15] Generally, soft-money advocates tended to emphasize the national character of greenbacks which, unlike gold, could not be manipulated by foreign economic powers; they argued that "specie currency brought with it detrimental foreign influences such as classism and monarchy."[16]

Hard-money advocates, when talking about the merits of a gold currency, often couched their argument in almost metaphysical terms. In the economic imaginary of gold advocates, gold by virtue of its sheer materiality was the natural embodiment of soundness. It was both money, a signifier, and as such, formal and abstract, as well as a material commodity, or "the commodity it would be if it weren't money." It thus represented an intermediate position between a barter economy and a money economy,[17] embodying both "fiscal and social stability," an ideal antidote to the instability of complex market relations.[18] At the same time, the arguments made by the hard-money faction relied on a model of specie flow that purported to address the issue of volume and money supply. According to Hugh McCulloch, under a true gold standard, money could never be too plentiful: "Coin, being the circulating medium of the world, flows from one country to another in obedience to the law of trade, which prevents it from becoming anywhere, for any considerable period, excessive in amount; when this law is not interfered with by legislation, the evils of an excessive currency are corrected by the law itself."[19]

This argument, while not new (it was first formulated by David Hume), became more prominent in the currency debates in the aftermath of the panic of 1873. According to John Eadie, a member of the New York Chamber of Commerce, gold was "the common property of the nations," continuously circulating from one country to the next, "thus changing prices and the volume of trade and commerce in that nation, as well as in all others closely connected with it by commercial intercourse. There is thus created a community of nations, with a current money constituting the standard of value of all the property and commodities of the people in the civilized world."[20]

It was thus not least the international, even potentially global character, of gold that made it such an attractive standard of money. The underlying notion of the world market was an idealized one where one nation's gain was not another's loss but, rather, where harmony prevailed. In this perspective, there could never be too much or too little money in any one place since the free flow of specie would immediately correct any imbalances.[21] This natural equilibrium was a consequence of the very size of the global money market, as the *Economist*, an unflinching defender of the gold standard, explained shortly after the panic: "Under a metallic currency, this augmenting reserve can be replenished from the store of the precious metals in the whole world. But under a system of inconvertible paper of limited amount there is no such comprehensive field in which to seek the sources of replenishment."[22] Crucially, this argument implied that global economic integration in the form of a worldwide standard of value made panics, insofar as these were caused by monetary factors, less likely, since there could never be an excess or a shortage of money.[23] Countries that did not participate in this form of global economic interaction were, by implication, more prone to financial crises. "The uniformity in value and appearance of our paper currency," one American writer argued, "the cheapness and ease with which domestic remittances are made, the fact that it pays debts, and, in appearance at least, discharges all the functions of money, are considerations which foster the error, that, as a nation, we are so absolute in our independence and so peculiar in our situation, that the laws of political economy are silent and inoperative."[24] The corollary to this argument, made more than a year after the September panic, was that America's monetary insulation had caused this most recent financial disaster. But only very rarely was this made explicit. Instead, American commentators and theorists extolled gold's international character without making a connection between America's place in the international monetary order and the panic's causes.

The same argument was made by Austrian observers in the immediate aftermath of the crisis.[25] Austria had left the silver standard and issued irredeemable paper currency on several occasions during the previous decades.

When, during the first half of the 1860s, the government embarked on a policy of deflation with the goal of resuming specie payments, the resulting downward pressure on prices coincided with an economic depression that only ended when the war with Prussia forced the government, in 1866, once again to expand the supply of paper money. The resulting premium on silver, coupled with a series of unusually good harvests, allowed Austria to export large quantities of grain, triggering an economic boom that finally ended in 1873.[26]

This experience, however, did not dampen their enthusiasm for gold. Rather, following the crash, many observers felt that past experiments with paper money were to blame for Austria's economic woes. The crash, it seemed, had proved that the growth of the past years had been fictitious, and that paper money had created artificial values. Their arguments were in many respects similar to those made by Americans: in their opinion, a nonmetallic monetary system was fundamentally unsound, and a return to a gold or silver standard was necessary to prevent future crises. According to parliamentarian Joseph Neuwirth, whose account of Austria's *Spekulationskrisis* garnered widespread attention, the issue of international monetary integration was crucial in explaining the adverse role Austria's paper money had played both in spawning and prolonging the financial and economic crisis. It was obvious, Neuwirth claimed, that Austria's crises differed from those in other countries in the former's "strictly localized character." While developments in international capital markets were certain to affect Austria's domestic market, this relationship was very much one-sided, since shocks originating in Austria hardly ever reverberated beyond its borders. The reason for this, according to Neuwirth, was to be found in its currency: "We are isolated, cut off from abroad, and the wall enclosing us is our paper money, our devalued currency."[27] Where countries shared a common metallic currency, Neuwirth argued, shocks and crises were more easily absorbed, since interest rates set by national central banks in response to such events regulated the flow of money, quickly correcting any imbalances and ultimately restoring a healthy equilibrium:

> This is a process which is continually happening under our eyes and which in fact comprises the mystery of the interconnectedness of the international markets of the big international economic sphere [*Wirthschaftsgebiet*]. From this healing process without which the recurrence of crises in general, more specifically of those of a localized character, would be much more common than we in fact have the opportunity to observe, we in Austria-Hungary are completely excluded.[28]

While in normal times, foreign investors were happy to buy Austrian securities and provide Austrian speculators with capital, they were quick to withdraw their loans as soon as a crisis broke out. In times of distress, Austrians could therefore not expect help from abroad. Neuwirth pointed to the German experience to prove his point: There too, speculation had been rampant, yet the subsequent downturn had not nearly been as awful as in Vienna. The notion that its paper currency partially insulated Austria from the international market and that this insulation was a source of instability was echoed by others. Thus one author described Austria's "fictitious currency" as an "insulation stool" (*Isolierschemel*), while another noted that only the adoption of the gold standard would enable Austria to attract serious foreign investors.[29] When bemoaning Austria's "isolation," commentators were not oblivious to the fact that capital (especially German capital) had in fact flowed across borders and into Austria in the run-up to the panic. But they believed that this flow was of an artificial and unhealthy kind, a one-way street, as it were, that failed to dry up even as markets were overheating.[30]

In Germany, the question of which currency the newly unified Empire should adopt had already been settled in favor of gold when the panic broke in 1873. A law mandating the minting of federal gold coins had been passed in December 1871; in July 1873, it was decided that the motley state currencies would be replaced by a unified federal gold currency.[31] The National Liberal parliamentarian Ludwig Bamberger, perhaps the most prominent German gold advocate of his time, asserted that only gold was a true international currency, one that had "a value in itself" that was "not determined inside the borders of the country but only on the world market."[32] The transatlantic financial crises of 1873 did not threaten this dominant German progold consensus. This seems remarkable given the fact that just a few years earlier, the Prussian Bank had drawn attention to the issue of the gold standard and international contagion. Following the international monetary conference of 1867, whose delegates had proposed an international gold-based coinage, officials had argued that adopting the gold standard would make Germany more vulnerable to the destabilizing influence of the British money market and its periodically recurring crises.[33] One can imagine that the transnational reach of the panics of 1873 might have revived this skepticism toward gold, but by then, the progold consensus was too firmly entrenched to be seriously challenged.

Nevertheless, monetary questions loomed large in the debate over what had caused the financial crisis. The peace treaty of Versailles had stipulated that the French war indemnity of five billion francs would partially be payable in gold, meaning that the government would no longer have to buy gold on the world market in order to introduce the new currency. Rather, it was now in a position to introduce the new coins without simultaneously having to retire the old silver ones from circulation. Consequently, the German money stock increased sharply. Contemporary observers argued that this sudden injection of capital fueled the speculative bubble and led to overinvestment and inflation.[34] According to this view, people had been led to believe that the transfer of mere signs of wealth constituted a transfer of real wealth and were blind to the fact that true value could only be created through labor and commerce. The government had encouraged and enabled this behavior by using the money to retire government debt, thus depriving investors of safe securities.[35] This type of criticism tended to focus exclusively on the French reparations and did not acknowledge the role of the currency reform, especially the government's failure to retire silver coins from circulation while minting new gold coins (some also pointed to the growing number of irredeemable bank notes).[36]

Some argued that the effects of this sudden influx of gold had been more or less identical to what many American, German, and Austrian commentators considered to be the dangers of an artificial paper currency. Thus an American observer claimed that the German experience proved that "a large increase of the specie circulation of a country is likely to be attended by fully as many evils as an expansion of paper currency."[37] Erwin Nasse explicitly argued that Germany, in 1872, had found itself in "abnormal" monetary conditions, as had the United States, Austria, and France. Although the high degree of international economic integration allowed speculation based on misguided expectations of future returns to spread more easily, an international metallic standard would have mitigated the worst excesses. Had it not been for the incoming gold, the country would have experienced monetary stringency by the end of 1872, providing a timely check on the speculative mood. But since both Austria and the United States were on an inconvertible currency, the circulating medium had not been able to flow outward and the natural healing powers had not been allowed to take effect: "Only these conditions, the transfer of billions and the paper currency in large parts of the world can explain . . . that the price equilibrium of different commodities and countries could have been disturbed so thoroughly."[38]

Most observers, then, concluded that a lack of transnational monetary integration had been one of the major causes of the crisis.[39] This argument did not come with significant policy implications since the monetary debate in Germany had already been settled in favor of gold. Paradoxically, the very measure that had made the transition feasible in the first place also served to illustrate what many considered to be the dangers of an irredeemable currency, though this contradiction was hardly ever made explicit.

Policy-makers and commentators in all three countries, then, were eager to join the gold standard precisely because it was an *international* system, which they expected would guarantee monetary stability. The international aspect of gold as a global currency, however, was to be purely economic; it did not entail any kind of political cooperation.[40] Currency theorists believed that the gold standard was, by its very nature, an international currency that was already in place, waiting, as it were, for countries to join so it could realize its global potential. Indeed, one key argument in favor of the gold standard was that it ensured international *economic* integration without requiring international *political* agreements.[41] This is why Ludwig Bamberger, for example, could argue that a unilateral move to gold by the German Reich constituted a *national* solution while he also praised gold as a truly *international* currency.[42] Thus, an awareness of global interconnectedness was clearly part of the currency debates during this period. But they rested on a clear distinction between the desirability of economic integration on the one hand and the undesirability of international political cooperation on the other.[43]

Of course, the argument made by proponents of the gold standard that only gold as an international currency would ensure an adequate supply of money ignored an important fact: For while the amount of gold available was largely determined by natural factors and could, theoretically, become so scarce relative to demand that flows would slow to a minimum, an elastic national paper currency that was not redeemable in gold could always be adjusted to current demand. Why were gold advocates oblivious to this fact, or why did they choose to ignore it? One reason is that even though gold production and supply fluctuated, depending on when and where new gold was discovered, this type of fluctuation occurred arbitrarily and could not be engineered by institutions. Where paper money was regulated by national institutions (or in the case of free banking, by private banks printing their own bank notes), by contrast, the supply of paper money fluctuated in line with political or private interests, which was not necessarily in the interest of the economy as a whole, and therefore more prone to abuse. In the American case, the Treasury's inept management of the money supply in the run-up to the panic of 1873 had seemingly proved the point. It was only after Cooke's failure and the panic on the money market that William Richardson had begun rereleasing greenbacks into the system. By then, however, the damage had been done. Focused as the American financial community was on Richardson's actions and the state of the money market, they may well have come to the conclusion that a monetary system so heavily dependent on the actions of one individual was flawed, and that a quasiautomatic regulation of money flows was vastly preferable.[44]

But if gold advocates took such an idealized view of global specie flows, it is worth asking why they did not believe that the same mechanism would regulate the flow of a national currency within that nation's borders. A nation with its own inconvertible paper money, gold advocates implied, had no external outlet if it ever suffered from an excess of money; the laws of supply and demand could not work their healing powers since no other country had use for a foreign currency. But this argument was not exactly self-evident, for there was, as far as this aspect of the monetary system was concerned, no structural difference between the functioning of a national market and that of a global market. There was, prima facie, no reason to believe that economic activity and demand for money could not vary from place to place within one and the same country in the same way it varied between different countries in the world, just as there was no reason to believe that a national currency should not flow between different regions within a country in the same way that it moved between different parts of the world. The fact that proponents of the gold standard were oblivious to this indicates that they saw national economies as homogenous wholes, where the same monetary conditions existed throughout. The global economy, by contrast, was seen to consist of distinct but mutually complimentary parts. This (implicit) belief that a national currency could not "flow" within one country according to the law of supply and demand was especially surprising in the American case since the uneven distribution of money within the United States was a common topic of discussion and manifested itself in significant interest rate differentials between different parts of the country.[45]

In this respect, the arguments advanced by gold proponents displayed an understanding of the relationship between the national and the global economy that differed considerably from other contemporary conceptions of internationalism and the "world of nations." Thus Christopher Hill has argued that American (as well as French and Japanese) accounts of national history during the last third of the nineteenth century conceived the world as a world *of nations*, specifically as a world divided by "systems of national markets and national states."[46] Similarly, a characteristic feature of nineteenth century internationalism (of which gold was "one of the most powerful signifiers") was a belief that it would be achieved by cooperation between nations.[47] According to such beliefs, internationalism was a continuation and extension of national experiences and institutions. Gold advocates, by contrast, relied on quite different assumptions. According to them, an international gold currency did not merely replicate on a global level what had already been proven to work on a national level. Rather, they argued that national currencies were inherently deficient and that only gold, an international currency by its very nature, would allow for a *world-wide flow* of money and thus bring into being a market, a system of flows governed by the law of supply and demand. In other words, the international market for currency was not an extension of national markets but the *only* possible realization of the idea of a perfect monetary system in accordance with the law of supply and demand.

This vision of a world-wide monetary system, however, also relied on unspoken assumptions that somewhat belied its claim to global harmony. For gold advocates generally believed that gold would only become a truly global currency in the distant future, once all nations had advanced to Western levels of commerce and culture. Until then, "civilized" nations would trade in gold, while economically less advanced nations such as India would use silver. This "orientalist" concept of metallic standards was both practical and ideological in nature. On a practical level, the argument went, gold was so valuable that even very small gold coins could not be used in small-scale transactions, while silver, being the cheaper metal, would require the shipment of vast amounts of coins, making it impractical for large-scale transactions in trade between wealthy nations. At the same time, such practical arguments were enmeshed with culturalist assumptions. Many Western currency theorists for example believed that Indians were culturally inclined to hoard precious metals. They could therefore not be trusted to handle a gold currency, which required a continuous flow of gold to wherever it was needed most. Silver, then, was considered the inferior metal and thus adequate for the needs of poor, under-developed countries.[48] This orientalist view of metallic standards of course ignored the fact that hoarding was not a phenomenon unknown to Americans and other supposedly "advanced nations." Noting that the French people "seem to have made it a rule of life, for several generations, to accumulate sup-plies of the precious metals," one writer observed that during the most recent panic, "something like the same rule appeared to have made an impression upon the minds of our own people, in the hoarding of our government legal tender paper money."[49]

This conflation of practical and ideological arguments was characteristic of much of the monetary debate during the 1870s. Proponents of the gold stan-dard propounded a vision of a global currency order that promised efficiency, stability, and harmony, a vision that relied on the exclusion of those who were perceived as culturally inferior. Within this vision, the panics of 1873 were depicted as instances of disorder. But this disorder within civilized nations of the West, gold advocates believed, stemmed not from cultural infe-riority but from a disregard for the universal laws of commerce. The experience of the panics was thus subsumed under preexisting notions of what consti-tuted a global standard of values, and experiences that might have questioned this narrative were discounted. Isolation, rather than integration, was seen to have caused the crisis.

To some extent, this may be explained by the fact that Americans in 1873 had been mostly unaware that the failure of Jay Cooke and the New York stock market panic had reverberated widely across Europe. Consequently, they rarely argued explicitly that their panic had been caused by isolation, even though this idea was the logical corollary to the notion that gold was a global currency. Ger-man and Austrian observers, by contrast, while not neglecting domestic fac-tors in their narratives, were quite certain that the New York panic had made a major impression on European investors. Yet as the memory of the Septem-ber and October events faded, and people began exploring structural factors rather than immediate triggers, they, too, attributed major importance to their countries' monetary isolation. All in all, then, the issue of transnational transmission of financial panics only rarely came up in monetary debates dur-ing the 1870s.[50]

German and Austrian (and, albeit indirectly, American) gold advocates thus harnessed the panic to make the argument that only a global gold currency would stave off future panics. Countries would thereby put an end to their monetary isolation and enter into exchange with other countries, thus creating a harmonious global flow of gold that would allow neither scarcity nor excess. This vision was couched in terms of universality, harmony, and balance while simultaneously subscribing to notions of civilization and cultural and economic inferiority; the world order it envisioned was an asymmetric one.

At the same time, however, the consensus that isolation rather than integration had caused the crisis was not complete. Some commentators and policy intellectuals indeed made the opposite case. "The larger the dimensions of commercial trade, the bigger the space through which commercial relations expand, the more difficult it becomes to determine with approximate certainty . . . the markets' solidity," the protectionist campaigner Franz Stöpel argued. "For this reason, that what we call world market is an unpredictable thing."[51] For Stöpel, it followed that national markets required protection in the shape of tariffs. Julius Faucher, an avid free trader, made an argument that was structurally very similar to Stöpel's, though it was cast in more specific monetary terms. According to Faucher, the changing nature of the bill of exchange in international trade could explain the causes of overspeculation. In earlier times, a bill of exchange had been tied to a specific commodity. Now, however, bills of exchange circulating in international trade were devoid of any material basis. This naturally led to periodical cycles of overproduction.[52] The relationship between an expanding world market and the economy's propensity to overproduction was not new, of course; Henry Carey and others had been popularizing this idea for years.[53]

Given this history, it seems remarkable that the theory was not more popular in the aftermath of 1873. Of course, the world market and free trade did come under attack during these years. But these attacks mostly originated not with those analyzing the panic's causes but those trying to combat its effects on trade. Thus, while there was a consensus of sorts that the panic had been caused by a lack of transnational (monetary) entanglement, and that a *greater* degree of interconnectedness was therefore desirable, many observers and policy-makers at the same time sought to discourage international trade, specifically imports, in order to counter the effects of deflation and international competition.[54] In this debate over protectionism and free trade, a view of the world market emerged that was very different from that sketched by gold advocates. According to protectionists (who by the end of the decade had largely succeeded in destroying the dominant discursive position enjoyed by free trade ideology in previous periods), modern industrial nations were engaged in a war-like conflict where battles were not fought with armies and battle ships but with the weapons of industrial and trade policies.[55] In Germany, this notion was popularized by the well-known protectionist politician Wilhelm von Kardorff in his pamphlet *Gegen den Strom*, in which the author claimed that a misguided belief in the superiority of free trade would not only make Germany poorer but also defenseless.[56]

This antagonistic view of the world market was diametrically opposed to that propagated by gold advocates. Where protectionists described the world market for goods as a zero sum game in which one country's gain was another country's loss, proponents of the gold standard held that in an ideal gold-based monetary system, no country could, by definition, ever have too much or too little currency. From their perspective, countries did not compete for gold but interacted as part of a harmonious whole in which any disequilibrium would immediately be corrected for the benefit of all. Considering these stark differences, it seems all the more remarkable that protectionist policies made such headway while the progold consensus remained largely intact during the 1870s.

Occasionally, the same antagonistic rhetoric that was typical of protectionist arguments could be heard from critics of the gold standard. Bismarck, who disliked the gold standard but opposed international bimetallism for practical reasons, believed that the world's limited supply of gold meant that nations had to compete with one another to obtain a sufficient amount.[57] But in Germany at least, the optimistic notion of international monetary cooperation championed by proponents of the gold standard was never seriously challenged in this period, even though the transition to gold did not go as smoothly as planned.[58] In 1879 the government, fearing the fiscal implications of a large-scale silver sale in a world of rapidly declining silver prices (itself of course partially brought on by Germany's monetary policies), suddenly decided to suspend the sale of its silver reserves and to stop withdrawing silver coins from circulation. In the same year, the plunging price of silver compelled the Austrian government to prohibit the private minting of silver coins. In 1892, Austria also finally made the transition to gold.[59] Germany remained on what came to be known as a "limping" gold standard or bimetallic currency until 1907. Silver coins continued to circulate as legal tender, and their value in relation to gold was fixed at a ratio of 1:15.5.[60] In the United States, too, gold advocates largely prevailed. Though opposition to the gold standard was decidedly more pronounced than in Germany, resumption was largely achieved in 1879. In a nod to proponents of bimetallism, a strictly limited remonetization of silver was implemented with the Bland-Allison Act of 1878, and the newly formed Greenback Party fielded its own presidential candidate with some success in the election of 1876. In 1890, the Sherman Silver Purchase Act expanded the remonetization of silver, though gold still remained dominant. But despite these limited successes, neither paper currency nor bimetallism was ever a serious option, and the progold consensus remained largely intact.

Even during the "great debate" of the 1880s and 1890s, when the gold standard did come under sustained attack, the theoretically most plausible alternative, international bimetallism, was never realistically in reach. To a large extent, this was a function of path dependency: Once major countries were on the gold standard, a transition to bimetallism was difficult to engineer, especially since any unilateral move towards bimetallism would have attracted masses of silver to that country's mint, and thus exposed it to exploitation.[61] For this reason, international bimetallism on the basis of a contractually fixed ratio of silver to gold was the only viable option. It was this idea in particular that provoked the ire of gold enthusiasts. Such contracts, they argued, would constitute an unacceptable infringement of national sovereignty. Of course, the gold standard also subjected nations to an international system that curtailed their autonomy in monetary matters, a fact that, unsurprisingly, progold commentators preferred to ignore.[62] Even during the 1880s and 1890s, then, an era in which contemporaries were acutely aware of the acrimonious nature of international economic competition, the idea of the gold standard mostly managed to maintain its association with progress and harmony, while bimetallism was branded as coercive.

In the United States, the theory that the gold standard would prevent the recurrence of panics held firm until 1907, when a financial crisis once again erupted in New York, despite the fact that the gold standard appeared to be in "good working order." Only then did legislators begin seriously entertaining the idea that the banking system rather than the currency was at fault, and the establishment of a lender of last resort in the shape of the Federal Reserve followed in due course.[63] In Germany and Austria, authorities were largely successful in managing the money supply, and major financial crises did not recur until well after the First World War, thus, essentially, vindicating the notion that the French indemnity, an anomalous one-off event, was responsible for the *Gründerkrach* of 1873.

International Capital Flows and National Cultures

Compared to the currency question, international capital flows received rather less attention from economic theorists in the aftermath of the panic. Those German and American writers who did address the issue, however, mostly concluded such transfer of capital was in the interest of both the exporting and importing party, and refrained from blaming it for the financial panic. It would nevertheless take several years for German capital exports to pick up once more.

In December 1873, the American ambassador to Germany informed the secretary of the treasury in a widely publicized letter that "[b]etween fifty and sixty [American] securities . . . have failed to pay their interest as it became due.

This has had an unhappy effect upon the public financial opinion," and a return to specie payments was necessary to restore the confidence of German investors.[64] Others noted that while the effects of such capital imports were not altogether positive, they were nevertheless necessary. According to one author, Americans, after the end of the Civil War, "seeing plenty around them, never realized they were using the products of labor other than their own . . . Extravagance and wasteful investments followed, and the panic of 1873 came at last." But, the author concluded, "it is the normal condition of a young and growing country like the United States to demand capital for new enterprises. We shall then ever have a European debt . . . as long as our rate of profit is higher."[65] Writing in the *Chronicle*, editor William Dana concurred with this view, claiming that in the next ten years Europeans were likely to invest more than the "many hundreds of millions" of the past decade: "In this anticipated current of capital from Europe lies one of the instrumentalities relied on by those who look for a revival."[66] Criticizing those who decried the sale of bonds abroad "as a payment of tribute to foreigners," another commentator claimed the relationship between creditor and debtor nation was no different from that between individuals in a commercial society: "If one man can pay interest to another, why may not one nation pay interest to another, without, in either case, any idea of tribute or degradation entering in the bargain."[67]

Most Germans and Americans, then, defended the principle and practice of international investments, even as these slowed to a trickle. Despite occasional calls for a ban of foreign securities from German exchanges, policy-makers never regarded such a measure as a realistic or sensible option. As one journal explained, it was misleading to attribute the losses realized by German investors in foreign securities to their supposedly "alien" character, since many German securities had declined even more in value. Where a country grew steadily wealthier and interest rates declined amid a plethora of capital, it was only natural and reasonable for money to leave the country, and as long as investors were smart enough to realize their gains when times were good, capital export would not amount to a drain of national resources—on the contrary.[68] Just as the "cosmopolitanism" of English capital had served that country well in the past, the journal told its readers, German investors and the German nation as a whole would likewise profit from a greater openness to foreign ventures.[69] In addressing the issue of capital flows, commentators rarely suggested that it might have been responsible for spreading the crisis.[70]

But in spite of this affirmative view of transnational economic integration, the accounts and interpretations of the panic of 1873 that were published in the 1870s can hardly be considered truly transnational in outlook. Their main organizing principle remained the nation, a clearly delineated, though not insulated, entity. Max Wirth, who published a revised edition of his monumental *Geschichte der Handelskrisen* in 1874, emphasized that events of world historical importance had preceded and caused the most recent crisis: "In the annals of history no period is known during which in an equally short period of time an equally great number of state-economic [*staatswirthschaftliche*] events of world-shattering scope succeeded one another as during the past four years."[71] But despite this grandiose-sounding opening, he did not trace the spatial ramifications of these "world-shattering" events (the wars in Europe, the French indemnity, the introduction of the German gold standard) in much detail. As he saw it, the crisis had been caused by developments in Austria, Germany, and the United States, while France and England had not played a role. The rapid growth of international trade and the growing commercial ties between Germany and America constituted the panic's precondition and context.[72] While Wirth devoted a few pages each to the crisis in Egypt, Russia, and South America, the "world" that had been "shattered" consisted of little more than (parts of) Europe and North America. Still, compared to other accounts of the 1873 crisis, Wirth's was fairly inclusive. Joseph Neuwirth's book, by contrast, only alluded to the American panic in passing which, he claimed, for a while seemed to portend the approaching of a "big world crisis."[73] This larger dimension however went unexplored and Neuwirth repeatedly emphasized the local, clearly delineated character of the Austrian crisis.[74]

American observers, for their part, did not seem entirely unaware of the continental European ramifications of Jay Cooke's failure. What had largely failed to register with Americans in the last months of 1873—that stock exchanges in Germany and Austria had crashed in response to the news from New York— became the subject of theoretical reflection in the years that followed. Writing in 1876, the American economist Charles Franklin Dunbar noted:

> With improved facilities for intercourse, the economic ties between countries have been vastly multiplied and strengthened . . . Every pulsation in the financial system is felt alike on each side of the Atlantic. A crisis in London has its instant counterpart here, and the great revulsions which periodically sweep over the commercial world may begin, almost as chance may dictate, in New York or in Vienna.[75]

Dunbar did not explicitly mention the Vienna panic here but, in picking the Austrian capital as an example, seemed to suggest that he had the most recent panic of 1873 in mind.

By mid-1874, indeed, it had become clear that America was not the only country suffering from the effects of the previous year's financial distress. "The dullness of business," the *Chronicle* observed in May, "is not peculiar to ourselves . . . England is complaining of it. France is complaining of it. So are Germany and Austria, and other countries." This fact prompted William Dana, the editorial's author, to dismiss calls for government action. Since the crisis was an international phenomenon, or so his reasoning went, it was hardly sensible to expect national governments to come to business's rescue. Any such efforts were bound to be futile, Dana concluded.[76] *Bankers' Magazine* also noted these similarities: "The case of Europe is in effect our own." The same "events and changes" that had prompted the American panic had also affected Europe.[77] In these and other articles, however, and much like Wirth's interpretation, it was not made clear how exactly this relationship between the individual crises was to be construed: was there one root cause, one all-encompassing development that had swept over many countries and regions? Or were there many parallel developments that displayed common features but also important differences?

These questions prompted some to examine which role, if any, a country's "national character" or "culture" had played in bringing about the crisis. Most American commentators dismissed the notion that their most recent panic was a manifestation of American peculiarities. "In our late affair," one author maintained, "we certainly did not approach the violence and insanity which prevailed on the bourse in the Austrian capital last summer."[78] One prominent commentator, however, suggested that cultural factors (a potentially broader category than national peculiarities) may well have played a role. Horace White, who like many others observed that the financial and economic crisis seemed to have largely bypassed France, claimed that speculative manias and panics were a peculiarly "Anglo-Saxon-Teutonic" phenomenon. "The reason," White argued, "is simply that the Frenchman is very little addicted to going in debt, very little inclined to speculate . . . Where these national habits exist . . . the fuel of financial crises is wanting." Given what he saw as the civilizing influence of the "Anglo-Saxon race," he considered it "humiliating" that they could not "subsist without sowing the wind and reaping the whirlwind of a financial crisis, two or three times in each generation."[79] Though White stopped well short of describing overspeculation as a universal phenomenon, such observations nevertheless served to undercut a popular narrative about the peculiarities of American capitalism. Here, it seemed, the American way of doing business was neither faster nor more given to extremes than its European counterparts.

In Germany, not all commentators took a similarly universalizing view. Some indeed suggested that the crash was essentially an alien phenomenon whose roots lay in other countries. Thus Otto Glagau, whose sensationalist and anti-Semitic account of the crisis was widely read, claimed that speculation was originally a Parisian phenomenon, and, somewhat incoherently, noted that while corporate fraud had not gone quite as far in Germany as in America, it was only a matter of time before it would do so.[80] Adolf Berliner's account of the crisis—in this respect similar to Glagau—also described German speculation as an originally French and American import that, however, was quickly assimilated into the spirit of the German people.[81]

The German-Austrian economist and politician Albert Schäffle followed Joseph Neuwirth's lead in analyzing the Vienna panic almost exclusively from a national perspective. The fictitious values created on the Austrian bourse, he claimed, were directly derived from specifically Austrian fictions. One such "fiction" was the country's paper currency. More importantly, however, its political system was based on an artificial electoral system. The result was a parliamentarian minority government funded by a liberal oligarchy that did not represent the majority of Austrians. Consequently, the more "fictitious . . . the unnatural political centralization, the bigger and more deleterious the financial and economic swindle will be that proliferates around it."[82]

Another account by Benno Weber proceeded along similar lines while attributing greater importance to religious-political factors. In his interpretation, specifically Austrian conflicts regarding questions of national and religious allegiance had prevented citizens from familiarizing themselves with economic questions.[83] The "intellectual laziness and mendacity" that Weber (in terms reminiscent of the *Kulturkampf*) deemed prevalent in the Austrian people was, he maintained, a direct consequence of the Catholic restoration. He conceded that the economic downturn had affected Protestant and Catholic countries alike, displaying what he described as an "intimate, though not easily explicable relationship" between the Vienna crash and the rest of Europe.[84] Weber's awareness of the transnational nature of capital markets clearly did not preclude an analysis in terms of national culture. Even H. v. Marschall, writing in *Der Welthandel*, a publication whose very name indicated its claim to a global perspective, adopted an almost exclusively Austrian point of view, though he did note in passing that the "founding fever" had also engulfed Europe and the United States, which, he conceded, could be considered a mitigating circumstance.[85] Unlike Germany and America, this still largely agrarian country was far removed from the vanguard of that unifying force, global capitalism, making the search for national peculiarities seemingly all the more plausible.

While these authors interpreted the panic by comparing it to similar contemporaneous events, others looked to the past: Was this panic different, or was it, fundamentally, a mere reenactment of old experiences? Wirth, while identifying many characteristics familiar from earlier crises, nevertheless maintained that the present one was bigger and deeper than anything the world had seen before. But only the panic's European causes were unique. Unlike the French indemnity and Germany's transition to gold, the underlying American cause—overspeculation in railroads—had many precedents in recent history.[86]

On the other side of the Atlantic, in October 1874, the editors of *Bankers' Magazine* expressed befuddlement at the prostration of business, noting that "in every previous panic the inflation has been in mercantile credits; while last year mercantile credits were unusually sound."[87] In the following issue, it was reported that according to Bonamy Price, the British economist, overinvestment in fixed capital, especially railroads, had caused America's most recent panic.[88] This, too, suggested that it differed in crucial respects from earlier ones. In 1877, when confidence had still not returned, the editors affirmed their assessment that "the panic of 1873, differed in essential points from the financial revulsions which were before on the record." The problem, they claimed, lay neither with credit nor with currency but, rather, with capital that was lying dormant both in Europe and America, unable or unwilling to provide business with much-needed stimulation.[89]

Most theorists, however, rejected the idea that 1873 was fundamentally different. Some conceded that certain features, such as the French indemnity, were unusual, but they nevertheless maintained that the most recent crisis had evolved according to the same general patterns and mechanisms that had been operative in earlier crises of the nineteenth century.[90] Friedrich Engels argued in 1878 that the world was witnessing the effects of a crisis of overproduction (a *crise pléthorique*), the sixth since 1825.[91] In this, he followed Karl Marx, for whom crises necessarily resulted from the law of diminishing returns. In the long run, this would spell the end of capitalism, and the most recent crisis was just another step toward its inexorable demise. In this perspective, of course, any peculiarities the most recent crisis might display were irrelevant, and consequently, neither Marx nor Engels published a detailed account of the crises of 1873.

In the history of business cycle theories, both of the Marxist and non-Marxist variety, 1873 was not a watershed event. Economists integrated the panic and ensuing depression into already existing conceptions of overinvestment, overproduction, and underconsumption. While the late 1870s saw a gradual shift in popular discourse toward a stronger emphasis on underconsumption as a cause of the *economic* depression,[92] the financial panics of 1873 generally reinforced the idea that such crises were but a phase in a longer cycle of periodical upswings and downturns. By the turn of the century, economists such as Knut Wicksell and Alfred Marshall would describe this cycle with considerable sophistication.[93] From this perspective, neither the nation nor the question of economic interconnectedness was a relevant category.

Conclusion

In the aftermath of the panic, economic theorists sought to explain its causes by pointing to the role of monetary factors. In all three countries, it seemed, an excess of currency, either in the form of irredeemable paper money or in the form of two simultaneously circulating metallic currencies, had fostered speculation and enabled the creation of artificial values. The remedy, therefore, was to be found in the introduction of a gold currency, which, in future, would prevent both monetary excess and scarcity. But while this idea was popular on both sides of the Atlantic, there was also a telling difference in how exactly this idea was spelled out: German and Austrian theorists explicitly argued that their panics had been caused by monetary insulation, while American theorists were much less likely to argue that their financial crisis had been caused by the lack of an external outlet for greenbacks. What gold proponents in all three countries had in common, however, was that they wished to replace the excessive, the intangible, and unreal with something concrete and material. In this sense, then, the currency debates examined here can be seen as instances of translating the experience of financial markets from something impalpable and opaque, as embodied by an excess of (paper) money, into something real and tangible, as embodied by the gold standard. Crucially, the notion that a gold standard would render financial markets transparent by making capital flows responsive to supply and demand and independent of institutional control also relied on a rendering of the national into the *transnational*. This suggests that conceptualizing financial markets was not unidirectional. Substituting a national framework with a transnational one could appear just as effective in reducing opacity as conceptual "nationalization."

The affirmative view of transnational economic integration and global markets was evident also in the largely affirmative writings on transnational investment. At the same time, the nation and national categories also retained some importance in the theoretical writings on financial panics during that decade, which mostly focused on one country; and even those that did not, nevertheless, use the nation as an entity to structure their narratives.

CHAPTER 5

CAPITALISM, CONSPIRACY, CORRUPTION, AND THE MORAL ECONOMY OF A FINANCIAL CRISIS

E xplaining financial markets in terms of the abstract flow of money, as economic theorists did, left little room for concrete actors and their motives. Yet to many contemporaries in the aftermath of the panic, it seemed imperative to analyze the causes and consequences of the crisis not just in systemic terms but also in terms of individual moral responsibility. Who, they asked, had stood to gain from the speculative bubble? Who lost out, and why? This chapter addresses how people attempted to make sense of the havoc wrought by financial markets, and the narratives and interpretative frameworks they employed to relate their own economic misfortunes to the actions of individual promoters, bankers, and politicians. The multiplication of values in the run-up to the panic, the rapid economic growth, followed by a sudden, sharp downturn in which many lost first their savings, and then their livelihoods, prompted contemporaries to reflect on the causes of the panic in distinctly moral terms. The ensuing debates revolved around notions of a moral economy according to which the crisis was the result neither of misfortune nor of abstract economic forces but of many individual acts of deception and fraud, and of a wider societal decay.[1] While notions of morality and legitimacy informed debates and reactions in all three countries, there were also significant differences, as this chapter shows. The question of whether investors, and especially those of small means, were to blame for their misfortune was debated on both sides of the Atlantic but was especially acrimonious in Germany and Austria. Charges of corruption were common in all three countries, but only in Germany did these take the form of a full-blown conspiracy theory with distinctly racialized elements. In this second section of the chapter, I will therefore focus on the German case and refer to the Austrian and American case to highlight these contrasting features.

A "Rich Man's Panic"?

"The recent decline in the value of railway shares has been very great. Before the panic, I bought Lake Shore @ 91—present value 73 1/2. N. Y. Central 99 @ 104—to day 89 @ 91 – Rock Island 108—now selling @ 90—Panama I paid 111 1/2 now 90," Edward N. Tailer wrote in his diary in late September, while the panic was still raging.[2] As stock and bond markets crashed, and investors and speculators rushed to liquidate their assets, observers wondered whether this shrinkage of values was real, or whether it merely signified a destruction of paper wealth, which had always been artificial in character. Initially, many believed that only those who had speculated on the stock exchange would suffer losses. "Thousands of persons had," the *New York Times* noted, "during the last few months, placed the hard earnings of a life time in 'stock margins,' and one fine morning saw them all remorselessly swept away in the final settlement. It is the old story, which is repeated ad nauseam on the New York exchange year after year." If "professional persons, women, mechanics, clerks, and others of every class" now found themselves "beggared," it was only because they had refused to learn the lesson of previous generations, the journalist concluded.[3] In December, even as signs of a commercial crisis were multiplying, one writer expressed his belief that the panic had been a mere "rich man's panic," one that only affected a "set of men who form a potent community of their own, who buy and sell constantly on the stock exchange." The recent storm, he confidently asserted, had "passed lightly over the merchant and the farmer, the manufacturer and the mechanic." The panic, he hoped, would turn out to be a force of poetic justice. Artificial, illegitimate wealth would be wiped out, while those who had always kept their distance from the stock exchange, the producers of real values, would be spared.[4]

In earlier panics, philosophers and the clergy had frequently interpreted the losses suffered as God's direct retribution for the human sin of greed. With every new panic, however, such religious interpretations seemed less and less relevant, and by 1873, explanations of economic misfortune were largely secular.[5] Secularization brought new conundrums: was financial hardship the result of individual failings or of larger economic forces?[6] The notion that failure was the result of an individual's misjudgment provided a forceful narrative on both sides of the Atlantic.[7] Yet in times of crisis, it appeared less compelling. Thus when Alwin Waltz, a certified broker at the Berlin Stock Exchange, committed suicide in October, it was noted that this respectable member of Berlin's financial community would surely have been able to pay all his debts had he been given just a little more time, and had circumstances been more auspicious.[8]

As many people soon discovered, far from being an agent of poetic justice, the panic in many instances reinforced old inequities and produced new inequalities. The stockbroking firm of Hume & Van Emburgh managed to significantly increase its fortune and in February 1874 was reported to be "in good credit," having "made a large amount of money, . . . being on the right side of the fence, when the panic came."[9] Indeed, almost as soon as the panic had begun, experienced speculators such as Jay Gould lost no time in salvaging the most valuable objects from the its wreck, while younger men such as Harriman and Frick, who were later to become some of Wall Street's most influential players, "plunged in to wrest many a prize from the financially dead and dying."[10] At the same time, stories detailing the fate of panic victims were multiplying. In Germany, the *Berliner Tageblatt* reported that a once-wealthy owner of several carriages had now been reduced to destitution, having been advised, when times were good, to sell his carriages to a corporation for a sum of 3,000 taler and join the company as a salaried employee. After signing the contract, however, he had discovered that the shares he had been promised would have to be deposited with the company as a security, and now that it had gone into receivership, "the once wealthy man is practically a beggar, and the almost worthless shares are part of the [bankruptcy] assets."[11] The article's title ("One of the Many") suggested that his fate was representative of that of many other victims of the panic.

Even more disquieting was the fact that the crisis was touching those who had never made speculative investments. As early as June, the Carinthian chamber of commerce had noted that the crisis no longer only affected "unviable and fraudulent companies" but had also brought down a reputable business and a bank that until recently had enjoyed the very best credit and had business relations with members of all classes.[12] In October, a Berlin paper reported that charitable endowments and the trustees of orphans were, in consequence of the financial turmoil, unable to find sufficient gilt-edged [*depositalfähige*] securities in which to invest the money entrusted to them.[13] In late November, it was reported that even members of the educated and privileged classes, who had previously been able to find employment with banks and insurance companies, had been made redundant and were now reduced to copying voter lists in the local magistrate's bureau of Berlin. But there, too, they would be no longer needed once the elections were over, and many were anxiously awaiting what the new year would bring.[14]

In Austria, one parliamentarian exclaimed in the debate on proposed state aid to businesses that one only needed to ask the farmer "who can no longer sell his products, the grocer who has lost customers, and the cobbler and tailor who have had to stop their work, and you will be told whether the stock exchange, industry, and commerce are interrelated."[15] Many members of the opposition, however, refused to believe that the Liberal government had the best interests of the lower and middle classes at heart when proposing a program of government loans to businesses. Rather, critics argued, the proposed bill was designed to bail out financiers and speculators, and Liberals were disingenuous in their evocation of the plight of craftsmen and small merchants. "These millions," Georg von Schönerer, a newly elected Liberal parliamentarian and self-professed advocate of the "man on the street," exclaimed during the debate, "would not help the people but the banks." Schönerer, soon to become one of Austria's most notorious anti-Semites, seized the opportunity to denounce his fellow Liberals as responsible for the growing economic calamity.[16] After a first failed attempt, the bill was passed by the Liberal majority, but many Austrians agreed that it represented a victory for financial circles.[17] In May the following year, Prussian legislators confronted a similar dilemma when they debated a bill that would enable the state to guarantee interest payments on securities of the Nordbahn Company. Following a passionate speech by Eduard Lasker, the well-known National Liberal politician and critic of railroad corruption, the bill was voted down, as parliamentarians feared the optics of providing state aid to a company that had been founded under dubious circumstances.[18]

In the United States, meanwhile, observers also noted the intimate links between the stock exchange, banks, brokers and ordinary businesses. "The wholly upright and honorable business firms who have gone down in the crash, are victims to the terror caused by a few unprincipled speculators," the *Churchman* wrote. If one railroad king destroyed another, that was of no concern to the public. But the way things stood now, they were "disturbing private supplies which reach to everyman's dwelling."[19] One farmer feared that his community would be among the hardest hit, since the decline in prices would squeeze his margins further and force him to sell below the costs of production.[20] To some, this interdependency seemed, if no longer as mysterious as it had in past crises, nevertheless deeply iniquitous—not simply a fact of modern life to be born with equanimity but a profoundly moral issue. There was, in the words of one commentator, "no question that this blind and helpless dependence on the conduct of others with whom one's relations are solely commercial, is one of the most weakening and corrupting agencies to which human character can be exposed."[21]

Labor leaders had long held that manual labor was inherently more virtuous, and more productive, than the ownership of the means of production, let alone of financial instruments. Prior to the panic, this "theme of the aristocracy of toil" (Daniel Rodgers) was promoted mainly by denouncing those capitalists who were workers' most direct antagonists—the "'non-working' owners of small workshops who ensured that producers remained dependent on his capital and forced an unfair price war onto small competitors," ruining them in the process. In the years preceding the panic, labor periodicals had occasionally condemned stock exchange speculators but had not made them the focus of their rhetoric. But beginning in 1873, the financial capitalist for a while became the dominant *Feindbild* in German labor circles.[22] Already prior to the September panic, the German *Neue Social-Demokrat* had noted that workers and members of the lower middle classes were bearing the brunt of the financial downturn, an observation that would come up repeatedly during the following years as the crisis dragged on. In early 1875, the paper reported growing unemployment among factory workers, noting that they had to bear the consequences of the panic, "whereas no speculator or industrialist would dream of sharing with the workers some of the profits made from overproduction prior to the crash."[23] On the other side of the Atlantic, the *Workingman's Advocate*, a Chicago labor newspaper, had observed a similar development as early as October 1873. The "general disposition on the part of capitalists to reduce the wages of workingmen" was, it claimed, "inexplicable and unjustifiable . . . Why is it, we ask, that the working man, who is the least able to bear it, should be made to suffer the first permanent loss?" In November, it noted that industrial classes produced values "but seldom hold cutthroat securities. These," it continued in terms markedly stronger, "are all in the hands of bankers and brokers, or in other words, in the hands of the hyenas of the financial class."[24] Somewhat paradoxically, then, the antagonism between labor and capital became a subject in labor circles only after the years of overspeculation and high interest rates had ended, and capital itself was undergoing a crisis.[25]

Where farmers and laborers were concerned, the case for moral outrage was not difficult to see. These people had, after all, not speculated in dubious securities, and it was hard to fault them for having indirect relations with banks and other institutions affiliated with the stock exchange, since this was an inevitable consequence of producing, buying, and selling in a monetary market economy. But while such observations and arguments seemed self-evident in the pages of religious publications, agricultural, and labor journals, and in liberal-reformist magazines, the question looked different from the perspective of those who were closer to Wall Street.[26] Thus the *Chronicle* argued that farmers (or at least, certain groups of farmers) had only themselves to blame. For many months before the panic broke, they had instigated protests against the railroads on whose services they relied, trying to force them to lower their rates. This, the *Chronicle* alleged, had scared investors into losing confidence in railroads, thus precipitating a panic whose consequences were now affecting the whole country.[27]

But what about those investors, big and small, who had bought railroad bonds and other securities in the hope of reaping a large profit? Should they, too, be considered blameless victims? Or did they bear some responsibility for

their misfortune? Wall Street was, as one journal argued, "the outlet of the speculative feeling of the financial sentiment of the whole people," and just as the
elated national mood of the past years had found expression in the frenzied
trading on the New York Stock Exchange, the present depression would not
spare those "men and women of every station of life, scattered from ocean to
ocean, and from Lake Superior to the Gulf" whose names had been entered into
Wall Street's ledgers when times still seemed good.[28] However cunning the promoters had been, these investors had bought their stocks and bonds voluntarily.
The "petty shopkeeper" in a Connecticut village who had put all his savings into
Northern Pacific bonds had acted recklessly and was now paying the price, the
writer suggested. Likewise, when the *Berliner Tageblatt* reported on the suicide
of a clockmaker and council member in the small town of Demmin, who had
discovered that his life's savings ("not significant but arduously acquired"),
which he had invested almost entirely with Quistorp's companies, were largely
destroyed, the writer did not say that the man had only himself to blame.[29] But
neither did he explicitly exculpate the man as a victim of unfortunate circumstances, unlike the case of the broker Alwin Waltz just a few weeks earlier.

Not everyone bought into this perspective. After all, the notion that securities trading was a rigged affair and that large operators and speculators held
an unfair advantage on the stock exchange was, if less widespread than in previous decades, still a common one.[30] From this perspective, small-time investors bore only little responsibility for their misfortune since they had never had
a fair chance of assessing the value of the securities they had been led to purchase and, unlike experienced operators, were not in a position to anticipate
or engineer a downturn on the market. "It is one of the peculiarities of stock
ownership," Franz Perrot, a German writer and politician, argued "that stocks,
as long as they are yielding and continuously promising a large profit, remain
in the hands of the privileged; but that they are quickly distributed to the general public as soon as they are about to decline in value."[31] "The sad thing that
follows these crises is not the ruin of the great Houses," one American writer
noted in a similar vein, "but the distress which falls upon thousands of persons in moderate circumstances, who have been led by their confidence in these
great Houses to invest their small means of support in unsound or worthless
securities. . . . Thousands of families who were comfortably off before are in
poverty now."[32]

It is not possible to assess whether small investors were indeed disproportionately harmed as a result of the panic. The available (anecdotal) evidence suggests this may well have been the case. Following the panic, the Northern
Pacific Company received letters from investors describing how they had first
invested their modest means in the company and then lost almost everything.
Among the writers were a disabled soldier, an Episcopalian minister, and a man
who had been forced to leave America and return to his home country after

losing his job in 1873.[33] In Germany, a butcher, a saddler, and a railroad employee testified in a criminal trial in the city of Brunswick, describing how they had purchased shares in a local company, believing they were making a promising long-term investment.[34] This was not uncommon: Of the 647 initial subscribers to shares of the Pommersche Centralbahn, a company that quickly went bankrupt, 291 had subscribed shares for merely 200 talers. Most of them were provincial craftsmen and farmers.[35] Similarly, one investor from a small village near Heidelberg claimed in a letter to the parliamentarian Eduard Lasker that many of the securities of the ailing Nordbahn Company had been placed with private and small capitalists who had now formed a committee, hoping to retrieve their investment. He himself had invested in the railroad because it had received a license from the Prussian state, and because some of the entrepreneurs involved were high-ranking state officials. As a Southern German, moreover, he was grateful to his Northern brothers for securing Germany's victory in the Franco-Prussian War. At no point, he claimed, had his motivations been of a speculative nature.[36] Whether such protestations were true or not hardly mattered. Investors were clearly convinced that their intentions had always been pure, not greedy, and their indignation at the perceived injustice was very real.

For Americans, the question of whether or not small investors bore most of the responsibility for their losses was complicated by the fact that traditional investment outlets for the lower and middle classes—namely, savings banks and trust companies—had experienced significant problems of their own and were clearly not the obvious choice for safe investments they had always been made out to be.[37] In the 1860s and early 1870s, the number of depositors and the size of deposits in savings banks had grown steadily. At the same time, even before the panic struck, some savings banks had been widely criticized for their careless, sometimes reckless management of deposits.[38] In November 1871, two such institutions, the Bowling Green Savings Bank and the Guardian Savings Institution in New York City, failed, something which, as one observer noted, could not come as a surprise to anyone familiar with the development of savings banks in recent years. Many of the newer institutions were, he explained, "creatures of speculators, who desired places for themselves and their favorites, or designed thereby to facilitate their own selfish ends by gaining control of large sums of money."[39] Less than two years later, it was reported that the secretary of the Brooklyn Trust Company, a well-known figure on Wall Street, had defrauded investors out of almost $200,000. Although the institution was not deemed to be in danger of failing, the *Chronicle* concluded that it would be necessary in future to strengthen "Trust Companies and Savings Banks and other fiduciary institutions."[40]

The September panic and its aftermath only reinforced this point, as many "fiduciary institutions" came under intense pressure. In early October, it was reported that the city's savings banks had been under "the severest strain," but that now the worst seemed to be over.[41] Because savings banks could require depositors to give notice before withdrawing funds and availed themselves of this privilege as soon as they sensed the danger of bank runs, they were less vulnerable to bank runs and suspensions than other financial institutions.[42] Some savings banks were nevertheless forced to suspend. On September 28, from Louisville, Arkansas, it was reported that several savings banks "conducted and owned chiefly by Germans, with large lines of German depositors" had closed.[43] But this, one observer insisted in December, had been an almost exclusively western phenomenon; in the eastern states, all savings banks had, with just one exception, stood firm.[44] There therefore seemed reason to believe that savings banks deposits were indeed safer than most other financial assets.

Such hopes, however, were soon to be disappointed, as it became clear that savings banks were plagued by long-standing problems that predated the panic and were now brought to the fore. The most notorious case was that of the Freedman's Bank, which failed in 1874 and whose fate, it turned out, had been intimately tied up with that of Jay Cooke's bank and the Northern Pacific Railroad Company. Chartered in 1865, the bank had been designed to safely invest the savings of freedpeople who, following failed attempts by the federal government to provide them with landed property, were to use their accumulated savings to eventually realize their goal of landed independence. Although depositors were promised that the bank's directors would invest their savings with a minimum of risk involved, the bank's charter nevertheless permitted investment in railroad bonds, and from 1870 onward, Henry Cooke, brother of Jay and the bank's finance chairman, freely availed himself of this privilege, buying Northern Pacific bonds and loaning money to his brother's bank against yet more bonds. In many instances, he also made investments decisions that were clearly in breach of the charter, such as loans to individuals and corporations, as well as to himself, against stocks and bonds of dubious value, and sometimes without any collateral. Henry Cooke was eventually ousted from the bank in 1872, but the damage had already been done. When Cooke & Co. failed, the bank's enormous liabilities could no longer be papered over. In early 1874, it was declared insolvent, and on July 2 closed its doors for good.[45]

The Freedman's Bank was not to remain the only savings bank to fail in the Northeast (although its fate was most clearly tied to the event that had triggered the panic: the failure of Cooke & Co.). Throughout the 1870s, several others followed suit, eventually spurring a legislative response that placed stringent regulations on trustees and directors in order to better protect small savers from the risks of the financial market.[46] The new laws effectively amounted to an admission that financial markets *had* failed small savers, that there had never been such a thing as a safe asset, and that the panic really had produced blameless victims.[47]

In both Germany and Austria, by contrast, savings banks stood firm and remained largely unaffected by the financial crisis. Although Austrian savings banks probably lost a certain share of savings to the speculative *Maklerbanken*, they were never in acute danger, and savings banks in Berlin steadily increased their deposits during the early 1870s.[48] But while these developments were rarely commented on, two prominent episodes involving a large number of small speculators garnered a great deal of attention and prompted commentators to reflect on the moral responsibility of members of the lower classes. In Vienna, Johann Baptist Placht had lured several thousand people to part with their savings by inviting them, in prominently placed newspaper advertisements, to participate in small *Consortien*, each consisting of one hundred members. These were asked to give their money to Placht, who would invest it in stocks during a period of six months, after which their initial investment would be returned to them along with a handsome dividend, a promise he appeared to make good on several occasions. When the stock exchange crashed in May, however, it quickly became clear that the trades had been largely fictitious and that Placht had, in fact, been operating a Ponzi scheme. In February 1874, Placht was indicted on charges of fraud and embezzlement and sentenced to six years in prison.[49]

In reporting on the trial, commentators pointed out that Placht's case bore a striking resemblance to that of Adele Spitzeder, a former actress who had gained notoriety in 1871 and 1872 by operating what soon came to be known as the Dachauer Bank. Spitzeder had lured thousands of people of moderate means from Munich and its hinterland to deposit their savings by promising extraordinarily high returns, which Spitzeder, much like Placht, had advertised in several newspapers. Unlike the latter, however, she did not claim to be investing the money in stocks and never gave any indication as to how she intended to turn a profit. Although many liberal papers had quickly and repeatedly denounced Spitzeder as a dangerous fraud, she managed to continue her scheme until November 1872, when local authorities finally intervened and arrested her on charges of fraud. A large part of the assets were never recovered, leaving many of her customers destitute. Spitzeder, too, was sentenced to several years in prison. The episode was widely reported in local and national newspapers and left many observers wondering just how far the speculative spirit had spread.[50]

Indeed, a distinguishing feature of both cases was that Spitzeder and Placht had mostly catered to people on the lower rungs of society—to small farmers, farm laborers, domestic servants, craftsmen, civil servants, and soldiers—and had counted more women than men among their customers.[51] Both the prosecutor and the judge in the Placht trial explicitly stated that, though the defendant had actively misled his customers, their gullibility and greed, and the general "gambling mania" that had become a distinguishing feature of the age had to be considered mitigating factors.[52] Following this line of argument, one Austrian reporter agreed that the trial had revealed the "shocking truth" about the "passions of the people": "The greed which motivated the play's hero at the same time revealed itself as the mainspring of his victims. Only by virtue of this remarkable conjuncture of passions did the contribution to the history of morality [*Sittengeschichte*], which the Placht trial furnished, become possible."[53]

Placht and Spitzeder were not the only ones to stand trial for their role in the speculative bubble of the 1870s. Beginning in 1873, several German promoters were charged with deceiving the public by creating fictitious "bubble companies" (*Schwindelunternehmungen*) in order to line their pockets. Unlike Placht and Spitzeder, the defendants in these trials were formerly well-to-do merchants and bankers. While some of their victims were similarly privileged, others were of much more modest means. In one of the earliest cases, it was reported that the defendants had persuaded the workers of the factory they had incorporated to purchase shares, which had then lost most of their value.[54] In another, the witnesses summoned included a railroad employee and a saddler.[55] Public interest in the trials was intense, as many hoped they would provide an antidote to the iniquities produced by the financial crash and the ensuing economic downturn.[56] When Kaiser Wilhelm, worried that the trials were damaging the reputation of German businesses, asked his justice minister whether he might intervene to put an end to investigations, the minister noted that this would surely alarm public opinion.[57] An intervention by the government would have been especially contentious as one of the prosecutors in the Berlin trials, Hermann von Tessendorf, also led the prosecution of leading Social Democrats for their role in organizing the city's workers. In at least one case, a Social Democrat had directly addressed Tessendorf in court, demanding to know why, rather than going after workers' associations, he did not indict "fraudulent promoters."[58]

Ultimately, the government refrained from intervening, and most of the trials resulted in convictions. In the end, for all the attention they garnered, the "promoter trials," as they were commonly known, did little to settle the question of individual responsibility in the realm of public opinion. Many cases had not gone to trial in the first place, and even where convictions were secured, this was only on appeal, after lower courts had initially acquitted the defendants.[59] Indeed, the legal issues at stake were complicated and contested, and the lengthy and sometimes opaque legal deliberations and opinions could not reflect a widespread perception that a large number of promoters were clearly and unequivocally culpable.

More complicated still was the question of whether small shareholders bore any responsibility for their fate. In the United States, the story of the Freedman's Bank and other savings institutions showed how easily industrious and modest people of small means could fall prey to the machinations of unscrupulous financiers, and there seems to have been, on the whole, less inclination to point to the greed and recklessness of small investors. The Placht trial in Austria and the Spitzeder trial in Germany, by contrast, proved that even maids, civil servants, and craftsmen had not been immune to the lure of financial markets.[60] These and the German promoters' trials suggest that the debate over personal responsibility for the panic was more intense in the two European countries than in the United States, where there were no similarly spectacular trials.

The economic and spiritual wounds the panic had inflicted were deep, and the prolonged economic downturn of the 1870s only intensified the experience of social strife and conflict. In Germany, Otto von Bismarck accused the labor movement of deliberately standing in the way of economic recovery by radicalizing destitute laborers and sowing discord, an accusation that laid the ground for the anti-Socialist laws of 1878.[61] In the United States, meanwhile, the economic elite increasingly convinced itself that workers presented a threat to their economic and political power, an impression that was reinforced by the nationwide labor uprisings of 1877.[62] In this atmosphere of social strife, questions of individual responsibility, human agency, and the moral dimension of capitalism continued to occupy the public of all three countries. During the 1870s, more and more people began asking whether the financial panic was a symptom of a wider and more profound societal decay. What if, they wondered, the buck stopped not with shareholders or even promoters but, instead, with the society at large—and, indeed, the system of capitalism and economic liberalism itself?

Cultures of Corruption

"Men quickly translated the crash into a political and moral indictment of the whole society. Corruption became the charge of the day."[63] This observation, made by Fritz Stern many years ago in describing German reactions to the crash, can easily be extended to the two other countries examined here. In all three societies, the notion that the panic had revealed profound political, social, and cultural conflicts was a common one, and frequently crystallized in the charge of corruption.[64]

In 1873, a case of political corruption became, for the first time, a scandal on a hitherto unseen scale in Germany. The National Liberal parliamentarian Eduard Lasker was the first prominent politician to expose the intimate nexus between railroads and the state, and its corrosive effect on public morality, when he attacked several prominent Prussian Conservatives in a series of widely noticed parliamentary speeches in early 1873. Specifically, he charged Hermann Wagener, a senior civil servant and close ally of Bismarck, with using his position to obtain concessions for railway companies he had founded. As a promoter, Lasker claimed, Wagener had paid himself and his copromoters a handsome reward, even though this would have been illegal according to the revised corporation law of 1870, which at the time in question had been passed but had not gone into effect. Several other legal restrictions had been evaded, Lasker charged, but the minister of commerce had seen to it that Wagener's companies could proceed unhindered. Two other Prussian aristocratic Conservatives, Prince Calixt Biron of Kurland and Prince Wilhelm Malte zu Putbus, similarly came under attack for their involvement with railway projects in the East. These, too, had been legally questionable and many investors had suffered heavy losses when their defects had become known. Bethel Henry Strousberg, the railway entrepreneur who had been responsible for the construction of many Prussian railways in the previous decade, featured prominently in Lasker's exposé as the original creator of the system underlying Putbus's and Biron's operations. The whole "Strousberg system," Lasker claimed, was inherently fraudulent and needed to end.[65]

Lasker's speeches were widely reported on and won him much praise from prominent individuals and small investors alike. In the months following the revelations, he not only received numerous letters of congratulation but also some from anonymous correspondents detailing the alleged misdeeds of railroad entrepreneurs whom Lasker had, they believed, omitted to mention.[66] Lasker had called for a parliamentary investigation into the Prussian government's railway concession system, but it was instead decided to set up a royal commission on which Lasker served as one of two parliamentary representatives.[67] The commission's report was issued in late 1873 and concluded that the practice of planning and constructing railroads was abstruse and, from the state's perspective, inefficient. Those flaws, however, were not merely the result of questionable decisions taken by individual ministers and civil servants. Rather, the system itself was at fault in that it gave too much power to private interests. Henceforth, the state should prioritize the "needs of public transport" over the question of profitability.[68] By then, Minister of Commerce Heinrich Friedrich von Itzenplitz had been forced to stand down, and Hermann Wagener had resigned his civil service post and Reichstag seat; he was later sentenced to 1,800,000 marks damages in a civil suit arising out of the railway's bankruptcy.[69] Putbus and Biron, by contrast, suffered no comparable consequences, although the former's involvement in one dubious enterprise, the Nordbahn, received renewed attention in May 1874, when Lasker again publicly accused the aristocrat of illicit dealings. Putbus angrily denied any wrongdoing and, after first suggesting he would press charges against Lasker, instead asked that a military tribunal (*Ehrengericht*) exonerate him. The tribunal obliged in due course, and the ruling was published in January the following year.[70]

   While Lasker was widely credited with having exposed a particularly egre-
gious case of corruption, the question of whether to allow civil servants to
engage in the promotion or operation of corporations had already been the subject of debates in the Reichstag. In 1872, the government had introduced a bill
to regulate the affairs of civil servants of the Reich, which had included a paragraph stipulating that any civil servant seeking a salaried sideline (including
as a member of a corporate board of directors) required an authorization from
his superiors. When the bill was debated on the floor of the Reichstag in April
and June 1872, several parliamentarians objected to this provision on the
grounds that it did not go far enough. In the end, an amendment passed that
prohibited civil servants, altogether, from joining the boards of, or otherwise
working for, corporations in return for direct or indirect remuneration.[71] During the debates, one parliamentarian, Count Ballestrem, warned that the present-day "feverish addiction" to making money was also affecting civil servants,
who were being seduced to take from the "large cornucopia of mammonism"
by joining the boards of corporations. This, he maintained, could lead to a
"general demoralization" and a conflict of interests.[72] While the proposed remedy (a stricter regulation of civil servants' activities) still relied on the traditional German narrow notion of corruption, Ballestrem's choice of words
("general demoralization") already indicated a transformation in the discourse on corruption as a more encompassing decay. This would become
increasingly evident in the following years.[73]
   The amended version of the "Law Regarding the Legal Conditions of Civil
Servants of the Reich" was passed in March 1873, with Lasker's revelations still
fresh in people's minds.[74] Soon, the Prussian legislature followed suit. The lower
chamber had first been presented with a draft bill in January 1873, six days after
Lasker's speech. The bill failed to gain support in the upper chamber. In 1874, a
law was passed prohibiting all Prussian civil servants from founding a corporation or working for one as a director or board member. By explicitly prohibiting the promotion of corporations, the final version of the Prussian law went
further than the equivalent paragraph in the federal law, a difference that may
well have been a reaction to the widespread criticism of railroad promoters,
unleashed by Lasker's speeches and the stock market crash in September 1873.
During the debate, a member of the Prussian upper chamber, Count von der
Schulenburg-Beetzendorf, pointed out that legislators had not deemed it necessary to apply the same rules to members of parliament, who could continue
their work as promoters and directors of corporations, even though they, too,
thereby risked a potential conflict of interest.[75] One contemporary observer esti-
mated that around five hundred Prussian civil servants—whose economic
position had been in decline since mid-century—would be negatively affected
"in their financial condition and social standing."[76] Despite such objections, the
bill was signed into law in June.[77]

While legislators chose not to prevent parliamentarians from promoting corporations, public disapproval of the misdeeds of aristocratic representatives was very real, as the case of two other prominent aristocrats and their involvement with Bethel Henry Strousberg shows. Strousberg, whom Lasker had angrily denounced in his speeches as the creator of a fraudulent "system" of railroad financing, was by then no longer the successful and admired figure he had been during the 1860s.[78] Having built several railroads in quick succession and established himself as Prussia's leading railway entrepreneur, Strousberg began looking out for new ventures and, in 1868, was commissioned by the Romanian government to build several railway lines. In order to raise money for this risky and capital-intensive project, Strousberg teamed up with several well-known Silesian magnates (Hugo Duke of Ujest, Victor Duke of Ratibor, and Karl Count Lehndorff-Steinort) to form a consortium for the sale of Romanian railway bonds, which were placed with thousands of investors in Prussia and beyond. The enterprise soon turned out to be costlier than anticipated, and in early 1871, it was announced that the company would not meet the promised interest payments. The Romanian government, having previously guaranteed the payment of interest in the event of default, refused to make good on its promise (the contract's wording left much room for interpretation), and thousands of investors big and small saw themselves threatened with heavy losses. Kaiser Wilhelm, fearing for the livelihood of his aristocratic friends, insisted that they not lose their investment. At Bismarck's behest, Bleichröder and Adolph Hansemann of the Disconto-Gesellschaft eventually agreed to step in and extend generous loans to the new company that they had founded to take over the interests of Strousberg's company, as well as to Ratibor and Ujest.[79]

The wealthy and well-connected, it seemed, had been spared while the small investor had lost out, a fact that was not lost on the public, as would quickly become clear. Ratibor had stood as a Reichstag candidate of the Freikonservative Partei in the election of 1871 but was defeated by a little-known candidate of the Catholic Zentrum Party, who, following the introduction of universal male suffrage for Reichstag elections, had been able to mobilize the support of many newly enfranchised Catholic voters. The result had enraged Liberals and Conservatives alike, who attributed it to the undue influence of priests, conveniently ignoring the widespread public outrage at Ratibor's role in the Romanian affair.[80] During the 1873 election, the Zentrum issued an appeal excoriating its political opponents for their dealings as promoters and claiming that its own candidates had always steered clear of such activities. The *Schlesische Volkszeitung* specifically accused Ratibor and Ujest of having colluded with Strousberg to rob the lower and middle classes of their hard-earned savings.[81] This tactic was employed repeatedly by Zentrum candidates in electoral campaigns in the following years.[82] The outrage at aristocratic promoters was not confined to Catholics. In early 1875, Eduard Lasker received a letter from a Protestant pastor angrily denouncing Prince Putbus. Were courts really powerless to force Putbus, who had sullied his "princely name" by willfully defrauding honest men, to reimburse his victims, the writer demanded to know? He and his son, he explained, had placed their trust in Putbus's aristocratic title, and now they had lost their savings while Putbus had escaped unscathed, having abused their trust and his position in society in order to enrich himself. Another correspondent observed that Lasker had failed to bring down Putbus, and that, instead, "many thousand innocent victims still remain and many tears are still to be dried."[83]

The stream of accusations continued throughout the decade. In 1874, the popular magazine *Die Gartenlaube* began publishing a series of articles by Otto Glagau, a journalist and former liberal, in which he set out to name and expose the many promoters of corporations, who, in the past years, had enriched themselves by swindling small investors.[84] The articles were later expanded and collected in a book whose first edition was published in 1876. In the preface, Glagau described his exposé as an indictment of the "corruption" in society, the press, and in parliament. All three, he claimed, had been contaminated and needed to be cleansed.[85] The notion that the public had only itself to blame for the greed it had displayed during the speculative bubble was nothing more than a convenient myth. According to Glagau, Strousberg's maneuvers had spawned an entire school of promoters, many of them Jewish, who had brought his system to perfection during the past period of swindle.[86] The book named some of the most active and notorious promoters and described their actions in great detail. In this, Glagau went much further in his accusations than Lasker had done (whom Glagau accused of focusing selectively on conservative offenders and sparing his Liberal allies).[87] Where Lasker had taken care to specify which laws and regulations Wagener and others had skirted or violated in their dealings, Glagau indicted a much larger group, accusing more than a hundred persons of illicit dealings. They had been aided, Glagau claimed, by the municipal government of Berlin, which had sold valuable land to reckless speculators, by civil servants who had been happy to serve on the boards of dubious bubble companies, and by a servile press dependent on income from advertising.[88]

Accusing the press of corruption was not exactly new. Others had leveled similar charges. The press, they claimed, had failed to warn investors of Heinrich Quistorp's dubious enterprises, and journalists had reaped a handsome profit from advertisements, all while luring innocent investors into buying the shares of worthless bubble companies.[89] In doing so, journalists had violated the "holy spirit" of their profession.[90] But what set Glagau's book apart from others was that he took these charges and combined them with a long list of alleged wrongdoers, creating a potent brew of insinuation, pseudo-specificity, and moral outrage.[91] As subsequent publications and debates would show,

Glagau did not change the discourse of corruption singlehandedly but channeled widespread sentiments into something stronger, a narrative of general moral decay and widespread greed and dishonesty.

The appeal of this narrative was evident in public reactions to Glagau's book. Glagau noted the many letters of support he had received and wrote a second volume, which appeared in 1877.[92] His revelations became the subject of a Reichstag debate when a parliamentarian for the Catholic Zentrum Party attempted to use some of Glagau's material to attack the National Liberal parliamentarian and former mayor of the city of Osnabrück, Johannes Miquel. Miquel, it was claimed, had, as director—and following his resignation from this post in August 1873, member of the supervisory board (*Aufsichtsrat*)—of a large and well-known bank, the Disconto-Gesellschaft, engaged in morally dubious speculations, a charge that was echoed even by some liberal newspapers. Following the debate, Miquel resigned both from the board and from parliament.[93]

Glagau's attacks also inspired other publicists to write similar exposés. In 1875, the publicist and parliamentarian Franz Perrot published several articles in the conservative Protestant *Kreuzzeitung*, denouncing Bismarck and his National Liberal allies for having sold out German interests to Jewish interests in return for financial gain. Perrot had previously written books and articles critical of corporations and the stock exchange but only now couched his criticism in explicitly anti-Semitic terms. The chief instigator, he claimed, was Gerson von Bleichröder, Bismarck's Jewish banker. Glagau had identified Bleichröder as one of the major promoters but, unlike Perrot, had not claimed he was the main culprit. Now, the banker took center stage.[94]

Increasingly, the discourse on corruption took a decidedly anti-Jewish turn. The Catholic *Germania* published a series of articles denouncing the prevailing "Jewish economy" (*Judenwirtschaft*) and accused Bismarck of having launched the anti-Catholic culture war (*Kulturkampf*) in order to deflect from his association with Bleichröder. In 1876, a pamphlet by Otto von Diest-Daber, a former deputy of the Prussian Diet, alleged that Bismarck had, in return for cheap stocks, granted certain privileges to a joint stock company founded by a Bleichröder-led consortium (a charge that was later refuted).[95] Rudolph Meyer, a conservative publicist, repeated this allegation in his 1877 exposé *Politische Gründer*, in which he set out to prove that two "consortiums," one led by Bleichröder and the other by the Disconto-Gesellschaft, had, in the 1860s, set out to monopolize the market for mortgages and personal loans, to seize control of German railways, and to unload masses of worthless securities onto public investment funds. In the process, they had corrupted "one civil servant and member of parliament after another." Corruption had become so rampant that German society was now easy prey for social democracy. Although Meyer, perhaps in an attempt to feign objectivity, noted that both Jews and Christians had participated in this process, he reserved his most vicious invectives for the former: "Jewry and its agents are permeating all influential circles. The Foreign Office is teeming with full and half-semites. The entire press is beholden to the promoters."[96] Meyer concluded that the only solution was to do away with the present corrupt liberal system in its entirety—without, however, saying what should replace it.

Within just a few years the discourse on corruption had shifted: Lasker had attacked individuals and corroborated his accusations with detailed and specific evidence. Glagau's exposé was broader in scope, and his anti-Jewish invectives showed that he was not content with indicting individuals but targeted an entire group—Jewish promoters and financiers—who, he alleged, had plundered the German people with the help of a few Christian aristocrats.[97] If this did not amount to a full-blown conspiracy theory, it did prepare the ground for one, as the publications by Perrot, Meyer, and others would subsequently show. Their obsessive denunciation of Bleichröder's relationship with Bismarck hinged on the notion that it embodied, *pars pro toto*, the pernicious hold of Jewish interests on German political and economic life. This in turn implied, these authors maintained, that the liberal principles on which the economic system was built were inequitable and illegitimate, which also marked a notable shift in the discourse on corruption.[98] Liberalism was, in this perspective, a rapacious Jewish ideology designed to further Jewish interests.

To denote this link, Meyer had coined the term "Golden International," which quickly became a popular rallying cry of social conservatives and anti-Semites. The eponymous best-selling book by Carl Wilmanns, published in 1876, spelled out this belief in detail. According to Wilmanns, the liberal ideology was dishonest in its application of the principle of free competition since it was applied only to labor and real estate but not to the capital market, which was monopolized by Jewish-dominated banks and stock exchanges. Financial capital, he noted, was privileged in all spheres of legislation, and the "honest merchant" was forced to abandon "principles of solid commerce." Owners of landed property, laborers, and urban traders were all in danger of impoverishment.[99] But while anti-Semites aggressively denounced liberalism, they were less than clear when it came to specifying which kind of economic order should replace it. Some called for the nationalization of certain sectors of the economy while, at the same time, socialism was anathema.[100] While Wilmanns called for reforms to stave off the otherwise inevitable revolution, it was unclear what reform meant beyond curtailing the power of the stock exchange through more stringent regulations. By the second half of the 1870s, then, it was no longer only shareholders, promoters, and bankers who were under attack but the principles of economic liberalism itself. These debates had been triggered by the experience of the financial crisis. At the same time, they must also be seen against the backdrop of the slowdown in economic growth and social strife during that decade. The moral economy that emerged from these debates was one that denounced, from a moral point of view, what was alleged to be the dishonesty, selfishness, and greed of the capitalist, non-producing class.

This combination of anticapitalism, anti-Semitism, and antiliberalism was not new, of course. It had originated in the High Middle Ages, when Jews in Central Europe had been driven out of agriculture and into trade and money lending, as the Church began issuing increasingly strident anti-interest proclamations, and the emerging guilds explicitly excluded Jews. In the early nineteenth century, German-speaking conservatives had combined this stereotypical image of Jews as usurers with accusations that Jews were acting as agents of political and economic liberalism.[101] Already in the 1850s, Hermann Wagener (Bismarck's later-to-be-disgraced ally) had propagandistically harnessed these charges in order to rally members of the old *Mittelstand*, who saw themselves under threat from liberal economic reforms (small owners of landed property, small traders, and urban artisans) to the conservative cause.[102] But it was only in the 1870s that these anti-Semitic, anticapitalist, and antiliberal tropes became widespread. This popularity was, according to historians of anti-Semitism, due not only to that decade's economic crisis but also a result of German unification. The process of political unification entailed a heightened intensity of communication between hitherto relatively isolated conservative political groups, and an increased competition between political parties. At the same time, it seemed to many as though national integration remained incomplete and under threat from social and religious strife.[103] From this perspective, the *Feindbild* of the Jewish-liberal capitalist could seem like a welcome scapegoat and instrument of social cohesion. Thus the idea that Jews were responsible for promoter fraud was embraced by certain Catholic groups too. Following the publication of anti-Jewish invectives by Catholic papers in 1875, Catholic publishers continued to maintain for decades that Jews had instigated the *Kulturkampf* in an attempt to deflect from their role in promoting share fraud.[104] On the Left, too, hostility to Jewish capitalists was by no means unknown. Social Democrats had long considered capital an immoral form of property that deprived workers of the fruits of their labor, frequently equating capitalists, whom they deemed lazy and fraudulent, with "the Jew."[105] Possibly inspired by Glagau, Franz Mehring, a rising politician of the Left, in 1876, first attacked Julius Schweitzer, a well-known financial reporter for his undisclosed financial interests and, allegedly, biased reporting. Mehring then initiated proceedings against Leopold Sonnemann, editor of the *Frankfurter Zeitung*, charging him with abusing his position of trust in order to promote companies in which he had a financial stake. (Sonnemann had denied these accusations and called them "libelous," whereupon Mehring sued Sonnemann.) The lower court concluded in its verdict that Sonnemann's financial interests never compromised his or his paper's integrity, and noted instances in which the paper had criticized companies in which Sonnemann had invested. The appeals court, however, while ultimately upholding the ruling, agreed with Mehring that Sonnemann had behaved dishonorably in accepting money from companies. The much-publicized trials showed how influential Glagau's accusations were, even among some members of the Left.[106] Although Social Democrats explicitly denounced anti-Semitism, they often at the same time protested that they were by no means philo-Semitic and that many Jews were, in fact, involved in immoral practices of exploitation.[107]

In Austria, as in Germany, the first much-publicized charges of corruption preceded the financial crisis. In 1870, Minister of the Interior Karl Giskra had been forced to resign in response to charges that he had abused his position as codirector of the Lemberg-Czernowitz Railroad. In 1872, a book setting out to expose the pervasive corruption of Austrian society and politics was published anonymously in Leipzig. In the following years, it would be reprinted several times.[108] The author's definition of corruption was a broad one and encompassed not only the manifold connections between the country's press, politicians, and businessmen but also Austria's concordat with the Vatican in the wake of the Crimean War and the servility of Austrian art critics. The largest part of his book was devoted to the favors that he alleged were routinely exchanged between journalists and promoters, as well as between railroads and parliamentarians. "Promoter fraud," he acknowledged, had become an "international disease" but one which afflicted Austria even more than other countries. Only in France, he claimed, were people similarly prepared to accept corruption as an inevitable fact of life.[109]

The book's prosecutorial tone and wide-ranging indictment struck a chord, and the public's outrage only grew when the stock market crashed and economic calamity took hold. The ruling Liberal Party came under particular scrutiny for its intimate ties with railroad companies in which many of its parliamentarians held positions as members of the governing board. (The practice had been common across the political spectrum, but most prominent board member-parliamentarians were Liberals simply because they dominated the Viennese Reichsrat.) In March 1873, a Prague newspaper published the first of several extensive lists naming Liberal board members to much public attention. The "party of the constitution" (Verfassungspartei), as they proudly called themselves, had, it seemed to many, become the "party of the board of directors" (Verwaltungsratspartei). Since many leading journalists—most famously, those of the *Neue Freie Presse*—were also in the liberal camp, and enjoyed similarly intimate ties with corporations, the charges of corruption, coupled with a steep economic downturn from May 1873 onward, presented a grave threat to the party's hegemony.[110]

Thus when Viktor Ofenheim Ritter von Ponteuxin, director of the Lemberg-Czernowitz-Jassyer railroad, was indicted for fraud in early 1875 (following his arrest in December 1873), Liberals hoped the trial would allow them to distance themselves from their image as the Verwaltungsratspartei. Ofenheim, the defendant, had been a leading financier and promoter whose influence and business ties ranged far and wide. A member of the Viennese Jewish bourgeoisie, he had headed a road whose interest payments were guaranteed by the government but which was notorious for accidents and disruptions. For all these reasons, Ofenheim, who was charged with fraud in nine cases as well as with negligence in construction, seemed to embody the nefarious connections between finance, railroads, and politics. Because Ofenheim was rumored—despite strenuous protestations to the contrary—to be coowner of the *Neue Freie Presse*, many considered the liberal press a de facto codefendant. Unlike in Germany, however, where similar trials had ended in convictions, Ofenheim was acquitted, following a series of sensational depositions, including those of one former minister president and five ministers.[111] Not surprisingly, the public (and even the royal court) greeted the verdict with disgust.[112] The Liberal Party's attempt at salvaging its reputation had spectacularly backfired: not only did the defendant walk free but the parade of well-known witnesses testifying to the intimate links between business and government only reinforced the party's already tarnished image as hopelessly corrupt.

Charges of corruption continued to be leveled throughout the following years. In 1877, an anonymous pamphlet alleged that the Liberal Auersperg administration had engaged in several transactions with corporations that had hurt shareholders, creditors, and the entire people.[113] The pamphlet, which was quickly seized by censors in Prague, detailed several such alleged wrongdoings, many of which by now had a familiar ring to them. Thus one government-protected institution was alleged to have issued 1,000,000 florins' worth of debentures (*Pfandbriefe*) on the basis of faked debt obligations; another bank had falsely certified the placement and sale of 5,000,000 florins' worth of shares when in fact no money had been paid in; and board members of another company had transferred shares trading at 29 percent at par value to the bank they represented. Recounting these allegations, the author of another anonymous pamphlet, published in the same year and addressed to Julius Glaser, the minister of justice, asked why Viennese prosecutors had failed to investigate these charges. It appeared, he argued, that Glaser had first sought to suppress the allegations by having censors in Prague seize the pamphlet. Now, Viennese prosecutors were conspicuously reluctant to investigate those responsible, presumably, the author suggested, because their superior, the minister of justice, did not wish to see his colleagues in the cabinet become the subject of criminal investigations.[114]

As was Ofenheim, the incriminated minister of justice was a baptized Jew. In this respect, they could be seen to be representative of the Austrian Liberals who counted many German Austrian Jews among their parliamentarians and ministers. Already before the crash, Catholic newspapers had identified Jews with liberalism, and denounced both as rapacious and fraudulent.[115] Similarly, the post-1873 indictment of the Verwaltungsratspartei, and the attacks leveled against the Auersperg administration were frequently tinged with anti-Semitism, a sentiment that also underlay the often-repeated allegation that the House of Rothschild had engineered the crash to rid itself of unwelcome competition. Both the involvement of Jewish figures such as Ofenheim and the lack of involvement, as in the case of Rothschild, were, according to this mindset, evidence of wicked Jewish machinations.[116] Despite such allegations, however, none of the widely circulating pamphlets and exposés on corruption were as openly anti-Semitic as those of Glagau and Meyer, and no figure in Austrian public life was invested with the same kind of conspiratorial power as Bleich-röder was in Germany.

If, in Germany and Austria, corruption only became a subject of intense public debates in the early 1870s, the American discourse on the subject, as it would come to dominate debates in the 1870s, had a longer history, one that went to back to the days of the Civil War. Faced with the task of financing a war effort on a previously unknown scale, the federal government had expanded drastically, and, with higher revenues and expenses, the opportunities for corruption and cronyism had grown. If this constellation in itself did not necessarily lead to a rise in corruption compared to the prewar era, it did allow opposition party members to denounce a war effort they opposed for other reasons by pointing to its supposedly corrosive effect on public morality. In the post-Civil War era, the charge of corruption became a potent political weapon during Reconstruction, when Democrats—and, following their lead, the first generations of historians of the Reconstruction era—denounced Republican rule in the South as an "era of corruption presided over by unscrupulous 'carpetbaggers' from the North, unprincipled Southern white 'scalawags,' and ignorant freedmen."[117] At the same time, many Americans came to believe that for all the courage displayed during the war years, the nation's political and moral body had suffered profoundly, and that a spirit of self-reliance and hard work had given way to speculation, ostentation, and extravagance, an impression that was fostered and sustained by a new class of special newspaper correspondents, who, acutely conscious of their newly elevated status and power to influence public opinion, began to see politicians primarily as "men fit to be exposed."[118]

In the years leading up to the panic, and much as in Germany and Austria, the most widely scandalized charges of corruption were leveled against railroad directors and railroad-friendly legislators. One of the most notorious railroads, the Erie, in the state of New York, became the subject of a widely read exposé by Charles Adams Jr. and Henry Adams, two well-known liberal reformers. The Adams' indictment of the Erie's rapacious directors, and of the venal legislators and judges who colluded with them, was underpinned by a belief that the country's "great corporations" were "fast emancipating themselves from the State to their own control, while individual capitalists, who long ago abandoned the attempt to compete with them, will next seek to control them. . . . The individual will hereafter be engrafted on the corporation."[119] Other states saw themselves confronted with similar problems. In Pennsylvania, corruption among state legislators had resulted in a groundswell of constitutional revision in the early 1870s, which came to fruition in 1873. The following year, a general incorporation act was passed.[120]

The debate on corruption, then, had become a central element of public discourse by the early 1870s. The most notorious scandal of the age, however, one that contemporaries would come to consider as an embodiment of all that was wrong with American politics, erupted in 1872, when the speculative bubble was in full swing. Again, it was the dealings between politicians and railroad corporations that caused widespread public outrage. But whereas the Erie scandal had exposed the venality of state and municipal authorities, the Crédit Mobilier scandal, as it quickly became known, centered on a railroad, the Union Pacific, which had been chartered by federal legislators. Because the Pacific Railway Act of 1864 forbade the sale of railroad securities below par as a means of raising capital, the promoters of the Union Pacific had founded a construction company, the Crédit Mobilier, to evade this restriction and attract the capital required to build the railroad. The Crédit Mobilier, whose directors were also the directors of the Union Pacific, accepted railroad bonds at face value in return for its construction work but sold them to investors below par, thus turning a profit by building at a lower cost than it had charged the railroad company, much as Strousberg had done in Prussia.

The scandal was touched off when, in 1872, the *New York Sun* (one of several powerful metropolitan papers that no longer depended on a political party for financial support) accused Congressman Oakes Ames of bribing his colleagues in Congress by selling them shares in the Crédit Mobilier. Himself a member of the Pacific Railroad Committee, Ames had assigned a contract to the company to help build the line. By selling company shares to fellow members of Congress, the *Sun* alleged, he had bribed them in order to secure favors for the Union Pacific. Faced with an incensed public, Congress set out to investigate the charges. The committee tasked with investigating Ames and his incriminated colleagues concluded that while the former was indeed guilty of offering bribes, the latter, with one exception, were not guilty of accepting them, even though the fact that shares had been sold was disputed by no one. The committee recommended that Ames and one congressman be expelled from Congress, but the required two-thirds majority could not be mustered. Instead, they were censured.[121]

Not surprisingly, the panic that followed just a few months later was widely considered by many commentators to be an inevitable consequence of widespread corruption. In November 1873, one writer claimed that the panic "is not understood when it is traced to its immediate causes." The real, long-term cause, he argued, was a pervasive distrust that had been building up for many years: "The distrust we feel to be in the air has been caused by fraud, by corruption, by the most shameless breaches of trust, and by open dishonesty." Railroad directors, trust companies, and members of Congress had all behaved fraudulently, and "never before have the intimate relations between Wall Street and the Treasury been made so manifest." The *International Review*, too, stressed that the panic's remote causes were to be found in the "spirit of speculation" brought on by the Civil War and by plundering contractors and corrupt politicians. The fundamental disease afflicting the nation was its moral fabric, and its most conspicuous symptoms were to be found in New York City, "our great commercial centre . . . where is found . . . concentrated and intensified, all that is best and worst in American life." Here, the ordinary merchant, confronted with the omnipresent display of luxury and extravagance, was continuously exposed to the temptations of Wall Street, and from there, the "contagion of [his] bad example affects every boy in the store, and every man on the street, and spreads through all departments of trade, and all ramifications of society." In this account, corruption was not merely a political phenomenon, or even one pertaining solely to the relationship between businessmen and elected officials, but affected the very essence of business itself, and by extension, of society at large. No business institution, however, was more corrupt than Wall Street.[122]

Other commentators challenged the notion of widespread business immorality. One noted that the panic, far from epitomizing or revealing a pervasive distrust, was in fact an exception, and not in any way a consequence of a peculiarly American way of doing business: "Nowadays . . . we transact business by faith rather than by sight. The idea is notably progressive. Subject to abuses and betrayals and in danger from the vulture Panic, its operation is in the main successful, and it reflects honor on our business communities." According to this argument the sheer number of business transactions taking place every day belied the idea that distrust was pervasive. In a paper and credit economy, mutual trust was, after all, a necessity, the lubricant that held everything together. The panic was therefore nothing more than the deliberate creation of a small clique on Wall Street, and would not be of any consequence to the large majority of businessmen.[123] But such spirited defenses of business morals were relatively rare. Too entrenched, it seems, was the notion that modern business and immorality went hand in hand and that the mercantile virtues of yore no longer had a place in the modern world where fortunes were acquired not through long, arduous work but through quickly executed speculative schemes.[124] Following the panic, commentators had, at first, been eager to stress that American commercial relations remained sound, but this had more to do with a desire to gainsay the rapidly multiplying evidence that trade and industry were entering a phase of contraction than with a conscious effort at defending the reputation of the American business community.[125] "The panic of 1873 suddenly sobered people," one observer noted more than two years later. "We view with a sort of melancholy satisfaction the process of liquidation, as it is called, which is going on in the commercial world. . . . There has been a complete breakdown of the conventional barriers which formerly restricted men in their modes of making money."[126]

Of course, when it came to corruption, newspapers were not blameless. Railroad promoters extended their favors not only to political office holders but also to journalists who acted as agents and lobbyists in return for money and free passes and promoted companies in their papers on whose advertisements they relied for revenue.[127] Yet this intimate nexus between journalists and railroad corporations received comparatively little attention in the aftermath of the panic. The *New York Sun* noted in October 1873 that those deceived by Jay Cooke were "the intelligent classes, who read newspapers, mingle in affairs, and have constant access to information," but such scattered observations did not prompt a systematic reflection on journalists' role in fostering the speculative bubble.[128]

Comparison and Conclusion

The "moral and social dislocation" wrought by the coming of capitalism was, as Fritz Stern once remarked, a "common experience in the world," but it was also one that assumed national peculiarities.[129] The experience of dislocation was felt acutely in the aftermath of the panic, and many believed that their misfortunes could not be explained in terms of anonymous market forces. Rather, they required an interpretation in terms of individual moral responsibility. This quest for individual culpability promised to render transparent and intelligible the experience of the destructive potential of financial markets.

The moral economies produced by the crisis were diverse and relied on different cultures and trajectories. In all three countries, notions of corruption informed responses and reactions to the panic. At the same time, there were significant differences. Thus the fact that many of those accused of corruption in Austria and Germany were members of the nobility may well have intensified the sense of injustice among the panic's middle-class victims, underlining the fact that even in a period of rapid economic transformation, old status privileges remained very much intact. The main difference, however, was surely the racialization that became a distinguishing feature of German debates on corruption during the second half of the 1870s. During this period, Gerson von Bleichröder in particular, and Jews in general, were claimed to be the major corrupting force in German political and economic life to which Bismarck and his ministers had succumbed. Meyer and other writers identified the corruption of political and economic life as one grand scheme devised by Jews and for Jews. While German perceptions of the issue focused closely on Bismarck and his relationship to Bleichröder, it was nevertheless depicted as something all-encompassing, a defining feature of political and economic life. The Bismarck-Bleichröder nexus embodied something larger, though what that was exactly was not spelled out in much detail.[130] One could argue that at this point the narrative had come full circle. What had begun as an attempt to translate the experience of financial markets as an anonymous, overwhelming force into terms of individual actions and personal responsibility evolved into a conspiracy theory that was itself expansive, even potentially transnational in nature. According to this narrative, financial markets were engineered by the actions of a collective entity vis-à-vis which outsiders were, once again, powerless. In this sense, then, the narrative responded to the desire of translating economic forces into human actions while at the same time accounting for the experience of the panic as something large and overwhelming. At the same time, and somewhat paradoxically perhaps, the fact that the crisis itself had been a transnational phenomenon did not figure prominently in these accounts of a Jewish conspiracy.

In Austria, too, many considered the panic a product of corruption, a corruption that was thought to be centered in the Liberal Party. The liberal economic and political order, consequently, came under attack. But while anti-Semitic racialization played a role in this discourse, it was not as pronounced as in Germany. The anonymous exposés of corruption did not single out individual Jews, or Jews as a collective, as responsible for Austria's decay. Since it has been observed that the history of anti-Semitism in Germany and Austria followed a very similar trajectory, this difference seems remarkable.[131] The main reason for this difference, it is plausible to assume, was the fact that economic anti-Semitism had been a mainstay of Prussian social conservative ideology since the late 1850s, something for which there was no Austrian equivalent.[132] In Austria, then, it was the Liberal Party that was seen to embody corruption, and the party's partly Jewish character was merely one of several attributes that was seen to define it.

In the United States, anti-Jewish stereotypes of the European tradition were by no means unknown, and Jewish Americans were frequently met with suspicion by the Christian majority; Jewish peddlers and traders were regularly depicted as dishonest and fraudulent. Following the Civil War, the critique of banks and banking leveled by agrarians was, in some instances, of an anti-Semitic nature. These instances, however, remained exceptions.[133] The postwar debate on corruption was thus not racialized the way the German debate was. Corruption was considered to be endemic, something affecting state legislatures as well as judiciaries, the federal government, and both chambers of Congress. But the alleged pervasiveness was of a different quality. It was, fundamentally, nothing more than the sum of many individual acts of bribery. There was no mastermind, Jewish or otherwise, behind them. Those decrying corruption, moreover—journalists and, more importantly, liberal reformers—also proposed specific remedies, such as civil service reform, a return to specie payments, and financial disclosure requirements.[134] It is true that during the 1870s, the independent American metropolitan press launched accusations of corruption almost as a matter of course, occasionally even without factual evidence. But at the same time, the fact that some of these proposals were enacted into law (to varying degrees of success) suggests that the discourse on corruption, shrill as it sometimes appeared, pointed to some very real deficiencies, as historians have readily acknowledged. For this there was no German equivalent. The accusations leveled by the German "antiliberal muckrakers," lacking "dignity and decorum," had a phantasmatic quality to them that went beyond mere hyperbole. Not surprisingly, they did not come with specific policy proposals.[135] In the United States, then, criticism of corruption brought reform; in Germany (and, later, in Austria), the combination of anticapitalism, anti-Semitism, and antiliberalism gave rise, from the late 1870s onward, to an anti-Semitic movement that, even after it ceased to be successful on the electoral level, profoundly shaped politics and society in both countries.[136]

I cannot attempt, here, to answer the question *why* the German critique of liberal capitalism assumed a racialized, conspiratorial quality in a way the American discourse did not, since this would surely require a book of its own. As a way of concluding, it may, however, be relevant to recall an argument made in the first chapter in order to show how these diverging paths were *consistent* with discursive patterns that preceded the panic: German stock market reports differed from American ones in that the former were cast in an impersonal, anonymous language while the latter were highly personalized and often revolved around well-known, easily identifiable public figures. These figures, moreover, were not only speculators but also railroad entrepreneurs. Because of this connection, Wall Street seemed connected to the "real," productive economy in a way that was not evident from the market reports on German stock exchanges. And while one could argue that it was precisely the fact that Wall Street appeared to be under the control of a few well-known cliques that might have encouraged an interpretation of the panic as a conspiracy, it is important to bear in mind that conspiracy theories thrived not on what was well-known, out in the open, but on what was alleged to go on secretly, in the background. In this respect, the anonymizing language of German stock market reports was entirely consistent with a conspiracy theory while the American language was not.[137] At the same time, the connection evident in American reports between financial speculation and the "real" economy could not easily have been reconciled with anti-Semitic tropes of Jewish financiers as work-shy and unproductive while German reports contained no such obvious stumbling blocks. This comparative angle suggests that the genealogy of anti-Semitism in German-speaking countries, as it emerged in the 1870s, should include not just the writings of professed anti-Jewish ideologues but must also take into account a wider financial discourse that made such anti-Semitic conspiracy theories seem superficially plausible. Seen this way, the proliferation of these anti-Jewish tropes appears not just as the product of an already existing reservoir of ideas but also of certain broader structures of financial discourse.

CHAPTER 6

CRIMINALIZING PROMOTERS, PROTECTING SHAREHOLDERS

I f corruption crusaders are to be believed, the speculative bubble and ensuing crisis revealed a fundamental rottenness in society. In stark contrast to such wholesale indictments, many policy-makers and legal experts in Germany and Austria believed that the inflation of values had been the result of inadequate legal provisions, and during the 1870s and 1880s engaged in a drawn-out debate about possible remedies. These debates, which will be examined in this chapter, hinged on the belief that the state, by virtue of its legislating power, had the means to rein in financial markets for the benefit of its citizens. Financial markets were thus seen as an institution that, despite its expansive nature, was responsive to national laws and institutional frameworks. The German debate on the responsibility of shareholders and promoters did, eventually, lead to policy responses that transformed the character of corporation law and investment practices. American corporation law, by contrast, did not see similarly momentous changes.

In Germany, several promoters were put on trial during the 1870s. These trials, it will be argued in the first part, revealed that there was little agreement among judges and legal experts regarding the legality of some of the practices that had become widespread among promoters during the early 1870s. Partly in response to this legal uncertainty, but also to prevent a recurrence of speculative excess, German policy-makers agreed that a wholesale reform of German corporation law was needed, and far-reaching changes were finally enacted in 1884. Although the corporation laws of other countries were frequently mentioned in this debate, the 1884 law, unlike its predecessors, showed few traces of foreign influences, American law being especially conspicuous in its absence. The final part of this chapter examines American developments in corporation law to explore why, during the 1870s and 1880s, there was no similar reform movement. The focus will be on Germany and the United States, mainly because developments in Austria were, in many respects, similar to those in Germany so that a detailed three-country comparison would suffer from repetitiveness. I will, however, touch on Austrian developments where they help shed light on certain aspects of my argument.

Promoters in the Court of Law

In Prussia, 857 new corporations were founded after the enactment of the new corporation law in mid-1870. Just four and a half years later, by the end of 1874, 123 had gone into liquidation and another 37 were in receivership.[1] To many observers, these numbers suggested that a significant number of the new corporations had been little more than "bubble companies" (*Schwindelunternehmungen*), that is, companies whose sole purpose had been to line promoters' pockets and which at no point had possessed anything resembling a viable long-term business plan. Promoters had used them for their own gain by paying up only a small amount of the company's nominal capital and then immediately selling the shares at a premium to investors, thus allowing them to turn a considerable profit. In many cases, promoters had deliberately overvalued a company's tangible assets, and, on the basis of this artificial valuation, issued large amounts of watered stock.[2] Not surprisingly, the German bear market dragged on for many years, only recovering at the end of the decade.[3]

From a legal point of view, however, it was not entirely clear whether the promoters of such short-lived corporations had actually committed a criminal offense. The law, it seemed, provided no clear guidance as to where to draw the line between legal (if ethically dubious) business practices and outright fraud. Replying to an inquiry by Kaiser Wilhelm, who worried that prosecutors were displaying an excessive zeal in going after promoters, the minister of justice noted that between 1872 and late 1876, prosecutors at Berlin's municipal court (*Stadtgericht*) had launched a total of ninety-eight investigations against promoters of which fifty-eight had been completed. Of those completed, forty-nine proceedings had been closed, while nine had resulted in formal charges, which in turn had resulted in eight convictions and one acquittal. In most cases, defendants were charged with fraud as well as with violating Article 249, nos. 1 and 3, of the Corporation Act of 1870, according to which it was a punishable offense for members of the supervisory board (*Aufsichtsrat*) and board of directors to make knowingly false statements regarding the amount of subscribed or paid-up capital, or to deliberately misrepresent the financial condition of their company.[4]

To the minister, these numbers suggested that prosecutors had shown neither too much nor too little zeal in pursuing promoters. The fact that so few promoters had been formally charged, he noted, was not evidence of undue leniency on the part of the prosecuting authorities but simply proved that "*criminal* manipulations even in dubious companies had been the exception." While some believed that the "promoter trials" amounted to a blanket criminalization of what were merely standard business practices, prosecutors were, he maintained, quite capable of identifying outright fraud, and the government would be well advised not to interfere with ongoing investigations.[5]

The jurisdiction of German criminal courts in cases of "promoter fraud" during the 1870s suggests that the matter was not as unambiguous as the minister believed. First, in these cases, most promoters were charged with deceiving shareholders by awarding themselves undisclosed promoters' fees, thus misrepresenting the value of a company's assets. But if the mere existence of undisclosed promoter fees—a practice that was widely believed to have been very common during the early 1870s—constituted sufficient grounds for an indictment, this suggests that prosecutors were inconsistent in their approach and dropped several investigations in cases that may well have resulted in convictions. Second, the question of what exactly constituted a "criminal manipulation" in this matter was a contested one, and not all courts applied the same standards. Where promoters were charged with fraud, prosecutors argued that they had deliberately misled shareholders in order to enrich themselves. The fraud, it was alleged, occurred when promoters bought assets (factories, real estate, machinery, etc.), established a corporation, and then, as directors of that same corporation, exchanged a certain amount of stock for these assets, which, prosecutors charged, did not reflect their true value. While the question of how to accurately value capital assets was, of course, open to debate, promoters were said to have defrauded shareholders by misrepresenting the price they had paid for the assets. The company's prospectus would state the price that had been paid without noting that a significant share of the money (in some cases up to a third) had not been paid to the seller but had ended up in the promoters' pockets.

While it was not per se illegal or illegitimate for promoters to charge a fee for their services, prosecutors argued, to claim that a certain price had been paid to a seller when the actual price had been lower amounted to a deliberate misrepresentation. Since shareholders had based their assessment of a company's value and profitability on the price mentioned in the prospectus, the losses they incurred when the company's share price plummeted was a consequence of this initial misrepresentation. Promoters who engaged in this practice therefore gained a pecuniary advantage and were guilty of fraud.

To make their case, prosecutors had to prove several things: that promoters had engaged in deliberate misrepresentation, that they had done so in order to line their pockets, and that the misrepresentation had induced their victims to engage in actions that resulted in financial losses to them. Regarding the "promoter profit," most courts agreed that official statements to the effect that assets had been purchased at a certain price were knowingly false if the seller had received less than the stated price. In most cases, such transactions had not been made directly between the seller and the corporation but had comprised two distinct transactions: the first one between the seller and the promoters or a middleman, and the second one between the middleman, or the promoters as private individuals, and the corporation, which, of course, was itself represented by the promoters who had founded it and appointed themselves directors.[6] In one case, a judge acquitted the defendants on the grounds that the corporation and the promoters were, legally speaking, two distinct entities, and since the promoters had indeed been paid the full price for the property, the prospectus was accurate, regardless of whether the initial owner had actually received a lower sum.[7] Most courts, by contrast, did not accept this line of reasoning, and one judge even explicitly argued that the two-part maneuver had been unnecessary from a practical point of view and had therefore been designed to obscure the true nature of the purchase, thus proving the defendants' criminal intent to deceive.[8]

To show that promoters had actively misled shareholders into buying shares, prosecutors presented witnesses who told the court that, had they been aware of the size of the "promoter profit," this would have negatively affected their assessment of the company's value and would have discouraged them from subscribing to its shares. In one case, a judge noted that it was impossible to prove directly that shareholders had been motivated to subscribe exclusively by the prospectus since these were "inner operations" (*innerliche Vorgänge*). But, he further argued, it was plausible to assume that the information in the prospectus had been at least a partial factor, all the more so since the shares had been issued at a premium of 5 percent, and it was reasonable for shareholders to believe that this premium was calculated to defray the costs of the incorporation, including any fees to promoters.[9]

Generally, the conviction rate in promoter trials appears to have been high: defendants were found guilty in eight of the nine cases cited by the minister, and four other cases cited in an 1876 set of cases also, ultimately, resulted in convictions, in some cases overturning acquittals by lower courts. Still, courts failed to establish uniform standards regarding the criminality of "promoter fraud." Thus two trials in Brunswick ended with acquittals that were later upheld by appellate courts.[10] Structurally, they were similar to other trials, but the presiding judge, embracing a line of argument other judges had explicitly rejected, ruled that the defendants had not engaged in fraud by omitting to state the size of their "promoter profit" in the company's prospectus.[11] A salient feature of the Brunswick trial was that the prosecutor presented witnesses whose modest background (as artisans and salaried employees) could be seen as representing the very worst speculative excesses of the past years, when dabbling in securities had ceased being the preserve of the wealthy. In denying they had been victims of fraud, the judge's verdict may well have expressed a belief that where class differences were in danger of eroding, as they had been in the early 1870s, the lower middle classes responsible for such disorder would and should bear the consequences, and must not look to the legal system when seeking redress.

Civil courts, too, adopted different standards. In a case that was brought first before the municipal and then the appellate court in Berlin, the plaintiff argued that he had been sold shares under false pretenses since he had not been made aware of the promoter profit, and he asked the court that the promoters take back the shares they had sold him and reimburse him. The lower court ruled against the plaintiff, noting, first, that he had not shown that his purchase had been motivated by the information in the prospectus, and second, that he had erroneously equated the purported price of the company's main asset, a factory, with its value, an error that, the judges ruled, had not been caused by the prospectus but by the plaintiff's mistaken identification of the terms "price" and "value."[12] The appellate court then overturned this ruling, noting that the basic issues of the case had already been adjudicated in a criminal court. The plaintiff, the court observed, had never said he had been deceived as to the factory's "absolute" value. Rather, he had been deceived about its "relative" value—that is, the value it had been assigned when sold to the company.[13] Finally, the supreme commercial court of the Reich (Reichsoberhandelsgericht [ROG]) sided with the lower court, ruling in June 1877 that keeping the promoter profit secret was permissible as long as the public assumed its existence or the possibility of its existence. It had not been proven, the court argued, that the promoters had kept their profit a secret in order to mislead potential shareholders, nor had the plaintiff shown that his erroneous assumption regarding the price had motivated his decision to purchase shares.[14]

Ultimately, these contradictory judgments showed that judges found it hard to agree on a standard of economic rationality. For some, a rational investor might conceivably buy shares in a company whose directors had awarded themselves a generous fee. Other judges found this notion implausible. In his memorandum to Kaiser Wilhelm, the minister of justice had expressed concern that where civil liability was concerned, courts seemed to be ruling against promoters, and that more decisions of a similar nature would be handed down in future, causing further disquiet in commercial circles.[15] The ROG's 1877 verdict shows that he need not have worried. Rejecting the reasoning of criminal courts, it argued, in essence, that all the talk of fraud and criminality was misplaced, that no one had been duped, and that shareholders had only themselves to blame. A single ruling could not, of course, sway public opinion and dispel the widespread impression that shareholders had been the victims of criminal operations by greedy entrepreneurs. What the deliberations in criminal and civil courts did show, however, was that there was no real consensus regarding issues of shareholder protection and promoter liability, and that, to avoid similar confusion and ambiguity in future, corporation law would have to be reformed. Such a reform, lawmakers and legal experts agreed, would have to ensure that the business practices that had attracted so much ire would henceforth be prohibited. In future, the law would better protect shareholders from being swindled and discourage the formation of bubble companies.

Reforming Corporation Law

The most recent overhaul of the corporation law had been passed in June 1870 and had constituted a significant departure from past practices: With the exception of railroads and credit banks, promoters now no longer required a license (*Konzession*) to establish a corporation. In keeping with the liberal zeitgeist, the reform had been premised on the idea that shareholders would no longer rely on the state in assessing a corporation's quality and profitability but would, instead, exercise their own judgment. This idea provided a practical solution to the backlog of applications that had been threatening to overwhelm the Prussian authorities.[16] Lawmakers had been well aware that the reform was not without risk and the transition to the new system might lead to a period of instability. They reasoned that "the influence of the money market, of political cycles, of the prospering or failure of individual large corporations . . . on the flourishing of a possible share fraud [*Aktienschwindel*] is decidedly more significant."[17]

The fears did not take long to materialize. As early as 1871, the *Deutsche Handelsblatt*, organ of the Deutsche Handelstag, published several critical assessments of the new law and of the numerous new corporations that had been created since its passage. Although the authors cautioned against hasty changes to the reform, they nevertheless triggered a debate that was to continue well into the next decade.[18] As discussed in the previous chapter, many commentators came to believe that the law had failed to protect guileless small-time shareholders from rapacious promoters, and while such black-and-white representations were certainly somewhat simplistic,[19] the underlying diagnosis of an informational asymmetry between promoters and investors was accurate.

Following Eduard Lasker's speeches in early 1873, the government began taking firsts steps towards a possible overhaul and wrote to representatives of the German chambers of commerce to solicit their opinion. In October 1873, the

Verein für Socialpolitik, a recently established association of academics devoted to developing and proposing reforms to correct what they perceived to be excesses of "Manchester liberalism," debated the flaws of the present system and possible remedies at its annual conference. While there was no consensus on what exactly a reform ought to achieve, it was widely agreed that the system in its current form had proven inadequate.[20] In this, the Verein was not alone: in the following years, both lawyers and economists published numerous studies on corporation law reform. It was not until 1884, however, that their efforts finally bore fruit, and a reform was passed. Unlike its predecessor, it was the result of a detailed, drawn-out public debate.[21]

Both legislators and scholars of corporation law agreed that reformers should look to the corporation laws of other European countries when designing the new system. Thus Felix Hecht argued that "in accordance with recent trends of German academic research, the new corporation law will have to comprehensively consult the modern European corporation legislation for purposes of comparison."[22] The idea was not a new one: the reform of 1870 had looked to the relevant French laws of 1856 and 1867 for inspiration. Since it seemed that the French model had not been able to adequately protect shareholders, many commentators now came to believe that Germany would do well to heed the principles of the English system.[23]

Given that many commentators believed that the reformed law of 1870 had played a significant role in creating the speculative bubble, it made sense to adopt a comparative approach. Germany, along with other countries, had experienced a financial crisis, while others had not seen a bubble of similar proportions. A comparative approach thus promised something resembling an experimental set-up that would allow commentators and policy-makers to disentangle causation and correlation. As early as 1871, the *Deutsche Handelsblatt* had suggested as much when it compared German and English regulations and concluded that while the English law was not as skittishly prescriptive as its German counterpart, both countries had nevertheless seen similar excesses of corporation-related fraud.[24] In other articles, too, the *Handelsblatt*'s authors argued that the proliferation of corporations was part of a worldwide economic boom, and that for the time being at least it would be wrong to believe that changes to national legislation would be able to check this movement.[25]

Following the crash, comparative arguments were made in order to distinguish between essential and incidental factors in the emergence of a bubble. Thus many commentators noted that the Austrian case proved that bubble companies could flourish even where promoters still required a government license. Returning to the system of special charters would therefore not solve the problem. (Austria had never made the transition to the general charter system.) France and England, however, remained the main points of reference for most commentators. Even though both countries had not seen a crisis of overspeculation in corporations in the early 1870s, many still considered their past experiences of crises relevant to the German debate. When it came to reforming corporation law, it seemed, concomitance mattered less than structural similarities, be they in the past or in the present.

Somewhat surprisingly, the American system played almost no role in this debate. In his report for the Verein für Socialpolitik, Heinrich Wiener alluded to the District of Columbia's 1870 law and noted that under this law, as in England, a corporation only became a legal entity when a minimum of seven promoters signed a certificate and registered it. Unlike in Germany, only railroads required a minimum amount of subscribed and paid-up capital.[26] Most commentators, however, ignored this and other American laws. As the legal historian Jan von Hein has noted, the extensive comparative part of the 1884 bill not only included detailed accounts of the corporation laws of several European countries but also contained a discussion of Venezuelan law. The laws of the American states, by contrast, did not merit even a brief mention.[27]

The fact that most commentators passed over the American laws and instead focused on France and England seems all the more remarkable in view of the close succession of the German and American financial crises in 1873, which might have prompted Germans to familiarize themselves with the American system of incorporation. Why, then, did this not happen? One possible explanation is that the heterogeneity of American laws on this subject jarred with the "ideal of national codification dominating German legal thought following the achievement of German unification towards the end of the nineteenth century."[28] But while this explanation seems plausible, it is not quite consistent with the fact that the laws of individual Swiss cantons did feature in the 1884 bill. Another possible explanation is a pragmatic one: German scholars may simply have not had access to the statutes of the American states.[29]

Whatever the reason, the history of the German corporation law of 1884 suggests a debate that had long closed itself off from the American experience so thoroughly that even the nearly simultaneous panics of 1873 left no trace. It is less than clear whether a detailed examination of American laws by legislators and jurists would have produced a different result. For all the detailed knowledge of European legislations on display both in scholarly debates and the final bill, the practical significance of specific clauses and regulations remained largely unexplored. While some authors, as noted previously, briefly alluded to speculative bubbles in other countries, this line of argument remained superficial. The question, for example, of whether the seemingly superior English legislation had produced a more stable growth of corporations was never subjected to a solid empirical examination. Compared to earlier revisions of corporation law, the authors of the 1884 bill were mostly concerned with refining and improving the already established principles of German corporation law and responding to recent German experiences.[30]

The overriding goal of the 1884 revision was to better protect shareholders from losses without imposing undue burdens on corporations and thus hampering economic growth.[31] The approach was twofold. Legislators prescribed a minimum share value of 1,000 marks in order to prevent small capitalists from investing in companies without giving the matter sufficient thought. In contrast to this paternalistic approach, legislators also aimed to improve corporate self-governance by providing large shareholders with greater rights and better informational resources to encourage them to take an active role in the company's affairs. The process of incorporation would henceforth require detailed, publicly accessible documentation, including the promoters' names and any fees and privileges they had received. Promoters were also required to draw up a detailed contract of association before inviting subscriptions from external investors.[32] These provisions, legislators believed, would henceforth prevent promoters from illicitly lining their pockets.

The law also strengthened the power of shareholder assemblies and allotted one vote per share, thus ending the previous practice of excluding small shareholders from voting.[33] To discourage the practice of stock watering, a company's capital could only be increased when the full nominal value of its initial capitalization had been paid in. The new law also recalibrated the role of the supervisory board (Aufsichtsrat) and specified its duties, not only expressly prohibiting dual membership in the supervisory board and the board of directors but also allowing the company to sue the former for damages when it failed to fulfill its functions.[34] Another important new provision was that shareholders would henceforth be liable for the full nominal value of their shares. Previously, shareholders had been permitted to pay only 40 percent of a share's value and then apply for a "liberation" (Liberierung) of the remaining 60 percent so that their liabilities to the corporation and its creditors were significantly lower than their nominal share in the company. This practice, as the Reichsoberhandelsgericht had noted in its report on corporation law reform, constituted an "anomaly" and had encouraged investors to carelessly subscribe to shares of newly incorporated companies and use them to engage in the "most ruinous stockjobbery."[35] Abolishing this practice, legislators believed, would encourage long-term investments and, ultimately, economic stability.

For the drafters of the 1884 bill, these stipulations followed from the experience of the bubble years.[36] In many respects, the 1884 bill was more independent of European models than its predecessors. One legal historian has even argued that its "clear national character" constitutes a caesura, marking the beginning of a "'diversification' of European corporation law."[37] In response to this argument, others have stressed that foreign law was not ignored but closely examined, as evidenced by the Materialien part of the bill. "In corporation law, more than in any other legal or economic field," the authors of the bill noted, "national legislation is closely linked with foreign legislation."[38] Most legal historians nevertheless agree that the 1884 reform was achieved through a process of adjusting the already existing German corporation law, and that foreign models were no longer decisive. This, according to von Hein, was also the result of a heightened awareness on the legislators' part that one could not simply pry laws from a context that had evolved over a long period of time in order to graft them onto a new and different system. The authors of the report by the Reichsoberhandelsgericht had stated this quite explicitly when, in discussing the relevance of foreign corporation laws for the German debate, they cautioned that "foreign legal provisions" were not "panaceas" against the abuses Germany had seen, and that serious reform proposals ought not to focus on individual provisions but, instead, had to propose an "entirety of provisions emerging from one unified system."[39] With the 1884 reform, then, legislators acknowledged that path dependency precluded the straightforward adoption of foreign practices.

But this interpretation, while not implausible, obscures a process of legislative transfer that was crucial to the 1884 reform and, to some extent, negates the prevailing view of the nationalization of German corporation law. For several clauses of the German 1884 bill were taken from two similar Austrian bills that had been debated in 1868, 1874, and 1881. While never passed into law, they had clearly been studied by German legislators.[40] As in Germany, the number of new corporations had risen sharply in Austria during the late 1860s and early 1870s.[41] As early as 1869, the Austrian parliament had debated a bill to reform the country's corporation law. Its goal was to do away with the state licensing of corporations, and to impose stricter regulations regarding incorporation, as well as improving shareholder protection. Several of the regulations that were proposed in this debate (pertaining to greater transparency of incorporation, control of promoters through the supervisory board and board of directors, shareholder meetings, and the rights of minority shareholders) were later adopted by German legislators. (Other Austrian stipulations, by contrast—such as the liability of promoters for the contents of the prospectus and the election of a representative of minority shareholders—did not make it into the German bill.) Two factors facilitated this legislative transfer: First, the abuses of corporation law that characterized the early 1870s in Austria and Germany were similar. Second, Austria had adopted the provisions of the General German Commercial Code (*Allgemeines Deutsches Handelsgesetzbuch*) of 1861 in 1863, and the problem of path dependency was hence less acute.[42]

But while the efforts of German policy-makers, finally and albeit somewhat belatedly, bore fruit, the various Austrian reform efforts remained inconclusive.[43] As early as March 1872, the Austrian government had issued a decree stipulating that certain types of corporations could only issue new shares when the old shares were fully paid up. Because the authorities failed to enforce this decree, however, the speculative fever was not dampened.[44] Following the crash, reformers stepped up their efforts but encountered stubborn resistance from those who worried that a reform might hamper future incorporations. In 1874, a bill was passed in the Abgeordnetenhaus but was scuttled when it reached the Herrenhaus. In 1882, another reform bill was introduced in the Abgeordnetenhaus but was not voted on.[45]

Although these efforts, ultimately, proved futile, legislators successfully passed a stock exchange reform bill in 1875. Its provisions amounted to a wholesale reform of the institution: the Vienna bourse now became a largely autonomous and self-administered body that wrote its own statutes with minimum supervision by the state-appointed stock exchange commissioner. For the first time, stock exchange transactions were made enforceable, thus improving the status of creditors. While the law did not realize all its goals (illegal trading sites, for example, were nominally banned but nevertheless continued to exist), it did bring a marked improvement in the regulation of securities trading.[46]

In Berlin, the stock exchange also saw reforms in response to the abuses of the *Gründerjahre*. These were devised and implemented by its directorate who—once it had become clear that the government would not make promoters liable for the content of prospectuses—in 1881 decided to tighten regulations regarding the listing of shares. Promoters were now required to submit a prospectus containing information about the company's business and finances. Only when the bourse's experts had concluded that the information met its requirements would the company's shares be allowed to trade on the exchange. In 1885, the Berlin regulations were adopted by the Frankfurt bourse.[47]

In the history of German corporation law, then, the 1870s constituted a watershed. In the United States, the panic of 1873 did not engender similar responses. Promoters were not indicted for fraud, and states did not pass sweeping overhauls of their corporation laws. Most American states had, by the early 1870s, done away with the system of special charters (in which each corporation was chartered individually by the state legislature) and passed general incorporation acts, thus allowing promoters to incorporate a company by meeting a certain set of requirements. In the United States, too, the number of incorporations had increased during the late 1860s and early 1870s, albeit not as sharply as in Germany and Austria.[48] Following the crash, prices on the NYSE plummeted, prompting the *New York Times* to observe that "professional persons, women, mechanics, clerks, and others of every class find now that the savings of a life have gone up."[49] But while many commentators agreed that overspeculation in railroads had been a major cause of the crisis,[50] and around two hundred railroads went into receivership during the 1870s, the public did not charge promoters with creating "bubble companies." This was not surprising. Investment in railroads during this period had, to a large extent, taken the form of bonds secured by liens. Here, the charge of "stock watering" (the common American term for issuing stocks in excess of a company's capital, as

German promoters had done when misrepresenting the price they had paid for assets sold to their corporation) did not apply.

Why did bubble companies proliferate in Germany and Austria but not in the United States? Were American corporation laws in this respect more sophisticated, better designed to discourage promoters from establishing corporations for short-term speculative purposes? In two important respects, this seems to have been the case. First, according to the prevalent "trust fund" doctrine and the influential New York general incorporation acts of the 1840s and 1850s, shareholders were doubly liable for the company's debts if the amount of capital actually paid up was lower than the nominal value of their shares. Where this was the case (where, in other words, the stock was "watered"), the principle of limited liability did not apply.[51] This principle stood in marked contrast to the German practice of *Liberierung*, which was abolished with the 1884 reform.

Second, if this principle of liability in the United States discouraged shareholders from buying stock cheaply for speculative short-term purposes, other provisions applied a similar principle of liability to directors and promoters. Generally, the common law doctrine of fraud—according to which sellers of property were prohibited from misrepresenting its value to buyers—applied to the sale of securities, whether or not the statutes of corporation law explicitly stated as much.[52] According to American legal opinion, promoters who created "bubble companies" by publishing "false statements" to misrepresent the value of the company's stock were "liable directly in damages in an action for deceit brought by any innocent party who, on the faith of the public representations and of the statements of the certificate, has purchased from third parties, and paid for, shares of the stock."[53] State legislatures, moreover, sought to discourage fraud by promoters and directors by means of statutory provisions. Thus the New York statutes stipulated that a railroad corporation's articles of association could only be "filed and recorded in the office of the secretary of state, until at least one thousand dollars of stock for every mile of railroad proposed to be made is subscribed thereto, and ten per cent paid thereon in good faith, and in cash." Three directors were required to confirm this in the form of an affidavit to be included with the articles of association, a provision aimed at enforcing transparency and accountability on the part of directors.[54] Similar provisions existed in other states.[55]

The New York statutes of 1848 also stipulated that for certain corporations (manufacturing, mining, mechanical, and chemical) only cash could be used to pay for the capital stock. This, the reasoning went, would prevent promoters from issuing stock in excess of the company's assets. Because this law proved too restrictive, however, it was amended in 1853 to allow the exchange of certain types of property for stock.[56] This raised the problem of how to accurately assess the value of the property in question. Addressing this question, one legal writer, in 1879, noted that "if the promoters of a corporation of this character shall, with a view to defraud, fill up the capital stock by putting in property at grossly exorbitant values, they are not to be exempted from the personal liability imposed by the statute." But, he continued, this should not apply where promoters made an "honest error of judgment" since "upon the question of the value of property, and more especially that adapted to mining, mechanical, and manufacturing purposes, a very wide difference of opinion may honestly exist among the most intelligent men familiar with such operations."[57] Given this predicament, the legislature of Massachusetts, a state with a large number of corporations, decreed that stock could be issued for property but aimed to curtail abuses of this practice by stipulating that officers and a majority of directors "make a sworn statement that described and valued the property and [that] the Commissioner of Corporations had to certify that, in his opinion, the valuation was reasonable." In New Jersey, too, a demonstrably wrong valuation would make directors liable for damages to injured shareholders.[58]

German promoters had argued that their "promoter profit" was justified as a fee for their services in incorporating a company and assuming financial risk in the process. In the United States, when this and similar issues came before courts, they tended to rule against promoters, holding that the "executive committee of a corporation" had "no right to vote money to themselves, in addition to their regular compensation, for their services as promoters and origina-tors of the company . . . the granting of large sums for such purposes, affords good reason for the appointment of a receiver."[59] Regarding the issue that had triggered the German promoter trials of the 1870s, American courts ruled that the position of promoters was one of "trust and confidence." Therefore, they could not, when buying property to form a company, profit from such sales.[60]

But while statutes and rulings allowed the authors of legal treatises to distill them into a body of law that appeared to discourage the formation of bubble companies and protect shareholders from deceitful practices by promoters and directors, it is difficult to assess how effective they were in practice. Many of the cases adjudicated came before the courts as a result of bankruptcy proceed-ings, and shareholders' capital would often have already been pilfered by pro-moters and directors. A ruling in favor of their interests would not necessarily have helped them recover their assets.[61] While the actual effectiveness of stat-utes and precedents governing "promoter fraud" is thus difficult to determine, it is nevertheless clear that the issue did not attract much public attention in the aftermath of the panic, especially not when compared to later periods.[62] During 1890s, by contrast, watered stock and large promoter profits did become hotly debated topics, as corporations went through a process of enormous expansion by swallowing competitors and flooding financial markets with masses of shares. It was only then that many observers accused the new mega-corporations of issuing watered stock to cover the fees of promoters and bankers, and several witnesses appeared before Congress in 1898 to testify on the widespread use of this practice. (Unlike in Germany and Austria, however, promoters were usually paid in stock, not in cash.)[63] This merger movement in American business in turn relied on changes in statutes and legal opinion regarding the valuation of assets. As a result of these changes, corporations were no longer prohibited from owning the stock of another corporation, and directors were given the exclusive right to value any property their corporation bought without being liable to creditors and shareholders.[64]

In the realm of corporation law, then, the 1870s were not a period of reform. This is not to say, however, that corporation law did not continue to evolve, as it had done in previous decades. Rather, the changes that did take place were not the result of a systematic effort by lawmakers but happened in a haphazard fashion. Unlike in Germany, where reforms focused on the principle of shareholder protection, one cannot easily subsume the American developments under one clear guideline. Some key elements of this process can nevertheless be identified. Beginning in the 1860s, many American commentators came to believe that directors of corporations—especially where railroads were concerned—had amassed too much power to the detriment of shareholders. This process coincided with a change in the pattern of shareholder voting rights. In earlier decades, minority shareholders had been protected by "prudent-mean voting rights," whereby small shareholders were allotted a share of votes that was disproportionately large compared to the number of shares they owned. This principle was increasingly replaced by the one-vote-per-share rule (laid down in many state statutes from the 1850s onward) which allowed the owner(s) of the majority of shares to overrule small shareholders at meetings. Reacting to this development and to concerns about the rights of minority shareholders, many states from the 1870s onward introduced the principle of cumulative voting, permitting shareholders to distribute their total votes (the number of shares multiplied by the number of directors) to elect a single candidate to represent them on the board, thus allowing them, so the theory went, better access to information.[65]

While this development, at least in theory, strengthened the rights of (minority) shareholders, it did not address the problem of how the power of directors might be curtailed and returned to the corporation's owners. Following the crash, many observers came to believe that the railroads' troubles stemmed not least from mismanagement by dishonest and greedy directors. This belief, however, did not result in statutory reforms that would have addressed the problem. When the state of New York, in the late 1870s, established a commission to investigate railroads, one aim was to place restrictions on the power of directors. In its final report, the commission recommended an amendment to the 1850 act governing the formation and regulation of railroad corporations. To address the managerial abuse of proxy voting (where managers paid shareholders to vote on their behalf), the commission suggested ending this practice altogether and counting only votes that were personally cast by stockholders. Furthermore, it recommended that corporations should only be allowed to increase their capital stock if two-thirds of their stockholders concurred, and the state engineer and surveyor (and later, a to-be-established board of railroad commissioners) gave their approval. Officers and directors who violated this provision were to be "punished by imprisonment not less than six months and by fine not exceeding one thousand dollars."[66] The suggestion that a particular kind of corporate fraud be criminalized is perhaps where the American debate (if not practice) most closely mirrored contemporary German developments. Though the problem of excessive executive power in corporations remained unresolved, the commission's report shows that policymakers displayed an awareness of the importance of strengthening shareholder rights as a means of improving corporate governance. The 1870s and even more so the decades that followed did not, however, see a strengthening but, rather, a further erosion of shareholder rights. One of the main reasons for this development was that corporations were a state matter. Because it was in a state's fiscal interests to encourage the formation of corporations under its jurisdiction, state legislatures began to dilute their incorporation acts in order to make them more attractive for promoters and directors. In the ensuing "race to the bottom," shareholder rights almost inevitably fell by the wayside, a trend that was only partially stopped with the antitrust legislation of the 1890s.

Given that prior to the panic, the American rate of incorporation had not risen as rapidly as in Germany and Austria, and overinvestment in railroads had mainly been in bonds (see chapter 1), the relative absence of criticism leveled at promoters is, perhaps, not surprising. Still, bondholders did not fare much better than shareholders in the aftermath of the panic. During the 1870s, many roads defaulted on their interest payments and courts appointed receivers who were tasked with administering the company and its assets so as to preserve, as far as possible, creditors' interests. While the legal institution of receivership was an old one, it was first applied on a wide scale to railroads during the 1870s (all in all, 220 roads representing 30 percent of all mileage were affected), a time when state and federal statutes had little or nothing to say on the matter. It was thus left to the courts to decide what was and was not permissible. The crux of the matter was that railroad receivers, unlike those of other companies, could not simply sell off assets one by one in order to pay creditors from the proceeds. Rather, to preserve the value of a railroad, it had to be kept in operation. This practice became generally accepted during the 1870s.[67]

States did not feel compelled to enact legislation to better protect bondholders mainly because railroads served a public good and could not simply cease operating without causing significant disruption to the economy. For creditors, this meant that the capital they had invested in railroads could not be withdrawn. It is worth noting that injured creditors were disproportionately likely to be Europeans, whose means of exerting political pressure on American state governments were limited.[68] Thus, bondholders during the 1870s saw their interest payments delayed or cancelled. In some cases, mortgage bonds were replaced with less secure income bonds. In others, bondholders managed to harness their power to put pressure on directors and thus secure at least some of the interest they had been promised, such as when a group of German investors in the Oregon and California Railroad elected a representative and banded together with American bondholders to oust the railroad's president and take over the company. Such instances of successful self-organization aside, however, bondholders continued to be disempowered well into the 1880s and beyond.[69]

While widespread bankruptcies and receiverships did not force the state's hand in the legislative realm, they did lead to an increased role for financial intermediaries in the management of railroads and, indirectly, in the protection of investors, continuing and accelerating a development that had already been underway prior to the panic. Responding to investor pressures, many bankers during the 1870s joined a railroad's board, using their influence to align its day-to-day operations with the interests of stockholders and bondholders, a practice that became more and more common toward the end of the century.[70] By the early 1900s, bankers acted both as underwriters for major securities issues and, through voting trusts and in their capacity as board members, as monitors of the railroads' operations, thus serving not only their own interests but also those of stockholders and bondholders.[71] In this respect, the American development bore similarities to the German case: In Germany, too, investment banks from the 1870s onward would increasingly assume a prominent role in monitoring corporations.[72]

Finally, in one important area of the economy, the 1870s did see major legislative activity: that of railroads and railroad rates. Overinvestment in railroads in the late 1860s and early 1870s had led to the construction of so many railroads that the ensuing economic downturn produced a situation of fierce competition. Many railroad owners and managers came to believe that only federal legislation would be able to prevent a ruinous race to the bottom in which railroads competed for traffic by offering ever lower rates. The first calls for railroad regulation, however, preceded the panic. In Illinois, Iowa, Minnesota, and Wisconsin, farmers as well as merchants had, beginning in the 1860s, leveled vociferous attacks on railroads for their allegedly discriminatory business practices in which roads charged different customers different rates for what appeared to be similar services. In response to such public pressure, several state legislatures passed laws (the so-called Granger laws) that aimed to outlaw such practices.[73]

Following the panic, the movement for stricter railroad regulation shifted to New York. Initially, many New York merchants came to believe that the Granger laws had scared off railroad investors and thus helped cause the panic.[74] According to this interpretation, railroad regulation had been passed to accommodate the radical farmers' interest in low and equal transportation rates, an interpretation that ignored the fact that in many cases, western merchants, not farmers, had been the main force behind the movement to rein in railroads. This antiregulation stance, embraced by many members of the New York business community who feared for their railroad investments, began to crumble in the mid-1870s. Railroad directors, realizing that competition was driving down rates to levels that would sooner or later put their railroads out of business, formed pooling agreements, ironically not least with the aim of convincing European investment bankers of the viability of eastern railroads as investment objects. This provoked the ire of New York merchants and farmers, who then banded together to pressure legislators into reining in what they regarded as the railroads' extortionate practices. In 1882, the state legislature responded by establishing a commission that was tasked with ending rate discrimination; and in 1887, after state initiatives in New York and elsewhere had proved largely futile, Congress established the Interstate Commerce Commission (ICC), thus for the first time providing a federal body with the power to regulate railroads.[75] While the ICC mostly failed to achieve its goals, its creation by legislators indicates that federal legislation pertaining to corporations was neither impossible nor inconceivable in the 1880s. The lack of corresponding legislation regarding stockholders and bondholders shows that the 1873 crisis simply did not engender the same sense of urgency that the rate wars of the 1870s did.

Conclusion

The different responses in Germany, Austria, and the United States in the realm of legislation and jurisdiction reflected the diverse nature of the crisis and its causes. In Germany, it was caused by overspeculation in railroads and also, to a significant extent, industrial and banking corporations. Many were liquidated in the years following the panic, leaving shareholders with little or nothing. In many cases, it emerged that promoters had incorporated a company purely for the sake of making a quick profit. In order to better protect shareholders and discourage the formation of bubble companies, German legislators passed a major reform of corporation law whose principles would shape the German economy well into the following century.

In the United States, by contrast, the issue of promoter fraud was not a topic of public debate in the 1870s. While the American laws governing the process of incorporation appear to have been better designed than their German counterpart, it is difficult to assess how effective they were in practice. More significantly, the bubble on financial markets in the early 1870s had been concentrated not in stock but in railroad bonds. These railroad companies did see high rates of receiverhip but were not liquidated. Instead, they were restructured, often with the help of investment bankers, and continued to operate.[76] Unlike the German companies that had been established by deceitful promoters, the American railroads served a clearly identifiable purpose and in many cases eventually evolved into viable businesses.

The fact that the United States, despite high rates of receivership, did not see a push for a reformed corporation law may also reflect the fact that such a reform would have presented American legislators with much greater challenges. Whereas in Germany economic legislation and policy making were national matters, in the United States they remained mostly in the hands of state legislatures. Although the American federal government gained certain powers in the realm of economic regulation following the Civil War, many areas—corporation law among them—remained matters of state legislation. For this reason, the United States did not see the emergence of a unified, nationally regulated market, as Germany had. In the realm of corporation law, this resulted in a race to the bottom that left shareholders with little protection. While this development was the result of state competition, it also reflected the fact that any movement for greater shareholder protection could not have presented shareholders' claims to a single, easily identifiable body. Rather, American interest groups were generally forced to look to many different state governments, thus weakening and splintering their influence and visibility.[77]

One line of argument, it seems worth noting, was practically absent in all three countries—namely, the notion that international competition precluded the possibility of an effective national regulation and legislation of corporations and securities markets. Rather, underpinning the arguments made by legislators and legal experts, was a belief that financial markets could and should be reined in through national laws and national institutional frameworks. In this respect, the interconnectedness of the panics of 1873 left few traces in the debates among legal experts, whose confidence in the power of national legislation and the regulatory state remained firmly intact. More than twenty years later, by contrast, Max Weber would argue that the proposed partial German ban on futures trading would hamper his country's international competitiveness.[78]

CONCLUSION

During the early 1870s, investors, bankers, journalists, and theorists engaged in manifold speculations: in financial speculations that spun a web of transactions and liabilities, and in interpretative speculations whose purpose it was both to contain and to render intelligible the aggregate result of many individual financial speculations—namely, the bubble and the panic. These interpretative speculations relied on three structurally similar mechanisms: transforming the abstract into the personal and individual, the virtual and intangible into the tangible and material; and the transnational into the national and local. The double nature of finance as both something that individuals engage in and as an aggregate, expansive force that assumes an agency transcending that of individuals was in evidence even before the panic. As financial markets and stock exchanges grew, a process that accelerated toward the end of the 1860s, investment manuals of the period normalized securities trading as a rational and productive activity, performed by individuals combining qualities of rational calculation with intuitive insight. This normalization of finance translated its abstract quality into the personal and individual, just as the volume of capital flows was rapidly expanding. At the same time, financial writers cast the stock exchanges that channeled these increasingly transnational flows of capital as institutions characterized by national customs and practices.

In a similar vein, journalists presented financial information and narratives to their readers, suggesting that future profits could be calculated and measured using the numbers neatly arranged in columns and spreadsheets. Finance thus appeared as an ordered activity, controllable by individuals. Yet this mode of presentation and narration lacked structure and intelligibility and was therefore more likely to induce in investors a state of indecision rather than the desired active, calculating attitude. At the same time, when it came to overseas investments, journalists signaled to their readers a sense of unease at the physical distance between an investor who might reside in a small German town, and the object of investment, such as a yet-to-be-built railroad in the American West. The expansive nature of transatlantic capital flows transcended the horizon of investors and journalists. This again invited a logic of personification: the honorable banker, financial writers suggested, could be trusted; concrete and real, his name provided a measure of security and intelligibility in the virtual world of financial information.

All the while, throughout 1871 and most of 1872, prices on the stock exchange were rising. An ever-growing number of advertisements for newly issued securities was evidence of an atmosphere of exuberance, and investors felt induced to jump on the bandwagon, thus creating a self-reinforcing momentum of rising prices. Here, already, it could seem as if financial markets were becoming increasingly decoupled and removed from the control of individuals. Observers scoured the horizon for warning signs, wondering whether a sudden eruption on financial markets might lead to a destruction of values, bringing down trade and commerce with them. No longer, it seemed, could rational individual action control the might of markets. Finance seemed to have taken on a life of its own and threatened to unleash its devastating power. Yet even where observers warned of a crisis, this was construed as a national or at most European event. They did not anticipate a crisis of transatlantic or worldwide proportions. The logic of interpretation operating on the eve of the crisis was one of nationalization. When the crisis broke, first in May in Vienna, then in New York in September, the transnational reach of financial markets suddenly assumed new visibility. Some in Germany and Austria at first continued to strenuously deny the relevance of American events, but the very act of denial itself testified to the fear of transnational contagion. By October the crisis had spread both nationally and transnationally and from the stock exchanges and national capitals to trade and commerce in small towns and rural areas. Economic actors likened these events to a "storm" or "hurricane," depicting financial markets as an uncontainable force. At the same time, there remained the possibility that purposeful human action might provide an antidote to this force, as some investors and entrepreneurs seized the opportunity to turn a profit. Overall, however, the overarching impression and experience was that financial markets defied not only individual control but also, for the time being at least, an interpretative framework that relied on causality, agency, and representation.

This was the impression that set the stage for the interpretative speculations that followed the crisis. Attempting to make sense of the experience of panic and render it intelligible, the structure of these speculations relied on established strategies but assumed a new intensity and visibility. Economic theorists debated the role of monetary factors in causing the panic. The Austrian and American paper currencies, they argued, and the abnormal glut of money on German capital markets caused by the payment of French reparations, had fostered financial speculation and the creation of artificial values. The lesson of the panic, therefore, was to resume specie payments by adopting the gold standard, which would create an international currency in which there could never be too much or too little money in any one nation, since the laws of supply and demand would guarantee an efficient distribution of the world's gold resources. The world market for gold would absorb any excess and channel money to where it was scarce. Financial markets, according to this reasoning, would be contained through "materialization": paper money, which was virtual, intangible, and artificial, would be replaced by gold, which was material, tangible, and real. At the same time, financial speculation would be cured not by national containment but by expansion, by creating an *international* currency. This clashed with a competing strategy of containment and interpretation—nationalization—showing that the mechanisms were distinct and not necessarily commensurate.

Debates on monetary policy addressed systemic issues. Competing with this was another mode of interpretation according to which the widespread economic calamity was the result of individual acts of wrongdoing, of the behavior of greedy and reckless individuals, and financial markets were in need of containment through the principles of a moral economy. This interpretation relied on a logic of personification: It identified individuals whose moral failings had brought on the crisis. In Germany, personification combined with conspiracy theories and racialization to form a narrative according to which Jewish financiers had conspired to corrupt and subdue parliaments, judiciary, and civil service. Bismarck's Jewish banker, Gerson von Bleichröder, was seen to personify this nexus. This combination was a specifically German phenomenon; neither Austria (where the dominant Liberal Party was widely perceived as corrupt) nor the United States (where the financial panic was regarded by many as a result of venality among businessmen and legislators) saw the development of an equally powerful full-blown conspiracy. German stock markets had—unlike in America—always been described in an anonymous, impersonal language, and it may well have been this aura of mystery and anonymity that invited speculation on secret machinations and lent such speculation a certain plausibility.

The final chapter of this study explored a third strategy of containment: that of restraining financial markets through national legislation. The German corporation law of 1870 was widely blamed for having enabled a proliferation of speculative bubble companies, many of which were liquidated in the aftermath of the panic. Legislators believed that more stringent regulations would help prevent a recurrence of such excess and, to this end, wrote a bill that was signed into law in 1884. Modeled in part on an Austrian bill, which had also been written in response to the panic, the 1884 law signaled a departure from French and British models and marked the nationalization of German corporation law. This strategy of containing financial markets through national legislation complemented rather than competed with the monetary internationalization that had already occurred. The American states, by contrast, saw no need for a similar overhaul of corporation law. While contemporaries were critical of the growing power of directors at the expense of shareholders, the fact that economic regulation remained in the hands of states triggered a race to the bottom in which shareholders ultimately lost out.

The speculative bubble and the financial crises of 1873, then, illustrate how contemporaries sought to contain finance both conceptually, by interpreting it and translating it into narratives, and practically, by calling for the adoption of a specie standard or by strengthening legal protections for shareholders. At the same time, however, we can observe significant differences between the countries most affected by the crisis. Perceptions of transnational connections varied depending on American, German, or Austrian viewpoints. The growth of stock exchanges was part of a global structure. Yet Wall Street was seen by Americans as a quintessentially American institution. When casting their glance abroad, Americans were most likely to look to London and took little interest in securities trading in continental Europe. Germans, by contrast, displayed a strong fascination with Wall Street, which they regarded with a mixture of awe and revulsion. This asymmetry was established before the panic and remained in place even during the momentous autumn of 1873. While Austrians and Germans, following a brief period of denial, acknowledged the effect American events were having on their markets, Americans themselves remained largely oblivious to these distant reverberations. Where journalists noted the distress among European investors, they did not describe it as having been caused by the New York panic. At the same time, the monetary contraction that took place throughout the United States, as bank failures spread down the eastern seaboard and into the West, did produce an impression of *national* economic integration, which stood in marked contrast to the awareness of internal division that had long been a central element of American politics. It may, in fact, have been this long-standing issue of sectionalism that focused the minds of American commentators inward: in a country so preoccupied with the specter of internal division, America's sense of its place in global capitalism was, perhaps, less likely to emerge.[1] This was evident, too, in the currency debate in which American gold advocates argued in favor of a globally flowing currency without admitting the corollary that America's recent panic had been the result of monetary isolation.

Austrians, unlike Americans, were acutely aware of foreign influences on the Austrian money market, an awareness that, we may assume, was at least partly the result of the country's rapidly growing volume of foreign trade, which doubled between 1868 and 1873. Prior to the panic, Austrians frequently noted the effect of developments on the Berlin bourse on their home market, and when prices in Vienna tumbled in May 1873, they widely believed this to be a local event, unlikely to strongly affect foreign markets. With the failure of Jay Cooke, the Vienna bourse was dealt another harsh blow, and prices began falling once again in response to developments in New York and Berlin. At the same time, however, many Austrian commentators and theorists, in the aftermath of the panic, argued that Austria's crisis was the result of a peculiar form of monetary isolation. The country's irredeemable currency, according to this theory, had led to a glut of money which, because it could not flow abroad, had produced an excess of artificial values. Rather than forming part of an international monetary system based on the laws of supply and demand, Austria had found itself in a state of one-sided dependence, a passive recipient of German capital but lacking any independent agency. This notion of Austrian isolation was reflected in the idea voiced by other commentators in the aftermath of the panic that national Austrian peculiarities—an immature attitude toward money, an artificial constitutional system, the backwardness of Catholic restoration—accounted for its unusual force and peculiar shape.

In Germany, commentators both before and after the panic were well aware of the influence of foreign developments. The very concept of a *Weltwirtschaft* had, after all, been coined by German writers at least since the 1860s. German commentators registered developments on foreign bourses and their effects on German markets and widely believed that the German panic of 1873 had been triggered by Jay Cooke's failure. At the same time, however, German responses to, and interpretations of, the panic relied heavily on national frameworks. A recurrence of the panic, legal experts and legislators believed, could be prevented by more effective national regulations, and the reforms that were finally put in place were more independent of foreign models than any of their predecessors. Popular conspiracy theories, too, ignored the panic's transnational dimension. Instead, their proponents first accused individuals and then German Jews, as a collective, of having conspired to corrupt national institutions and defraud ordinary Germans. One might argue that this conspiracy theory was potentially global in nature, but only in later years would it evolve into a narrative of a "world" Jewry. In the 1870s, this global dimension was, at most, hinted at.

Given these discrepancies and differences, to what extent was the crisis of 1873 a moment of global consciousness? The observation that the experience and perception of this transnational crisis was shaped by national conditions does not in itself countermand the idea of 1873 as a global moment. The dialectic of global processes and local and national forms of adaptation has, after all, come to be regarded as an inherent feature of the process of globalization. Can we therefore think of the panics of 1873 as a "global moment": an event that contemporaries perceived as both epochal and of global significance, investing them with a symbolic meaning that went beyond any immediately obvious structural changes they produced?[2]

Certainly, the panics of 1873 were not global in the sense of being a topic of discussion not just in the West but also in Asia, Latin America, and Africa. But contemporaries nevertheless readily used semantics of the global, describing the transnational connections they witnessed as encompassing the entire world. What is more, they frequently stressed the newness of interconnectedness, of living in a shrinking world, believing that this set their world apart from earlier periods, a belief that is, to this day, a recurring theme in discourses of globalization.[3] If such metaphors of the global were, strictly speaking, precisely that and in this sense inaccurate, we may also interpret them as indicators of an anticipatory awareness of the expansive nature of capitalism that would, in subsequent decades, indeed span to different degrees of intensity the entire globe. At the same time, as we have seen, this awareness of interconnectedness was uneven and more pronounced in Germany and Austria than in the United States. This discrepancy confirms that globalization in the second half of the nineteenth century was an uneven process, characterized by lumpiness and asymmetries. The events of 1873 show that this unevenness was not merely a feature of the relationship between the capitalist core and the periphery but existed even within the West, both in terms of discourse and of practices.

One might be tempted to consider this truncated global consciousness, as it were, a nineteenth-century phenomenon, characteristic of an age and a mentality in which traditional attitudes competed with a mindset still seeking to grasp but not ready to completely affirm the newness of globalized financial markets. But perhaps it is better thought of as an effect of the virtual nature of finance itself, which almost always compels a measure of translation and interpretation to become intelligible, a feature that distinguishes financial crises from other potentially global events such as wars or natural disasters. These, too, of course, are interpreted and appropriated within national frameworks. But they do not require a rendering in terms of what they are not, nor do they challenge notions of representation, agency, and causality in the way the experience of financial markets seems to do. For this reason, it would be promising to explore how global consciousness was transformed in the countries examined here during the Great Depression, when the specter of overproduction and falling prices for commodities became dominant themes in debates on tariff policy and the world economy.[4] Was the intense awareness of international competition during these years perhaps more conducive to global consciousness than virtual financial flows had been?

It was not only the degree of worldwide interconnectedness that contemporaries in the 1870s perceived as a new, epoch-defining feature. Much more so than today, finance in the final third of the nineteenth century still maintained an air of novelty; the complex world of stock exchanges, capital flows and corporations was still juxtaposed with the market place of yore, a place of personalized interaction, the transition from which many believed had happened so rapidly that it formed part of living memory, a narrative that coexisted rather than competed with nascent theories of the business cycle.

If, today, globalization has still not shed its association with novelty, the same cannot be said of finance. Rather, many commentaries on the most recent crisis were couched in terms of recurrence, implicitly arguing that when it comes to finance, there really is nothing new under the sun. Yet, while the cyclical element of finance and financial crises cannot be denied, it is worth asking in which respect the expansion of the financial sector in the early 1870s differed from later instances of the same phenomenon: "Finance is capitalism's repetition compulsion in times of crisis, yet every repetition is different."[5] One such difference arguably concerns the issue of complexity. Finance and banking seem to lend themselves to descriptions of complexity that can easily be harnessed to obfuscate power relations, a feature that has been highlighted with regard to both early and late twentieth century discourses on finance.[6] During the period examined here, such arguments were not altogether absent. Thus Walter Bagehot, in his treatise on the money market, explicitly set out to counter the notion of finance's impalpability and abstraction.[7] Yet Bagehot's statement is probably best understood as an expression of stylistic aspiration rather than an accurate summary of contemporary financial discourse. In the financial press and in economic treatises of the early 1870s, at least, arguments of complexity were rarely adduced to counter critics of the financial system.

One explanation for this absence might be that the strategies of translation examined here never amounted to a full-blown *critique* of finance against which arguments of complexity might have been used as a weapon. The gold standard and a reformed national legislation were strategies of containment that were not, fundamentally, critical of the financial system but sought to harmonize it by curbing its worst excesses. Discourses of demoralization, corruption, and conspiracy theories, by contrast, could not address finance as a system precisely because of their focus on individual action and morality. If labor publications, post-1873, were increasingly critical of financiers and their power, this criticism, too, remained largely focused on individuals and was thus inchoate. It was only in the early twentieth century, when finance capitalism was replacing industrial capitalism, that writers such as the Austrian-born Rudolf Hilferding—and in the United States, Louis Brandeis—formulated extended critiques of finance's power.[8] These critiques were responses to processes that had begun with the crash, when large banks in Austria and Germany had moved to oust or take over competitors, resulting in a large-scale concentration of the banking system. This, combined with the growing presence of bank directors on corporate boards, Hilferding argued, would eventually result in finance capital's complete control of production. In the United States, the Great Merger Movement of the late nineteenth century produced industrial corporations of a hitherto unseen size, a process that was engineered by the nation's leading investment bankers. Bankers and promoters were charged with overcapitalizing the new corporations in order to award themselves handsome fees. J. P. Morgan's network of banks, insurance companies, and trust companies came under heavy public scrutiny, leading to a congressional investigation. Here, too, it was alleged that interlocking directorates among industrial firms and investment banks were monopolizing production to the detriment of the public. The 1914 Clayton Act aimed to reduce the influence of banks on corporate boards, but it was only in the 1930s that banks and the securities market would see a wholesale reform. In Germany, public criticism of "banking power" (*Bankenmacht*) was altogether less intense.[9] Jacob Riesser's account of the *German Great Banks and their Concentration* appeared in several editions in quick succession. In it, the banker and politician aimed to dispel the notion that there was anything nefarious about the large banks' power.[10]

If financialization occurs in cycles, as one prominent account has argued, it seems worth examining if the same holds true of discursive and practical strategies aimed at translating, accounting for, and criticizing the power of financial markets.[11] In the twenty-first century, a critical account of financial markets would surely need to grapple with the seemingly ever-increasing complexity and thus lack of transparency of banks, and their power to camouflage and suppress basic market signals.[12] It would also have to be mindful of the historically racialized element that often accompanied claims of finance's ostensibly antithetical relationship to production. Whether such a critique can, ultimately, amount to more than a temporary containment of finance remains to be seen.

NOTES

Introduction

1. Henry Villard, *Memoirs of Henry Villard, Journalist and Financier: 1835–1900*, vol. 2 (Boston: Houghton, Mifflin, 1904), 268.
2. Dietrich G. Buss, *Henry Villard: A Study of Transatlantic Investments and Interest, 1870–1895* (New York: Arno Press, 1978), 20–27.
3. Henry Villard to Gardner Colby, July 9, 1872, Letter Book, vol. 1a, Henry Villard Collection, Baker Library, Harvard Business School.
4. On Villard's later career, see Alexandra Villard de Borchgrave and John Cullen, *Villard: The Life and Times of an American Titan* (New York: Doubleday, 2001).
5. Gottfried Keller, "Das verlorene Lachen," in *Gottfried Keller: Gesammelte Werke: Historisch-kritische Ausgabe*, ed. Walter Morgenthaler, vol. 5 (Basel: Stroemfeld, 2000 [1874]), 321. All translations from German primary and secondary sources are mine unless otherwise indicated.
6. Charles P. Kindleberger, *Historical Economics: Art or Science?* (New York: Harvester Wheatsheaf, 1990), 341. Scott Mixon has speculated that "the deteriorating balance sheets of U.S. railroads" sparked the crash in Vienna. See Mixon, "The Crisis of 1873: Perspectives from Multiple Asset Classes," *Journal of Economic History* 68 (2008): 753. But the bourse in Vienna never listed American bonds.
7. Scott Reynolds Nelson, *A Nation of Deadbeats: An Uncommon History of America's Financial Disasters* (New York: Alfred A. Knopf, 2012), 164. On the New York money market in 1873, see Oliver M. W. Sprague, *History of Crises under the National Banking System* (Washington, DC: Government Printing Office, 1910), 32f.
8. Walter Bagehot, *Lombard Street: A Description of the Money Market* (London: King, 1873), 1.
9. Joseph Vogl, *The Specter of Capital* (Stanford: Stanford University Press, 2014), 12.

10.   *Oxford English Dictionary*, s.v. "speculation (*n.*)," accessed April 19, 2018, http://www
.oed.com/view/Entry/186113?redirectedFrom=speculation#eid.

11.   Karl Marx and Frederick Engels, *The Communist Manifesto* (London: Verso, 2012
[1888]), 39.

12.   Charles P. Kindleberger and Robert Z. Aliber, *Manias, Panics, and Crashes: A History
of Financial Crises*, 6th ed. (Basingstoke: Palgrave Macmillan, 2011), 28. Studies of these
earlier crises include Sarah Alice Kidd, *The Search for Moral Order: The Panic of 1819
and the Culture of the Early American Republic* (PhD diss., University of Missouri,
2003); Jessica M. Lepler, *The Many Panics of 1837: People, Politics, and the Creation of
a Transatlantic Financial Crisis* (New York: Cambridge University Press, 2013); Gerhard Ahrens, *Krisenmanagement 1857: Staat und Kaufmannschaft in Hamburg während
der ersten Weltwirtschaftskrise* (Hamburg: Verlag Verein für Hamburgische
Geschichte, 1986); James L. Huston, *The Panic of 1857 and the Coming of the Civil War*
(Baton Rouge: Louisiana State University Press, 1987); Charles W. Calomiris and Larry
Schweikart, "The Panic of 1857: Origins, Transmission, and Containment," *Journal of
Economic History* 51 (1991): 807–834; Hans Rosenberg, *Die Weltwirtschaftskrise 1857–
1859: Mit einem Vorbericht* (Göttingen: Vandenhoeck & Ruprecht, 1974). While these
panics were transnational in scope, they either did not affect the European continent
or, as in the case of 1857, not to the same extent as those of 1873. See ibid., 128–130.

13.   Ann Fabian, "Speculation on Distress: The Popular Discourse of the Panics of 1837 and
1857," *Yale Journal of Criticism* 3 (1989): 127–142. On nineteenth-century definitions of
"panic," "crisis," and related terms, see Daniele Besomi, "Naming Crises," in *Crises
and Cycles in Economic Dictionaries and Encyclopaedias*, ed. Daniele Besomi (London:
Routledge, 2012), 54–132. For an exploration of literary "panic texts" see David A. Zimmerman, *Panic! Markets, Crises, and Crowds in American Fiction* (Chapel Hill: University of
North Carolina Press, 2006).

14.   This element of crystallization retains something of the original Greek meaning of the
term "crisis," which could denote both a situation of parting as well as a situation
requiring a decision. See Reinhart Koselleck, "Krise," in *Geschichtliche Grundbegriffe:
Historisches Lexikon zur politisch-sozialen Sprache in Deutschland*, vol. 3, ed. Otto
Brunner, Werner Conze, and Reinhart Koselleck (Stuttgart: Klett-Cotta, 1982), 617–650.

15.   Youssef Cassis, "Economic and Financial Crises," in *Capitalism: The Reemergence of
a Historical Concept*, ed. Jürgen Kocka and Marcel van der Linden (London: Bloomsbury, 2016), 22. For a brief survey of the historiography of crises see ibid., 19–22.

16.   Mixon, "Crisis of 1873," argues that American investors' behavior in 1873 was rational.

17.   Sprague, *History of Crises*. This remains a standard work of reference. For a more recent
account and interpretation with new data see Elmus Wicker, *Banking Panics of the
Gilded Age* (Cambridge: Cambridge University Press, 2000).

18.   Charles P. Kindleberger, *Manias, Panics, and Crashes: A History of Financial Crises*
(New York: Basic Books, 1978), 10. Joseph Schumpeter, too, described business
cycles with reference to an underlying model according to which cycles and crises were
driven by credit and technological innovation. At the same time, he stressed that
"general history (social, political, and cultural), economic history, and more particularly
industrial history are not only indispensable but really the most important contribu-
tors to the understanding of our problem. All other materials and methods, statistical
and theoretical, are only subservient to them and worse than useless without them."
See Joseph A. Schumpeter, *Business Cycles: A Theoretical, Historical, and Statistical
Analysis of the Capitalist Process*, 2 vols. (New York: McGraw Hill, 1939), 13. The oldest
studies of the business cycle date back to the nineteenth century: Clément Juglar, *Des*

Crises commerciales et de leur retour périodique en France, en Angleterre et aux États-Unis (Paris, 1861); William Stanley Jevons, "Commercial Crises and Sun Spots," *Nature* 19 (1878): 33–37.

19. Samuel Rezneck, "Distress, Relief, and Discontent in the United States during the Depression of 1873–78," *Journal of Political Economy* 58 (1950): 494–512; Hans Rosenberg, *Große Depression und Bismarckzeit: Wirtschaftsablauf, Gesellschaft und Politik in Mitteleuropa* (Berlin: de Gruyter, 1967). For a more recent assessment of the 1873–1879 period on the basis of quantitative and qualitative material see Margrit Grabas, "Die Gründerkrise von 1873/79—Fiktion oder Realität? Einige Überlegungen im Kontext der Weltfinanz- und wirtschaftskrise 2008/2009," *Jahrbuch für Wirtschaftsgeschichte* 52, no. 1 (2011): 69–96. On the Austrian crash, see Herbert Matis, *Österreichs Wirtschaft 1848–1913: Konjunkturelle Dynamik und gesellschaftlicher Wandel im Zeitalter Franz Josephs I.* (Berlin: Duncker & Humblot, 1972), 155–218, 302–325; Joseph Neuwirth, *Die Spekulationskrisis von 1873* (Leipzig: Duncker & Humblot, 1874).

20. Nicolas Barreyre, "The Politics of Economic Crisis: The Panic of 1873, the End of Reconstruction and the Realignment of American Politics," *Journal of the Gilded Age and Progressive Era* 10 (2011): 403–424.

21. This brief period is the focus of two older studies: E. Ray McCartney, *Crisis of 1873* (Minneapolis: Burgess, 1935); Erhard Hübener, *Die deutsche Wirtschaftskrisis von 1873* (Berlin: Ebering, 1905).

22. On economic crises as catalysts for political transformations, see William H. Sewell Jr., "Economic Crises and the Shape of Modern History," *Public Culture* 24 (2012), 305–308.

23. Schumpeter, *Business Cycles*, 1:336f.; A. Sartorius von Waltershausen, *Die Entstehung der Weltwirtschaf: Geschichte des zwischenstaatlichen Wirtschaftslebens vom letzten Viertel des achtzehnten Jahrhunderts bis 1914* (Jena: Gustav Fischer, 1931), 290–293; Kindleberger, *Historical Economics*, 310; though see Nelson, *Nation of Deadbeats*, 148–168.

24. Britain, France, and Latin America did not experience financial turmoil on a similar scale. See Philip L. Cottrell, "Domestic Finance, 1860–1914," in *The Cambridge Economic History of Modern Britain*, vol. 2, ed. Roderick Floud and Paul Johnson (Cambridge: Cambridge University Press, 2004), 277; Luc Marco, "Les faillites en France pendant la longue stagnation," in *La longue stagnation en France: L'autre grande depression 1873–1897*, ed. Yves Breton, Albert Broder, and Michel Lutfalla (Paris: Editions economica, 1997), 110f.; Carlos Marichal, *A Century of Debt Crises in Latin America: From Independence to the Great Depression, 1820–1930* (Princeton: Princeton University Press, 1989), 98–125. The Italian crisis of 1873 was small in scope and effect, and not connected to international financial markets. See Giuseppe Conti, "Il crac del 1873," in *Crisi e scandali bancari nella storia d'Italia*, ed. Paolo Pecorari (Venice: Istituto Veneto di Scienze, Lettere ed Arti, 2006), 29–66.

25. Hans Pohl, *Aufbruch der Weltwirtschaft: Geschichte der Weltwirtschaft von der Mitte des 19. Jahrhunderts bis zum Ersten Weltkrieg* (Stuttgart: Franz Steiner, 1989), 158.

26. Charles Bright and Michael Geyer, "Where in the World Is America? The History of the United States in the Global Age," in *Rethinking American History in a Global Age*, ed. Thomas Bender (Berkeley: University of California Press), 76.

27. The now-classic definition of the term is in Anthony Giddens, *Consequences of Modernity* (Cambridge: Polity Press, 1991), 64: globalization is the "intensification of worldwide social relations which link distant localities in such a way that local happenings are shaped by events occurring many miles away and vice versa." A seminal historical

account is Kevin H. O'Rourke and Jeffery G. Williamson, *Globalization and History: The Evolution of a Nineteenth-Century Atlantic Economy* (Cambridge, Mass.: MIT Press, 1999). On globalization in imperial Germany, see, for example, Sebastian Conrad, *Globalisation and Nation in Imperial Germany* (Cambridge: Cambridge University Press, 2010); Julia Laura Rischbieter, *Mikro-Ökonomie der Globalisierung: Kaffee, Kaufleute und Konsumenten im Kaiserreich 1870–1914* (Cologne: Böhlau, 2011); Cornelius Torp, *The Challenges of Globalization: Economy and Politics in Germany, 1860–1914* (New York: Berghahn, 2014). For the United States see, for example, Marc-William Palen, *The "Conspiracy" of Free Trade: The Anglo-American Struggle over Empire and Economic Globalization, 1846–1896* (Cambridge: Cambridge University Press, 2016); Andrew Zimmerman, *Alabama in Africa: Booker T. Washington, the German Empire, and the Globalization of the New South* (Princeton: Princeton University Press, 2010). There are no book-length studies on globalization and nineteenth-century Austria. Two recent articles that place Austrian history in a transnational perspective are Alison Frank, "The Children of the Desert, and the Laws of the Sea: Austria, Great Britain, the Ottoman Empire, and the Mediterranean Slave Trade in the Nineteenth Century," *American Historical Review* 117 (2012): 410–444; Quinn Slobodian, "How to See the World Economy: Statistics, Maps, and Schumpeter's Camera in the First Age of Globalization," *Journal of Global History* 10 (2015): 307–332.

28. Frederick Cooper, *Colonialism in Question: Theory, Knowledge, History* (Berkeley: University of California Press, 2005), 95, 11. The more astute theorists of globalization never made such assumptions. See Giddens, *Consequences of Modernity*, 64f.

29. Kevin O'Rourke and Jeffrey G. Williamson, *Globalization and History*. See also the contributions in *Globalization in Historical Perspective*, ed. Michael D. Bordo, Alan M. Taylor, and Jeffrey G. Williamson (Chicago: University of Chicago Press, 2003). For a succinct summary of nineteenth-century globalization see also Jürgen Osterhammel, and Niels P. Petersson, *Globalization: A Short History* (Princeton: Princeton University Press, 2005), 57–90.

30. Sebastian Conrad, *What Is Global History?* (Princeton: Princeton University Press, 2016), 99.

31. In describing this dialectic, Christopher Bayly has argued that the phase he calls "modern globalization" was characterized by a development in which "rapidly developing connections . . . created many hybrid polities, mixed ideologies, and complex forms of global economic activity" while at the same time often heightening the sense of difference. Christopher A. Bayly, *The Birth of the Modern World, 1780–1914* (Malden, Mass.: Blackwell, 2004), 1.

32. AHR Conversation, "On Transnational History," participants: Christopher A. Bayly, Sven Beckert, Matthew Connelly, Isabel Hofmeyr, Wendy Kozol, and Patricia Seed, *American Historical Review* 111 (2006): 1453f.

33. Conrad, *What Is Global History?*, 190–204.

34. Ibid., 109–111; Christof Dejung and Niels P. Petersson, "Introduction: Power, Institutions, and Global Markets—Actors, Mechanisms, and Foundations of Worldwide Economic Integration, 1850–1930," in *The Foundations of Worldwide Economic Integration. Power, Institutions, and Global Markets, 1850–1930*, ed. Christof Dejung and Niels P. Petersson (Cambridge: Cambridge University Press, 2013), 1–17.

35. Antony G. Hopkins, "Introduction," in *Global History: Interactions between the Universal and the Local*, ed. Antony G. Hopkins (Basingstoke: Palgrave Macmillan, 2006), 12.

36. A. G. Kenwood and A. L. Lougheed, *The Growth of the International Economy: An Introductory Text*, 3rd. ed. (London: Routledge, 1992), 61. The most visible manifestation

of this was perhaps the laying of the transatlantic cable in 1866. See Simone M. Müller, *Wiring the World: The Social and Cultural Creation of Global Telegraph Networks* (New York: Columbia University Press, 2016).

37. If the historiography of globalization has taken a turn away from the strictly economic in recent years, much the same can be said of the historiography of capitalism. See, for example, Kenneth D. Lipartito, "Reassembling the Economic: New Departures in Historical Materialism," *American Historical Review* 121 (2016): 101–139; Jeffrey Sklansky, "Labor, Money, and the Financial Turn in the History of Capitalism," *Labor: Studies in the Working-Class History of the Americas* 11 (2014): 32–46; Jürgen Kocka, "Writing the History of Capitalism," *Bulletin of the German Historical Institute* 47 (Fall 2010): 7–24; "Interchange: The History of Capitalism," *Journal of American History* 101, no. 2 (September 2014): 504–536.

38. Heinz-Gerhard Haupt and Jürgen Kocka, "Comparison and Beyond: Traditions, Scope, and Perspectives of Comparative History," in *Comparative and Transnational History. Central European Approaches and New Perspectives*, ed. Heinz-Gerhard Haupt and Jürgen Kocka (New York: Berghahn Books, 2009), 1–30.

39. Jürgen Kocka, "Einleitung," in *Gibt es einen deutschen Kapitalismus? Tradition und globale Perspektiven der sozialen Marktwirtschaft*, ed. Volker R. Berghahn and Sigurt Vitols (Frankfurt am Main: Campus, 2006), 9–21. See also the other contributions in this volume as well as Colleen A. Dunlavy and Thomas Welskopp, "Myths and Peculiarities: Comparing U.S. and German Capitalism," *German Historical Institute Bulletin* 41 (2007): 33–64.

1. Setting the Stage: Institutions and Cultures of Speculation in the 1860s and Early 1870s

1. Albert G. Kenwood and Alan L. Lougheed, *The Growth of the International Economy: An Introductory Text*, 3rd ed. (London: Routledge, 1992), 12–23, quotation at 61. Economic development in the Western world was not, of course, uniform. France was still reeling following its defeat in the Franco-Prussian War, while Great Britain, having seen a period of overspeculation in the mid-1860s, did not witness a similar upsurge in securities trading as the countries discussed here. See Wolfram Fischer, *Expansion—Integration—Globalisierung: Studien zur Geschichte der Weltwirtschaft* (Göttingen: Vandenhoeck & Ruprecht, 1998), 82.

2. *Bericht über den Handel und die Industrie von Berlin im Jahre 1872, nebst einer Uebersicht über die Wirksamkeit des Aeltesten-Collegiums vom Mai 1872 bis Mai 1873 erstattet von den Aeltesten der Kaufmannschaft von Berlin*, 1, Landesarchiv Berlin, A Rep. 200–01, Nr. 593.

3. On French reparations and their impact on the German capital market, see chapter 4.

4. Herbert Matis, *Österreichs Wirtschaft 1848–1913: Konjunkturelle Dynamik und gesellschaftlicher Wandel im Zeitalter Franz Josephs I.* (Berlin: Duncker & Humblot, 1972), 155–158.

5. Mark Twain and Charles Dudley Warner, *The Gilded Age: A Tale of Today* (Seattle: University of Washington Press, 1968 [1873]), 125.

6. Sven Beckert, *The Monied Metropolis: New York City and the Consolidation of the American Bourgeoisie, 1850–1896* (Cambridge: Cambridge University Press, 2001), 145f., 150f.

7. "The End of an Era of Speculation," *Nation*, June 30, 1870.

8. Rendigs Fels, *American Business Cycles, 1865–1897* (Chapel Hill: University of North Carolina Press, 1959), 97.
9. Hans Pohl, *Aufbruch der Weltwirtschaft: Geschichte der Weltwirtschaft von der Mitte des 19. Jahrhunderts bis zum ersten Weltkrieg* (Stuttgart: Franz Steiner, 1989), 325f.
10. Hans-Ulrich Wehler, *Deutsche Gesellschaftsgeschichte*, vol. 3 (Munich: Beck, 1995), 73.
11. Albert Fishlow, "Transportation in the 19th and Early 20th Centuries," in *The Cambridge Economic History of the United States*, vol. 2, ed. Stanley L. Engerman and Robert E. Gallman (Cambridge: Cambridge University Press, 1996–2000), 584ff.
12. Eduard März, *Österreichische Industrie- und Bankpolitik in der Zeit Franz Josephs I: Am Beispiel der k. k. priv. Österreichischen Credit-Anstalt für Handel und Gewerbe* (Vienna: Europa-Verlag, 1968), 140, 143; David F. Good, *The Economic Rise of the Habsburg Empire, 1750–1914* (Berkeley: University of California Press, 1984), 164.
13. Dolores Greenberg, *Financiers and Railroads, 1869–1889: A Study of Morton, Bliss and Company* (Newark: University of Delaware Press, 1980), 43f.; Vincent P. Carosso, *Investment Banking in America* (Cambridge, Mass.: Harvard University Press, 1970), 1–28; März, *Industrie- und Bankpolitik*, 42f., 71, 122; Volker Wellhöner and Harald Wixforth, "Finance and Industry," in *Germany: A New Social and Economic History*, vol. 3, ed. Sheilagh Ogilvie (London: Arnold, 2003), 156f.; Carsten Burhop, *Die Kreditbanken in der Gründerzeit* (Stuttgart: Franz Steiner, 2004), 107–123.
14. Walter E. Mosse, *Jews in the German Economy: The German-Jewish Economic Élite, 1820–1935* (Oxford: Clarendon Press, 1987), 133.
15. New York, vol. 200, p. 400 SS, R. G. Dun & Co. Credit Report Volumes, Baker Library, Harvard Business School; George Opdyke and Company records, Letter Book, March–May 1872, New York Historical Society.
16. Matis, *Österreichs Wirtschaft*, 207. According to stock exchange officials, only one third of all securities bought and sold were listed in the official table of stocks and bonds. See ibid. The number refers to the number of securities, not of companies.
17. Markus Baltzer, *Der Berliner Kapitalmarkt nach der Reichsgründung 1871: Gründerzeit, internationale Finanzmarktintegration und der Einfluss der Makroökonomie* (Berlin: Peter Lang, 2007), 27.
18. Robert E. Wright, "Capitalism and the Rise of the Corporation Nation," in *Capitalism Takes Command: The Social Transformation of Nineteenth-Century America*, ed. Michael Zakim and Gary J. Kornblith (Chicago: University of Chicago Press 2012), 149.
19. *Financial Review* (1873), 52–54.
20. George Herberton Evans Jr., *Business Incorporations in the United States, 1800–1943* (New York: National Bureau of Economic Research, 1949), 11.
21. *Financial Review* (1873), 31; *Financial Review* (1876), 48f. O'Sullivan counts 141 railroad bonds for 1873. See O'Sullivan, *Dividends of Development. Securities Markets in the History of US Capitalism, 1866–1922* (Oxford: Oxford University Press, 2016), 29.
22. Beckert, *Monied Metropolis*, 192–195; Annemarie Lange, *Berlin zur Zeit Bebels und Bismarcks: Zwischen Reichsgründung und Jahrhundertwende* (Berlin: Dietz, 1972), 156–171; Philipp Reick, *"Labor is Not a Commodity!": The Movement to Shorten the Workday in Late Nineteenth-Century Berlin and New York* (Frankfurt am Main: Campus, 2016); Lothar Machtan, *Streiks und Aussperrungen im Deutschen Kaiserreich* (Berlin: Colloquium Verlag, 1984); Helmut Konrad, "Deutsch-Österreich: Gebremste Klassenbildung und importierte Arbeiterbewegung im Vielvölkerstaat," in *Europäische Arbeiterbewegungen im 19. Jahrhundert: Deutschland, Österreich, England und Frankreich im Vergleich*, ed. Jürgen Kocka (Göttingen: Vandenhoeck & Ruprecht, 1983), 106–128.

23. "Notes from Berlin," *Nation*, February 22, 1872; Kristin Poling, "Shantytowns and Pioneers beyond the City Wall: Berlin's Urban Frontier in the Nineteenth Century," *Central European History* 47 (2014), 260.

24. Lange, *Berlin*, 122–138.

25. Beckert, *Monied Metropolis*, 174, 182.

26. Wolfgang Renzsch, *Handwerker und Lohnarbeiter in der frühen Arbeiterbewegung: Zur sozialen Basis von Gewerkschaften und Sozialdemokratie im Reichsgründungsjahrzehnt* (Göttingen: Vandenhoeck & Ruprecht, 1981), 163f.

27. Jürgen Kocka, *Arbeitsverhältnisse und Arbeiterexistenzen: Grundlagen der Klassenbildung im 19. Jahrhundert* (Bonn: Dietz, 1990), 369f.

28. Franz Baltzarek, *Die Geschichte der Wiener Börse: Öffentliche Finanzen und privates Kapital im Spiegel einer österreichischen Wirtschaftsinstitution* (Vienna: Verlag der Österreichischen Akademie der Wissenschaften, 1973), 19.

29. Walter Werner and Steven T. Smith, *Wall Street* (New York: Columbia University Press, 1991), 28; Steve Fraser, *Wall Street: A Cultural History* (London: Faber & Faber, 2005), 13, 33.

30. Rainer Gömmel, "Entstehung und Entwicklung der Effektenbörsen im 19. Jahrhundert bis 1914," in *Deutsche Börsengeschichte*, ed. Hans Pohl (Frankfurt am Main: Knapp, 1992), 135, 191; Christof Biggeleben, *Das "Bollwerk des Bürgertums": Die Berliner Kaufmannschaft 1870–1920* (Munich: Beck, 2006), 67.

31. Baltzarek, *Wiener Börse*, 62–65, 75; Annelies Rohrer, *Die Wiener Börse und ihre Besucher in den Jahren 1867–1875* (PhD diss., Vienna University, 1971), 241, 251.

32. Geheimes Staatsarchiv Preußischer Kulturbesitz, I. HA Rep. 151, Finanzministerium HB, Nr. 1267.

33. Hellmut Gebhard, *Die Berliner Börse von den Anfängen bis zum Jahre 1896* (Berlin: R. L. Prager, 1928), 137. There are no recent monographs on the Berlin exchange, though see Michael Buchner, *Die Spielregeln der Börse: Institutionen, Kultur und die Grundlagen des Wertpapierhandels in Berlin und London, ca. 1860–1914* (PhD diss., Heidelberg University, 2017).

34. "Beschränkung des Börsenbesuchs," *Berliner Tageblatt*, January 18, 1872.

35. Ranald C. Michie, *The London and New York Stock Exchanges, 1850–1914* (London: Allen & Unwin, 1987), 194.

36. Stuart Banner, *Anglo-American Securities Regulation: Cultural and Political Roots, 1690–1860* (Cambridge: Cambridge University Press, 1998), 174.

37. Robert Sobel, *The Big Board: A History of the New York Stock Market* (New York: Free Press, 1965), 44, 72–82; Michie, *London and New York*, 203.

38. Margaret G. Myers, *The New York Money Market: Origins and Development* (New York: Columbia University Press, 1931), 299.

39. Baltzarek, *Wiener Börse*, 9, 19, 50f., 63.

40. Gebhard, *Berliner Börse*, 53.

41. Myers, *New York Money Market*, 280.

42. Carl Gareis, *Die Börse und die Gründungen nebst Vorschlägen zur Reform des Börsenrechts und der Actiengesetzgebung* (Berlin: Habel, 1874), 20; August Saling, *Die Börsen-Papiere: Erster Theil: Die Börse und die Börsen-Geschäfte*, 2nd expanded ed. (Berlin, 1871), 101–110; Moriz Rubrom, *Neues Wiener Börse-Buch: Handbuch der Speculation*, 3rd improved and rev. ed. (Vienna, 1873), 26–30.

43. Otto Swoboda, *Börse und Actien. Eine ausführliche Besprechung der Börse und der an denselben vorkommenden Arten von Geschäften, des Actienwesens und der auf dasselbe bezüglichen Gesetze, sowie sämmtlicher an Deutschen Börsen courshabenden in- und

ausländischen Werthpapiere (Cologne: Wilh. Hassel 1869), 21; Geheimes Staatsarchiv Preußischer Kulturbesitz, I. HA Rep. 120, Ministerium für Handel und Gewerbe, C IX 1 (Innerer Handel, Generalia) Nr. 28, Bd. 1, fol. 93; Gebhard, *Berliner Börse*, 59.

44. Myers, *New York Money Market*, 300.

45. Anton Negrin, *Die Entwicklung der Wiener Börse (Effektensektion): Von ihrer Gründung bis zum Ausbruch des Weltkriegs (1771–1914): Eine betriebswirtschaftliche Untersuchung*, Teildruck (PhD diss., Vienna, Hochschule für Welthandel, 1937), 1f.

46. Geheimes Staatsarchiv Preußischer Kulturbesitz, I HA Rep. 77, Tit. 945, Nr. 51, Bd. 1, fol. 90. In return, WTB was granted preferential use of the telegraphic bureau and an annual subsidy of 100,000 talers. See Jürgen Wilke, *Grundzüge der Medien- und Kommunikationsgeschichte*, 2nd ed. (Cologne: Böhlau, 2008), 247.

47. Edith Dörfler and Wolfgang Pensold, *Die Macht der Nachricht: Die Geschichte der Nachrichtenagenturen in Österreich* (Vienna: Molden, 2001), 141. The telegraph was first used to transmit stock exchange quotations from Vienna to the provinces in 1849. See Josef Reindl, *Der Deutsch-Österreichische Telegraphenverein und die Entwicklung des deutschen Telegraphenwesens 1850–1871: Eine Fallstudie zur administrativ-technischen Kooperation deutscher Staaten vor der Gründung des Deutschen Reiches* (Frankfurt am Main: Peter Lang, 1993), 138.

48. Theodor Karras, "Telegrapheneinrichtungen in Oesterreich-Ungarn," *Archiv für Post und Telegraphie* 10 (1883): 306.

49. Menaham Blondheim, *News over the Wires: The Telegraph and the Flow of Public Information in America, 1844–1897* (Cambridge, Mass.: Harvard University Press, 1994), 173.

50. Michie, *London and New York*, 186. For a skeptical contemporary view, see "Ueber den Einfluss politischer Ereignisse auf die Bildung des Tagespreises der Effekten," *Zeitschrift für Kapital und Rente* 5 (1869).

51. Christopher Hoag, "The Atlantic Telegraph Cable and Capital Market Information Flows," *Journal of Economic History* 66 (2006): 342–353.

52. "The Railway Monitor: Investments in Small Amounts," *Commercial and Financial Chronicle*, October 12, 1872; Robert E. Wright, *Corporation Nation* (Philadelphia: University of Pennsylvania Press, 2014), 85. On securities holdings among wealthy investors, see James Lester Sturm, *Investing in the United States, 1798–1893: Upper Wealth-Holders in a Market Economy* (New York: Arno Press 1977), 52.

53. Rubrom, *Handbuch der Speculation*, 22.

54. Banner, *Securities Regulation*, 36, 145–158, 201–221; Hanns Leiskow, *Spekulation und öffentliche Meinung in der ersten Hälfte des 19. Jahrhunderts* (Jena: Fischer, 1930), 29; Karl Neidlinger, *Studien zur Geschichte der deutschen Effektenspekulation von ihren Anfängen bis zum Beginn der Eisenbahnspekulation* (Jena: Fischer, 1930), 78; Helen J. Paul, *The South Sea Bubble: An Economic History of Its Origins and Consequences* (London: Routledge, 2011), 13.

55. Banner, *Securities Regulation*, 220.

56. Pierre-Joseph Proudhon, *Manuel du spéculateur à la bourse* (Paris: Garnier Frères, 1854), 4–36.

57. Alexander Engel, "Vom verdorbenen Spieler zum verdienstvollen Spekulanten. Ökonomisches Denken über Börsenspekulation im 19. Jahrhundert," *Jahrbuch für Wirtschaftsgeschichte* 54, no. 2 (2013): 57f.

58. Gustav Cohn, *Die Börse und die Spekulation* (Berlin, 1868), 16.

59. Engel, "Ökonomisches Denken," 60.

60. "Der Lieferungshandel (Zeitkauf)," *Welthandel* (1871).

61. Engel, "Ökonomisches Denken," 49f.

62. "The Bank as a Promoter of Speculation," *Bankers' Magazine*, March 1872.

63. New York, vol. 200, p. 400 SS, R. G. Dun & Co. Credit Report Volumes, Baker Library, Harvard Business School.

64. New York, vol. 201, p. 500 SS, R. G. Dun & Co. Credit Report Volumes, Baker Library, Harvard Business School.

65. Alex Preda, "The Rise of the Popular Investor: Financial Knowledge and Investing in England and France, 1840–1880," *Sociological Quarterly* 42 (2001): 205–232.

66. Alex Preda, *Framing Finance: The Boundaries of Markets and Modern Capitalism* (Chicago: University of Chicago Press, 2009), 3.

67. John Hickling & Co., *Men and Idioms of Wall Street: Explaining the Daily Operations in Stocks, Bonds and Gold* (New York, 1875), 19.

68. Barnes Garrison & Co., *Key to Success in Wall Street* (New York [1870s]), 2, 6; Urs Stäheli, *Spektakuläre Spekulation: Das Populäre der Ökonomie* (Frankfurt am Main: Suhrkamp, 2007), 76.

69. James K. Medbery, *Men and Mysteries of Wall Street* (Westport, Conn.: Greenwood Press, 1968 [1870]), 11.

70. Henry Hamon, *New York Stock Exchange Manual, Containing Its Principles, Rules, and Its Different Modes of Speculation* (New York, 1865 [reprint: 1970]), 142; L. W. Hamilton & Co., *Stock Speculation* (New York, 1875), 5.

71. Rubrom, *Handbuch der Speculation*, 71f.

72. Ibid., 138.

73. Hamilton & Co., *Stock Speculation*, 30; Hickling & Co., *Men and Idioms*, 6f.

74. Hamilton & Co., *Stock Speculation*, 30; Hickling & Co., *Men and Idioms*, 6; see also Tumbridge & Co., *Secrets of Success in Wall Street* (New York, 1875), 11f.

75. Hickling & Co., *Men and Idioms*, 5.

76. Rubrom, *Handbuch der Speculation*, 156; Jacob Kautsch, *Allgemeines Börsenbuch nebst Usancen der Berliner, Frankfurter und Wiener Börse: Ein Handbuch für Capitalisten, Financiers und Bankbeamte* (Stuttgart, 1874), 59; Saling, *Börsen-Papiere: Erster Theil*, 85.

77. Hamilton & Co., *Stock Speculation*, 31; Barnes Garrison & Co., *Key to Success*, 5.

78. Barnes Garrison & Co., *Key to Success*, 5f. See also Kautsch, *Allgemeines Börsenbuch*, 139.

79. Medbery, *Men and Mysteries*, 118f.; Hickling & Co., *Men and Idioms*, 7; Hamon, *Manual*, 142. According to the latter, "cool-headed" speculators are also the most "fortunate" ones—as though they, too, owe their success largely to fate.

80. Hickling & Co., *Men and Idioms*, 8.

81. Tumbridge & Co., *Secrets of Success*, 30.

82. Barnes Garrison & Co., *Key to Success*, 12.

83. Medbery, *Men and Mysteries*, 211.

84. The few female brokers that did operate on Wall Street were ostracized. See Fraser, *Wall Street*, 88f.; Irene Finel-Honigman, *A Cultural History of Finance* (Abingdon: Routledge, 2010), 58–63. In Vienna and Berlin, female brokers were unknown during this period.

85. David Anthony, *Paper Money Men: Commerce, Manhood, and the Sensational Public Sphere in Antebellum America* (Columbus: Ohio State University Press, 2009), 4, 104–106.

86. On manliness and financial markets, see also Marieke De Goede, "Mastering 'Lady Credit': Discourses of Financial Crisis in Historical Perspective," *International Feminist Journal of Politics* 2 (2000), 58–81; Stäheli, *Spektakuläre Spekulation*, 274–277. Both authors emphasize the notion that speculators, in order to be successful, must control their desires, a notion that is less prominent in the texts analyzed here. Conversely,

Gilded Age financial guides for women were also characterized by an underlying tension—namely, in order to be successful, a woman investor would have to "cultivate masculine qualities," rendering her "less attractive to men." See George Robb, *Ladies of the Ticker. Women and Wall Street from the Gilded Age to the Great Depression* (Urbana: University of Illinois Press, 2017), 24.

87. Fraser, *Wall Street*, 42, 85.

88. The most famous corner was Jay Gould's gold corner in 1869. See Maury Klein, *The Life and Legend of Jay Gould* (Baltimore: Johns Hopkins University Press, 1986), 100–114.

89. "Anarchy in Wall Street," *New York Times*, October 19, 1872.

90. Edward J. Renehan Jr., *Commodore: The Life of Cornelius Vanderbilt* (New York: Basic Books, 2007), 290.

91. "The recent 'Corner,' and What Started It," *Commercial and Financial Chronicle*, November 30, 1872.

92. See, for example, "The Stock Market," *Stockholder*, December 27, 1871.

93. "Capital in Wall Street," *Stockholder*, December 5, 1871.

94. Toward the end of the century, this depiction of the market as personalized increasingly became confined to the pages of popular magazines. See Peter Knight, "Reading the Market: Abstraction, Personification and the Financial Column of *Town Topics* Magazine," *Journal of American Studies* 46 (2012): 7.

95. Wilhelm Liebknecht, *Letters to the Chicago Workingman's Advocate November 26, 1870–December 2, 1871*, ed. Philip S. Foner (New York: Holmes & Meier, 1982), 90.

96. "Impresario James Hirschfeld," *Berliner Tageblatt*, January 20, 1872.

97. "Wiener Börse," *Neue Freie Presse*, morning ed., January 4, 1872.

98. Joachim Borchart, *Der europäische Eisenbahnkönig Bethel Henry Strousberg* (Munich: Beck, 1991), 145–159.

99. See, for example, "Ein Mann aus eigener Kraft," *Welthandel* (1871): 31–37. On Strousberg's system, see Borchart, *Eisenbahnkönig*, 50f., 77.

100. Colleen A. Dunlavy, *Politics and Industrialization: Early Railroads in the United States and Prussia* (Princeton: Princeton University Press, 1994), 50.

101. State involvement had been considerable in the 1830s and 1840s but had declined thereafter. See James W. Ely Jr., *Railroads and American Law* (Lawrence: University Press of Kansas, 2001), 16f.

102. Carl Fürstenberg, *Die Lebensgeschichte eines deutschen Bankiers 1870–1914*, ed. Hans Fürstenberg (Berlin: Ullstein, 1931), 213f.

103. "Berliner Cours-Bericht," *Berliner Tageblatt*, January 8 and 15, 1873; "Wiener Börse," *Neue Freie Presse*, morning ed., March 1, 1872; "Wiener Börse," *Neue Freie Presse*, morning ed., April 18, 1872.

104. This contrasts with the 1880s when the market page in the *New York Herald* began arguing "that the market would be better off if outside investors helped rally the market into action, to prevent it from becoming merely the plaything of professional traders." See Peter Knight, *Reading the Market: Genres of Financial Capitalism in Gilded Age America* (Baltimore: Johns Hopkins University Press, 2016), 35.

105. "Berliner Börse," *Aktionär*, February 11, 1872.

106. "Börsenrundschau vom 27: Dezember bis 3. Januar," *Berliner Tageblatt*, January 5, 1873; "Cours-Bericht," *Berliner Börsen-Zeitung*, evening ed., June 11, 1872; "Berliner Börse," *Aktionär*, January 26, 1873. Quotation in "Vermischte Nachrichten: (Der Reklameschwindel in Berlin)," *Aktionär*, September 22, 1872.

107. Medbery, *Men and Mysteries*, 341f.

108. Preda, *Framing Finance*, 189.

109. Hermann Hirschbach, *Von der Börse, oder: Der Geist der Speculation* (Quedlinburg, 1864), 54.

110. Cohn, *Börse und Spekulation*, 24; Gustav Cohn, "Nachtrag zu dem Aufsatze über 'Zeitgeschäfte und Differenzgeschäfte,'" *Jahrbücher für Nationalökonomie und Statistik* 9 (1867): 76.

111. "Zur Lage," *Aktionär*, January 8, 1871.

112. Henning Albrecht, *Antiliberalismus und Antisemitismus: Hermann Wagener und die preußischen Sozialkonservativen 1855–1873* (Paderborn: Schöningh, 2010), 236.

113. Matis, *Österreichs Wirtschaft*, 208; Gömmel, "Effektenbörse," 182.

114. Hirschbach, *Von der Börse*, 15f.

115. Frh. v. Dankelmann, "Die systematische Spoliation des Effektenbesitzes auf dem Gebiet des Staatskredits und des Aktienwesens," *Zeitschrift für Kapital und Rente* 9 (1873): 6.

116. "Vermischte Nachrichten," *Aktionär*, January 19, 1873.

117. "James Fisk, Jr., ein Muster unseres 'Shoddytums,'" *Im Neuen Reich* 2, no. 1 (1872): 436–440.

118. "James Fisk, der Fürst von Erie," *Grenzboten* 31, no. 1 (1872): 257.

119. Wolfgang Helbich, "Different, But Not Out of This World: German Images of the United States between Two Wars, 1871–1914," in *Transatlantic Images and Perceptions: Germany and America Since 1776* (Cambridge: Cambridge University Press, 2007), ed. David E. Barclay and Elisabeth Glaser-Schmidt, 129. This was often contrasted with "German Idealism, Culture, Depth, *Gemüt*, and *Gemütlichkeit*" in ibid.

120. "Volkswirthschaftliche Revue," *Oesterreichischer Oekonomist*, January 4, 1873.

121. "Corners on London," *Stockholder*, September 2, 1873.

122. "The Vienna Panic," *New York Times*, July 12, 1873.

123. "Stock Gambling in Vienna," *New York Times*, June 16, 1873.

2. The Virtual World of Financial Information and the Making of a Bubble

1. Eve Rosenhaft, "Herz oder Kopf: Erfahrungsbildung beim Kauf von Aktien und Witwenrenten im norddeutschen Bildungsbürgertum des späten 18. Jahrhunderts," *Historische Anthropologie* 14 (2006): 351.

2. Henrietta M. Larson, *Jay Cooke: Private Banker* (Cambridge, Mass.: Harvard University Press, 1936), 125–128.

3. Wayne Parsons, *The Power of the Financial Press: Journalism and Economic Opinion in Britain and America* (Aldershot: Elgar, 1989), 24.

4. Douglas Steeples, *Advocate for American Enterprise: William Buck Dana and the Commercial and Financial Chronicle* (Westport: Greenwood Press, 2002), xxii, 41–43.

5. David P. Forsyth, *The Business Press in America, 1750–1865* (Philadelphia: Chilton Books, 1964), 110.

6. Alfred D. Chandler, *Henry V. Poor: Business Editor, Analyst, and Reformer* (Cambridge, Mass.: Harvard University Press, 1956), 224.

7. Joachim Kirchner, *Das deutsche Zeitschriftenwesen: Seine Geschichte und seine Probleme*, Part 2, *Vom Wiener Kongress bis zum Ausgang des 19. Jahrhunderts* (Wiesbaden: Otto Harrassowitz, 1962), 184.

8. Emil Dovifat, *Die Zeitungen* (Gotha: Flamberg, 1925), 61f.

9. *Berliner Börsen-Zeitung*, July 1, 1865, quoted in *75 Jahre Berliner Börsen-Zeitung. 1. Juli 1855—1. Juli 1930*, ed. Friedrich Bertkau and Arnold Killisch von Horn (Berlin: Berliner Börsen-Zeitung und Verlag, 1930), 25.

10. Kirchner, *Das deutsche Zeitschriftenwesen*, 183; Bertkau and Killisch von Horn, *Berliner Börsen-Zeitung*, 14.

11. Bertkau and Killisch von Horn, *Berliner Börsen-Zeitung*, 14.

12. Peter de Mendelssohn, *Zeitungsstadt Berlin: Menschen und Mächte in der Geschichte der deutschen Presse* (Berlin: Ullstein, 1959), 63–71.

13. "Die systematische Spoliation des Effektenbesitzes," *Zeitschrift für Kapital und Rente* 9 (1873): 14.

14. Bertkau and Killisch von Horn, *Berliner Börsen-Zeitung*, 28–31; Ursula E. Koch, *Berliner Presse und europäisches Geschehen 1871* (Berlin: Colloquium, 1978), 16.

15. Johann Winckler, *Die periodische Presse Oesterreichs: Eine historisch-statistische Studie* (Vienna, 1875), 188–190.

16. Josef Reich, *Die Wiener Presse und der Wiener Börsenkrach von 1873 im wechselseitigen Förderungsprozess* (PhD diss., Vienna University, 1947), 36–39.

17. Winckler, *Periodische Presse*, 190, 187 (quotation).

18. Gertrud Fischer, *Die Zeitungsannonce der Wr. Presse vor u. nach dem Börsenkrach von 1873* (PhD diss., Vienna University, 1937), 52.

19. Reich, *Wiener Presse*, 31.

20. This point is echoed by contemporary economic historians who tend to stress the role of the financial press as an agent of market integration. See, for example, Lance E. Davis and Robert E. Gallman, *Evolving Financial Markets and International Capital Flows* (Cambridge: Cambridge University Press, 2001), 276, 303, and passim.

21. Richard White, "Information, Markets, and Corruption: Transcontinental Railroads in the Gilded Age," *Journal of American History* 90 (2003): 26, 36.

22. Joachim Borchart, *Der europäische Eisenbahnkönig Bethel Henry Strousberg* (Munich: Beck, 1991), 107f.; Heinrich Wuttke, *Die deutschen Zeitschriften und die Entstehung der öffentlichen Meinung: Ein Beitrag zur Geschichte des Zeitungswesens*, 2nd ed. (Leipzig, 1875), 18f.; Robert Radu, *Auguren des Geldes: Eine Kulturgeschichte des Finanzjournalismus in Deutschland 1850–1914* (Göttingen: Vandenhoeck & Ruprecht, 2017), 117f.

23. Herbert Matis, *Österreichs Wirtschaft 1848–1913: Konjunkturelle Dynamik und gesellschaftlicher Wandel im Zeitalter Franz Josephs I* (Berlin: Duncker & Humblot, 1972), 218.

24. *Berliner Börsen-Zeitung*, evening ed., 1st suppl., January 9, 1872.

25. Reich, *Wiener Presse*, 64f. Contemporaries regarded such deals as an open secret.

26. *Prospectus: Einladung zum Abonnement auf die Berliner Börsen-Correspondenz für Producte, Fonds & Effecten*, signed by Carl Guthschmidt and Leopold Lassar, November 1856, Geheimes Staatsarchiv Preußischer Kulturbesitz, I. HA Rep. 77, Ministerium des Innern, Tit. 54a, Nr. 27 (emphasis in original).

27. See, for example, the advertisement for the *Börsen-Zeitung*'s rival paper, the *Berliner Börsen-Courier*, in the *Berliner Tageblatt*, January 19, 1873, and "Das Emissions-Geschäft und sein Publikum," *Aktionär*, April 16, 1871.

28. *Stockholder*, November 17, 1863, quoted in Forsyth, *Business Press*, 110; "The 'Chronicle' for 1872," *Commercial and Financial Chronicle*, January 6, 1872.

29. "Berlin, den 1. Juni," *Berliner Börsen-Zeitung*, evening ed., June 1, 1872.

30. *Berliner Börsen-Zeitung*, evening ed., extra suppl., January 11, 1872.

31. "Extra Chronicle—New Table Pages," *Commercial and Financial Chronicle*, October 28, 1871.

32. "The Railway Monitor," *Commercial and Financial Chronicle*, November 25, 1871.
33. "Money Market," *Independent*, November 30, 1871.
34. "Eisenbahn-Betriebseinnahmen im Monat Mai 1871," *Neue Freie Presse*, June 16, 1871.
35. Carsten Burhop, *Die Kreditbanken in der Gründerzeit* (Stuttgart: Franz Steiner, 2004), 29f.
36. Caitlin C. Rosenthal, "From Memory to Mastery: Accounting for Control in America, 1750–1880," *Enterprise and Society* 14, no. 4 (2013): 13.
37. White, "Information, Markets, and Corruption": 32; Alfred D. Chandler, *The Visible Hand: The Managerial Revolution in American Business* (Cambridge, Mass.: Harvard University Press, 1977), 109–120.
38. Richard White, *Railroaded: The Transcontinentals and the Making of Modern America* (New York: Norton, 2011), 69; Jonathan Barron Baskin, "The Development of Corporate Financial Markets in Britain and the United States, 1600–1914: Overcoming Asymmetric Information," *Business History Review* 62 (1988): 227.
39. Theodore M. Porter, *The Rise of Statistical Thinking, 1820–1900* (Princeton: Princeton University Press, 1986).
40. Patricia Cline Cohen, *A Calculating People: The Spread of Numeracy in Early America* (Chicago: University of Chicago Press, 1982), 117, 205.
41. "Investments," *Commercial and Financial Chronicle*, February 22, 1873.
42. "Briefkasten der Redaktion," *Berliner Tageblatt*, October 10, 1872.
43. "Briefkasten der Redaktion," *Berliner Tageblatt*, October 10, 5, 9, 15, 17, and 19, 1872.
44. "Über Kapitalanlage und Vermögensverwaltung," *Zeitschrift für Kapital und Rente* 10 (1874): 752f.
45. Hermann Reuchlin to H. H. Meier, May 7, 1872, in *Im Neuen Reich 1871–1890: Politische Briefe aus dem Nachlaß liberaler Parteiführer*, ed. Paul Wentzcke (Bonn: Kurt Schroeder, 1926), 49.
46. On trust as a lubricant of social relations in complex modern societies, see, for example, Anthony Giddens, *Consequences of Modernity* (Cambridge: Polity Press, 1991), 26–35; Niklas Luhmann, *Vertrauen. Ein Mechanismus der Reduktion sozialer Komplexität*, 2nd rev. ed. (Stuttgart: Ferdinand Enke, 1973), 25–27.
47. Henry Villard to Wright, January 2, 1872, Letter Book, vol. 1b, Henry Villard Collection, Baker Library, Harvard Business School.
48. Henry Villard to William Larson, July 18, 1872, Letter Book, vol. 1a, Henry Villard Collection, Baker Library, Harvard Business School.
49. Henry Villard to William Larson, February 10, 1874, Letter Book, vol. 1, Henry Villard Collection, Baker Library, Harvard Business School.
50. On Taylor, see Daniel Hodas, *The Business Career of Moses Taylor. Merchant, Finance Capitalist, and Industrialist* (New York: New York University Press, 1976).
51. Helen B. Des Chapelles to Moses Taylor, July 8, 1872, box 32, letters D, Moses Taylor Papers, New York Public Library (NYPL).
52. R. M. del Castillo to Moses Taylor, April 30, 1873, box 34, folder 'Castillo,' Moses Taylor Papers, NYPL.
53. Hodas, *Moses Taylor*, 22f.
54. E. A. Brooks to Moses Taylor, February 23, 1872, box 32, folder Be–Bu; L. G. de Heredia to Moses Taylor, February 5, 1872, box 32, letters H–I, Moses Taylor Papers, NYPL.
55. "Die Gründung von deutschen Banken im Jahr 1871," *Zeitschrift für Kapital und Rente* 8 (1872): 75.
56. "Houston and Texas Central," *Commercial and Financial Chronicle*, June 8, 1872. See also "Investments," *Commercial and Financial Chronicle*, January 4, 1873.

57. "A Useful and Honorable Enterprise," *Stockholder*, March 28, 1871; see also "Hannibal & St. Joseph RR," *Stockholder*, December 24, 1872.

58. Scott A. Sandage, *Born Losers: A History of Failure in America* (Cambridge, Mass.: Harvard University Press, 2005), 144.

59. Hartmut Berghoff, "Markterschließung und Risikomanagement: Die Rolle der Kreditauskunfteien und Agenturen im Industrialisierungs- und Globalisierungsprozess des 19. Jahrhunderts," *Vierteljahrsschrift für Sozial- und Wirtschaftsgeschichte* 92 (2005): 148–151; James H. Madison, "The Evolution of Commercial Credit Reporting Agencies in Nineteenth-Century America," *Business History Review* 48 (1974): 167; Rowena Olegario, *A Culture of Credit. Embedding Trust and Transparency in American Business* (Cambridge, Mass.: Harvard University Press, 2006), 2.

60. Berghoff, "Markterschließung und Risikomanagement": 156–158.

61. Monika Pohle Fraser, "Bankiers und 'Hasardeure'—Die Rolle bürgerlicher Tugenden im Bankgeschäft, 1800–1912," in *Bankiers und Finanziers—sozialgeschichtliche Aspekte*, ed. Harald Wixforth (Stuttgart: Franz Steiner, 2004), 57–79.

62. William Maden to Moses Taylor, June 24, 1873, box 34, folder M–Mc, Moses Taylor Papers, NYPL.

63. Richard Slotkin, *The Fatal Environment: The Myth of the Frontier in the Age of Industrialization, 1800–1890* (New York: Atheneum, 1985), 283–288.

64. For a discussion of similar issues in the British context, see Gary B. Magee and Andrew S. Thompson, *Empire and Globalisation: Networks of People, Goods and Capital in the British World, c. 1850–1914* (Cambridge: Cambridge University Press, 2010), 185–198.

65. White, *Railroaded*, 38.

66. Baskin, "Asymmetric Information," 215–219.

67. George Opdyke to Messrs. Yoke & Defer, March 21, 1872, Letter Book, March–May 1872, George Opdyke and Company records, New York Historical Society (NYHS).

68. George Opdyke to Messr. Wilson Colston & Co., March 15, 1872, Letter Book, March–May 1872, George Opdyke and Company records, NYHS.

69. Lance E. Davis and Robert J. Cull, "International Capital Movements, Domestic Capital Markets, and American Economic Growth, 1820–1914," in *The Cambridge Economic History of the United States*, vol. 2, ed. Stanley L. Engerman and Robert E. Gallman (Cambridge: Cambridge University Press, 2000), 784. Another reason, the authors argue, is that the NYSE imposed relatively strict trading rules, which prevented many companies from listing their stock there (see ibid.). More recently, Mary O'Sullivan has argued that listing requirements in the 1870s were "not nearly as demanding as has been claimed." See O'Sullivan, *Dividends of Development. Securities Markets in the History of US Capitalism, 1866–1922* (Oxford: Oxford University Press, 2016), 47.

70. Mira Wilkins, *The History of Foreign Investment in the United States to 1914* (Cambridge, Mass.: Harvard University Press, 1989), 110–115.

71. Ibid., 115; Henry Villard to Winslow, Lanier & Co., October 24, 1871, Letter Book, vol. 1b, Henry Villard Collection, Baker Library, Harvard Business School.

72. Ernst Hostmann, "Einige Betrachtungen über das Finanzwesen der Gegenwart," *Zeitschrift für Kapital und Rente* 8 (1872): 8 (emphasis in original).

73. April 20, 1870, Geheimes Staatsarchiv Preußischer Kulturbesitz, I. HA Rep. 120, Ministerium für Handel und Gewerbe, C IX 1, Nr. 28, Bd. 1, 40.

74. May 6, 1870, ibid., 42. The railroad defaulted the following year, see Jonas Minoprio, *Die Frankfurter Börse: Handbuch für Banquiers, Makler und Capitalisten enthaltend*

eingehende Erklärung aller an der Frankfurter Börse gültigen Usancen und gehandelten Papiere (Frankfurt am Main: F. Boselli'sche Buchhandlung, 1873), 353.

75. May 7, 1870, ibid., 51–55. (The files of the German consulate in New York during this period have not been preserved.)

76. "Frankfurter Börse," *Aktionär*, February 27, 1870.

77. "Frankfurter Börse," *Aktionär*, March 6, 1870.

78. Larson, *Jay Cooke*, 260–263, 295–298.

79. Ellis P. Oberholtzer, *Jay Cooke: Financier of the Civil War*, vol. 2 (Philadelphia: George W. Jacobs & Co., 1907), 214–223.

80. "Amerikanische Post," *Aktionär*, February 26, 1871.

81. Matthew Simon, *Cyclical Fluctuations and the International Capital Movements of the United States, 1865–1897* (New York: Arno Press, 1978), 162f.

82. Frh. v. Danckelmann, "Transatlantisches," *Zeitschrift für Kapital und Rente* 5 (1869): 303. German papers nevertheless occasionally relied on American newspaper articles. See, for example, the translation of an article from the *New York Daily Tribune* in *Berliner Börsen-Zeitung*, evening ed., December 5, 1871.

83. "Amerikanische Post," *Aktionär*, June 4, 1870.

84. Report dated November 25, 1874, New York, vol. 384, p. 500 Y, R. G. Dun & Co. Credit Report Volumes, Baker Library, Harvard Business School; Radu, *Auguren des Geldes*, 78.

85. According to Scott Mixon, informational barriers made European investors lose confidence in American bonds in 1872. But as the examples given show, the German investing public was very conscious of the informational asymmetry already in 1870. See Mixon, "The Crisis of 1873: Perspectives from Multiple Asset Classes," *Journal of Economic History* 68 (2008): 748–753.

86. "Frankfurter Börse," *Aktionär*, April 16, 1871. See also "Frankfurter Börse," *Aktionär*, October 1, 1871; "Berlin, 4. Januar," *Berliner Börsen-Zeitung*, evening ed., January 4, 1872. Frh. v. Danckelmann, "Die systematische Spoliation des Effektenbesitzes," *Zeitschrift für Kapital und Rente* 9 (1873): 45.

87. "Californien: Land und Leute; von Robert von Schlagintweit," *Aktionär*, October 1, 1871. Poor's statistical manual of American railroads, by contrast, received a highly unfavorable review. See "Poor's E.-B.-Handbuch," *Aktionär*, August 27, 1871.

88. Notable exceptions were made for mines, maritime companies, and banks. See, for example, Frh. v. Danckelmann, "Die Aktien und Obligationen der deutsch-österreichischen Dampfschiffahrts-Gesellschaften," *Zeitschrift für Kapital und Rente* 6 (1870): 6; "Die Gründung von deutschen Banken im Jahr 1871," *Zeitschrift für Kapital und Rente* 8 (1872): 74f.

89. Alexander Schmidt, *Reisen in die Moderne: Der Amerika-Diskurs des deutschen Bürgertums im europäischen Vergleich* (Berlin: Akademie Verlag, 1997), 91f.; Adam I. P. Smith, "Land of Opportunity?" in *America Imagined: Explaining the United States in Nineteenth-Century Europe and Latin America*, ed. Axel Körner, Nicola Miller, and Adam I. P. Smith (New York: Palgrave Macmillan, 2012), 38; Kenneth D. Rose, *Unspeakable Awfulness: America through the Eyes of European Travelers, 1865–1900* (New York: Routledge, 2014), 222–255. German travelers had written admiringly about the transcontinentals in the 1860s. See Hans Lange, *Die Wirtschaft der Vereinigten Staaten von Amerika in der Sicht des deutschen Reisenden* (PhD diss., Göttingen University, 1967), 20f.

90. *Aktionär*, June 25, 1871.

91. *Berliner Börsen-Zeitung*, evening ed., April 16, 1871.

92. "Frankfurter Börse," *Aktionär*, August 18, 1872.

93. Pamphlet dated July 16, 1870, quoted in Oberholtzer, *Jay Cooke*, 187.

94. S. McClean & Co. to H. Kreisman, October 10, 1870, RG 84, Records of Foreign Service Posts, Consular Posts, Berlin, Germany, vol. 014, National Archives, College Park, Maryland (emphasis in original).

95. Henry Villard to I. B. Thayer, December 11, 1871, Letter Book, vol. 1b, Henry Villard Collection, Baker Library, Harvard Business School.

96. White, *Railroaded*, 52.

97. William S. Hancock to Jay Cooke, January 11, 1870, quoted in Oberholtzer, *Jay Cooke*, 169f.

98. Roberts's Preliminary Report, dated Philadelphia, September 25, 1869, quoted in Oberholtzer, *Jay Cooke*, 156.

99. Ray Allen Billington, *Land of Savagery, Land of Promise: The European Image of the American Frontier in the Nineteenth Century* (New York: Norton, 1981), 129–140.

100. Walter Nugent, *Crossings: The Great Transatlantic Migrations, 1870–1914* (Bloomington: Indiana University Press, 1992), 63–72. A large number of German migrants during this period were rural inhabitants of the eastern provinces who intended to become independent farmers.

101. David Montgomery, *The Fall of the House of Labor: The Workplace, the State, and American Labor Activism, 1865–1925* (Cambridge: Cambridge University Press, 1987), 66; Walter Licht, *Working for the Railroad: The Organization of Work in the Nineteenth Century* (Princeton: Princeton University Press, 1983), 221–224.

102. White, *Railroaded*, 29f.; see also James H. Ducker, *Men of the Steel Rails: Workers on the Atchison, Topeka & Santa Fe Railroad, 1869–1900* (Lincoln: University of Nebraska Press, 1983), 27

103. Oberholtzer, *Jay Cooke*, 154.

104. John Maynard Keynes, *A General Theory of Employment, Interest, and Money* (London: Macmillan, 1936), 161f.

105. Jakob Tanner, "Wirtschaftskurven: Zur Visualisierung des anonymen Marktes," in *Ganz normale Bilder: Historische Beiträge zur visuellen Herstellung von Selbstverständlichkeit*, ed. David Gugerli and Barbara Orland (Zurich: Chronos, 2002), 144–148.

106. "Berliner Börse," *Aktionär*, March 6, 1870.

107. "Frankfurter Börse," *Aktionär*, April 3, 1870.

108. For a survey of reports on these topics in Berlin papers, see Koch, *Berliner Presse*, 137–152, 301–355.

109. "Statistik der Aktiengesellschaften," *Aktionär*, March 3, 1872, 1st suppl.

110. "Berlin, den 11. Ocotober," *Berliner Börsen-Zeitung*, evening ed., October 11, 1872; "Aus Westphalen," *Berliner Börsen-Zeitung*, evening ed., 1st suppl., October 3, 1872; *Berliner Börsen-Zeitung*, evening ed., March 15, 1872.

111. "Finanzieller Rückblick," *Presse*, December 30, 1871. For similar assessments see, for example, "Wien, den 31. December 1871," *Neue Freie Presse*, January 1, 1871; "Wiener Börsenwoche," *Neue Freie Presse*, December 31, 1871.

112. "Eisenbahnstatistik nach Ländern," *Presse*, August 26, 1871.

113. "Roundout and Oswego Railroad," *American Railroad Journal*, May 27, 1871.

114. "Railroad consolidation again successful," *Commercial and Financial Chronicle*, October 21, 1871.

115. The same arguments had been made in the 1850s and 1860s, see Chandler, *Henry Varnum Poor*, 95; Larson, *Jay Cooke*, 131.

116. This view of America echoed the ideology of American exceptionalism, see Dorothy Ross, *The Origins of American Social Science* (New York: Cambridge University Press, 2001), 22–50.
117. "Notes on the Money Market," *Bankers' Magazine*, July 1872.
118. "Railroad Investments," *Nation*, August 15, 1872.
119. Carl Gareis, *Die Börse und die Gründungen nebst Vorschlägen zur Reform des Börsenrechts und der Actiengesetzgebung* (Berlin: Habel, 1874), 24.
120. "Berlin, 13. Januar 1872," *Berliner Börsen-Zeitung*, evening ed., January 13, 1872. See also similar articles on January 5, 8, and 12, 1872 (all evening ed.).
121. "Berlin, 15. Januar," *Berliner Börsen-Zeitung*, evening ed., January 15, 1872.
122. This number is based on prospectuses in the *Börsen-Zeitung*'s evening ed. between April 18 and 24, 1871 and April, 2–8, 1872 respectively.
123. Fischer, *Zeitungsannonce*, 10f. Fischer notes that the downturn in advertising began in the first half of 1873, well before the crash.
124. "Vermischte Nachrichten (Der Reklameschwindel in Berlin)," *Aktionär*, September 22, 1872.
125. See the advertisements in *Presse*, March 1, 1872, 10. For other examples see Fischer, *Zeitungsannonce*, 53–74.
126. *Presse*, June 2, 1872, 10.
127. *Neue Freie Presse*, morning ed., November 1, 1872, 15.
128. The figures are 5, 6, 4, 4, and 4 for the issues of June 1, 8, 15, 22, and 29, 1871 respectively, and 11, 9, 8, and 7 for the issues of June 6, 13, 20, and 27, 1872 respectively. Some of the 1872 advertisements were by banks offering more than one type of bond.

3. Predicting and Experiencing the Panics of 1873

1. Gerson von Bleichröder to N. M. Rothschild and Sons, February 13, 1873, Rothschild Archive London (RAL) XI/64/0: 1873.
2. "Sucht, ohne Arbeit reich zu werden," *Berliner Tageblatt*, January 18, 1872. See also "A Plea for Resumption," *New York Times*, June 12, 1873.
3. Max Wirth, *Geschichte der Handelskrisen*, 2nd rev. and improved ed. (Frankfurt am Main: J. D. Sauerländer, 1874), 5.
4. Clément Juglar, *Des Crises commerciales et de leur retour périodique en France, en Angleterre et aux États-Unis* (Paris: Guillaume et Cie., 1862); Philippe Gilles, *Histoire des crises et des cycles économiques: Des crises industrielles du 19e siècle aux crises financières actuelles*, 2nd ed. (Paris: Armand Colin, 2009), 68–74.
5. Harald Hagemann, "Introduction," in *Business Cycle Theory: Selected Texts, 1860–1930*, vol. 1, ed. Harald Hagemann (London: Pickering & Chatto, 2002), xii; Jürgen Kromphardt, "Konjunktur- und Krisentheorie in der 2: Hälfte des 19. Jahrhunderts," in *Studien zur Entwicklung der ökonomischen Theorie*, vol. 7, ed. Bertram Schefold (Berlin: Duncker & Humblot, 1989), 13.
6. Harry E. Miller, "Earlier Theories of Crises and Cycles in the United States," *Quarterly Journal of Economics* 38 (1924): 312; Paul Barnett, *Business-Cycle Theory in the United States, 1860–1900* (Chicago: University of Chicago Press, 1941), 86–88. It was only in the late 1870s that, in the popular press at least, theories of underconsumption were to gain greater currency.
7. Max Wirth, *Geschichte der Handelskrisen*, 1st ed. (Frankfurt am Main, 1852), 151. Adolf Wagner in 1866 also emphasized the "growing globalization of capital." Vitantonio

Gioia, "Adolf Wagner: Economic Crises, Capitalism and Human Nature," in *Crises and Cycles in Economic Dictionaries and Encyclopaedias*, ed. Daniele Besomi (London: Routledge, 2012), 313f.

8. Juglar, *Crises commerciales*, 13 (translation mine).
9. Eugen von Bergmann, *Geschichte der nationalökonomischen Krisentheorien* (Stuttgart: W. Kohlhammer, 1895), 135f.
10. Juglar, *Crises commerciales*, 5 (translation mine); Henry Carey, *Financial Crises: Their Causes and Effects* (Philadelphia: Baird, 1860), 4.
11. Hans Pohl, *Aufbruch der Weltwirtschaft: Geschichte der Weltwirtschaft von der Mitte des 19. Jahrhunderts bis zum Ersten Weltkrieg* (Stuttgart: Franz Steiner, 1989), 20.
12. Herbert Blume, *Gründungszeit u. Gründungskrach mit Beziehung auf das deutsche Bankwesen* (Danzig: Kasemann, 1914), 27; Karl Helfferich, *Georg von Siemens: Ein Lebensbild aus Deutschlands großer Zeit*, vol. 1 (Berlin: Julius Springer, 1923), 220.
13. Ernst Hostmann, "Einige Betrachtungen über das Finanzwesen der Gegenwart," *Zeitschrift für Kapital und Rente* 8 (1872): 13.
14. "Die E.-B.-Bauten in den Vereinigten Staaten," *Aktionär*, 3rd suppl., October 2, 1872.
15. "Frankfurter Börse," *Aktionär*, October 6, 1872.
16. Werner Siemens to Wilhelm Siemens, September 21, 1872, in Conrad Matschoß, *Werner Siemens: Ein kurzgefaßtes Lebensbild nebst einer Auswahl seiner Briefe, aus Anlass der 100. Wiederkehr seines Geburtstages*, vol. 2 (Berlin: Julius Springer, 1916), 376f.; "Frankfurter Börse," *Aktionär*, November 17, 1872; "Berlin, den 3. Januar 1873," *Berliner Börsen-Zeitung*, January 3, 1873, evening ed., 9. On the French indemnity, see chapter 4.
17. Markus Baltzer, "Cross-Listed Stocks as an Information Vehicle of Speculation: Evidence from European Cross-Listings in the Early 1870s," *European Review of Economic History* 10 (2006): 301–327.
18. "Berlin, den 8. October 1872," *Berliner Börsen-Zeitung*, evening ed., October 8, 1872.
19. Gerson von Bleichröder to N. M. Rothschild and Sons, November 21, 1872, RAL XI/64/0: 1872.
20. "Berliner Cours-Bericht," *Berliner Tageblatt*, January 8, 1873.
21. "Volkswirthschaftliche Revue," *Oesterreicher Oekonomist*, January 4, 1873.
22. On Lasker's speech, see chapter 5.
23. Gerson von Bleichröder to N. M. Rothschild and Sons, April 19, 1873, RAL XI/64/0: 1873.
24. See, for example, "Wiener Börse vom 3. Januar 1872," *Neue Freie Presse*, morning ed., January 4, 1872.
25. "Die Börse gegenüber Handel und Industrie," *Oesterreichischer Oekonomist*, January 11, 1873.
26. Joseph Neuwirth, *Die Spekulationskrisis von 1873* (Leipzig: Duncker & Humblot, 1874), 75–82.
27. Jutta Pemsel, "Die Wiener Weltausstellung von 1873," in *Traum und Wirklichkeit: Wien, 1870–1930* (Vienna: Historisches Museum der Stadt Wien, 1985), 62–67.
28. Neuwirth, *Spekulationskrisis*, 83–99.
29. "Börsen- und Geldverhältnisse in Wien," *Berliner Börsen-Zeitung*, evening ed., May 9, 1873.
30. "Misstrauen," *Berliner Börsen-Zeitung*, evening ed., May 15, 1873.
31. Baltzer, *Berliner Kapitalmarkt*, 102.
32. "Frankfurter Börse," *Aktionär*, June 15, 1873.
33. Werner Siemens to Wilhelm Siemens, May 17, 1873, in Matschoß, *Werner Siemens*, 415.

34. "Berliner Börse," *Aktionär*, August 3, 1873.

35. Gerson von Bleichröder to N. M. Rothschild and Sons, August 26, 1873, RAL XI/64/0: 1873.

36. "Volkswirthschaftliche Revue: Die Chancen des Welthandels (aus dem 'Deutsch-amerikanischen Oekonomist')," *Oesterreichischer Oekonomist*, June 28, 1873; "Zur ökonomischen Situation," *Oesterreichischer Oekonomist*, July 5, 1873.

37. Ranald C. Michie, *The City of London: Continuity and Change, 1850–1990* (Basingstoke: Macmillan, 1992), 72–78.

38. Jay Sexton, *Debtor Diplomacy: Finance and American Foreign Relations in the Civil War Era, 1837–1873* (Oxford: Oxford University Press, 2005), 190–228.

39. "The Coming Financial Storm," *New York Times*, December 16, 1871. See also "Notes from England," *New York Times*, December 4, 1872.

40. "Our Financial Prophets and Their Vagaries," *Commercial and Financial Chronicle*, May 25, 1872; "Our Foreign Commerce and the Export of Gold," *Commercial and Financial Chronicle*, August 3, 1872.

41. "Our Railroads and Their Foreign Bondholders," *Commercial and Financial Chronicle*, December 21, 1871.

42. "German Capital and Our Money Market," *Commercial and Financial Chronicle*, January 11, 1873. See also "Notes on the Money Market," *Bankers' Magazine*, December 1872; "American Bonds in Germany," *Railroad Gazette*, August 2, 1873.

43. "The Money Market," *New York Tribune*, May 17, 1873.

44. "Financial," *Independent*, May 22, 1873. The article noted that while there was no direct connection between Vienna and New York, the latter might well be affected via Berlin or London.

45. August Belmont to N. M. Rothschild and Sons, May 13, 15, and 16, 1873, RAL XI/62/23B.

46. Clipping in Edward N. Tailer Diaries, entry of June 4, 1873, New York Historical Society (NYHS).

47. August Belmont to N. M. Rothschild and Sons, June 5, 1873, RAL XI/62/23B.

48. August Belmont to N. M. Rothschild and Sons, March 27, 1873, RAL XI/62/23A.

49. The Committee of the Treasury Minute Book, vol. 35, Bank of England Archive, does not record the reasoning behind this decision.

50. Scott Reynolds Nelson, *A Nation of Deadbeats: An Uncommon History of America's Financial Disasters* (New York: Alfred A. Knopf, 2012), 164. Nelson claims that the failure of the *Maklerbanken* was caused by their investments in Austro-Hungarian exports, which declined in value when large amounts of cheap American wheat entered the European markets and depressed prices. I have not been able to confirm this. It seems unlikely that these banks, specializing as they did in short-term transactions on the stock exchange, would have invested in export goods.

51. August Belmont to N. M. Rothschild and Sons, May 20 and 27, June 10, 1873, RAL XI/62/23B. Commercial paper rates in New York City averaged 11.4 percent in April, 8.12 percent in May, and 6.83 percent in June. See *Historical Statistics of the United States, 1789–1945* (Washington, DC: US Department of Commerce, 1949), 347.

52. "Money Market & City Intelligence," *Times* (London), August 22, 1873; "Money Market and City Intelligence," *Times* (London), September 26, 1873.

53. "The Vienna Panic," *New York Times*, June 12, 1873.

54. See chapter 4.

55. Irwin Unger, *The Greenback Era: A Social and Political History of American Finance, 1865–1879* (Princeton: Princeton University Press, 1964), 115; David M. Gische, "The New York City Banks and the Development of the National Banking System,

1860–1870," *American Journal of Legal History* 23 (1979): 29; R. McCarter to James B. Jermain, December 15, 1871, box 15, folder 28, Warshaw Collection of Business Americana, National Museum of American History.

56. Richard White, *Railroaded: The Transcontinentals and the Making of Modern America* (New York: Norton, 2011), 81.

57. J. P. Morgan Jr. to Pierpont Morgan, April 3, 1873, Letterpress Copybook 1873–1880, ARC 120, Pierpont Morgan Papers, Pierpont Morgan Library Archives.

58. "Financial Dangers," *Commercial and Financial Chronicle*, February 1, 1873; "Our Safeguards against Panic," *Commercial and Financial Chronicle*, April 26, 1873; "The Strength of Our Financial System," *Commercial and Financial Chronicle*, May 3, 1873; "The Languor of the Money Market," *Commercial and Financial Chronicle*, May 17, 1873; "How to Prevent Panics," *Commercial and Financial Chronicle*, June 21, 1873.

59. Oliver M. W. Sprague, *History of Crises under the National Banking System* (Washington, DC: Government Printing Office, 1910), 32f.

60. "Notes on the Money Market," *Bankers' Magazine*, August 1873.

61. Henrietta M. Larson, *Jay Cooke: Private Banker* (Cambridge, Mass.: Harvard University Press, 1936), 323, 340f.; Ellis P. Oberholtzer, *Jay Cooke: Financier of the Civil War*, vol. 2 (Philadelphia: George W. Jacobs, 1907), 233–235.

62. Michael J. Lubetkin, *Jay Cooke's Gamble: The Northern Pacific Railroad, the Sioux, and the Panic of 1873* (Norman: University of Oklahoma Press, 2006), 270.

63. White, *Railroaded*, 81; Lees & Waller to Mills, Ralston, and Bell, December 7, 1872, quoted in ibid., 79; C. P. Huntington to M. Hopkins, March 10 and 19, 1871, quoted in ibid., 82.

64. Lubetkin, *Jay Cooke's Gamble*, 93, 103, 113, 138–142, 160, 182–184, 244ff.

65. Larson, *Jay Cooke*, 396f.

66. "Wall Street," *New York Commercial Advertiser*, September 15, 1873.

67. "The Panic," *New York Times*, September 19, 1873.

68. Vincent P. Carosso, *The Morgans: Private International Bankers, 1854–1913* (Cambridge, Mass.: Harvard University Press, 1987), 181.

69. Allan Nevins and Milton Halsey Thomas, eds., *The Diary of George Templeton Strong: Post-war Years, 1865–1875* (New York: Macmillan, 1952), entry of September 19, 1873.

70. Gische, "New York City Banks," 54; Elmus Wicker, *Banking Panics of the Gilded Age* (Cambridge: Cambridge University Press), 2.

71. Unger, *Greenback Era*, 214.

72. Sprague, *History of Crises*, 47. In 1873, Boston, Baltimore, Cincinnati, St. Louis, and New Orleans, for the first time, also made use of the loan certificate system. See Fritz Redlich, *The Molding of American Banking: Men and Ideas*, part 2, *1840–1910* (New York: Hafner, 1951), 164f.

73. "How It Commenced," *Stockholder*, September 23, 1873. Informal trading continued outside the NYSE's premises.

74. The argument that the clearing house's "power to equalize or pool the reserves of the NYCH banks" effectively turned it into a central bank was first made by Sprague. More recently, this argument has been further elaborated by Wicker who argues that while in 1873, the stock of total reserves was inadequate, the suspension of cash payments was "probably unnecessary, but, given the knowledge available, understandable." See Wicker, *Banking Panics*, xiv, 17.

75. George Opdyke to A. M. Palmer, September 18, 1873, Letter Book, September–December 1873, George Opdyke and Company records, NYHS.

76. "The Panic," *New York Times*, September 19, 1873.

77. "Lying Rumors and Conservative Journalism," *New York Journal of Commerce*, September 25, 1873.

78. See the letters to various correspondents in Opdyke's Letter Book, September–December 1873, 36, 38, 39, 66, 73, and others, George Opdyke and Company records, NYHS.

79. George Opdyke to J. H. Gould, September 30, 1873, Letter Book, September–December 1873, George Opdyke and Company records, NYHS.

80. George Opdyke to J. D. Knox, September 30, 1873, Letter Book, September–December 1873, George Opdyke and Company records, NYHS.

81. August Belmont to N. M. Rothschild and Sons, September 23, 1873, RAL XI/62/23C.

82. See chapter 1. Belmont was known on Wall Street for his sexual prowess. See Steve Fraser, *Wall Street: A Cultural History* (London: Faber & Faber), 88.

83. Edwin J. Perkins, "In the Eyes of the Storm: Isaac Seligman and the Panic of 1873," *Business History* 56 (2014): 1137.

84. Strong, Diary, entries of September 22 and 23, 1873; M. Taylor to Federico Alter, September 25, 1873, box 60, Letter Book, August 11–November 18 1873, Moses Taylor Papers, New York Public Library (NYPL); Simon F. Mackie to [illegible], September 25, 1873, Letter Book, March 1873–January 1874, Robert Mackie and Son records, NYHS.

85. Moses Taylor to Heidegger Trelles & Co., September 30, 1873, box 60, Letter Book, August 11–November 18, 1873, Moses Taylor Papers, NYPL.

86. Wicker, *Banking Panics*, 21. Despite the fact that New York banks continued to freely advance funds to country banks, the degree of loan and deposit contraction experienced by national banks in the interior turned out to be twice as large as that of their counterparts in New York. See ibid.

87. "Akron Items," *Daily Cleveland Herald*, September 27, 1873.

88. "The Financial Crisis," *Daily Arkansas Gazette*, September 27, 1873; "From Louisville," *Daily Arkansas Gazette*, September 28, 1873.

89. "French Gossip," *New York Times*, October 6, 1873.

90. Ibid.

91. Letter dated September 30, 1873, Records of Foreign Service Posts, Diplomatic Posts, Germany, vol. 207, National Archives, College Park, Maryland.

92. On contemporary, often contradictory, assessments of telegraphy's role during the panic, see Hannah Catherine Davies, "Spreading Fear, Communicating Trust: Writing Letters and Telegrams during the Panic of 1873," *History and Technology* 32 (2016): 159–177; Dwayne Winseck, "Double-Edged Swords: Communications Media and the Global Financial Crisis of 1873," in *International Communication and Global News Networks. Historical Perspectives*, ed. Peter Putnis, Chandrika Kaul and Jürgen Wilke (New York: Hampton Press, 2011), 55–81.

93. "Berlin, den 20. September 1873," *Berliner Börsen-Zeitung*, evening ed., September 20, 1873.

94. "Berliner Börse," *Vossische Zeitung*, September 20, 1873.

95. "Wiener Börse," *Neue Freie Presse*, morning ed., September 26, 1873.

96. "Berliner Börse," *Vossische Zeitung*, September 22, 1873.

97. "Der amerikanische Krach" *Oesterreichischer Oekonomist*, September 27, 1873.

98. "Der amerikanische Krach," *Aktionär*, September 28, 1873.

99. The BOE adjusted its rate a total of twenty-four times in 1873, and six times alone between September and November 1873 in order to prevent an excessive drain of gold from its vaults. The rate peaked at 9 percent in November. See John Clapham, *The Bank*

of England: A History, vol. 2 (Cambridge: Cambridge University Press, 1970 [1944]), 293–298.

100. "Business Notes," Economist, September 27, 1873.
101. "Wien, 20. September," Neue Freie Presse, morning ed., September 21, 1873.
102. "Berlin, den 23. September 1873," Berliner Börsen-Zeitung, evening ed., September 23, 1873; "Berliner Börse," Vossische Zeitung, September 24, 1873; "Deutsches Reich," Rostocker Zeitung, October 9, 1873; "Preußische Bank," Neue Freie Presse, morning ed., October 18, 1873.
103. "Quistorp'sche Institute," Berliner Börsen-Zeitung, evening ed., September 30, 1873.
104. "Handels- und Verkehrsnachrichten," Vossische Zeitung, October 8, 1873.
105. "Handels- und Verkehrsnachrichten," Vossische Zeitung, October 11, 1873; "Banken," Vossische Zeitung, October 15, 1873.
106. Quistorp had not, in fact, emigrated to the United States to return in 1867. Rather, he had gone into business with his brother, the successful entrepreneur Johannes Quistorp, in 1866, before embarking on his own projects two years later. See Willy Bark, Chronik von Alt-Westend, mit Schloß Ruhwald, Spandauer Bock und Fürstenbrunn (F. G. Mittler & Sohn: Berlin 1937), 30; Friedrich Bartels, "Kommerzienrat Johannes Quistorp," Pommern: Zeitschrift für Kultur und Geschichte 51 (2013): 40–46.
107. "Die Quistorp-Affaire," Neue Freie Presse, morning ed., October 10, 1873.
108. On "German capitalism," see Volker R. Berghahn, "Das 'deutsche Kapitalismus-Modell' in Geschichte und Geschichtswissenschaft," in Gibt es einen deutschen Kapitalismus? Tradition und globale Perspektiven der sozialen Marktwirtschaft, ed. Volker R. Berghahn and Sigurt Vitols (Frankfurt am Main: Campus, 2006), 23–43. In fact, the twenty-nine corporations the Quistorp Bank had founded and promoted were active not only in real estate construction but also in transport and industry. See Wirth, Geschichte der Handelskrisen (1874), 527f.
109. "Industrie und Handel," Berliner Tageblatt, October 4, 1874; "Falliments in Süddeutschland," Berliner Tageblatt, October 8, 1873; "Mecklenburgische Nachrichten," Rostocker Zeitung, October 11, 1873; Wirth, Geschichte der Handelskrisen (1874), 658.
110. "Die amerikanische Krise," Neue Freie Presse, morning ed., October 2, 1873.
111. "Wiener Börsenwoche," Neue Freie Presse, morning ed., September 28, 1873.
112. "Wiener Börsenwoche," Neue Freie Presse, morning ed., October 5, 1873.
113. "Zur Lage," Neue Freie Presse, morning ed., October 17, 1873.
114. "Der bisherige Verlauf der Krise," Oesterreichischer Oekonomist, October 4, 1873.
115. "Die amerikanische Krise," Neue Freie Presse, morning ed., September 23, 1873.
116. "Wiener Börsenwoche," Neue Freie Presse, morning ed., September 28, 1873.
117. Neuwirth, Spekulationskrisis, 173, 177, 187f.; Eduard März, Österreichische Industrie- und Bankpolitik in der Zeit Franz Josephs I: Am Beispiel der k. k. priv. Österreichischen Credit-Anstalt (Vienna: Europa-Verlag, 1968), 181.
118. "Probable Effects of the Panic in Europe," New York Journal of Commerce, October 4, 1873.
119. August Belmont to N. M. Rothschild and Sons, October 30, 1873, RAL XI/62/23D.
120. "Abroad," Chicago Tribune, September 29, 1873.
121. "A Big Failure in Berlin," Daily Evening Bulletin, November 19, 1873.
122. Margaret Schabas, The Natural Origins of Economics (Chicago: University of Chicago Press, 2005), 119–141; Nicolas Barreyre, Gold and Freedom: The Political Economy of Reconstruction (Charlottesville: University of Virginia Press, 2015), 71.
123. "Is the Outlook Hopeful?," Commercial and Financial Chronicle, September 20, 1873
124. Wicker, Banking Panics, 11.

125. Thomas Ewing to J. P. Weethie, September 22, 1873, Letter Book, March 10, 1873–October 20, 1874, Thomas Ewing Family Papers, Library of Congress; Alexander Brown to R. Hutting, September 27, 1873, Letter Book, August 18–November 10, 1873, box 58, Alexander Brown & Sons records, Library of Congress.

126. George Opdyke to M. B. Bonnifield, October 7, 1873; George Opdyke to Fox, Lyster and Roe, November 7, 1873, Letter Book, September–December 1873, George Opdyke and Company records, NYHS.

127. August Belmont to N. M. Rothschild and Sons, September 26, 1873, RAL XI/62/23C.

128. Alexander Brown to William Lamb, October 3, 1873, Letter Book, August 18–November 10, 1873, box 58, Alexander Brown & Sons records, Library of Congress.

129. August Belmont to N. M. Rothschild and Sons, October 7, 1873, RAL XI/62/23D.

130. "What Will Congress Do?," *Stockholder*, November 4, 1873.

131. Edward Neufville Tailer, Diary, entries of November 3 and December 30, 1873, and January 24, 1874, NYHS.

132. On the history and function of epistolary begging, see Scott Sandage, *Born Losers: A History of Failure in America* (Cambridge, Mass.: Harvard University Press, 2005), 228–251.

133. H. C. Conant to Alexander T. Stewart, January 15, 1874, box 10, folder 3; H. Young to Alexander T. Stewart, February 24, 1874, box 10, folder 6; C. W. Porter to Alexander T. Stewart, March 24, 1874, box 11, folder 1, Alexander Turney Stewart correspondence, NYPL.

134. According to Sandage, "epistolary begging letters employed the impersonal modes of human interaction that coincided with the integration of a national economy." See Sandage, *Born Losers*, 246.

135. J. Adam Tooze, *Statistics and the German State, 1900–1945: The Making of Modern Economic Knowledge* (Cambridge: Cambridge University Press, 2001), 10. See also Timothy Mitchell, "Economics. Economists and the Economy in the Twentieth Century," in *The Politics of Method in the Human Sciences*, ed. George Steinmetz (Durham, NC: Duke University Press, 2005), 126–141.

136. "Der amerikanische Krach," *Oesterreichischer Oekonomist*, September 27, 1873.

4. Flows of Paper, Flows of Gold: Theorizing the Panics

1. J. Adam Tooze, *Statistics and the German State, 1900–1945: The Making of Modern Economic Knowledge* (Cambridge: Cambridge University Press, 2001), 33.

2. Wilhelm I to Heinrich Achenbach, October 5, 1873, Nachlass Achenbach, Stadtarchiv Siegen.

3. "Staatshülfe für preußische Spekulanten," *Neuer Social-Demokrat*, October 1, 1873.

4. Lothar Höbelt, "Gründerzeit und Börsenschwindel: Politik und Wirtschaft in der liberalen Ära," in *Korruption in Österreich. Historische Streiflichter*, ed. Ernst Bruckmüller (Vienna: Wilhelm Braumüller, 2011), 78; Pieter Judson, *Exclusive Revolutionaries: Liberal Politics, Social Experience, and National Identity in the Austrian Empire* (Ann Arbor: University of Michigan Press, 1996), 176. On Austrian Liberals' subsequent disenchantment with free market principles, see ibid., 180f., and Wilhelm Wadl, *Liberalismus und soziale Frage in Österreich: Deutschliberale Reaktionen und Einflüsse auf die frühe österreichische Arbeiterbewegung* (Vienna: Verlag der Österreichischen Akademie der Wissenschaften, 1987), 145.

176 4. Flows of Paper, Flows of Gold

5. Edward Chase Kirkland, *Dream and Thought in the Business Community, 1860–1900* (Ithaca: Cornell University Press, 1956), 1–28; Walter T. K. Nugent, *Money and American Society, 1865–1880* (New York: Free Press, 1968), 26 (quotation).

6. See, for example, August Belmont to N. M. Rothschild and Sons, September 23, 1873, Rothschild Archive, London (RAL) XI/62/23C; "Will Wall Street Recover?," *Commercial and Financial Chronicle*, September 27, 1873.

7. Erwin Nasse, "Ueber die Verhütung der Produktionskrisen durch staatliche Fürsorge," *Jahrbuch für Gesetzgebung, Verwaltung und Volkswirtschaft im Deutschen Reich* 3 (1879): 174. See also Max Wirth, *Geschichte der Handelskrisen*, 2nd ed. (Frankfurt am Main: Sauerländer, 1874), xxi; John G. Sproat, *"The Best Men": Liberal Reformers in the Gilded Age* (New York: Oxford University Press, 1968), 8, 151.

8. Irwin Unger, *The Greenback Era: A Social and Political History of American Finance, 1865–1879* (Princeton: Princeton University Press, 1964), 3. For an account that examines both Reconstruction and the money question in their myriad intersections see Nicolas Barreyre, *Gold and Freedom: The Political Economy of Reconstruction* (Charlottesville: University of Virginia Press, 2015).

9. Unger, *Greenback Era*, 44–50, 60–68; Robert Sharkey, *Money, Class, and Party: An Economic Study of Civil War and Reconstruction* (Baltimore: Johns Hopkins University Press, 1959), 105–111, 221–267; Gretchen Ritter, *Goldbugs and Greenbacks: The Antimonopoly Tradition and the Politics of Finance in America* (Cambridge: Cambridge University Press, 1997), 5

10. Unger, *Greenback Era*, 46.

11. Richard F. Bensel, *Yankee Leviathan: The Origins of Central State Authority in America, 1859–1877* (Cambridge: Cambridge University Press, 1990), 318.

12. Charles Calomiris, "Greenback Resumption and Silver Risk: The Economics and Politics of Monetary Regime Change in the United States, 1862–1900," in *Monetary Regimes in Transition*, ed. Michael D. Bordo and Forrest Capie (Cambridge: Cambridge University Press, 1994), 96.

13. Nicolas Barreyre, "The Politics of Economic Crisis: The Panic of 1873, the End of Reconstruction and the Realignment of American Politics," *Journal of the Gilded Age and Progressive Era* 10 (2011), 413; Francis A. Walker, *International Bimetallism* (New York: Henry Holt, 1896), 177.

14. Anonymous, *The Finances: Panics and Specie Payments, "Facts Speak"* (Philadelphia: John Campbell & Son, 1874), iii, 9, 18; "Our Currency," *American Manufacturer and Iron World*, November 6, 1873.

15. Paul Keith Conkin, *Prophets of Prosperity: America's First Political Economists* (Bloomington: Indiana University Press, 1980), 303f.; Jeffrey Sklansky, *The Soul's Economy: Market Society and Selfhood in American Thought, 1820–1920* (Chapel Hill: University of North Carolina Press, 2002), 80–90.

16. Ritter, *Goldbugs and Greenbacks*, 96, 101; Barreyre, *Gold and Freedom*, 68.

17. Walter Benn Michaels, *The Gold Standard and the Logic of Naturalism* (Berkeley: University of California Press, 1987), 147f.

18. David Anthony, *Paper Money Men: Commerce, Manhood, and the Sensational Public Sphere in Antebellum America* (Columbus: Ohio State University Press, 2009), 21, 30.

19. Quoted in Nugent, *Money and American Society*, 36.

20. John Eadie, *Panics in the Money Market and Recovery from Their Effect: Being an Inquiry into the Practical Working of the Monetary Systems of America and Europe, Past and Present, and the Phenomena of Speculations, Revulsions and Panics* (New York: J. M. Amerman, 1873), 8.

21. See, for example, William G. Sumner, *A History of American Currency* (New York: Henry Holt, 1875), 250 and passim; Secretary Babcock to the United States Senate, December 7, 1874, *Journal of the Senate of the United States*, vol. 70, 9.

22. "Lessons of the American Monetary Crisis," *Economist*, September 27, 1873. The passage was quoted affirmatively in "The Week," *Nation*, October 9, 1873.

23. As was common in the nineteenth century, this view failed to take into account deposits and monetary substitutes. See Unger, *Greenback Era*, 36f.

24. "The Currency and the Panic," *Bankers' Magazine*, February 1, 1875.

25. "Die amerikanische Krise," *Neue Freie Presse*, morning ed., October 2, 1873.

26. Reinhard Kamitz, "Die österreichische Geld- und Währungspolitik von 1848 bis 1948," in *Hundert Jahre österreichischer Wirtschaftsentwicklung*, ed. Hans Mayer (Vienna: Springer, 1949), 143; Herbert Matis, *Österreichs Wirtschaft 1848–1913: Konjunkturelle Dynamik und gesellschaftlicher Wandel im Zeitalter Franz Josephs I* (Berlin: Duncker & Humblot, 1972), 155–158. Some contemporaries believed that deflation had harmed Austria's economy. While some historians concur with this assessment, others stress the role of nonmonetary factors. See Clemens Jobst, *Die Bank, Das Geld, Der Staat: Nationalbank und Währungspolitik in Österreich 1816–2016* (Frankfurt am Main: Campus, 2016), 81.

27. Joseph Neuwirth, *Die Spekulationskrisis von 1873* (Leipzig: Duncker & Humblot, 1874), 372f.

28. Ibid., 372.

29. Bruno Weber, *Einige Ursachen der Wiener Krisis vom Jahre 1873* (Leipzig: Veit, 1874), 26; Moritz Linder, *Die Asche der Millionen: Vor, während und nach der Krise vom Jahre 1873* (Vienna: Wilhelm Frick, 1883), 103; Walther Lotz, "Die Währungsfrage in Oesterreich-Ungarn und ihre wirtschaftliche und politische Bedeutung," *Jahrbuch für Gesetzgebung, Verwaltung und Volkswirtschaft im Deutschen Reich* 13 (1889): 38.

30. According to Yeager, the Austrian case in the nineteenth century shows that fluctuating exchange rates and economic integration are not mutually exclusive. See L. B. Yeager, "Fluctuating Exchange Rates in the Nineteenth Century: The Experience of Austria and Russia," in *Monetary Problems of the International Economy*, ed. Robert A. Mundell and Alexander K. Swoboda (Chicago: University of Chicago Press: 1969), 61–89.

31. Karl Helfferich, *Geschichte der deutschen Geldreform*, vol. 1 (Leipzig: Duncker & Humblot, 1898), 235.

32. Quoted in Stanley Zucker, *Ludwig Bamberger. German Liberal Politician and Social Critic, 1823–1899* (Pittsburgh: University of Pittsburgh Press, 1975), 65.

33. Luca Einaudi, *Money and Politics: European Monetary Unification and the International Gold Standard (1865–1873)* (Oxford: Oxford University Press, 2001), 172–174. Modern econometric analysis suggests that these qualms were well founded. See Walter E. Huffman and James R. Lothian, "The Gold Standard and the Transmission of Business Cycles, 1833–1932," in *A Retrospective on the Classical Gold Standard, 1821–1931*, ed. Michael D. Bordo and Anna J. Schwartz (Chicago: University of Chicago Press, 1984), 455–507. Bank officials also feared reductions of dividends, increased international competition, and a loss of profits from the issue of paper money. See Einaudi, *Money and Politics*, 176.

34. Markus Baltzer, *Der Berliner Kapitalmarkt nach der Reichsgründung 1871: Gründerzeit, internationale Finanzmarktintegration und der Einfluss der Makroökonomie* (Berlin: Peter Lang, 2007), 5ff.; Ulrich Nocken, "Die Große Deflation: Goldstandard, Geldmenge und Preise in den USA und Deutschland 1870 bis 1896," in *Geld und*

Währung vom 16. Jahrhundert bis zur Gegenwart, ed. Eckart Schremmer (Stuttgart: Franz Steiner, 1993), 182; Anja Weigt, *Der deutsche Kapitalmarkt vor dem Ersten Weltkrieg—Gründerboom, Gründerkrise und Effizienz des deutschen Aktienmarktes bis 1914* (Frankfurt am Main: Knapp, 2005), 11f. It should be noted, however, that by October 1873, only 2.5 to 3 billion (out of 5 billion francs) can be said to have had a direct impact on German capital markets. See Gömmel, "Effektenbörsen," 154.

35. Ludwig Bamberger, "Die fünf Milliarden," *Preußische Jahrbücher* 31 (1873): 441–460; Adolf Soetbeer, *Die 5 Milliarden. Betrachtungen über die Folgen der großen Kriegsentschädigung für die Wirtschaftsverhältnisse Frankreichs und Deutschlands* (Berlin: Habel, 1874); Adolf Berliner, *Die wirtschaftliche Krisis, ihre Ursachen und ihre Entwicklung* (Hannover: Carl Meyer, 1878), 39.

36. Wirth, *Geschichte der Handelskrisen*, 4th ed. (Frankfurt am Main: J. D. Sauerländer, 1890), 458f.; Wilhelm Oechelhaeuser, *Die wirtschaftliche Krisis* (Berlin: Springer, 1876), 52–55, 70; Berliner, *Krisis*, 46. On German banks of issue, see Knut Borchardt, "Währung und Wirtschaft," in *Währung und Wirtschaft in Deutschland 1876–1975*, ed. Deutsche Bundesbank (Frankfurt am Main: Knapp, 1976), 10–12.

37. "Our Currency," *American Manufacturer and Iron World*, November 6, 1873.

38. Nasse, "Ueber die Verhütung der Produktionskrisen," 177, 181f., 186.

39. There were some exceptions but these were few and far between. See, for example, Joh. H. Becker, *Das Wesen des Geldes: Eine Studie über die Ursachen der Krisis* (Berlin, 1879). A broader German movement in favor of an expansion of the money supply would only develop in the 1880s. See Jörg Lichter, "Goldwährung oder Doppelwährung. Der Bimetallismusstreit im Deutschen Reich 1880 bis 1895," *Bankhistorisches Archiv* 22 (1996): 86–107.

40. According to the "consensus" view on the spread of the gold standard, "the movement to gold post-1873 was pragmatic at best, probably accidental, and certainly without careful deliberation by the international economic community." Ted Wilson, *Battles for the Standard. Bimetallism and the Spread of the Gold Standard in the Nineteenth Century* (Aldershot: Ashgate, 2000), 8.

41. Both international coinage and bimetallism, by contrast, would have necessitated an international multilateral agreement. See Martin H. Geyer, "One Language for the World: The Metric System, International Coinage, and the Rise of Internationalism, 1850–1900," in *The Mechanics of Internationalism: Culture, Society, and Politics from the 1840s to the First World War*, ed. Martin Geyer and Johannes Paulmann (Oxford: Oxford University Press, 2001), 89.

42. Guido Thiemeyer, "Die deutschen Liberalen, die Reichsgründung und die Entstehung des internationalen Goldstandards 1870–1873," in *Geschichte der internationalen Beziehungen: Erneuerung und Erweiterung einer historischen Disziplin*, ed. Eckart Conze (Cologne: Böhlau, 2004), 149.

43. This observation is not incompatible with Gallarotti's argument that the decision by several countries to adopt gold as their currency was a function of domestic institutions and preferences. See Guido M. Gallarotti, "The Scramble for Gold: Monetary Regime Transformation in the 1870s," in *Monetary Regimes in Transition*, ed. Michael D. Bordo and Forest Capie (Cambridge: Cambridge University Press, 1994), 17.

44. Bensel, *Yankee Leviathan*, 239–252, 264, 277, 294f. Bensel argues that American financiers' disappointment with Secretary Richardson led them to conclude that their interests would be better served if the management of the money supply were left to the BOE. It was this line of reasoning that explains their support of resumption. But

one must be cautious in equating their progold stance with confidence in the BOE's superior monetary policy skills. The primary sources cited by Bensel, indeed, make no mention of the BOE. It was a marked feature of the dominant model of global specie flows that it was couched in terms of immutable laws and disregarded the autonomous role of institutions.

45. John A. James, *Money and Capital Markets in Postbellum America* (Princeton: Princeton University Press, 1978).

46. Christopher L. Hill, *National History and the World of Nations: Capital, State, and the Rhetoric of History in Japan, France, and the United States* (Durham: Duke University Press, 2008), 270.

47. Geyer, "One Language for the World," 56; Martin H. Geyer and Johannes Paulmann, "Introduction: The Mechanics of Internationalism," in *The Mechanics of Internationalism: Culture, Society, and Politics from the 1840s to the First World War*, ed. Martin H. Geyer and Johannes Paulmann (Oxford: Oxford University Press, 2001), 1–25.

48. See, for example, "The Low Value of Silver and Its Effects on India," *Littell's Living Age*, March 4, 1876; Wilson, *Battles for the Standard*, 147–150.

49. Eadie, *Panics in the Money Market*, 41.

50. For a rare exception see "The Failures in England and Their Influence Here," *Commercial and Financial Chronicle*, June 19, 1875.

51. Franz Stöpel, *Die Handelskrisis in Deutschland* (Frankfurt am Main: Expedition des "Merkur," 1875), 7.

52. Julius Faucher, "Kurze Wechselziele zur Vorbeugung der Handelskrisen," *Vierteljahrschrift für Volkswirthschaft, Politik und Kulturgeschichte* 45 (1875): 21, 24.

53. See chapter 3.

54. A worldwide gold standard exacerbated international competition since it precluded the possibility of currency depreciation.

55. Andreas Etges, *Wirtschaftsnationalismus: USA und Deutschland im Vergleich (1815–1914)* (Frankfurt am Main: Campus, 1999), 309; Marc-William Palen, *The "Conspiracy" of Free Trade: The Anglo-American Struggle over Empire and Economic Globalization, 1846–1896* (Cambridge: Cambridge University Press, 2016), 84 and passim; Judson, *Exclusive Revolutionaries*, 180–183; Ivo Nikolai Lambi, *Free Trade and Protectionism in Germany, 1868–1879* (Wiesbaden: Franz Steiner, 1963), 96.

56. Wilhelm von Kardorff-Wabnitz, *Gegen den Strom! Eine Kritik der Handelspolitik des deutschen Reichs an der Hand der Carey'schen Forderungen* (Berlin: Springer, 1875), 45.

57. Steven P. Reti, *Silver and Gold: The Political Economy of International Monetary Conferences, 1867–1892* (Westport: Greenwood Press, 1998), 104.

58. Dieter Lindenlaub, "Die Glaubwürdigkeit einer neuen Währung: Die Einführung der Mark in Deutschland 1871–1876," *Bankhistorisches Archiv* 28 (2002): 21–39.

59. Matis, *Österreichs Wirtschaft*, 315f.

60. Harald Winkel, "Die Entwicklung der Geldtheorie in der deutschen Nationalökonomie des 19. Jahrhunderts und die Gründung der Reichsbank," in *Wissenschaft und Kodifikation des Privatrechts im 19: Jahrhundert*, vol. 5, ed. Helmut Coing and Walter Wilhelm (Frankfurt am Main: Klostermann, 1980), 21.

61. Gallarotti, "Scramble for Gold," 45.

62. Lichter, "Goldwährung oder Doppelwährung," 98f.

63. Hugh Rockoff, "Banking and Finance, 1789–1914," in *The Cambridge Economic History of the United States*, vol. 2, ed. Stanley L. Engerman and Robert E. Gallman (Cambridge: Cambridge University Press, 2000), 673.

64. "Our Credit Abroad: A Letter from Mr. George Bancroft to the Secretary of State," *Bankers' Magazine*, June 1874.

65. "The Foreign Indebtedness of the United States," *Harper's New Monthly Magazine*, June 1, 1879.

66. "Foreign Capital and Recuperation from Panics," *Commercial and Financial Chronicle*, April 10, 1875.

67. "Prospects of the Fall Trade," *Bankers' Magazine*, October 1874.

68. Frh. v. Danckelmann, "Kapitalanlage in ausländischen Wertpapieren," *Zeitschrift für Kapital und Rente* (1875).

69. Frh. v. Danckelmann, "Kosmopolitismus des englischen Kapitals," *Zeitschrift für Kapital und Rente* (1875).

70. "American Indebtedness Held in Europe," *Bankers' Magazine*, September 1878. For a more skeptical view of capital exports see Berliner, *Wirthschaftliche Krisis*, 21–26, 32. The American Greenback Party, which enjoyed a brief heyday in the second half of the 1870s, called for an end to foreign investment. See Wilson, *Battles for the Standard*, 92.

71. Max Wirth, *Die Reform der Umlaufsmittel im Deutschen Reiche: Ein Nachtrag zur "Geschichte der Handelskrisen"* (Frankfurt am Main, 1875), 1. For a similar assessment see "Ein Rückblick," *Zeitschrift für Kapital und Rente* 9 (1873), 678.

72. Wirth, *Geschichte der Handelskrisen*, 1874, 435ff., 455, 550.

73. Neuwirth, *Spekulationskrisis*, 172.

74. The same is true of Linder, *Die Asche der Millionen*. Other countries are briefly mentioned (9f.), but the main focus is on Austria.

75. Charles Franklin Dunbar, "Economic Science in America," *North American Review*, January 1876 (reprinted in Charles Franklin Dunbar, *Economic Essays*, ed. Oliver W. Sprague (London: Macmillan, 1904), 1–29.

76. "The Dullness of Business and Its Remedies," *Commercial and Financial Chronicle*, May 16, 1874.

77. "The Revival of Commercial Activity," *Bankers' Magazine*, May 1877.

78. "A Few Words about Some Recent Events," *Galaxy*, December 1873.

79. Horace White, "The Financial Crisis in America," *Fortnightly Review*, June 1876. See also Horace White, "Commercial Crises," in *Lalor's Cyclopedia of Political Science, Political Economy and Political History of the United States*, ed. John J. Lalor (New York: Maynard, Merrill, 1881), 524–530.

80. Otto Glagau, "Der Börsen- und Gründungsschwindel in Berlin: Gesammelte und stark vermehrte Artikel der 'Gartenlaube,'" vol. 1 (Leipzig: Frohberg, 1876), xv, 1ff. On Glagau, see also chapter 5.

81. Berliner, *Wirthschaftliche Krisis*, 15, 27, 45.

82. Albert Schäffle, "Der 'grosse Börsenkrach' des Jahres 1873," *Zeitschrift für die gesamte Staatswissenschaft* 30 (1874): 68, 74, 92.

83. On this, see also Linder, *Asche der Millionen*, 12.

84. Weber, *Ursachen der Wiener Krisis*, 5f., 113.

85. H. v. Marschall, "Ursache und Verlauf der Wiener Börsen-Katastrophe," *Welthandel* (1874), 1–6. See also Anton Wilhelm Neydl, *Die wirthschaftlichen Zustände Oesterreichs: Vortrag gehalten im Handels- und Gewerbe-Vereine Sechshaus* (Vienna: A. Hartleben, 1876), 18f., 42.

86. Wirth, *Geschichte der Handelskrisen*, 1870, 697–701.

87. "Prospects of the Fall Trade," *Bankers' Magazine*, October 1874.

88. "Bonamy Price on the Causation of Panics," *Bankers' Magazine*, November 1874; Daniel Rodgers, *The Work Ethic in Industrial America*, 2nd ed. (Chicago: University of Chicago Press, 2014), 116.

89. "The Financial Situation," *Bankers' Magazine*, June 1877.
90. Nasse, "Produktionskrisen," 147, 156; Adolf Wagner, *Grundlegung der politischen Ökonomie*, part 2, 3rd ed. (Leipzig: Winter, 1894), 144–148, quoted in Eugen von Bergmann, *Geschichte der nationalökonomischen Krisentheorien* (Stuttgart: W. Kohlhammer, 1895), 408.
91. Friedrich Engels, "Herrn Eugen Dühring's Umwälzung des Sozialismus," *Vorwärts*, May 26, 1878.
92. Rosanne Currarino, *The Labor Question in America: Economic Democracy in the Gilded Age* (Bloomington: Indiana University Press, 2011).
93. Jürgen Kromphardt, "Konjunktur- und Krisentheorie in der 2. Hälfte des 19. Jahrhunderts," in *Studien zur Entwicklung der ökonomischen Theorie*, vol. 7, ed. Betram Schofeld (Berlin: Duncker & Humblot, 1989), 20–25; Paul Barnett, *Business-Cycle Theory in the United States, 1860–1900* (Chicago: University of Chicago Press, 1941), 217–220.

5. Capitalism, Conspiracy, Corruption, and the Moral Economy of a Financial Crisis

1. My use of this term is inspired by E. P. Thompson's seminal essay "The Moral Economy of the English Crowd in the Eighteenth Century," *Past and Present* 50 (February 1971): 76–136. I follow Thompson in his argument that reactions to economic hardship must be interpreted in terms of custom and culture, and that these factors inform notions of what constitute legitimate practices on (financial) markets.
2. Edward Neufville Tailer, Diary, entry of September 26, 1873, New York Historical Society (NYHS).
3. "Silent Histories of the Stock Market," *New York Times*, October 1, 1873.
4. "A Few Words about Some Recent Events," *Galaxy*, December 1873.
5. Ann Fabian, "Speculation on Distress: The Popular Discourse of the Panics of 1837 and 1857," *Yale Journal of Criticism* 3 (1989): 127–142; Jessica M. Lepler, *The Many Panics of 1837: People, Politics, and the Creation of a Transatlantic Financial Crisis* (New York: Cambridge University Press, 2013), 218.
6. A recent study on Switzerland has found that the latter increasingly replaced the former in official analyses of bankruptcy cases during the 1860s. See Mischa Suter, *Rechtstrieb: Schulden und Vollstreckung im liberalen Kapitalismus 1800–1900* (Konstanz: Konstanz University Press, 2016), 99–106, 188–194.
7. Scott A. Sandage, *Born Losers: A History of Failure on America* (Cambridge, Mass.: Harvard University Press, 2005); Gerhard Hahn, *Ursachen von Unternehmermisserfolgen: Ergebnisse von Untersuchungen besonders im rheinischen Industriebezirk* (Cologne: Deutscher Industrieverlag, 1958), 49–51.
8. "Lokalnachrichten," *Berliner Tageblatt*, October 4, 1873; "Lokalnachrichten," *Berliner Tageblatt*, October 8, 1873.
9. New York, vol. 201, p. 500 S, R. G. Dun & Co. Credit Report Volumes, Baker Library, Harvard Business School.
10. Matthew Josephson, *The Robber Barons: The Great American Capitalists, 1861–1901* (New York: Harcourt, Brace, 1934), 170.
11. "Einer von den Vielen," *Berliner Tageblatt*, October 25, 1873.
12. "Local- und Provinzial-Nachrichten," *Klagenfurter Zeitung*, June 18, 1873.
13. "Städtisches," *Berliner Tageblatt*, October 25, 1873.
14. "Die Folgen der Geldkrisis," *Berliner Tageblatt*, November 29, 1873.

15. Quoted in "Verhandlungen des Reichsraths," *Presse*, November 24, 1873.
16. Michael Wladika, *Hitlers Vätergeneration: Die Ursprünge des Nationalsozialismus in der k.u.k. Monarchie* (Vienna: Böhlau, 2005), 74f.
17. Lothar Höbelt, "Gründerzeit und Börsenschwindel: Politik und Wirtschaft in der liberalen Ära," in *Korruption in Österreich: Historische Streiflichter*, ed. Ernst Bruckmüller (Vienna: Wilhelm Braumüller, 2011), 78.
18. "Berlin, den 13. Mai 1874," *Berliner Börsen-Zeitung*, evening ed., May 13, 1874.
19. "The Lesson of the Panic," *Churchman*, October 4, 1873.
20. "The Panic from a Farmer's Standpoint," *Western Rural*, December 13, 1873.
21. "The Workingman and the Panic," *Nation*, October 30, 1873. For a similar perspective see Julius Faucher, "Kurze Wechselziele zur Vorbeugung der Handelskrisen," *Vierteljahrschrift für Volkswirthschaft, Politik und Kulturgeschichte* 45 (1875): 19.
22. Daniel T. Rodgers, *The Work Ethic in Industrial America*, 2nd ed. (Chicago: University of Chicago Press, 2014), 176; Thomas Welskopp, *Das Banner der Brüderlichkeit: Die deutsche Sozialdemokratie vom Vormärz bis zum Sozialistengesetz* (Bonn: Dietz, 2000), 624f. See also Rosanne Currarino, *The Labor Question in America: Economic Democracy in the Gilded Age* (Bloomington: Indiana University Press, 2011), 15.
23. "Börse und Kleinbürgertum," *Neuer Social-Demokrat*, August 29, 1873; "Die Demoralisation der heutigen Gesellschaft," *Neuer Social-Demokrat*, November 16, 1873; "Der große Krupp," *Neuer Social-Demokrat*, January 8, 1873.
24. "The Panic and the Working Men," *Workingman's Advocate*, October 18, 1873; "The Financial Outlook," *Workingman's Advocate*, November 1, 1873.
25. On capital/labor antagonism and its role in historiography, see Jeffrey Sklansky, "Labor, Money, and the Financial Turn in the History of Capitalism," *Labor: Studies in the Working-Class History of the Americas* 11 (2014): 32–44, esp. 42f.
26. Liberal reformism, while embracing the political economy of orthodox liberalism, was critical of excessive speculation on Wall Street and fearful of the corrupting potential of exploitative capitalism. See John G. Sproat, *"The Best Men": Liberal Reformers in the Gilded Age* (New York: Oxford University Press, 1968), 6–19, 150–153.
27. "State and Railroad Bonds," *Commercial and Financial Chronicle*, September 20, 1873. The *Chronicle* was referring to the Granger's movement in the American West, whose activities had been widely reported on in the press. The notion that the Grangers were to blame for the panic became widely accepted in northeastern commercial and financial circles even though the railroad regulation movement had also emanated from, and been supported by, western commercial interests. See George H. Miller, *Railroads and the Granger Laws* (Madison: University of Wisconsin Press, 1971), 91; Lee Benson, *Merchants, Farmers, and Railroads: Railroad Regulation and New York Politics, 1850–1887* (New York: Russell & Russell, 1969 [1955]), 24–27, 67.
28. "Wall Street and the Crisis," *Old and New*, January 1, 1874.
29. "Ein neues Opfer des Quistorp'schen Konkurses," *Berliner Tageblatt*, November 5, 1873.
30. See chapter 1.
31. Franz Perrot, *Der Bank-, Börsen- und Actienschwindel: Eine Hauptursache der drohenden socialen Gefahr: Beiträge zur Kritik der politischen Oekonomie* (Rostock: Ernst Kuhn, 1876), 105f. See also Heinrich Beta, *Dichtkunst der Börse* (Berlin: Habel, 1873), 12–14, and Friedrich Spielhagen, *Sturmflut*, 16th ed., vol. 2 (Leipzig: Staackmann, 1902 [1877]), 75.
32. "The New York Panic," *Religious Magazine and Monthly Review*, October 1, 1873.
33. Richard White, "Information, Markets, and Corruption: Transcontinental Railroads in the Gilded Age," *Journal of American History* 90 (2003): 41.

34. *Verhandlungen des Strafprozesses, die Gründung des Braunschweiger Walzwerks betreffend, nebst Gutachten* (Braunschweig: Vieweg, 1878), 138. (The proceedings were published by the defendants' lawyers.)

35. *Sammlung sämmtlicher Drucksachen des Hauses der Abgeordneten aus der XII. Legislatur-Periode, I. Session: 1873–1874*, vol. 1 (Berlin: W. Moeser, 1874), 27–47. According to the parliamentary report on this and other enterprises, only a small part of the total share capital had been paid up. It is therefore not possible to quantify the exact volume of the shareholders' losses.

36. [Illegible] Duprée to Eduard Lasker, January 28, 1876, Eduard Lasker Papers, reel 36, Robert D. Farber University Archives and Special Collections, Brandeis University.

37. Sheldon Garon, *Beyond Our Means: Why Americans Spend while the World Saves* (Princeton: Princeton University Press, 2012), 89.

38. *Historical Statistics of the United States, 1789–1945* (Washington, DC: US Department of Commerce, 1949), 271.

39. "The Failure of Savings Banks," *Independent*, November 30, 1871.

40. "Trust Companies, Savings Banks, and Gold Speculators," *Commercial and Financial Chronicle*, August 30, 1873.

41. "The Savings Banks and the Crisis," *Commercial and Financial Chronicle*, October 4, 1873.

42. Oliver M. W. Sprague, *History of Crises under the National Banking System* (Washington, DC: US Government Printing Office, 1910), 51.

43. "From Louisville," *Daily Arkansas Gazette*, September 28, 1873.

44. [Untitled], *Appleton's Journal*, December 13, 1873.

45. Jonathan Levy, *Freaks of Fortune: The Emerging World of Capitalism and Risk in America* (Cambridge, Mass.: Harvard University Press, 2012), 140–146.

46. R. Daniel Wadhwani, "Protecting Small Savers: The Political Economy of Economic Security," *Journal of Policy History* 18 (2006): 127, 137ff.

47. Life insurance companies, too, failed in significant numbers during the 1870s, though not, in the main, as a result of the panic. See Sharon Ann Murphy, *Investing in Life: Insurance in Antebellum America* (Baltimore: Johns Hopkins University Press, 2010), 287–294.

48. Christian Dirninger, "Sparkassen und Staatsinterventionismus im Zusammenhang mit der Krise von 1873 in Österreich," in *Bankenkrisen in Mitteleuropa im 19. und 20. Jahrhundert*, ed. Richard Tilly (Stuttgart: Franz Steiner, 1999), 22–27; Herbert Krafft, *Immer ging es um Geld: Einhundertfünfzig Jahre Sparkasse in Berlin* (Berlin: Sparkasse der Stadt Berlin West, 1968), 75–77.

49. "Aus dem Gerichtssaale," *Neue Freie Presse*, morning ed., February 12, 1874.

50. Dirk Schumann, "Der Fall Adele Spitzeder 1872: Eine Studie zur Mentalität der 'kleinen Leute' in der Gründerzeit," *Zeitschrift für bayerische Landesgeschichte* 58 (1995): 991–1025.

51. Schumann, "Adele Spitzeder," 1002f.; "Das Falliment Placht," *Neues Fremden-Blatt*, May 21, 1873; "Die Börsenkrisis in der Provinz," *Neue Freie Presse*, May 24, 1873; "Placht und Spitzeder," *Local-Anzeiger der "Presse,"* February 11, 1874.

52. "Aus dem Gerichtssaale," *Neue Freie Presse*, morning ed., February 10, 1874; "Aus dem Gerichtssaale," *Neue Freie Presse*, morning ed., February 11, 1874.

53. "Aus dem Gerichtssaale," *Neue Freie Presse*, morning ed., February 12, 1874.

54. "Dummheit und Schlechtigkeit," *Neuer Social-Demokrat*, May 14, 1873.

55. *Verhandlungen des Strafprozesses, die Gründung des Braunschweigischen Walzwerks betreffend*, 138f.

56. Justinus Moeller, *Gründerprocesse: Eine criminalpolitische Studie* (Berlin: Julius Springer, 1876), iii.

57. "Die strafgerichtliche Verfolgung der bei der Gründung von Actiengesellschaften verübten Vergehen, Votum des Justizministers, Geheimes Staatsarchiv Preußischer Kulturbesitz," I. HA Rep. 77, Ministerium des Innern, Central-Bureau, Tit. 859, Nr. 60.

58. (Untitled), *Neuer Social-Demokrat*, April 14, 1875.

59. I examine the legal issues at stake in these trials in more detail in chapter 6.

60. Max Wirth, *Geschichte der Handelskrisen,* 2nd rev. and improved ed. (Frankfurt am Main: J. D. Sauerländer, 1874), 559.

61. Hans-Ulrich Wehler, *Deutsche Gesellschaftsgeschichte: Von der "Deutschen Doppelrevolution" bis zum Beginn des Ersten Weltkriegs 1849–1914* (Munich: C. H. Beck, 1995), 903f.

62. Sven Beckert, *The Monied Metropolis: New York City and the Consolidation of the American Bourgeoisie, 1850–1896* (Cambridge: Cambridge University Press, 2001), 209f., 232.

63. Fritz Stern, "Money, Morals, and the Pillars of Bismarck's Society," *Central European History* 3 (1970), 61.

64. On the history of the term, see Werner Plumpe, "Korruption: Annäherung an ein historisches und gesellschaftliches Phänomen," *Historische Zeitschrift* 48 (2009): 19–47.

65. Gordon R. Mork, "The Prussian Railway Scandal of 1873: Economics and Politics in the German Empire," *European Studies Review* 1 (1971), 36–38. On Strousberg and his system, see chapter 1.

66. See, for example, a letter signed by more than thirty names from Krojanke in Prussia, February 12, 1873, reel 36; and two anonymous letters, one dated April 5, 1873, and one undated (signed "civis"), reel 35, Eduard Lasker Papers, Robert D. Farber University Archives and Special Collections, Brandeis University.

67. Mork, "Prussian Railway Scandal," 40–44.

68. *Sammlung sämmtlicher Drucksachen des Hauses der Abgeordneten aus der XII: Legislatur-Periode, I. Session, 1873–1874,* vol. 1.

69. Fritz Stern, *Gold and Iron: Bismarck, Bleichröder, and the Building of the German Empire* (New York: Alfred A. Knopf, 1977), 242.

70. "Berlin, den 22. Januar 1875," *Berliner Börsen-Zeitung,* evening ed., January 22, 1875.

71. *Stenographische Berichte über die Verhandlungen des Deutschen Reichstags* (Berlin: Verlag der Buchdruckerei der 'Norddeutschen Allgemeinen Zeitung', 1872), April 25, 1872, 174.

72. *Stenographische Berichte, Reichstag,* June 4, 1872, 690. Fears of a general demoralization as a result of widespread fraud were also voiced on the Left. See "Die Demoralisation der heutigen Gesellschaft," *Neuer Social-Demokrat,* November 16, 1873.

73. On this, see Jens Ivo Engels, "Politische Korruption in der Moderne. Debatten und Praktiken in Großbritannien und Deutschland im 19. Jahrhundert," *Historische Zeitschrift* 282 (2006): 329. The term *Korruption* only became widespread in the German-speaking world in the last third of the nineteenth century. In English and French, the term had for a long time denoted not only the abuse of a public office for private gain but also decay and decomposition. See ibid., 316.

74. *Reichsgesetzblatt* (Berlin: Verlag des Gesetzsammlungsamtes, 1873), 61–90, § 16.

75. *Stenographische Berichte über die Verhandlungen des Preußischen Herrenhauses* (Berlin: W. Moeser, 1874), May 20, 1874, 416.

76. Franz Fischer, "Die Betheiligung der Staatsbeamten bei der Gründung und Verwaltung von Erwerbsgeselllschaften," *Die Gegenwart* 14, (1874): 213–215; Hansjoachim

Henning, *Die deutsche Beamtenschaft im 19. Jahrhundert: Zwischen Stand und Beruf* (Stuttgart: Franz Steiner, 1984), 89–96.

77. The full text of the law can be found in Carl Pfafferoth, *Preußische Beamten-Gesetzgebung: Enthaltend die wichtigsten Beamtengesetze in Preußen*, 3rd rev. ed. (Berlin: Guttentag, 1896), 34.

78. Rather, his by-now notorious name was used by Lasker to tarnish Strousberg's allies in the administration rather than the entrepreneur himself. See Joachim Borchart, *Der europäische Eisenbahnkönig Bethel Henry Strousberg* (Munich: C. H. Beck, 1991), 173.

79. Stern, *Gold and Iron*, 358–369; Borchart, *Eisenbahnkönig*, 123–162. In the end, investors in Strousberg's railroad, too, were able to retrieve their initial investment along with a respectable dividend. But a small investor losing his nerve and selling his securities before the deal was struck would have incurred a significant loss. See ibid., 162.

80. Margaret Lavinia Anderson, *Practicing Democracy: Elections and Political Culture in Imperial Germany* (Berkeley: University of California Press, 2000), 69–72.

81. Leonhard Müller, *Der Kampf zwischen politischem Katholizismus und Bismarcks Politik im Spiegel der Schlesischen Volkszeitung: Ein Beitrag zur schlesischen Kirchen-, Parteien- und Zeitungsgeschichte* (Breslau: Müller & Seiffert, 1929), 185–187.

82. Markus Raasch, *Der Adel auf dem Feld der Politik: Das Beispiel der Zentrumspartei in der Bismarckära (1871–1890)* (Düsseldorf: Droste, 2015), 262.

83. H. Niemeyer to Eduard Lasker, January 30, 1875; F. Benekendorff to Eduard Lasker, February 8, 1875, reel 36, Eduard Lasker Papers, Robert D. Farber University Archives and Special Collections, Brandeis University. The writers presumably reacted to the ruling of the military tribunal that had recently exonerated Putbus. The ruling had been made public in January (see above).

84. On Glagau's early years, see Daniela Weiland, *Otto Glagau und 'Der Kulturkämpfer': Zur Entstehung des modernen Antisemitismus im frühen Kaiserreich* (Berlin: Metropol, 2004), 43.

85. Otto Glagau, *Der Börsen- und Gründungsschwindel in Berlin: Gesammelte and stark vermehrte Artikel der "Gartenlaube,"* vol. 1 (Leipzig: Frohberg, 1876–1877), xxxv.

86. Earlier writings on Strousberg, by contrast, had barely mentioned his Jewish roots and rarely displayed anti-Jewish sentiments. See Ralf Roth, "Der Sturz des Eisenbahnkönigs Bethel Henry Strousberg: Ein jüdischer Wirtschaftsbürger in den Turbulenzen der Reichsgründung," *Jahrbuch für Antisemitismusforschung* 10 (2001): 87.

87. Glagau, *Börsen- und Gründungsschwindel*, vol. 1, xiv, 241.

88. Glagau, *Börsen- und Gründungsschwindel*, vol. 1, 145, 187, 317.

89. Heinrich Wuttke, *Die deutschen Zeitschriften und die Entstehung der öffentlichen Meinung: Ein Beitrag zur Geschichte des Zeitungswesens*, 2nd ed. (Leipzig: Krüger, 1875), 396; Bruno Weber, *Einige Ursachen der Wiener Krisis vom Jahre 1873* (Leipzig: Veit, 1874), 70.

90. Perrot, *Der Bank-, Börsen- und Actienschwindel*, 14 (quotation). See also Wuttke, *Entstehung der öffentlichen Meinung*, 179. On criticism of the German financial press and its reactions post-1873, see Robert Radu, *Auguren des Geldes: Eine Kulturgeschichte des Finanzjournalismus in Deutschland 1850–1914* (Göttingen: Vandenhoeck & Ruprecht, 2017), 127–153.

91. This "combination of vagueness and particularity in denunciations of conspiracy" was a standard feature of conspiracy theories popular during the French Revolution, and, it seems, of conspiracy theories in general. See Lynn Hunt, *Politics, Culture, and Class in the French Revolution* (Berkeley: University of California Press, 1984), 42.

92. Glagau, *Der Börsen- und Gründungsschwindel*, vol. 1, xv f.

93. Hans Herzfeld, *Johannes von Miquel: Sein Antheil am Ausbau des Deutschen Reiches bis zur Jahrhundertwende*, vol. 1 (Detmold: Meyer'sche Hofbuchhandlung, 1938), 373–375.

94. Stern, *Gold and Iron*, 187, 503; James F. Harris, "Franz Perrot: A Study in the Development of German Lower Middle Class Social and Political Thought in the 1870s," *Studies in Modern European History and Culture* 2 (1976): 73–106.

95. Stern, *Gold and Iron*, 503–506.

96. Rudolph Meyer, *Politische Gründer und die Corruption in Deutschland* (Leipzig: Bidder, 1877), 57, 111, 172–176, 183–185, 196, quotations at 176 and 111. Adolph Hansemann of the Disconto-Gesellschaft, Meyer noted, had intimate ties to Jewry because he had married a member of the Oppenheim family. See ibid., 22.

97. The alleged cooperation of Jews and aristocrats was itself a common anti-Jewish trope. See Franziska Schößler, *Börsenfieber und Kaufrausch: Ökonomie, Judentum und Weiblichkeit bei Theodor Fontane, Heinrich Mann, Thomas Mann, Arthur Schnitzler und Émile Zola* (Bielefeld: Aisthesis, 2009), 24.

98. Lasker had not questioned the system of the market economy. His goal was to ensure, through regulation and exposure, that public officials would not use their power for private gain, and to otherwise uphold liberal economic principles. See James F. Harris, *A Study in the Theory and Practice of German Liberalism: Eduard Lasker, 1829–1884* (Lanham: University of America Press, 1984), 94.

99. Carl Wilmanns, *Die "goldene" Internationale und die Nothwendigkeit einer socialen Reformpartei* (Berlin: Niendorf, 1876), 11, 35, 37, 39–52.

100. Adalbert Hahn, *Die Berliner Revue: Ein Beitrag zur Geschichte der konservativen Partei zwischen 1855 und 1875* (Berlin: Ebering, 1934), 202f.

101. Marcel Stoetzler, *The State, the Nation, and the Jews: Liberalism and the Antisemitism Dispute in Bismarck's Germany* (Lincoln: University of Nebraska Press, 2008), 193, 211.

102. Henning Albrecht, *Antiliberalismus und Antisemitismus: Hermann Wagener und die preußischen Sozialkonservativen 1855–1873* (Paderborn: Schöningh, 2010).

103. Werner Jochmann, *Gesellschaftskrise und Judenfeindschaft in Deutschland, 1870–1945* (Hamburg: Christians, 1988), 30–33; Shulamit Volkov, *Germans, Jews, and Antisemites: Trials in Emancipation* (New York: Cambridge University Press, 2006), 97.

104. Olaf Blaschke, *Katholizismus und Antisemitismus im Deutschen Kaiserreich* (Göttingen: Vandenhoeck & Ruprecht, 1997), 88.

105. Welskopp, *Banner der Brüderlichkeit*, 540, 622–637.

106. Radu, *Auguren des Geldes*, 135–137; Emil Dovifat, *Die Zeitungen* (Gotha: Flamberg, 1925), 66; Thomas Höhle, *Franz Mehring: Sein Weg zum Marxismus*, 2nd rev. ed. (Berlin (East): Rütten & Loening, 1958), 109–111. Other party leaders criticized Mehring's actions. See ibid., 115–117.

107. Lars Fischer, *The Socialist Response to Antisemitism in Imperial Germany* (Cambridge: Cambridge University Press, 2007). A more benign interpretation of Social Democracy"s role in this context is offered by Volkov, *Germans, Jews, and Antisemites*, 119–129.

108. Wilhelm Brauneder, "Die Korruption als historisches Phänomen," in *Korruption und Kontrolle*, ed. Christian Brünner (Vienna: Böhlau, 1981), 96–99.

109. Anonymous [W. Angerstein], *Die Corruption in Oesterreich: Ein Beitrag zur Charakteristik der österreichischen Verhältnisse* (Leipzig: Luckhardt, 1872), 6, 31, 37, 47.

110. Höbelt, "Gründerzeit und Börsenschwindel," 60, 65, 76.

111. Herbert Matis, *Österreichs Wirtschaft 1843–1913: Konjunkturelle Dynamik und gesellschaftlicher Wandel im Zeitalter Franz Josephs I.* (Berlin: Duncker & Humblot, 1972), 321–325; Höbelt, "Gründerzeit und Börsenschwindel," 72–74.

112. For public reactions to the trial see, for example, the overview in "Politische Ueber-sicht," *Vaterland*, March 1, 1875.

113. Anonymous, *Lasser, genannt Auersperg: Eine cisleithanische Zeitstudie* (Amberg: Habbel, 1877).

114. Anonymous, *Ein offenes Wort an Herrn Justizminister Dr. Glaser*, and *Vom Verfasser der Broschüre: "Lasser, genannt Auersperg"* (Amberg: Habbel, 1877). The author of these two anonymous publications is likely to have been Karl Vogelsang, a German convert to Roman Catholicism, who in 1875 was appointed editor of the conservative *Vaterland* and took a strong interest in social and economic problems. His goal was a restoration of the Christian economic order. See Peter Pulzer, *The Rise of Political Anti-Semitism in Germany and Austria*, rev. ed. (London: Peter Halban, 1988), 126f.

115. Hans Gruber, "Vom Agrarantisemitismus zum katholischen Antisemitismus im Vorarlberg des 19. Jahrhunderts," in *Katholischer Antisemitismus im 19. Jahrhundert: Ursachen und Traditionen im internationalen Vergleich*, ed. Olaf Blaschke and Aram Mattioli (Zurich: Orell Füssli, 2000), 325f. It was only in the 1890s that Catholic anti-Semites in the Vorarlberg began attributing omnipotent, conspiratorial power to Jews as agents of liberalism. See ibid., 328.

116. Pulzer, *Political Anti-Semitism*, 138.

117. Eric Foner, *Reconstruction: America's Unfinished Revolution, 1863–1877* (New York: Harper & Row, 1988), xix–xxii, quotation at xix.

118. Edward Chase Kirkland, *Industry Comes of Age: Business, Labor and Public Policy, 1860–1897* (New York: Holt, Rinehart & Winston, 1961), quotation at 25; Mark Wahlgren Summers, *The Era of Good Stealings* (New York: Oxford University Press, 1993), 61–63, quotation at 62. The fear of corruption was, of course, a central feature of republican ide-ology and had informed debates on the American political and economic order since colonial times.

119. Charles F. Adams Jr. and Henry Adams, *Chapters of Erie, and Other Essays* (Boston: James R. Osgood & Co., 1871), 12. The essay was first published in 1869.

120. Ari Hoogenboom, "Did Gilded Age Scandals Bring Reform?" in *Before Watergate: Problems of Corruption in American Society*, ed. Abraham S. Eisenstadt, Ari Hoogen-boom, and Hans L. Trefousse (Brooklyn: College Press, 1978), 128–130.

121. Scholars have argued that general influence peddling had indeed occurred, but that the shares had not been sold in return for any specific favor. See Maury Klein, *Union Pacific: Birth of a Railroad, 1862–1893* (New York: Doubleday, 1987), 291–303; Summers, *Era of Good Stealings*, 50–54.

122. "Politics," *Atlantic Monthly*, November 1873; "Our Late Panic," *International Review*, January 1874. For similar assessments along these lines see "The Lesson of the Autumn," *Harper's Weekly*, November 15, 1873; "Hard Times and Their Causes," *Her-ald & Presbyter*, December 17, 1873; "Twelve Blows and Their Echoes," *Money Safe*, April 1, 1874.

123. "A Few Words About Some Recent Events," *Galaxy*, December 1873.

124. See, for example, E. L. Godkin, "Commercial Immorality and Political Corruption," *North American Review* (July 1868): 253.

125. See chapter 3.

126. "The Political Use of Scandal," *Nation*, April 27, 1876.

127. White, "Information, Markets, and Corruption."

128. *New York Sun*, October 1873 (no day given), quoted in White, "Information, Markets, and Corruption," 41.

129. Stern, "Bismarck's Society," 51.

130. Meyer himself, ironically, would later jettison such personalized analyses in favor of structural and transnational ones. In the 1880s, he traveled to the United States in search of institutional explanations for America's growing economic might and published his findings in a book: Rudolph Meyer, *Ursachen der amerikanischen Concurrenz: Ergebnisse einer Studienreise* (Berlin: Barr, 1883).

131. Pulzer, *Political Anti-Semitism*, 121.

132. Henning Albrecht, "Preußen, ein 'Judenstaat': Antisemitismus als konservative Strategie gegen die 'Neue Ära'—zur Krisentheorie der Moderne," *Geschichte und Gesellschaft* 37 (2011): 459–467.

133. David A. Gerber, "Cutting Out Shylock: Elite Anti-Semitism and the Quest for Moral Order in the Mid-Nineteenth-Century American Market Place," *Journal of American History* 69 (1982): 615–637; Irwin Unger, *The Greenback Era: A Social and Political History of American Finance, 1865–1879* (Princeton: Princeton University Press, 1964), 210–212.

134. Mark Wahlgren Summers, *Party Games: Getting, Keeping, and Using Power in Gilded Age Politics* (Chapel Hill: University of North Carolina Press, 2004), 231–237; Hoogenboom, "Gilded Age Scandals," 132–140.

135. Stern, *Gold and Iron*, 509.

136. It became, as Shulamith Volkov famously argued, a "cultural code" of the right. See Volkov, *Germans, Jews, and Antisemites*, 115.

137. The American reasoning was metonymical: Wall Street was seen as controlled by greedy individuals, and this diagnosis could then be applied—precisely because Wall Street was considered a quintessentially American institution—to the society at large.

6. Criminalizing Promoters, Protecting Shareholders

1. Ernst Engel, *Die erwerbsthätigen juristischen Personen insbesondere die Actiengesellschaften im preussischen Staate* (Berlin: Verlag des Königlich-Preussischen Statistischen Bureaus, 1876), 19. According to a more recent compilation, 462 new corporations were listed on the Berlin Stock Exchange between 1870 and 1873. Unlike Engel's numbers, this statistic does not include companies that were not listed in Berlin or only existed for a very short period of time. See Markus Baltzer, *Der Berliner Kapitalmarkt nach der Reichsgründung 1871: Gründerzeit, internationale Finanzmarktintegration und der Einfluss der Makroökonomie* (Berlin: Peter Lang, 2007), 27.

2. Reichsoberhandelsgericht, "Gutachten über die geeignetsten Mittel zur Abhülfe der nach den Erfahrungen des Reichs-Oberhandelsgerichts bei der Gründung, der Verwaltung und dem geschäftlichen Betriebe von Aktienunternehmungen hervorgetretenen Uebelstände," March 31, 1877, in *Hundert Jahre modernes Aktienrecht: Eine Sammlung von Quellen und Texten zur Aktienrechtsreform von 1884 mit zwei Einführungen*, ed. Werner Schubert and Peter Hommelhoff (Berlin: de Gruyter, 1985), 160.

3. The market bottomed out in late 1875. According to one performance index, an investor lost, on average, 0.41 percent per year between January 1871 and December 1875. See Anja Weigt, *Der deutsche Kapitalmarkt vor dem Ersten Weltkrieg—Gründerboom, Gründerkrise und Effizienz des deutschen Aktienmarktes bis 1914* (Frankfurt am Main: Knapp, 2005), 94. Ronge, using a different methodology, calculates losses of around 26 percent between November 1872 and November 1875. See Ulrich Ronge, *Die langfristige Rendite deutscher Standardaktien. Konstruktion eines historischen Aktienindex ab Ultimo 1870 bis Ultimo 1959* (Frankfurt am Main: Peter

Lang, 2002), 63f., 212. Indices do not reflect the reality of investing during this period, as investors tended to buy shares of individual companies. In many cases, losses of individual investors would have been much higher.

4. "Die strafgerichtliche Verfolgung der bei der Gründung von Actiengesellschaften verübten Vergehen, Votum des Justizministers," October 16, 1876, Geheimes Staatsarchiv Preußischer Kulturbesitz, I. HA Rep. 77, Ministerium des Innern, Central-Bureau, tit. 859, Nr. 60. The relevant files of the municipal court have not been preserved.

5. Ibid., emphasis in original.

6. *Civil- und kriminalrechtliche Entscheidungen deutscher Gerichtshöfe in Gründungssachen*, vol. 1 (Berlin: Mitscher & Röstel, 1876), 60, 78, 112. For a similar case see also *Die Rechtsprechung des Königlichen Ober-Tribunals in Straf-Sachen*, vol. 17 (Berlin: Georg Reimer, 1876), 197f.

7. *Verhandlungen des Strafprocesses, die Gründung des Braunschweiger Walzwerks betreffend, nebst Gutachten* (Brunswick: Vieweg, 1878), 314.

8. *Civil- und kriminalrechtliche Entscheidungen*, 78f.

9. Ibid., 144–146, 159.

10. On the Brunswick trials, see also Norman-Mathias Pingel, "Gründerkrach in Braunschweig," *Braunschweigisches Jahrbuch für Landesgeschichte* 83 (2002): 223–232.

11. *Verhandlungen des Strafprocesses, die Gründung des Braunschweiger Walzwerks betreffend*, 311.

12. *Civil- und kriminalrechtliche Entscheidungen*, 24–28.

13. *Civil- und kriminalrechtliche Entscheidungen*, 38f. For the criminal proceedings, see ibid., 131–168.

14. *Entscheidungen des Reichsoberhandelsgerichts herausgegeben von den Räthen des Gerichtshofes*, vol. 22 (Stuttgart: Ferdinand Enke, 1878), 388, no. 90.

15. "Die strafgerichtliche Verfolgung der bei der Gründung von Actiengesellschaften verübten Vergehen, Votum des Justizministers," October 16, 1876, Geheimes Staatsarchiv Preußischer Kulturbesitz, I. HA Rep. 77, Ministerium des Innern, Central-Bureau, Tit. 859, Nr. 60.

16. Jan Lieder, "Die 1. Aktienrechtsnovelle vom 11. Juni 1870," in *Aktienrecht im Wandel*, vol. 1, *Entwicklung des Aktienrechts*, ed. Walter Bayer and Mathias Habersack (Tübingen: Mohr Siebeck, 2007), 323f.; Werner Schubert, "Die Abschaffung des Konzessionssystems durch die Aktienrechtsnovelle von 1870," *Zeitschrift für Unternehmens- und Gesellschaftsrecht* 2 (1981): 285–317.

17. *Stenographische Berichte über die Verhandlungen des Reichstages des Norddeutschen Bundes* (Berlin: F. Sittenfeld, 1870), 1. Legislatur-Periode, Session 1870, vol. 4, 650.

18. Boris Gehlen, *Der Deutsche Handelstag und die Regulierung der deutschen Wirtschaft* (Tübingen: Mohr Siebeck, forthcoming).

19. See, for example, "Ein Wort an kleinere Capitalisten," *Grenzboten* 2 (1872).

20. *Verhandlungen des Vereins für Socialpolitik am 12. und 18. October 1873* (Leipzig: Duncker & Humblot, 1874).

21. Passage of the reform was delayed until 1884 because policy-makers for many years failed to agree on whether it would be passed as a stand-alone law or as part of a reformed commercial code. The former position prevailed when Bismarck, in the context of the wider conservative turn in 1878–1879, personally advised the justice minister to draft a bill. See Werner Schubert, "Die Entstehung des Aktiengesetzes von 1884," in *Hundert Jahre modernes Aktienrecht*, ed. Schubert and Hommelhoff, 7–15, 20–22.

22. Felix Hecht, *Das Börsen- und Actienwesen der Gegenwart und die Reform des Actien-Gesellschafts-Rechts* (Mannheim: Schneider, 1874), 39.
23. Lieder, "Aktienrechtsnovelle," 331; Norbert Reich, "Die Entwicklung des deutschen Aktienrechts im 19. Jahrhundert," *Jus Commune* 2 (1969): 262; Hecht, *Actienwesen*, 39.
24. "Die Aktiengesellschaften in England,"*Deutsches Handelsblatt*, August 31, 1871.
25. Gehlen, *Der Deutsche Handelstag*.
26. Heinrich Wiener, Julian Goldschmidt, and Jakob Friedrich Behrend, *Zur Reform des Actiengesellschaftswesens: Drei Gutachten auf Veranlassung der Eisenacher Versammlung zur Besprechung der socialen Frage* (Leipzig: Duncker & Humblot, 1873), 6f. (n). See also Wilhelm Oechelhaeuser, *Die wirthschaftliche Krisis* (Berlin: Springer, 1876), 124.
27. Jan von Hein, *Die Rezeption US-amerikanischen Gesellschaftsrechts in Deutschland* (Tübingen: Mohr Siebeck, 2008), 89.
28. Hein, *Rezeption*, 91.
29. The bill's authors stressed that they had only been able to obtain the Swiss provisions with considerable difficulty. See Hein, *Rezeption*, 91.
30. Schubert, "Entstehung des Aktiengesetzes," 49f.
31. Schubert, "Entstehung des Aktiengesetzes," 50.
32. Peter Hommelhoff, "Eigenkontrolle statt Staatskontrolle—rechtsdogmatischer Überblick zur Aktienrechtsreform 1884," in *Hundert Jahre modernes Aktienrecht*, ed. Schubert and Hommelhoff, 66.
33. Despite this provision, many companies continued to curtail the rights of small shareholders, sometimes even excluding them from attending shareholder meetings. See Carsten Burhop, "Banken, Aufsichtsräte und Corporate Governance im Deutschen Reich (1871–1913)," *Bankhistorisches Archiv* 32 (2006), 1–25. Burhop also argues, however, that banks on corporate boards not only served their own interests but also those of small shareholders. See ibid., 22.
34. Sibylle Hofer, "Das Aktiengesetz von 1884—ein Lehrstück für prinzipielle Schutzkonzeptionen," *Aktienrecht im Wandel*, vol. 1, *Entwicklung des Aktienrechts*, ed. Walter Bayer and Mathias Habersack (Tübingen: Mohr Siebeck, 2007), 403–411.
35. Reichsoberhandelsgericht, "Gutachten," 11f.
36. As Carsten Burhop has shown, "giving shareholders voting and monitoring rights improved the stock market valuation and survival probability of banks during the economic crisis of the 1870s," suggesting that the relevant provisions in the 1884 reform reflected these developments. See Burhop, "No Need for Governance? The Impact of Corporate Governance on Valuation, Performance and Survival of German Banks During the 1870s," *Business History* 51 (2009), 569–601, quotation on 593.
37. Reich, "Entwicklung des Aktienrechts," 273.
38. Quoted in Hein, *Rezeption*, 89.
39. "Reichsoberhandelsgericht, Gutachten," 9, in *Modernes Aktienrecht*, ed. Schubert and Hommelhoff, 164; Eduard Pape, president of the ROG, to the minister of justice, quoted in ibid., 16.
40. In this paragraph I rely on Susanne Kalss, Christina Burger, and Georg Eckert, *Die Entwicklung des österreichischen Aktienrechts: Geschichte und Materialien* (Vienna: Linde, 2003), 162–188. Copies of two different drafts of the Austrian bill (one dated 1874; one dated 1882) can be found among the files of the department tasked with working on the German law at the Ministry for Trade. See Geheimes Staatsarchiv Preußischer Kulturbesitz, I. HA Rep. 120, Ministerium für Handel und Gewerbe, A XII 5 (Handelsgesellschaften) Nr. 1, Bd. 8, 11.

41. 1005 corporations were established between 1867 and 1873. See Herbert Matis, *Österreichs Wirtschaft. 1848–1913: Konjunkturelle Dynamik und gesellschaftlicher Wandel im Zeitalter Franz Josephs I.* (Berlin: Duncker & Humblot, 1972), 172f.

42. One element of the 1861 law which Austria chose not to adopt was the general charter (*Normativsystem*).

43. On the history of the bill and the internal debate among different branches of the government and judiciary, see Schubert, "Die Entstehung des Aktiengesetzes von 1884," 7–42.

44. Rainer Gömmel, "Entstehung und Entwicklung der Effektenbörsen im 19. Jahrhundert bis 1914," in *Deutsche Börsengeschichte*, ed. Hans Pohl (Frankfurt am Main: Knapp, 1992), 157.

45. Kalss, Burger, and Eckert, *Entwicklung des österreichischen Aktienrechts*, 183.

46. Gömmel, "Effektenbörse," 157; Kalss, Burger, and Eckert, *Entwicklung des österreichischen Aktienrechts*, 158f.

47. Wolfgang Schulz, *Das deutsche Börsengesetz: Die Entstehungsgeschichte und wirtschaftlichen Auswirkungen des Börsengesetzes von 1896* (Frankfurt am Main: Lang, 1994), 371–373.

48. George Herberton Evans, *Business Incorporations in the United States, 1800–1943* (New York: National Bureau of Economic Research, 1949), 11.

49. "Germany. Rumors of Financial Troubles—Heavy Fall in Stocks," *New York Times*, October 1, 1873. Stock prices plunged in the immediate aftermath of the crash but, according to one index, recovered in 1874, remained more or less flat in 1875, only to decline again in 1876 and 1877. In 1879 they were almost back to their peak of 1872. It appears that American shareholders did not experience the same protracted decline that many Germans did. See Susan B. Carter, Scott Sigmund Gartner, Michael R. Haines, Alan L. Olmstead, Richard Sutch, and Gavin Wright, eds., *Historical Statistics of the United States: Earliest Times to the Present*, millennial edition, vol. 3, *Economic Structure and Performance* (Cambridge: Cambridge University Press, 2006), 757.

50. "The Month," *Penn Monthly*, October 1873, and "How Railroads Should Be Financed and Built," *American Railroad Journal*, September 27, 1873.

51. Herbert Hovenkamp, *Enterprise and American Law, 1836–1937* (Cambridge, Mass.: Harvard University Press, 1991), 51–53; James Willard Hurst, *The Legitimacy of the Business Corporation in the Law of the United States, 1780–1970* (Charlottesville: University Press of Virginia, 1970), 27; Victor Morawetz, *A Treatise on the Law of Private Corporations*, 2nd ed., vol. 1 (Boston: Little, Brown & Co.), 1886, §§ 159–161.

52. Stuart Banner, *Anglo-American Securities Regulation: Cultural and Political Roots* (Cambridge: Cambridge University Press, 1998), 236.

53. Benjamin Vaughn Abbott, *A General Digest of the Law of Corporations: Presenting the American Adjudications Upon Public and Private Corporations of Every Kind, with a Full Selection of English Cases* (New York: Baker, Voorhis & Co., 1869), 795.

54. Quoted in George W. Cothran, *The Revised Statutes of the State of New York, as Altered by Subsequent Legislation*, vol. 2 (Albany: Banks & Brothers, 1875), Title XV, § 2.

55. Edward Chase Kirkland, *Men, Cities, and Transportation: A Study in New England History*, vol. 2 (Cambridge, Mass.: Harvard University Press, 1948), 323f.

56. Lawrence M. Friedman, *A History of American Law*, 3rd ed. (New York: Simon & Schuster, 2005), 392.

57. Potter Platt, *Treatise on the Law of Corporations: General and Local, Public and Private, Aggregate and Sole*, vol. 2 (New York: Banks & Brothers, 1879), 929.

58. Lawrence Mitchell, *The Speculation Economy: How Finance Triumphed over Industry* (San Francisco: Berret-Koehler, 2006), 45.

59. Abbott, *A General Digest of the English and American Cases*, 157. Abbot, however, also noted that a company could, once fully formed, compensate people for "acts . . . done in furtherance of their object" in the course of procuring a charter, suggesting corporations had a certain amount of leeway in deciding which actions merited compensation. See ibid., 170.

60. Abbott, *General Digest of the English and American Cases*, 297. Abbott cites *Pa. Supreme Ct.* 1869, McElhenny's Appeal, 61 Pa. St. 188, and S. P. 1869, Simons V. Vulcan Oil, &c., Co., in ibid., 202.

61. Friedman, *American Law*, 392. On American promoters' reputation for fraud, see Frederick A. Cleveland and Fred Wilbur Powell, *Railroad Promotion and Capitalization in the United States* (London: Longmans, Green & Co., 1909), 139f.

62. A search of the *New York Times* digital database shows that the term "bubble companies" comes up only eight times for the period 1870–1879 and is mostly used to describe British companies. The term "watered stock" comes up forty-three times during this period, which is much higher than in the previous decade (where the term is recorded only once) but significantly lower than in the following decade, where it appears 136 times.

63. Vincent P. Carosso, *Investment Banking in America* (Cambridge, Mass.: Harvard University Press, 1970), 45.

64. Mitchell, *Speculation Economy*, 45–56, 68.

65. Colleen A. Dunlavy, "Social Conceptions of the Corporation: Insights from the History of Shareholder Voting Rights," *Washington and Lee Law Review* 63 (2006), 1353, 1358–1362.

66. *Report of the Special Committee on Railroads, Appointed under a Resolution of the Assembly, February 28, 1879, to Investigate Alleged Abuses in the Management of Railroads Chartered by the State of New York* (Albany, 1880), 46 and appendix, 1f. (quotation) and 6.

67. Henry H. Swain, "Economic Aspects of Railroad Receiverships," *Economic Studies* 3 (April 1898), 56–61, 98; Gerald Berk, *Alternative Tracks: The Constitution of American Industrial Order, 1865–1917* (Baltimore: Johns Hopkins University Press, 1994), 25, 47–49. A different way of measuring default rates uses the percentage of total par value. By this measure, the crisis of the 1870s was the most severe of the last 150 years. Two years during this period had default rates of around 15 percent, the large majority of which were in the railroad sector. See Kay Giesecke, Francis A. Longstaff, Stephen Schaefer, and Ilya Strebulaev, "Corporate Bond Default Risk: A 150-year Perspective," *Journal of Financial Economics* 102 (2011), 236.

68. Matthew Simon, *Cyclical Fluctuations and the International Capital Movements of the United States, 1865–1897* (New York: Arno Press, 1978), 180–182.

69. Albro Martin, "Railroads and Equity Receivership: An Essay on Institutional Change," *Journal of Economic History* 34, no. 3 (1974), 686–688, 695f.; Dietrich G. Buss, *Henry Villard: A Study of Transatlantic Investments and Interest, 1870–1895* (New York: Arno Press, 1978), 30–55.

70. Dolores Greenberg, *Financiers and Railroads, 1869–1889: A Study of Morton, Bliss & Company* (Newark: University of Delaware Press, 1980), 44, 48, 82–114; Carosso, *Investment Banking in America*, 27–33.

71. Carola Frydman and Eric Hilt, "Investment Banks as Corporate Monitors in the Early Twentieth Century United States," *American Economic Review* 107 (2017), 1938–1970.

On voting trusts as a means of protecting bondholder interests, see Peter Tufano, "Business Failure, Judicial Intervention, and Financial Innovation: Restructuring U.S. Railroads in the Nineteenth Century," *Business History Review* 71 (1997), 1–40. Bradford DeLong has argued that the presence of J. P. Morgan or his associates on corporate boards led to a significant increase of the firm's common stock. See J. Bradford DeLong, "Did Morgan's Men Add Value?" in *Inside the Business Enterprise: Historical Perspectives on the Use of Information*, ed. Peter Temin (Chicago: University of Chicago Press 1991), 205–250.

72. The traditional view has long been that links between firms and banks were weaker in the United States than in Germany. See, for example, Charles Calomiris, "The Costs of Rejecting Universal Banking: American Finance in the German Mirror," in Calomiris, *U.S. Bank Deregulation in Historical Perspective* (Cambridge: Cambridge University Press, 2000), 212–279. It is worth noting that Calomiris's focus is on industrial firms, not on railroads. With regard to the latter, Carola Frydman and Eric Hilt have recently argued that, especially from 1893 onward, American railroads benefitted from permanent relationships with investment banks. See Frydman and Hilt, "Investment Banks as Corporate Monitors." For an account arguing that American banks actually had more influence than their German counterparts before 1914 see Jeffrey Fear and Christopher Kobrak, "Banks on Board. German and American Corporate Governance, 1870–1914," *Business History Review* 84 (2010): 703–736.

73. James Ely Jr., *Railroads and American Law* (Lawrence: University Press of Kansas, 2001), 86; George H. Miller, *Railroads and the Granger Laws* (Madison: University of Wisconsin Press, 1971), 86.

74. See, for example, "State and Railroad Bonds," *Commercial and Financial Chronicle*, September 20, 1873.

75. Lee Benson, *Merchants, Farmers, and Railroads: Railroad Regulation and New York Politics, 1850–1887* (New York: Russell & Russell, 1969 [1955]), 37–58, 67–156; Ely, *Railroads and American Law*, 71–91.

76. Richard White has emphasized the fraudulent aspects, especially of transcontinentals vis-à-vis investors and the public in the late nineteenth century. See Richard White, *Railroaded: The Transcontinentals and the Making of Modern America* (New York: Norton, 2011)—while arguably neglecting the more successful restructurings. See Eric Hilt, "Economic History, Historical Analysis, and the 'New History of Capitalism,'" *Journal of Economic History* 77 (2017), 523.

77. Colleen A. Dunlavy and Thomas Welskopp, "Myths and Peculiarities: Comparing U.S. and German Capitalism," *German Historical Institute Bulletin* 41 (2007): 33–64.

78. Max Weber, "Börsenwesen. Schriften und Reden 1893–1898," in *Max Weber Gesamtausgabe*, vol. 5.2, ed. Knut Borchardt (Tübingen: Mohr Siebeck, 2000), 868.

Conclusion

1. On the specter of internal division in American writings of that period, see Christopher L. Hill, *National History and the World of Nations: Capital, State, and the Rhetoric of History in Japan, France, and the United States* (Durham: Duke University Press, 2008).

2. Sebastian Conrad and Dominic Sachsenmaier, "Competing Visions of World Order: Global Moments and Movements, 1880s–1930s," in *Competing Visions of World Order:*

Global Moments and Movements, 1880s–1930s, ed. Sebastian Conrad and Dominic Sachsenmaier (New York: Palgrave Macmillan, 2007), 1–25.

3. Adam McKeown, "Periodizing Globalization," *History Workshop Journal* 61 (2007): 219.

4. Giovanni Arrighi, *The Long Twentieth Century: Money, Power, and the Origins of Our Time* (London: Verso, 2010 [1994]); Marc-William Palen, *The "Conspiracy" of Free Trade: The Anglo-American Struggle over Empire and Economic Globalization, 1846–1896* (Cambridge: Cambridge University Press, 2016).

5. Leigh Claire La Berge, *Scandals and Abstraction: Financial Fiction of the Long 1980s* (Oxford: Oxford University Press, 2015), 15.

6. Ibid.; Ewen H. H. Green, "The Influence of the City over British Economic Policy, c. 1880–1960," in *Finance and Financiers in European History*, ed. Youssef Cassis (Cambridge: Cambridge University Press, 1992), 202.

7. Walter Bagehot, *Lombard Street: A Description of the Money Market* (London: King, 1983), 1; see also "Money Gets More than Its Share," *Workingman's Advocate*, June 7, 1873.

8. Rudolf Hilferding, *Das Finanzkapital: Eine Studie zur jüngsten Entwicklung des Kapitalismus* (Vienna: Ignaz Brand, 1910); Louis D. Brandeis, *Other People's Money and How the Bankers Use It* (New York: Frederick A. Stokes, 1914).

9. Jeffrey Fear and Christopher Kobrak, "Banks on Board: German and American Corporate Governance, 1870–1914," *Business History Review* 84 (2010): 716f.

10. Jacob Riesser, *Die deutschen Großbanken und ihre Konzentration im Zusammenhang mit der Entwicklung der Gesamtwirtschaft in Deutschland*, several eds. (Jena: G. Fischer, 1905ff.) Riesser's study is to this day frequently cited in scholarly accounts of German banking history. For a recent comprehensive investigation of the role of banks in late nineteenth- and early twentieth-century Germany see Caroline Fohlin, *Finance Capitalism and Germany's Rise to Industrial Power* (Cambridge: Cambridge University Press, 2007).

11. Arrighi, *Long Twentieth Century*; on cyclical elements in the interpretation of financial markets see Peter Knight, *Reading the Market: Genres of Financial Capitalism in Gilded Age America* (Baltimore: Johns Hopkins University Press, 2016).

12. Harold James, "Finance Capitalism," in *Capitalism: The Reemergence of a Historical Concept* (London: Bloomsbury, 2016), 135. A recent example is the manipulation of the LIBOR rate by banks. See "Deutsche Bank to Pay $2.5 Billion Fine to Settle Rate-Rigging Case," *New York Times*, April 23, 2015.

BIBLIOGRAPHY

Archival Material

Baker Library, Harvard Business School
    Henry Villard Collection
    R. G. Dun & Co. Credit Report Volumes
Brandeis University, Robert D. Farber University Archives and Special Collections
    Eduard Lasker Papers
Geheimes Staatsarchiv Preußischer Kulturbesitz
    I. HA Rep. 77, Ministerium des Innern, Central-Bureau, Tit. 859, Nr. 27
    I. HA Rep. 120, Ministerium für Handel und Gewerbe, C IX 1 (Innerer Handel, Generalia) Nr. 28, Bd. 1
    I. HA Rep. 120, Ministerium für Handel und Gewerbe, A XII 5 (Handelsgesellschaften) Nr. 1, Bd. 8, 11
    I. HA Rep. 151, Finanzministerium, HB, Nr. 1267
Landesarchiv Berlin
    A Rep. 200–01 Korporation der Kaufmannschaft von Berlin
Library of Congress, Manuscript Division
    Alexander Brown and Sons Records
    Thomas Ewing Family Papers
National Archives at College Park, Maryland
    Records of Foreign Service Posts. Consular Posts. Berlin, Germany.
    Records of Foreign Service Posts. Diplomatic Posts. Germany.
National Museum of American History, Archives Center
    Warshaw Collection of Business Americana
New York Historical Society (NYHS)
    George Opdyke and Company Records
    Diary of Edward Neufville Tailer

Robert Mackie and Son Records
Brown Brothers Harriman Records
New York Public Library (NYPL), Rare Book and Manuscript Division
Moses Taylor Papers
Alexander Turney Stewart Correspondence
The Pierpont Morgan Library Archives
Pierpont Morgan Papers
Rothschild Archive, London (RAL)
Records of Nathan Mayer Rothschild and Sons, Correspondence Department
Stadtarchiv Siegen
Nachlass Achenbach

Periodicals

Der Aktionär (Frankfurt am Main)
American Railroad Journal
Atlantic Monthly
Bankers' Magazine
Berliner Tageblatt (Berlin)
Berliner Börsen-Zeitung (Berlin)
Chicago Tribune
Christian Union
Commercial and Financial Chronicle
Churchman
Daily Arkansas Gazette
Daily Cleveland Herald
Daily Evening Bulletin
Deutsch-amerikanischer Oekonomist
The Economist (London)
Financial Review
Galaxy
Die Gartenlaube (Leipzig)
Die Gegenwart (Berlin)
Die Grenzboten (Berlin)
Harper's New Monthly Magazine
Harper's Weekly
Independent (New York)
International Review
Iron Age
Journal of the Senate of the United States
Klagenfurter Zeitung (Klagenfurt)
Linzer Volksblatt (Linz)
The Nation
Neue Freie Presse (Vienna)
Neuer Social-Demokrat (Berlin)
New York Commercial Advertiser
New Yorker Handels-Zeitung
New York Journal of Commerce

New York Times
New York Tribune
North American Review
Der Oesterreichische Oekonomist (Vienna)
Old and New
Penn Monthly
Die Presse (Vienna)
Railroad Gazette
Rostocker Zeitung (Rostock)
The Stockholder
The Times (London)
Das Vaterland (Vienna)
Vorwärts (Leipzig)
Vossische Zeitung (Berlin)
Der Welthandel (Stuttgart)
Western Rural
Zeitschrift für Kapital und Rente (Stuttgart)

Printed Primary and Secondary Sources

Abbott, Benjamin Vaughn. *A General Digest of the Law of Corporations: Presenting the American Adjudications upon Public and Private Corporations of Every Kind, with a Full Selection of English Cases.* New York: Baker, Voorhis, 1869.
———. *A General Digest of the English and American Cases upon the Law of Corporations for the Ten Years from July 1868 to July 1878, with Acts of Congress.* New York: Baker, Voorhis, 1879.
Adams Jr., Charles F., and Henry Adams. *Chapters of Erie, and Other Essays.* Boston: James R. Osgood & Co., 1871.
AHR Conversation, "On Transnational History." Participants: C. A. Bayly, Sven Beckert, Matthew Connelly, Isabel Hofmeyr, Wendy Kozol, and Patricia Seed. *American Historical Review* 111, no. 5 (December 2006): 1441–1464.
Ahrens, Gerhard. *Krisenmanagement 1857: Staat und Kaufmannschaft in Hamburg während der ersten Weltwirtschaftskrise.* Hamburg: Verlag Verein für Hamburgische Geschichte, 1986.
Albrecht, Henning. *Antiliberalismus und Antisemitismus: Hermann Wagener und die preußischen Sozialkonservativen 1855–1873.* Paderborn: Schöningh, 2010.
———. "Preußen, ein 'Judenstaat': Antisemitismus als konservative Strategie gegen die 'Neue Ära'—Zur Krisentheorie der Moderne." *Geschichte und Gesellschaft* 37 (2011): 455–481.
Anderson, Margaret Lavinia. *Practicing Democracy: Elections and Political Culture in Imperial Germany.* Berkeley: University of California Press, 2000.
Anonymous [W. Angerstein]. *Die Corruption in Oesterreich: Ein Beitrag zur Charakteristik der österreichischen Verhältnisse.* Leipzig: Luchhardt'sche Verlagsbuchhandlung, 1872.
Anonymous. *The Finances: Panics and Specie Payments: "Facts Speak."* Philadelphia: John Campbell & Son, 1874.
Anonymous. *Ein offenes Wort an Herrn Justizminister Dr. Glaser: Vom Verfasser der Broschüre: "Lasser, genannt Auersperg."* Amberg: Habbel, 1877.
Anonymous. *Lasser, genannt Auersperg: Eine cisleithanische Zeitstudie.* Amberg: Habbel, 1877.

Anthony, David. *Paper Money Men: Commerce, Manhood, and the Sensational Public Sphere in Antebellum America.* Columbus: Ohio State University Press, 2009.

Arrighi, Giovanni. *The Long Twentieth Century: Money, Power and the Origins of our Times.* London: Verso, 2010 [1994].

Bagehot, Walter. *Lombard Street: A Description of the Money Market.* London: King, 1873.

Baltzer, Markus. "Cross-Listed Stocks as an Information Vehicle of Speculation: Evidence from European Cross-Listings in the Early 1870s." *European Review of Economic History* 10 (2006): 301–327.

——. *Der Berliner Kapitalmarkt nach der Reichsgründung 1871: Gründerzeit, internationale Finanzmarktintegration und der Einfluss der Makroökonomie.* Berlin: Peter Lang, 2007.

Baltzarek, Franz. *Die Geschichte der Wiener Börse: Öffentliche Finanzen und privates Kapital im Spiegel einer österreichischen Wirtschaftsinstitution.* Vienna: Verlag der Österreichischen Akademie der Wissenschaften, 1973.

Bamberger, Ludwig. "Die fünf Milliarden." *Preußische Jahrbücher* 31 (1873): 441–460.

Banner, Stuart. *Anglo-American Securities Regulation: Cultural and Political Roots, 1690–1860.* Cambridge: Cambridge University Press, 1998.

Bark, Willy. *Chronik von Alt-Westend, mit Schloß Ruhwald, Spandauer Bock und Fürstenbrunn.* F. G. Mittler & Sohn: Berlin, 1937.

Barnes Garrison & Co. *Key to Success in Wall Street.* New York [c. 1870s]. Baker Library, Harvard Business School.

Barnett, Paul. *Business-Cycle Theory in the United States, 1860–1900.* Chicago: University of Chicago Press, 1941.

Barreyre, Nicolas. "The Politics of Economic Crisis: The Panic of 1873, the End of Reconstruction and the Realignment of American Politics." *Journal of the Gilded Age and Progressive Era* 10 (2011): 403–424.

——. *Gold and Freedom: The Political Economy of Reconstruction.* Charlottesville: University of Virginia Press, 2015.

Bartels, Friedrich. "Kommerzienrat Johannes Quistorp." *Pommern: Zeitschrift für Kultur und Geschichte* 51 (2013): 40–46.

Baskin, Jonathan Barron. "The Development of Corporate Financial Markets in Britain and the United States, 1600–1914: Overcoming Asymmetric Information." *Business History Review* 62 (1988): 199–237.

Bayly, Christopher A. *The Birth of the Modern World, 1780–1914.* Malden, Mass.: Blackwell, 2004.

Becker, Joh. H. *Das Wesen des Geldes: Eine Studie über die Ursachen der Krisis.* Berlin: F. Graf Behr, 1879.

Beckert, Sven. *The Monied Metropolis: New York City and the Consolidation of the American Bourgeoisie, 1850–1896.* Cambridge: Cambridge University Press, 2001.

Bender, Thomas. *A Nation among Nations: America's Place in the World.* New York: Hill and Wang, 2006.

Bensel, Richard F. *Yankee Leviathan: The Origins of Central State Authority in America, 1859–1877.* Cambridge: Cambridge University Press, 1990.

Benson, Lee. *Merchants, Farmers, and Railroads: Railroad Regulation and New York Politics, 1850–1887.* New York: Russell & Russell, 1969 [1955].

Berghahn, Volker R. "Das 'deutsche Kapitalismus-Modell' in Geschichte und Geschichtswissenschaft." In *Gibt es einen deutschen Kapitalismus? Tradition und globale Perspektiven der sozialen Marktwirtschaft,* ed. Volker R. Berghahn and Sigurt Vitols, 23–43. Frankfurt am Main: Campus 2006.

Berghoff, Hartmut. "Markterschließung und Risikomanagement: Die Rolle der Kredit-auskunfteien und Agenturen im Industrialisierungs- und Globalisierungsprozess des 19. Jahrhunderts." *Vierteljahrsschrift für Sozial- und Wirtschaftsgeschichte* 92 (2005): 141–162.

Bergmann, Eugen von. *Geschichte der nationalökonomischen Krisentheorien.* Stuttgart: W. Kohlhammer, 1895.

Berk, Gerald. *Alternative Tracks: The Constitution of American Industrial Order, 1865–1917.* Baltimore: Johns Hopkins University Press, 1994.

Berliner, Adolf. *Die wirthschaftliche Krisis, ihre Ursachen und ihre Entwicklung.* Hannover: Carl Meyer, 1878.

Bertkau, Friedrich, and Arnold Killisch von Horn, eds. *75 Jahre Berliner Börsen-Zeitung, 1. Juli 1855 –1. Juli 1930.* Berlin: Berliner Börsen-Zeitung, 1930.

Besomi, Daniele. "Naming Crises." In *Crises and Cycles in Economic Dictionaries and Encyclopaedias,* ed. Daniele Besomi, 54–132. London: Routledge, 2012.

Beta, Heinrich. *Dichtkunst der Börse.* Berlin: Habel, 1873.

Biggeleben, Christof. *Das "Bollwerk des Bürgertums": Die Berliner Kaufmannschaft 1870–1920.* Munich: Beck, 2006.

Billington, Ray Allen. *Land of Savagery, Land of Promise: The European Image of the American Frontier in the Nineteenth Century.* New York: Norton, 1981.

Blaschke, Olaf. *Katholizismus und Antisemitismus im Deutschen Kaiserreich.* Göttingen: Vandenhoeck & Ruprecht, 1997.

Blondheim, Menahem. *News over the Wires: The Telegraph and the Flow of Public Information in America, 1844–1897.* Cambridge, Mass.: Harvard University Press, 1994.

Blume, Herbert. *Gründungszeit u. Gründungskrach mit Beziehung auf das deutsche Bankwesen.* Danzig: Kasemann, 1914.

Borchardt, Knut. "Währung und Wirtschaft." In *Währung und Wirtschaft in Deutschland 1876–1975,* ed. Deutsche Bundesbank, 3–55. Frankfurt am Main: Knapp, 1976.

Borchart, Joachim. *Der europäische Eisenbahnkönig Bethel Henry Strousberg.* Munich: Beck, 1991.

Borchgrave, Alexandra Villard de, and John Cullen. *Villard: The Life and Times of an American Titan.* New York: Doubleday, 2001.

Bordo, Michael D., Alan M. Taylor, and Jeffrey G. Williamson, eds. *Globalization in Historical Perspective.* Chicago: University of Chicago Press, 2003.

Brandeis, Louis D. *Other People's Money and How the Bankers Use It.* New York: Frederick A. Stokes, 1914.

Brauneder, Wilhelm. "Die Korruption als historisches Phänomen." In *Korruption und Kontrolle,* ed. Christian Brünner, 75–104. Vienna: Böhlau, 1981.

Bright, Charles, and Michael Geyer. "Where in the World Is America? The History of the United States in the Global Age." In *Rethinking American History in a Global Age,* ed. Thomas Bender, 63–100. Berkeley: University of California Press, 2002.

Buchner, Michael. *Die Spielregeln der Börse: Institutionen, Kultur und die Grundlagen des Wertpapierhandels in Berlin und London, ca. 1860–1914.* PhD diss., Heidelberg University, 2017.

Burhop, Carsten. *Die Kreditbanken in der Gründerzeit.* Stuttgart: Franz Steiner, 2004.

——. "Banken, Aufsichtsräte und Corporate Governance im Deutschen Reich (1871–1913)." *Bankhistorisches Archiv* 32 (2006): 1–25.

——. "No Need for Governance? The Impact of Corporate Governance on Valuation, Performance and Survival of German Banks during the 1870s." *Business History* 51 (2009): 569–601.

Buss, Dietrich G. *Henry Villard: A Study of Transatlantic Investments and Interest, 1870–1895.* New York: Arno Press, 1978.

Calomiris, Charles. "Greenback Resumption and Silver Risk: The Economics and Politics of Monetary Regime Change in the United States, 1862–1900." In *Monetary Regimes in Transition,* ed. Michael D. Bordo and Forrest Capie, 86–132. Cambridge: Cambridge University Press, 1994.

——. "The Costs of Rejecting Universal Banking: American Finance in the German Mirror." In Calomiris, *U.S. Bank Deregulation in Historical Perspective.* Cambridge: Cambridge University Press, 2000: 212–279.

Calomiris, Charles, and Larry Schweikart. "The Panic of 1857: Origins, Transmission, and Containment." *Journal of Economic History* 51 (1991): 807–834.

Carey, Henry. *Financial Crises: Their Causes and Effects.* Philadelphia: Baird, 1860.

Carosso, Vincent P. *Investment Banking in America.* Cambridge, Mass.: Harvard University Press, 1970.

——. *The Morgans: Private International Bankers, 1854–1913.* Cambridge, Mass.: Harvard University Press, 1987.

Carter, Susan B., Scott Sigmund Gartner, Michael R. Haines, Alan L. Olmstead, Richard Sutch, and Gavin Wright, eds. *Historical Statistics of the United States: Earliest Times to the Present,* millennial ed., vol. 3. Cambridge: Cambridge University Press, 2006.

Cassis, Youssef. "Economic and Financial Crises." In *Capitalism: The Reemergence of a Historical Concept,* ed. Jürgen Kocka and Marcel van der Linden, 13–32. London: Bloomsbury, 2016.

Chandler, Alfred D. *Henry V. Poor: Business Editor, Analyst, and Reformer.* Cambridge, Mass.: Harvard University Press, 1956.

——. *The Visible Hand: The Managerial Revolution in American Business.* Cambridge, Mass.: Harvard University Press, 1977.

Civil- und kriminalrechtliche Entscheidungen deutscher Gerichtshöfe in Gründungssachen. Heft 1. Berlin: Mitscher & Röstell, 1876.

Clapham, John. *The Bank of England: A History.* Vol. 2. Cambridge: Cambridge University Press, 1970 [1944].

Cleveland, Frederick A., and Fred Wilbur Powell. *Railroad Promotion and Capitalization in the United States.* London: Longmans, Green, 1909.

Cohen, Patricia Cline. *A Calculating People: The Spread of Numeracy in Early America.* Chicago: University of Chicago Press, 1982.

Cohn, Gustav. "Nachtrag zu dem Aufsatze über 'Zeitgeschäfte und Differenzgeschäfte.'" *Jahrbücher für Nationalökonomie und Statistik* 9 (1867): 377–428.

——. *Die Börse und die Spekulation.* Berlin: Lüderitz, 1868.

Conkin, Paul Keith. *Prophets of Prosperity: America's First Political Economists.* Bloomington: Indiana University Press, 1980.

Conrad, Sebastian. *Globalisation and the Nation in Imperial Germany.* Cambridge: Cambridge University Press, 2014.

——. *What Is Global History?* Princeton: Princeton University Press, 2016.

Conrad, Sebastian, and Dominic Sachsenmaier. "Competing Visions of World Order: Global Moments and Movements, 1880s–1930s." In *Competing Visions of World Order: Global Moments and Movements, 1880s–1930s,* ed. Sebastian Conrad and Dominic Sachsenmaier, 1–25. New York: Palgrave Macmillan, 2007.

Conti, Giuseppe. "Il crac del 1873." In *Crisi e scandali bancari nella storia d'Italia,* ed. Paolo Pecorari, 29–66. Venice: Istituto Veneto di Scienze, Lettere ed Arti, 2006.

Cooper, Frederick. *Colonialism in Question: Theory, Knowledge, History.* Berkeley: University of California Press, 2005.

Cothran, George W. *The Revised Statutes of the State of New York, as Altered by Subsequent Legislation,* vol. 2. Albany: Banks & Bros., 1875.

Cottrell, P. L. "Domestic Finance, 1860–1914." In *The Cambridge Economic History of Modern Britain.* Vol. 2, *Economic Maturity, 1860–1939,* ed. Roderick Floud and Paul Johnson, 253–279. Cambridge: Cambridge University Press, 2004.

Currarino, Rosanne. *The Labor Question in America: Economic Democracy in the Gilded Age.* Bloomington: Indiana University Press, 2011.

Danckelmann, Frh. v. "Transatlantisches." *Zeitschrift für Kapital und Rente* 5 (1869): 301–304.

Danckelmann, Frh. v. "Die Aktien und Obligationen der deutsch-österreichischen Dampfschiffahrts-Gesellschaften." *Zeitschrift für Kapital und Rente* 6 (1870): 1–47.

Danckelmann, Frh. v. "Die systematische Spoliation des Effektenbesitzes auf dem Gebiet des Staatskredits und des Aktienwesens." *Zeitschrift für Kapital und Rente* 9 (1873): 1–19.

Danckelmann, Frh. v. "Kapitalanlage in ausländischen Wertpapieren," *Zeitschrift für Kapital und Rente* 11 (1875): 713-718.

Danckelmann, Frh. v. "Kosmopolitismus des englischen Kapitals." *Zeitschrift für Kapital und Rente* 11 (1875): 393–398.

Davies, Hannah Catherine. "Spreading Fear, Communicating Trust: Writing Letters and Telegrams during the Panic of 1873." *History and Technology* 32 (2016): 159–177.

Davis, Lance E., and Robert J. Cull. "International Capital Movements, Domestic Capital Markets, and American Economic Growth, 1820–1914." In *The Cambridge Economic History of the United States,* vol. 2, ed. Stanley L. Engerman and Robert E. Gallman, 733–812. Cambridge: Cambridge University Press, 2000.

Davis, Lance E., and Robert E. Gallman. *Evolving Financial Markets and International Capital Flows.* Cambridge: Cambridge University Press, 2001.

Dejung, Christof, and Niels P. Petersson. "Introduction: Power, Institutions, and Global Markets—Actors, Mechanisms, and Foundations of Worldwide Economic Integration, 1850–1930." In *The Foundations of Worldwide Economic Integration: Power, Institutions, and Global Markets, 1850–1930,* ed. Christof Dejung and Niels P. Petersson, 1–17. Cambridge: Cambridge University Press, 2013.

DeLong, J. Bradford. "Did Morgan's Men Add Value?" In *Inside the Business Enterprise: Historical Perspectives on the Use of Information,* ed. Peter Temin, 205–250. Chicago: University of Chicago Press, 1991.

Dirninger, Christian. "Sparkassen und Staatsinterventionismus im Zusammenhang mit der Krise von 1873 in Österreich." In *Bankenkrisen in Mitteleuropa im 19. und 20. Jahrhundert,* ed. Richard Tilly, 13–48. Stuttgart: Franz Steiner, 1999.

Dörfler, Edith, and Wolfgang Pensold. *Die Macht der Nachricht: Die Geschichte der Nachrichtenagenturen in Österreich.* Vienna: Molden, 2001.

Dovifat, Emil. *Die Zeitungen.* Gotha: Flamberg, 1925.

Ducker, James H. *Men of the Steel Rails: Workers on the Atchison, Topeka and Santa Fe Railroad, 1869–1900.* Lincoln: University of Nebraska Press, 1983.

Dunbar, Charles Franklin. "Economic Science in America, 1776–1876." In Charles Franklin Dunbar, *Economic Essays,* ed. Oliver M. W. Sprague, 1–29. London: Macmillan, 1904.

Dunlavy, Colleen A. *Politics and Industrialization: Early Railroads in the United States and Prussia.* Princeton: Princeton University Press, 1994.

——. "Social Conceptions of the Corporation: Insights from the History of Shareholder Voting Rights." *Washington and Lee Law Review* 63 (2006): 1347–1388.

Dunlavy, Colleen A., and Thomas Welskopp. "Myths and Peculiarities: Comparing U.S. and German Capitalism." *German Historical Institute Bulletin* 41 (2007): 33–64.

Eadie, John. *Panics in the Money Market and Recovery from Their Effect: Being an Inquiry into the Practical Working of the Monetary Systems of America and Europe, Past and Present, and the Phenomena of Speculations, Revulsions and Panics*. New York: J. W. Amerman, 1873.

Eichengreen, Barry. *Elusive Stability: Essays in the History of International Finance, 1919–1939*. Cambridge: Cambridge University Press, 1990.

Einaudi, Luca. *Money and Politics: European Monetary Unification and the International Gold Standard (1865–1873)*. Oxford: Oxford University Press, 2001.

Ely Jr., James W. *Railroads and American Law*. Lawrence: University Press of Kansas, 2001.

Engel, Alexander. "Vom verdorbenen Spieler zum verdienstvollen Spekulanten: Ökonomisches Denken über Börsenspekulation im 19. Jahrhundert." *Jahrbuch für Wirtschaftsgeschichte* 54, no. 2 (2013): 49–69.

Engel, Ernst. *Die erwerbsthätigen juristischen Personen insbesondere die Actiengesellschaften im preussischen Staate*. Berlin: Verlag des Königlich Preussischen Statistischen Bureaus, 1876.

Engels, Friedrich. "Herrn Eugen Dühring's Umwälzung des Sozialismus." *Vorwärts*, May 26, 1878.

Engels, Jens Ivo. "Politische Korruption in der Moderne: Debatten und Praktiken in Großbritannien und Deutschland im 19. Jahrhundert." *Historische Zeitschrift* 282 (2006): 313–350.

Entscheidungen des Reichsoberhandelsgerichts herausgegeben von den Räthen des Gerichts. Stuttgart: Ferdinand Enke, 1872–1880.

Etges, Andreas. *Wirtschaftsnationalismus: USA und Deutschland im Vergleich (1815–1914)*. Frankfurt am Main: Campus, 1999.

Evans Jr., George Herberton. *Business Incorporations in the United States 1800–1943*. New York: National Bureau of Economic Research, 1949.

Fabian, Ann. "Speculation on Distress: The Popular Discourse of the Panics of 1837 and 1857." *Yale Journal of Criticism* 3 (1989): 127–142.

Faucher, Julius. "Kurze Wechselziele zur Vorbeugung der Handelskrisen." *Vierteljahrschrift für Volkswirthschaft, Politik und Kulturgeschichte* 45 (1875): 1–33.

Fear, Jeffrey, and Christopher Kobrak. "Banks on Board: German and American Corporate Governance, 1870–1914." *Business History Review* 84 (2010): 703–736.

Fels, Rendigs. *American Business Cycles, 1865–1897*. Chapel Hill: University of North Carolina Press, 1959.

Finel-Honigman, Irene. *A Cultural History of Finance*. Abingdon: Routledge, 2010.

Fischer, Franz. "Die Betheiligung der Staatsbeamten bei der Gründung und Verwaltung von Erwerbsgeselllschaften." *Die Gegenwart* 14 (1874): 213–215.

Fischer, Gertrud. *Die Zeitungsannonce der Wiener Presse vor und nach dem Börsenkrach von 1873*. PhD diss., Vienna University, 1937.

Fischer, Lars. *The Socialist Response to Antisemitism in Imperial Germany*. Cambridge: Cambridge University Press, 2007.

Fischer, Wolfram. *Expansion—Integration—Globalisierung: Studien zur Geschichte der Weltwirtschaft*. Göttingen: Vandenhoeck & Ruprecht, 1998.

Fishlow, Albert. "Transportation in the 19th and Early 20th Centuries." In *The Cambridge Economic History of the United States*, vol. 2, ed. Stanley L. Engerman and Robert E. Gallman, 543–642. Cambridge: Cambridge University Press, 2000.

Fohlin, Caroline. *Finance Capitalism and Germany's Rise to Industrial Power*. Cambridge: Cambridge University Press, 2007.

Foner, Eric. *Reconstruction: America's Unfinished Revolution, 1863–1877*. New York: Harper & Row, 1988.

Foreman-Peck, James. *A History of the World Economy: International Economic Relations since 1850*. Brighton: Harvester Press, 1983.

Forsyth, David P. *The Business Press in America, 1750–1865*. Philadelphia: Chilton Books, 1964.

Frank, Alison. "The Children of the Desert, and the Laws of the Sea: Austria, Great Britain, the Ottoman Empire, and the Mediterranean Slave Trade in the Nineteenth Century." *American Historical Review* 117 (2012): 410–444.

Fraser, Steve. *Wall Street: A Cultural History*. London: Faber & Faber, 2005.

Friedman, Lawrence M. *A History of American Law*. 3rd ed. New York: Simon & Schuster, 2005.

Frydman, Carola, and Eric Hilt. "Investment Banks as Corporate Monitors in the Early Twentieth Century United States." *American Economic Review* 107 (2017): 1938–1970.

Fürstenberg, Carl. *Die Lebensgeschichte eines deutschen Bankiers 1870–1914*, ed. Hans Fürstenberg. Berlin: Ullstein, 1931.

Gallarotti, Guido M. "The Scramble for Gold: Monetary Regime Transformation in the 1870s." In *Monetary Regimes in Transition*, ed. Michael D. Bordo and F. Capie, 15–67. Cambridge: Cambridge University Press, 1994.

Gareis, Carl. *Die Börse und die Gründungen nebst Vorschlägen zur Reform des Börsenrechts und der Actiengesetzgebung*. Berlin: Habel, 1874.

Garon, Sheldon. *Beyond Our Means: Why Americans Spend While the World Saves*. Princeton: Princeton University Press, 2012.

Gebhard, Hellmut. *Die Berliner Börse von den Anfängen bis zum Jahre 1896*. Berlin: R. L. Prager, 1928.

Gehlen, Boris. *Der Deutsche Handelstag und die Regulierung der deutschen Wirtschaft*. Tübingen: Mohr Siebeck, forthcoming.

Gerber, David A. "Cutting Out Shylock: Elite Anti-Semitism and the Quest for Moral Order in the Mid-Nineteenth-Century American Market Place." *Journal of American History* 69 (1982): 615–637.

Geyer, Martin H. "One Language for the World: The Metric System, International Coinage, and the Rise of Internationalism, 1850–1900." In *The Mechanics of Internationalism: Culture, Society, and Politics from the 1840s to the First World War*, ed. Martin H. Geyer and Johannes Paulmann, 55–92. Oxford: Oxford University Press, 2001.

Geyer, Martin H., and Johannes Paulmann, "Introduction: The Mechanics of Internationalism." In *The Mechanics of Internationalism: Culture, Society, and Politics from the 1840s to the First World War*, ed. Martin H. Geyer and Johannes Paulmann, 1–26. Oxford: Oxford University Press, 2001.

Giddens, Anthony. *Consequences of Modernity*. Cambridge: Polity Press, 1991.

Giesecke, Kay, Francis A. Longstaff, Stephen Schaefer, and Ilya Strebulaev. "Corporate Bond Default Risk: A 150-Year Perspective." *Journal of Financial Economics* 102 (2011): 233–250.

Gilles, Philippe. *Histoire des crises et des cycles économiques: Des crises industrielles du 19e siècle aux crises financières actuelles*. 2nd ed. Paris: Armand Colin, 2009.

Gioia, Vitantonio. "Adolf Wagner: Economic Crises, Capitalism and Human Nature." In *Crises and Cycles in Economic Dictionaries and Encyclopaedias*, ed. Daniele Besomi, 307–319. London: Routledge, 2012.

Gische, David M. "The New York City Banks and the Development of the National Banking System, 1860–1870." *American Journal of Legal History* 23 (1979): 21–67.

Glagau, Otto. *Der Börsen- und Gründungsschwindel in Berlin: Gesammelte und stark vermehrte Artikel der "Gartenlaube."* 2 vols. Leipzig: Frohberg, 1876–1877.

Godkin, E. L. "Commercial Immorality and Political Corruption." *North American Review* (July 1868): 253.

Goede, Marieke de. "Mastering 'Lady Credit': Discourses of Financial Crisis in Historical Perspective." *International Feminist Journal of Politics* 2 (2000): 58–81.

Gömmel, Rainer. "Entstehung und Entwicklung der Effektenbörsen im 19. Jahrhundert bis 1914." In *Deutsche Börsengeschichte*, ed. Hans Pohl, 135–207. Frankfurt am Main: Knapp, 1992.

Good, David F. *The Economic Rise of the Habsburg Empire, 1750–1914.* Berkeley: University of California Press, 1984.

Grabas, Margrit. "Die Gründerkrise von 1873/79—Fiktion oder Realität? Einige Überlegungen im Kontext der Weltfinanz- und wirtschaftskrise 2008/2009." *Jahrbuch für Wirtschaftsgeschichte* 52, no. 1 (2011): 69–96.

Grabbe, Hans-Jürgen. "Weary of Germany—Weary of America: Perceptions of the United States in Nineteenth-Century Germany." In *Transatlantic Images and Perceptions: Germany and America since 1776*, ed. David Barclay and Elizabeth Glaser-Schmidt, 65–86. Cambridge: Cambridge University Press, 2007.

Green, Ewen H. H. "The Influence of the City over British Economic Policy, c. 1880–1960." In *Finance and Financiers in European History*, ed. Youssef Cassis, 193–218. Cambridge: Cambridge University Press, 1992.

Greenberg, Dolores. *Financiers and Railroads, 1869–1889: A Study of Morton, Bliss & Company.* Newark: University of Delaware Press, 1980.

Gruber, Hans. "Vom Agrarantisemitismus zum katholischen Antisemitismus im Vorarlberg des 19. Jahrhunderts." In *Katholischer Antisemitismus im 19. Jahrhundert: Ursachen und Traditionen im internationalen Vergleich*, ed. Olaf Blaschke and Aram Mattioli, 317–335. Zurich: Orell Füssli, 2000.

Hagemann, Harald. "Introduction." In *Business Cycle Theory: Selected Texts, 1860–1930*, vol. 1, ed. Harald Hagemann, xvii–xxvii. London: Pickering & Chatto, 2002.

Hahn, Adalbert. *Die Berliner Revue: Ein Beitrag zur Geschichte der konservativen Partei zwischen 1855 und 1875.* Berlin: Ebering, 1934.

Hahn, Gerhard. *Ursachen von Unternehmermisserfolgen: Ergebnisse von Untersuchungen besonders im rheinischen Industriebezirk.* Cologne: Deutscher Industrieverlag, 1958.

Hamon, Henry. *New York Stock Exchange Manual, Containing Its Principles, Rules, and Its Different Modes of Speculation.* New York: J. F. Trow, 1865 [reprint: 1970].

Harris, James F. "Franz Perrot: A Study in the Development of German Lower Middle Class Social and Political Thought in the 1870s." *Studies in Modern European History and Culture* 2 (1976): 73–106.

——. *A Study in the Theory and Practice of German Liberalism: Eduard Lasker, 1829–1884.* Lanham: University of America Press, 1984.

Haupt, Heinz-Gerhard, and Jürgen Kocka. "Comparison and Beyond: Traditions, Scope, and Perspectives of Comparative History." In *Comparative and Transnational History: Central European Approaches and New Perspectives*, ed. Heinz-Gerhard Haupt and Jürgen Kocka, 1–30. New York: Berghahn Books, 2009.

Hecht, Felix. *Das Börsen- und Actienwesen der Gegenwart und die Reform des Actien-Gesellschafts-Rechts.* Mannheim: Schneider,1874.

Hein, Jan von. *Die Rezeption US-amerikanischen Gesellschaftsrechts in Deutschland.* Tübingen: Mohr Siebeck, 2008.

Helbich, Wolfgang. "Different, But Not Out of This World: German Images of the United States between Two Wars, 1871–1914." In *Transatlantic Images and Perceptions: Germany and America since 1776*, ed. David E. Barclay and Elisabeth Glaser-Schmidt, 109–129. Cambridge: Cambridge University Press, 2007.

Helfferich, Karl. *Geschichte der deutschen Geldreform*. Vol. 1. Leipzig: Duncker & Humblot, 1898.

Henning, Hansjoachim. *Die deutsche Beamtenschaft im 19. Jahrhundert: Zwischen Stand und Beruf.* Stuttgart: Franz Steiner, 1984.

Herzfeld, Hans. *Johannes von Miquel: Sein Antheil am Ausbau des Deutschen Reiches bis zur Jahrhundertwende.* Vol. 1. Detmold: Meyer'sche Hofbuchhandlung, 1938.

Hilferding, Rudolf. *Das Finanzkapital: Eine Studie zur jüngsten Entwicklung des Kapitalismus.* Vienna: Ignaz Brand, 1910.

Hill, Christopher L. *National History and the World of Nations: Capital, State, and the Rhetoric of History in Japan, France, and the United States.* Durham: Duke University Press, 2008.

Hilt, Eric. "History of American Corporate Governance: Law, Institutions, and Politics." *Annual Review of Financial Economics* 6 (2014): 1–21.

——. "Economic History, Historical Analysis, and the 'New History of Capitalism.'" *Journal of Economic History* 77 (2017): 511–536.

Hirschbach, Hermann. *Von der Börse, oder: Der Geist der Speculation.* Quedlinburg: Ernst'sche Buchhandlung, 1864.

Historical Statistics of the United States, 1789–1945. Washington, DC: U.S. Department of Commerce, 1949.

Hoag, Christopher. "The Atlantic Telegraph Cable and Capital Market Information Flows." *Journal of Economic History* 66 (2006): 342–353.

Höbelt, Lothar. "Gründerzeit und Börsenschwindel: Politik und Wirtschaft in der liberalen Ära." In *Korruption in Österreich: Historische Streiflichter*, ed. Ernst Bruckmüller, 60–80. Vienna: Wilhelm Braumüller, 2011.

Hodas, Daniel. *The Business Career of Moses Taylor. Merchant, Finance Capitalist, and Industrialist.* New York: New York University Press, 1976.

Hofer, Sibylle. "Das Aktiengesetz von 1884—ein Lehrstück für prinzipielle Schutzkonzeptionen." In *Aktienrecht im Wandel. Band I, Entwicklung des Aktienrechts*, ed. Walter Bayer and Mathias Habersack, 398–411. Tübingen: Mohr Siebeck, 2007.

Höhle, Thomas. *Franz Mehring: Sein Weg zum Marxismus.* 2nd rev. ed. Berlin: Rütten & Loening, 1958.

Hommelhoff, Peter. "Eigenkontrolle statt Staatskontrolle—rechtsdogmatischer Überblick zur Aktienrechtsreform 1884." In *Hundert Jahre modernes Aktienrecht: Eine Sammlung von Texten und Quellen zur Aktienrechtsreform 1884 mit zwei Einführungen*, ed. Werner Schubert and Peter Hommelhoff, 53–105. Berlin: de Gruyter, 1985.

Hoogenboom, Ari. "Did Gilded Age Scandals Bring Reform?" In *Before Watergate: Problems of Corruption in American Society*, ed. Abraham S. Eisenstadt, Ari Hoogenboom, and Hans L. Trefousse, 125–142. Brooklyn: College Press, 1978.

Hopkins, Antony G. "Introduction." In *Global History: Interactions between the Universal and the Local*, ed. Antony G. Hopkins, 1–38. Basingstoke: Palgrave Macmillan, 2006.

Hostmann, Ernst. "Einige Betrachtungen über das Finanzwesen der Gegenwart." *Zeitschrift für Kapital und Rente* 8 (1872): 1–15.

Hovenkamp, Herbert. *Enterprise and American Law, 1836–1937.* Cambridge, Mass.: Harvard University Press, 1991.

Hübener, Erhard. *Die deutsche Wirtschaftskrisis von 1873.* Berlin: Ebering, 1905.

Huffman, Walter E., and James R. Lothian. "The Gold Standard and the Transmission of Business Cycles, 1833–1932." In *A Retrospective on the Classical Gold Standard, 1821–1931*, ed. Michael D. Bordo and Anna J. Schwartz, 455–507. Chicago: University of Chicago Press, 1984.

Hunt, Lynn. *Politics, Culture, and Class in the French Revolution.* Berkeley: University of California Press, 1984.

Hurst, James Willard. *The Legitimacy of the Business Corporation in the Law of the United States, 1780–1970.* Charlottesville: University Press of Virgina, 1970.

Huston, James L. *The Panic of 1857 and the Coming of the Civil War.* Baton Rouge: Louisiana State University Press, 1987.

James, Harold. "Finance Capitalism." In *Capitalism: The Reemergence of a Historical Concept,* ed. Jürgen Kocka and Marcel van der Linden, 133–163. London: Bloomsbury, 2016.

James, John A. *Money and Capital Markets in Postbellum America.* Princeton: Princeton University Press, 1978.

Jevons, William Stanley. "Commercial Crises and Sun Spots." *Nature* 19 (1878): 33–37.

Jobst, Clemens. *Die Bank, das Geld, der Staat: Nationalbank und Währungspolitik in Österreich 1816–2016.* Frankfurt am Main: Campus, 2016.

Jochmann, Werner. *Gesellschaftskrise und Judenfeindschaft in Deutschland, 1870–1945.* Hamburg: Christians, 1988.

John Hickling & Co. *Men and Idioms of Wall Street: Explaining the Daily Operations in Stocks, Bonds and Gold.* New York, 1875. Baker Library, Harvard Business School.

Josephson, Matthew. *The Robber Barons: The Great American Capitalists, 1861–1901.* New York: Harcourt, Brace, 1934.

Judson, Pieter. *Exclusive Revolutionaries: Liberal Politics, Social Experience, and National Identity in the Austrian Empire.* Ann Arbor: University of Michigan Press, 1996.

Juglar, Clément. *Des Crises commerciales et de leur retour périodique en France, en Angleterre et aux États-Unis.* Paris: Guillaumin, 1861.

Kabisch, Thomas R. *Deutsches Kapital in den USA: Von der Reichsgründung bis zur Sequestrierung.* Stuttgart: Klett-Cotta, 1982.

Kalss, Susanne, Christina Burger, and Georg Eckert. *Die Entwicklung des österreichischen Aktienrechts: Geschichte und Materialien.* Vienna: Linde, 2003.

Kamitz, Reinhard. "Die österreichische Geld- und Währungspolitik von 1848 bis 1948." In *Hundert Jahre österreichischer Wirtschaftsentwicklung,* ed. Hans Mayer. Vienna: Springer, 1949.

Kardorff-Wabnitz, Wilhelm von. *Gegen den Strom! Eine Kritik der Handelspolitik des deutschen Reichs an der Hand der Carey'schen Forderungen.* Berlin: Springer, 1875.

Karras, Theodor. "Telegrapheneinrichtungen in Oesterreich-Ungarn." *Archiv für Post und Telegraphie* 10 (1883): 305–316.

Kautsch, Jacob. *Allgemeines Börsenbuch nebst Usancen der Berliner, Frankfurter und Wiener Börse: Ein Handbuch für Capitalisten, Financiers und Bankbeamte.* Stuttgart: Julius Meyer, 1874.

Keller, Gottfried. "Das verlorene Lachen." In *Gottfried Keller: Gesammelte Werke: Historisch-kritische Ausgabe,* ed. Walter Morgenthaler. 32 vols. Basel: Stroemfeld, 2000 (1874).

Kenwood, Alan G., and A. L. Lougheed. *The Growth of the International Economy: An Introductory Text.* 3rd ed. London: Routledge 1992 [1971].

Keynes, John Maynard. *A General Theory of Employment, Interest, and Money.* London: Macmillan, 1936.

Kidd, Sarah Alice. *The Search for Moral Order: The Panic of 1819 and the Culture of the Early American Republic.* PhD diss., University of Missouri, 2003.

Kindleberger, Charles P. *Manias, Panics, and Crashes: A History of Financial Crises.* New York: Basic Books, 1978.

——. *Historical Economics: Art or Science?* New York: Harvester Wheatsheaf, 1990.

Kindleberger, Charles P., and Robert Z. Aliber. *Manias, Panics, and Crashes: A History of Financial Crises*. 6th ed. Basingstoke: Palgrave Macmillan, 2011.

Kirchner, Joachim. *Das deutsche Zeitschriftenwesen: Seine Geschichte und seine Probleme*. Part 2, *Vom Wiener Kongress bis zum Ausgang des 19. Jahrhunderts*. Wiesbaden: Otto Harrassowitz, 1962.

Kirkland, Edward Chase. *Men, Cities, and Transportation: A Study in New England History*, vol. 2. Cambridge, Mass.: Harvard University Press, 1948.

——. *Dream and Thought in the Business Community, 1860–1900*. Ithaca: Cornell University Press, 1956.

——. *Industry Comes of Age: Business, Labor and Public Policy, 1860–1897*. New York: Holt, Rinehart and Winston, 1961.

Klein, Maury. *The Life and Legend of Jay Gould*. Baltimore: Johns Hopkins University Press, 1986.

——. *Union Pacific: Birth of a Railroad, 1862–1893*. New York: Doubleday, 1987.

Knight, Peter. "Reading the Market: Abstraction, Personification and the Financial Column of Town Topics Magazine." *Journal of American Studies* 46 (2012): 1–21.

——. *Reading the Market: Genres of Financial Fiction in Gilded Age America*. Baltimore: Johns Hopkins University Press, 2016.

Koch, Ursula E. *Berliner Presse und europäisches Geschehen 1871*. Berlin: Colloquium, 1978.

Kocka, Jürgen. *Arbeitsverhältnisse und Arbeiterexistenzen: Grundlagen der Klassenbildung im 19. Jahrhundert*. Bonn: Dietz, 1990.

——. "Einleitung." In *Gibt es einen deutschen Kapitalismus? Tradition und globale Perspektiven der sozialen Marktwirtschaft*, ed. Volker R. Berghahn and Sigurt Vitols, 9–21. Frankfurt am Main: Campus, 2006.

——. "Writing the History of Capitalism." *Bulletin of the German Historical Institute* 47 (2010): 7–24.

Konrad, Helmut. "Deutsch-Österreich: Gebremste Klassenbildung und importierte Arbeiterbewegung im Vielvölkerstaat." In *Europäische Arbeiterbewegungen im 19. Jahrhundert. Deutschland, Österreich, England und Frankreich im Vergleich*, ed. Jürgen Kocka, 106–128. Göttingen: Vandenhoeck & Ruprecht, 1983.

Koselleck, Reinhart. "Krise." In *Geschichtliche Grundbegriffe: Historisches Lexikon zur politisch-sozialen Sprache in Deutschland*, vol. 3, ed. Otto Brunner, Werner Conze, and Reinhart Koselleck, 617–650. Stuttgart: Klett-Cotta, 1982.

Krafft, Herbert. *Immer ging es um Geld: Einhundertfünfzig Jahre Sparkasse in Berlin*. Berlin: Sparkasse der Stadt Berlin West, 1968.

Kromphardt, Jürgen. "Konjunktur- und Krisentheorie in der 2. Hälfte des 19. Jahrhunderts." In *Studien zur Entwicklung der ökonomischen Theorie*, vol 7., ed. Bertram Schefold, 9–33. Berlin: Duncker & Humblot, 1989.

La Berge, Leigh Claire. *Scandals and Abstraction: Financial Fiction of the Long 1980s*. Oxford: Oxford University Press, 2015.

Lambi, Ivo Nikolai. *Free Trade and Protectionism in Germany, 1868–1879*. Wiesbaden: Franz Steiner, 1963.

Lange, Annemarie. *Berlin zur Zeit Bebels und Bismarcks: Zwischen Reichsgründung und Jahrhundertwende*. Berlin: Dietz, 1972.

Lange, Hans. *Die Wirtschaft der Vereinigten Staaten von Amerika in der Sicht des deutschen Reisenden*. PhD diss., Göttingen University, 1967.

Larson, Henrietta M. *Jay Cooke: Private Banker*. Cambridge, Mass.: Harvard University Press, 1936.

Lears, Jackson. *Something for Nothing: Luck in America*. New York: Penguin, 2003.

Leiskow, Hanns. *Spekulation und öffentliche Meinung in der ersten Hälfte des 19. Jahrhunderts*. Jena: Fischer, 1930.

Lepler, Jessica M. *The Many Panics of 1837: People, Politics, and the Creation of a Transatlantic Financial Crisis*. New York: Cambridge University Press, 2013.

Levy, Jonathan. *Freaks of Fortune: The Emerging World of Capitalism and Risk in America*. Cambridge, Mass.: Harvard University Press, 2012.

Licht, Walter. *Working for the Railroad: The Organization of Work in the Nineteenth Century*. Princeton: Princeton University Press, 1983.

Lichter, Jörg. "Goldwährung oder Doppelwährung: Der Bimetallismusstreit im Deutschen Reich 1880 bis 1895." *Bankhistorisches Archiv* 22 (1996): 86–107.

Liebknecht, Wilhelm. *Letters to the Chicago Workingman's Advocate November 26, 1870–December 2, 1871*. Ed. Philip S. Foner. New York: Holmes & Meier, 1982.

Lieder, Jan. "Die 1. Aktienrechtsnovelle vom 11. Juni 1870." In *Aktienrecht im Wandel*. Vol. 1, *Entwicklung des Aktienrechts*. Ed. Walter Bayer and Mathias Habersack, 318–386. Tübingen: Mohr Siebeck, 2007.

Lindenlaub, Dieter. "Die Glaubwürdigkeit einer neuen Währung: Die Einführung der Mark in Deutschland 1871–1876." *Bankhistorisches Archiv* 28 (2002): 21–39.

Linder, Moritz. *Die Asche der Millionen: Vor, während und nach der Krise vom Jahre 1873*. Vienna: Wilhelm Frick, 1883.

Lipartito, Kenneth D. "Reassembling the Economic: New Departures in Historical Materialism." *American Historical Review* 121 (2016): 101–139.

Lotz, Walther. "Die Währungsfrage in Oesterreich-Ungarn und ihre wirtschaftliche und politische Bedeutung." *Jahrbuch für Gesetzgebung, Verwaltung und Volkswirtschaft im Deutschen Reich* 13 (1889): 15–53.

Lubetkin, Michael J. *Jay Cooke's Gamble: The Northern Pacific Railroad, the Sioux, and the Panic of 1873*. Norman: University of Oklahoma Press, 2006.

Luhmann, Niklas. *Vertrauen: Ein Mechanismus der Reduktion sozialer Komplexität*, 2nd rev. ed. Stuttgart: Ferdinand Enke, 1973.

L. W. Hamilton & Co. *Stock Speculation*. New York, 1875. Baker Library, Harvard Business School.

Machtan, Lothar. *Streiks und Aussperrungen im Deutschen Kaiserreich*. Berlin: Colloquium Verlag, 1984.

Madison, James H. "The Evolution of Commercial Credit Reporting Agencies in Nineteenth-Century America." *Business History Review* 48 (1974): 164–186.

Magee, Gary B., and Andrew S. Thompson. *Empire and Globalisation: Networks of People, Goods and Capital in the British World, c. 1850–1914*. Cambridge: Cambridge University Press, 2010.

Marco, Luc. "Les faillites en France pendant la longue stagnation." In *La longue stagnation en France: L'autre grande depression 1873–1897*, ed. Yves Breton, Albert Broder, and Michel Lutfalla. Paris: Editions economica, 1997.

Marichal, Carlos. *A Century of Debt Crises in Latin America: From Independence to the Great Depression, 1820–1930*. Princeton: Princeton University Press, 1989.

Marschall, H. v. "Ursache und Verlauf der Wiener Börsen-Katastrophe." *Welthandel* (1874): 1–6.

Martin, Albro. "Railroads and Equity Receivership: An Essay on Institutional Change." *Journal of Economic History* 34 (1974): 685–709.

Marx, Karl, and Frederick Engels. *The Communist Manifesto*. London: Verso, 2012 [1888].

März, Eduard. *Österreichische Industrie- und Bankpolitik in der Zeit Franz Josephs I: Am Beispiel der k. k. priv. Österreichischen Credit-Anstalt für Handel und Gewerbe.* Vienna: Europa-Verlag, 1968.

Matis, Herbert. *Österreichs Wirtschaft 1848–1913: Konjunkturelle Dynamik und gesellschaftlicher Wandel im Zeitalter Franz Josephs I.* Berlin: Duncker & Humblot, 1972.

Matschoß, Conrad, ed. *Werner Siemens: Ein kurzgefaßtes Lebensbild nebst einer Auswahl seiner Briefe: Aus Anlass der 100. Wiederkehr seines Geburtstages.* Vol. 2. Berlin: Julius Springer, 1916.

McCartney, E. Ray. *Crisis of 1873.* Minneapolis: Burgess, 1935.

McKeown, Adam. "Periodizing Globalization." *History Workshop Journal* 61 (2007): 218–230.

Medbery, James K. *Men and Mysteries of Wall Street.* Westport, Conn.: Greenwood Press, 1968 [1870].

Mendelssohn, Peter de. *Zeitungsstadt Berlin: Menschen und Mächte in der Geschichte der deutschen Presse.* Berlin: Ullstein, 1959.

Meyer, Rudolph. *Politische Gründer und die Corruption in Deutschland.* Leipzig: Bidder, 1877.

——. *Ursachen der amerikanischen Concurrenz: Ergebnisse einer Studienreise.* Berlin: Bahr, 1883.

Michaels, Walter Benn. *The Gold Standard and the Logic of Naturalism.* Berkeley: University of California Press, 1987.

Michie, Ranald C. *The London and New York Stock Exchanges, 1850–1914.* London: Allen & Unwin, 1987.

——. *The City of London: Continuity and Change, 1850–1990.* Basingstoke: Macmillan, 1992.

Miller, George H. *Railroads and the Granger Laws.* Madison: University of Wisconsin Press, 1971.

Miller, Harry E. "Earlier Theories of Crises and Cycles in the United States." *Quarterly Journal of Economics* 38, no. 2 (1924): 294–329.

Minoprio, Jonas. *Die Frankfurter Börse: Handbuch für Banquiers, Makler und Capitalisten enthaltend eingehende Erklärung aller an der Frankfurter Börse gültigen Usancen und gehandelten Papiere.* Frankfurt am Main: F. Boselli'sche Buchhandlung, 1873.

Mitchell, Lawrence E. *The Speculation Economy: How Finance Triumphed over Industry.* San Francisco: Berret-Koehler, 2006.

Mitchell, Timothy. "Economics: Economists and the Economy in the Twentieth Century." In *The Politics of Method in the Human Sciences,* ed. George Steinmetz, 126–141. Durham: Duke University Press, 2005.

Mixon, Scott. "The Crisis of 1873: Perspective from Multiple Asset Classes." *Journal of Economic History* 68 (2008): 722–757.

Moeller, Justinus. *Gründerprocesse: Eine criminalpolitische Studie.* Berlin: Julius Springer, 1876.

Montgomery, David. *The Fall of the House of Labor: The Workplace, the State, and American Labor Activism, 1865–1925.* Cambridge: Cambridge University Press, 1987.

Morawetz, Victor. *A Treatise on the Law of Private Corporations.* 2nd ed., vol. 1. Boston: Little, Brown & Company, 1886.

Mork, Gordon R. "The Prussian Railway Scandal of 1873: Economics and Politics in the German Empire." *European Studies Review* 1 (1971): 35–48.

Mosse, Walter E. *Jews in the German Economy: The German-Jewish Economic Élite, 1820–1935.* Oxford: Oxford University Press, 1987.

Müller, Leonhard. *Der Kampf zwischen politischem Katholizismus und Bismarcks Politik im Spiegel der Schlesischen Volkszeitung: Ein Beitrag zur schlesischen Kirchen-, Parteien- und Zeitungsgeschichte.* Breslau: Müller & Seiffert, 1929.

Müller, Simone M. *Wiring the World: The Social and Cultural Creation of Global Telegraph Networks.* New York: Columbia University Press, 2016.

Murphy, Sharon Ann. *Investing in Life: Insurance in Antebellum America.* Baltimore: Johns Hopkins University Press, 2010.

Myers, Margaret G. *The New York Money Market: Origins and Development.* New York: Columbia University Press, 1931.

Nasse, Erwin. "Ueber die Verhütung der Produktionskrisen durch staatliche Fürsorge." *Jahrbuch für Gesetzgebung, Verwaltung und Volkswirtschaft im Deutschen Reich* 3 (1879): 145–189.

Negrin, Anton. *Die Entwicklung der Wiener Börse (Effektensektion): Von ihrer Gründung bis zum Ausbruch des Weltkriegs (1771–1914): Eine betriebswirtschaftliche Untersuchung, Teildruck.* Dissertation. Vienna: Hochschule für Welthandel, 1937.

Neidlinger, Karl. *Studien zur Geschichte der deutschen Effektenspekulation von ihren Anfängen bis zum Beginn der Eisenbahnspekulation.* Jena: Fischer, 1930.

Nelson, Scott Reynolds. *A Nation of Deadbeats: An Uncommon History of America's Financial Disasters.* New York: Alfred A. Knopf, 2012.

Neuwirth, Joseph. *Die Spekulationskrisis von 1873.* Leipzig: Duncker & Humblot, 1874.

Neydl, Ant. Wilhelm. *Die wirthschaftlichen Zustände Oesterreichs: Vortrag gehalten im Handels- und Gewerbe-Vereine Sechshaus.* Vienna: A. Hartleben, 1876.

Nocken, Ulrich. "Die Große Deflation: Goldstandard, Geldmenge und Preise in den USA und Deutschland 1870 bis 1896." In *Geld und Währung vom 16. Jahrhundert bis zur Gegenwart,* ed. Eckart Schremmer, 157–189. Stuttgart: Franz Steiner, 1993.

Nugent, Walter T. K. *Money and American Society, 1865–1880.* New York: Free Press, 1968.

——. *Crossings: The Great Transatlantic Migrations, 1870–1914.* Bloomington: Indiana University Press, 1992.

Oberholtzer, Ellis P. *Jay Cooke: Financier of the Civil War.* Vol. 2. Philadelphia: George W. Jacobs & Co., 1907.

Oechelhaeuser, Wilhelm. *Die wirthschaftliche Krisis.* Berlin: Springer, 1876.

Olegario, Rowena. *A Culture of Credit: Embedding Trust and Transparency in American Business.* Cambridge, Mass.: Harvard University Press, 2006.

O'Rourke, Kevin H., and Jeffrey G. Williamson. *Globalization and History: The Evolution of a Nineteenth-Century Atlantic Economy.* Cambridge, Mass.: MIT Press, 1999.

Osterhammel, Jürgen, and Niels P. Petersson. *Globalization: A Short History.* Princeton: Princeton University Press, 2005.

O'Sullivan, Mary. *Dividends of Development: Securities Markets in the History of US Capitalism, 1866–1922.* Oxford: Oxford University Press, 2016.

Ott, Julia C. *When Wall Street Met Main Street: The Quest for an Investor's Democracy.* Cambridge, Mass.: Harvard University Press, 2011.

Palen, Marc-William. *The "Conspiracy" of Free Trade: The Anglo-American Struggle over Empire and Economic Globalization, 1846–1896.* Cambridge: Cambridge University Press, 2016.

Parsons, Wayne. *The Power of the Financial Press: Journalism and Economic Opinion in Britain and America.* Aldershot: Elgar, 1989.

Paul, Helen J. *The South Sea Bubble: An Economic History of Its Origins and Consequences.* London: Routledge, 2011.

Pemsel, Jutta. "Die Wiener Weltausstellung von 1873." In *Traum und Wirklichkeit: Wien 1870–1930,* 62–67. Vienna: Historisches Museum der Stadt Wien, 1985.

Perkins, Edwin J. "In the Eyes of the Storm: Isaac Seligman and the Panic of 1873." *Business History* 56 (2014): 1129–1142.

Perrot, Franz. *Der Bank-, Börsen- und Actienschwindel: Eine Hauptursache der drohenden socialen Gefahr. Beiträge zur Kritik der politischen Oekonomie.* Rostock: Ernst Kuhn, 1876.

Pfafferoth, Carl. *Preußische Beamten-Gesetzgebung: Enthaltend die wichtigsten Beamtengesetze in Preußen.* 3rd rev. ed. Berlin: J. Guttentag, 1896.

Pingel, Norman-Mathias. "Gründerkrach in Braunschweig." *Braunschweigisches Jahrbuch für Landesgeschichte* 83 (2002): 223–232.

Platt, Potter. *Treatise on the Law of Corporations: General and Local, Public and Private, Aggregate and Sole.* Vol. 2. New York: Banks & Bros., 1879.

Plumpe, Werner. "Korruption: Annäherung an ein historisches und gesellschaftliches Phänomen." *Historische Zeitschrift* 48 (2009): 19–47.

Pohl, Hans. *Aufbruch der Weltwirtschaft: Geschichte der Weltwirtschaft von der Mitte des 19. Jahrhunderts bis zum Ersten Weltkrieg.* Stuttgart: Franz Steiner, 1989.

Pohle Fraser, Monika. "Bankiers und 'Hasardeure'—Die Rolle bürgerlicher Tugenden im Bankgeschäft, 1800–1912." In *Bankiers und Finanziers—sozialgeschichtliche Aspekte*, ed. Harald Wixforth, 57–79. Stuttgart: Franz Steiner, 2004.

Poling, Kristin. "Shantytowns and Pioneers beyond the City Wall: Berlin's Urban Frontier in the Nineteenth Century." *Central European History* 47 (2014): 245–274.

Porter, Theodore M. *The Rise of Statistical Thinking, 1820–1900.* Princeton: Princeton University Press, 1986.

Preda, Alex. "The Rise of the Popular Investor: Financial Knowledge and Investing in England and France, 1840–1880." *Sociological Quarterly* 42 (2001): 205–232.

——. *Framing Finance: The Boundaries of Markets and Modern Capitalism.* Chicago: University of Chicago Press, 2009.

Priemel, Kim Christian, "Spekulation als Gegenstand historischer Forschung." *Jahrbuch für Wirtschaftsgeschichte* 52, no. 2 (2013): 9–26.

Proudhon, Pierre-Joseph. *Manuel du Spéculateur à la Bourse.* Paris: Garnier Frères, 1854.

Pulzer, Peter. *The Rise of Political Anti-Semitism in Germany and Austria.* Rev. ed. London: Peter Halban, 1988.

Raasch, Markus. *Der Adel auf dem Feld der Politik: Das Beispiel der Zentrumspartei in der Bismarckära (1871–1890).* Düsseldorf: Droste, 2015.

Radu, Robert. *Auguren des Geldes: Eine Kulturgeschichte des Finanzjournalismus in Deutschland 1850–1914.* Göttingen: Vandenhoeck & Ruprecht, 2017.

Die Rechtsprechung des Königlichen Ober-Tribunals in Strafsachen. Berlin: Georg Reimer, 1861–1879.

Redlich, Fritz. *The Molding of American Banking: Men and Ideas.* Part 2, *1840–1910.* New York: Hafner, 1951.

Reich, Josef. *Die Wiener Presse und der Wiener Börsenkrach von 1873 im wechselseitigen Förderungsprozess.* PhD diss., Vienna University, 1947.

Reich, Norbert. "Die Entwicklung des deutschen Aktienrechts im 19. Jahrhundert." *Jus Commune* 2 (1969): 239–276.

Reichsoberhandelsgericht. "Gutachten über die geeignetsten Mittel zur Abhülfe der nach den Erfahrungen des Reichs-Oberhandelsgerichts bei der Gründung, der Verwaltung und dem geschäftlichen Betriebe von Aktienunternehmungen hervorgetretenen Uebelstände, March 31, 1877." In *Hundert Jahre modernes Aktienrecht: Eine Sammlung von Quellen und Texten zur Aktienrechtsreform von 1884 mit zwei Einführungen*, ed. Werner Schubert and Peter Hommelhoff, 157–262. Berlin: de Gruyter, 1985.

Reick, Philipp. *"Labor Is Not a Commodity": The Movement to Shorten the Workday in Late Nineteenth-Century Berlin and New York*. Frankfurt am Main: Campus, 2016.

Reindl, Josef. *Der Deutsch-Österreichische Telegraphenverein und die Entwicklung des deutschen Telegraphenwesens 1850–1871: Eine Fallstudie zur administrativ-technischen Kooperation deutscher Staaten vor der Gründung des Deutschen Reiches*. Frankfurt am Main: Peter Lang, 1993.

Renehan Jr., Edward J. *Commodore: The Life of Cornelius Vanderbilt*. New York: Basic Books, 2007.

Renzsch, Wolfgang. *Handwerker und Lohnarbeiter in der frühen Arbeiterbewegung: Zur sozialen Basis von Gewerkschaften und Sozialdemokratie im Reichsgründungsjahrzehnt*. Göttingen: Vandenhoeck & Ruprecht, 1981.

Report of the Special Committee on Railroads, Appointed under a Resolution of the Assembly, February 28, 1879, to Investigate Alleged Abuses in the Management of Railroads Chartered by the State of New York. Toronto: Globe, 1880.

Reti, Steven P. *Silver and Gold: The Political Economy of International Monetary Conferences, 1867–1892*. Westport, Conn.: Greenwood Press, 1998.

Rezneck, Samuel. "Distress, Relief, and Discontent in the United States during the Depression of 1873–78." *Journal of Political Economy* 58 (1950): 494–512.

Riesser, Jacob. *Die deutschen Großbanken und ihre Konzentration im Zusammenhang mit der Entwicklung der Gesamtwirtschaft in Deutschland*. Jena: Fischer, 1905ff.

Rischbieter, Julia Laura. *Mikro-Ökonomie der Globalisierung: Kaffee, Kaufleute und Konsumenten im Kaiserreich 1870–1914*. Cologne: Böhlau, 2011.

Ritter, Gretchen. *Goldbugs and Greenbacks: The Antimonopoly Tradition and the Politics of Finance in America*. Cambridge: Cambridge University Press, 1997.

Robb, George. *Ladies of the Ticker: Women and Wall Street from the Gilded Age to the Great Depression*. Urbana: University of Illinois Press, 2017.

Rockoff, Hugh. "Banking and Finance, 1789–1914." In *The Cambridge Economic History of the United States*, vol. 2, ed. Stanley L. Engerman and Robert E. Gallman, 643–684. Cambridge: Cambridge University Press, 2000.

Rodgers, Daniel T. *The Work Ethic in Industrial America*. 2nd ed. Chicago: University of Chicago Press, 2014.

Rohrer, Annelies. *Die Wiener Börse und ihre Besucher in den Jahren 1867–1875*. PhD diss., Vienna University, 1971.

Ronge, Ulrich. *Die langfristige Rendite deutscher Standardaktien: Konstruktion eines historischen Aktienindex ab Ultimo 1870 bis Ultimo 1959*. Frankfurt am Main: Peter Lang, 2002.

Rose, Kenneth D. *Unspeakable Awfulness: America through the Eyes of European Travelers, 1865–1900*. New York: Routledge, 2014.

Rosenberg, Hans. *Große Depression und Bismarckzeit: Wirtschaftsablauf, Gesellschaft und Politik in Mitteleuropa*. Berlin: de Gruyter, 1967.

——. *Die Weltwirtschaftskrise 1857–1859, mit einem Vorbericht*. Göttingen: Vandenhoeck & Ruprecht, 1974.

Rosenhaft, Eve. "Herz oder Kopf: Erfahrungsbildung beim Kauf von Aktien und Witwenrenten im norddeutschen Bildungsbürgertum des späten 18. Jahrhunderts." *Historische Anthropologie* 14 (2006): 349–369.

Rosenthal, Caitlin C. "From Memory to Mastery: Accounting for Control in America, 1750–1880." *Enterprise and Society* 14 (2013): 732–748.

Ross, Dorothy. *The Origins of American Social Science*. New York: Cambridge University Press, 2001.

Roth, Ralf. "Der Sturz des Eisenbahnkönigs Bethel Henry Strousberg: Ein jüdischer Wirtschaftsbürger in den Turbulenzen der Reichsgründung." *Jahrbuch für Antisemitismusforschung* 10 (2001): 86–112.

Rubrom, Moriz. *Neues Wiener Börse-Buch: Handbuch der Speculation.* 3rd improved and rev. ed. Vienna: Moriz Perles, 1873.

Saling, August. *Die Börsen-Papiere:* Part I., *Die Börse und die Börsengeschäfte.* 2nd expanded ed. Berlin, 1871.

Sammlung sämmtlicher Drucksachen des Hauses der Abgeordneten aus der XII: Legislatur-Periode, I. Session, 1873–1874, vol. 1. Berlin: W. Moeser, 1874.

Sandage, Scott A. *Born Losers: A History of Failure in America.* Cambridge, Mass.: Harvard University Press, 2005.

Schabas, Margaret. *The Natural Origins of Economics.* Chicago: University of Chicago Press, 2005.

Schäfer, Karl-Christian. *Deutsche Portfolioinvestitionen im Ausland 1870–1914: Banken, Kapitalmärkte und Wertpapierhandel im Zeitalter des Imperialismus.* Münster: Lit, 1995.

Schäffle, Albert. "Der 'grosse Börsenkrach' des Jahres 1873." *Zeitschrift für die gesamte Staatswissenschaft* 30 (1874): 1–94.

Schmidt, Alexander. *Reisen in die Moderne: Der Amerika-Diskurs des deutschen Bürgertums im europäischen Vergleich.* Berlin: Akademie Verlag, 1997.

Schößler, Franziska. *Börsenfieber und Kaufrausch: Ökonomie, Judentum und Weiblichkeit bei Theodor Fontane, Heinrich Mann, Thomas Mann, Arthur Schnitzler und Émile Zola.* Bielefeld: Aisthesis, 2009.

Schubert, Werner. "Die Entstehung des Aktiengesetzes von 1884." In *Hundert Jahre modernes Aktienrecht: Eine Sammlung von Quellen und Texten zur Aktienrechtsreform von 1884 mit zwei Einführungen,* ed. Werner Schubert and Peter Hommelhoff, 3–50. Berlin: de Gruyter, 1985.

Schulz, Wolfgang. *Das deutsche Börsengesetz: Die Entstehungsgeschichte und wirtschaftlichen Auswirkungen des Börsengesetzes von 1896.* Frankfurt am Main: Lang, 1994.

Schumann, Dirk. "Der Fall Adele Spitzeder 1872: Eine Studie zur Mentalität der 'kleinen Leute' in der Gründerzeit." *Zeitschrift für bayerische Landesgeschichte* 58 (1995): 991–1025.

Schumpeter, Joseph A. *Business Cycles: A Theoretical, Historical, and Statistical Analysis of the Capitalist Process.* 2 vols. New York: McGraw Hill, 1939.

Sewell, William H. "Economic Crises and the Shape of Modern History." *Public Culture* 24 (2012): 303–327.

Sexton, Jay. *Debtor Diplomacy: Finance and American Foreign Relations in the Civil War Era, 1837–1873.* Oxford: Oxford University Press, 2005.

Sharkey, Robert. *Money, Class, and Party: An Economic Study of Civil War and Reconstruction.* Baltimore: Johns Hopkins University Press, 1959.

Simon, Matthew. *Cyclical Fluctuations and the International Capital Movements of the United States, 1865–1897.* New York: Arno Press, 1978.

Sklansky, Jeffrey. *The Soul's Economy: Market Society and Selfhood in American Thought, 1820–1920.* Chapel Hill: University of North Carolina Press, 2002.

——. "Labor, Money, and the Financial Turn in the History of Capitalism." *Labor: Studies in the Working-Class History of the Americas* 11 (2014): 32–46.

Slobodian, Quinn. "How to See the World Economy: Statistics, Maps, and Schumpeter's Camera in the First Age of Globalization." *Journal of Global History* 10 (2015): 307–332.

Slotkin, Richard. *The Fatal Environment: The Myth of the Frontier in the Age of Industrialization, 1800–1890.* New York: Atheneum, 1985.

Smith, Adam I. P. "Land of Opportunity?" In *America Imagined: Explaining the United States in Nineteenth-Century Europe and Latin America*, ed. Axel Körner, Nicola Miller, and Adam I. P. Smith, 10–49. New York: Palgrave Macmillan, 2012.

Sobel, Robert. *The Big Board: A History of the New York Stock Market*. New York: Free Press, 1965.

Soetbeer, Adolf. *Die 5 Milliarden: Betrachtungen über die Folgen der großen Kriegsentschädigung für die Wirthschaftsverhältnisse Frankreichs und Deutschlands*. Berlin: Habel, 1874.

Spielhagen, Friedrich. *Sturmflut*. 16th ed. 2 vols. Leipzig: L. Staackmann, 1902 [1877].

Sprague, Oliver M. W. *History of Crises under the National Banking System*. Washington, DC: Government Printing Office, 1910.

Sproat, John G. *"The Best Men": Liberal Reformers in the Gilded Age*. New York: Oxford University Press, 1968.

Stäheli, Urs. *Spektakuläre Spekulation: Das Populäre der Ökonomie*. Frankfurt am Main: Suhrkamp, 2007.

Steeples, Douglas. *Advocate for American Enterprise: William Buck Dana and the Commercial and Financial Chronicle*. Westport, Conn.: Greenwood Press, 2002.

Stenographische Berichte über die Verhandlungen des Deutschen Reichstags. Berlin: Buchdruckerei der "Norddeutschen Allgemeinen Zeitung", 1871–1918.

Stenographische Berichte über die Verhandlungen des Preußischen Abgeordnetenhauses. Berlin: W. Moeser, 1866–1918.

Stenographische Berichte über die Verhandlungen des Preußischen Herrenhauses. Berlin: W. Moeser, 1866–1918.

Stern, Fritz. "Money, Morals, and the Pillars of Bismarck's Society." *Central European History* 3 (1970): 49–72.

——. *Gold and Iron: Bismarck, Bleichröder, and the Building of the German Empire*. New York: Alfred A. Knopf, 1977.

Stoetzler, Marcel. *The State, the Nation, and the Jews: Liberalism and the Antisemitism Dispute in Bismarck's Germany*. Lincoln: University of Nebraska Press, 2008.

Stöpel, Franz. *Die Handelskrisis in Deutschland*. Frankfurt am Main: Expedition des 'Merkur', 1875.

Strong, George Templeton. *The Diary of George Templeton Strong: Post-War Years, 1865–1875*. Ed. Allan Nevins and Milton Halsey Thomas. New York: Macmillan, 1952.

Sturm, James Lester. *Investing in the United States, 1798–1893: Upper Wealth-Holders in a Market Economy*. New York: Arno Press, 1977.

Summers, Mark Wahlgren. *The Era of Good Stealings*. New York: Oxford University Press, 1993.

——. *Party Games: Getting, Keeping, and Using Power in Gilded Age Politics*. Chapel Hill: University of North Carolina Press, 2004.

Sumner, William G. *A History of American Currency*. New York: Henry Holt, 1875.

Suter, Mischa. *Rechtstrieb: Schulden und Vollstreckung im liberalen Kapitalismus 1800–1900*. Konstanz: Konstanz University Press, 2016.

Swain, Henry H. "Economic Aspects of Railroad Receiverships." *Economic Studies* 3 (1898): 54–161.

Tanner, Jakob. "Wirtschaftskurven: Zur Visualisierung des anonymen Marktes." In *Ganz normale Bilder: Historische Beiträge zur visuellen Herstellung von Selbstverständlichkeit*, ed. David Gugerli and Barbara Orland, 129–158. Zurich: Chronos, 2002.

Thiemeyer, Guido. "Die deutschen Liberalen, die Reichsgründung und die Entstehung des internationalen Goldstandards 1870–1873." In *Geschichte der internationalen Beziehungen:*

Erneuerung und Erweiterung einer historischen Disziplin, ed. Eckart Conze, 139–167. Cologne: Böhlau, 2004.

Thompson, Edward P. "The Moral Economy of the English Crowd in the Eighteenth Century." *Past and Present* 50 (1971): 76–136.

Tooze, J. Adam. *Statistics and the German State, 1900–1945: The Making of Modern Economic Knowledge*. Cambridge: Cambridge University Press, 2001.

Torp, Cornelius. *The Challenge of Globalization: Economics and Politics in Germany 1860–1914*. New York: Berghahn Books, 2015.

Tumbridge & Co. *Secrets of Success in Wall Street*. New York, 1875. Baker Library, Harvard Business School.

Twain, Mark, and Charles Dudley Warner. *The Gilded Age: A Tale of Today*. Seattle: University of Washington Press, 1968 [1873].

Tufano, Peter. "Business Failure, Judicial Intervention, and Financial Innovation: Restructuring U.S. Railroads in the Nineteenth Century." *Business History Review* 71 (1997): 1–40.

Unger, Irwin. *The Greenback Era: A Social and Political History of American Finance, 1865–1879*. Princeton: Princeton University Press, 1964.

Verhandlungen des Strafprozesses, die Gründung des Braunschweiger Walzwerks betreffend, nebst Gutachten. Braunschweig: Vieweg, 1878.

Verhandlungen des Vereins für Socialpolitik am 12. und 18. October 1873. Leipzig: Duncker & Humblot, 1874.

Villard, Henry. *Memoirs of Henry Villard, Journalist and Financier: 1835–1900*, vol. 2. Boston: Houghton, Mifflin, 1904.

Vogl, Joseph. *The Specter of Capital*. Stanford: Stanford University Press, 2014.

Volkov, Shulamit. *Germans, Jews, and Antisemites: Trials in Emancipation*. New York: Cambridge University Press, 2006.

Wadhwani, R. Daniel. "Protecting Small Savers: The Political Economy of Economic Security." *Journal of Policy History* 18 (2006): 126–145.

Wadl, Wilhelm. *Liberalismus und soziale Frage in Österreich: Deutschliberale Reaktionen und Einflüsse auf die frühe österreichische Arbeiterbewegung*. Vienna: Verlag der Österreichischen Akademie der Wissenschaften, 1987.

Wagner, Adolf. *Grundlegung der politischen Ökonomie*. Part 2. 3rd ed. Leipzig: Winter, 1894.

Walker, Francis A. *International Bimetallism*. New York: Henry Holt, 1896.

Waltershausen, August Sartorius von. *Die Entstehung der Weltwirtschaft: Geschichte des zwischenstaatlichen Wirtschaftslebens vom letzten Viertel des achtzehnten Jahrhunderts bis 1914*. Jena: Fischer, 1931.

Weber, Bruno. *Einige Ursachen der Wiener Krisis vom Jahre 1873*. Leipzig: Veit, 1874.

Weber, Max. "Börsenwesen: Schriften und Reden 1893–1898." In *Max Weber Gesamtausgabe*, vol. 5.2, ed. Knut Borchardt. Tübingen: Mohr Siebeck, 2000.

Wehler, Hans-Ulrich. *Deutsche Gesellschaftsgeschichte*. Vol. 3, *Von der "deutschen Doppelrevolution" zum Ausbruch des Ersten Weltkriegs 1849–1914*. Munich: Beck, 1995.

Weigt, Anja. *Der deutsche Kapitalmarkt vor dem Ersten Weltkrieg—Gründerboom, Gründerkrise und Effizienz des deutschen Aktienmarktes bis 1914*. Frankfurt am Main: Knapp, 2005.

Weiland, Daniela. *Otto Glagau und 'Der Kulturkämpfer': Zur Entstehung des modernen Antisemitismus im frühen Kaiserreich*. Berlin: Metropol, 2004.

Wellhöner, Volker, and Harald Wixforth. "Finance and Industry." In *Germany: A New Social and Economic History*, vol. 3, ed. Sheilagh Ogilvie, 152–191. London: Arnold, 2003.

Welskopp, Thomas. *Das Banner der Brüderlichkeit: Die deutsche Sozialdemokratie vom Vormärz bis zum Sozialistengesetz*. Bonn: Dietz, 2000.

Wentzcke, Paul, ed. *Im Neuen Reich 1871–1890: Politische Briefe aus dem Nachlaß liberaler Parteiführer*. Bonn: Kurt Schroeder, 1926.

Werner, Walter, and Steven T. Smith. *Wall Street*. New York: Columbia University Press, 1991.

White, Horace. "The Financial Crisis in America." *Fortnightly Review*, June 1876, 810–829.

——. "Commercial Crises." In *Lalor's Cyclopedia of Political Science, Political Economy and Political History of the United States*, ed. John J. Lalor, 524–530. New York: Maynard, Merrill, 1881.

White, Richard. "Information, Markets, and Corruption: Transcontinental Railroads in the Gilded Age." *Journal of American History* 90 (2003): 19–43.

——. *Railroaded: The Transcontinentals and the Making of Modern America*. New York: Norton, 2011.

Wicker, Elmus. *Banking Panics of the Gilded Age*. Cambridge: Cambridge University Press, 2000.

Wiener, Heinrich, Julian Goldschmidt, and Jakob Friedrich Behrend. *Zur Reform des Actiengesellschaftswesens: Drei Gutachten auf Veranlassung der Eisenacher Versammlung zur Besprechung der socialen Frage*. Leipzig: Duncker & Humblot, 1873.

Wilke, Jürgen. *Grundzüge der Medien- und Kommunikationsgeschichte*. 2nd ed. Cologne: Böhlau, 2008.

Wilkins, Mira. *The History of Foreign Investment in the United States to 1914*. Cambridge, Mass.: Harvard University Press, 1989.

Wilmanns, Carl. *Die "goldene" Internationale und die Nothwendigkeit einer socialen Reformpartei*. Berlin: Niendorf, 1876.

Wilson, Ted. *Battles for the Standard: Bimetallism and the Spread of the Gold Standard in the Nineteenth Century*. Aldershot: Ashgate, 2000.

Winckler, Johann. *Die periodische Presse Oesterreichs: Eine historisch-statistische Studie*. Vienna: Leopold Sommer, 1875.

Winkel, Harald. "Die Entwicklung der Geldtheorie in der deutschen Nationalökonomie des 19. Jahrhunderts und die Gründung der Reichsbank." In *Wissenschaft und Kodifikation des Privatrechts im 19. Jahrhundert*, vol. 5, ed. Helmut Coing and Walter Wilhelm, 1–26. Frankfurt am Main: Klostermann, 1980.

Winseck, Dwayne. "Double-Edged Swords: Communications Media and the Global Financial Crisis of 1873." In *International Communication and Global News Networks: Historical Perspectives*, ed. Peter Putnis, Chandrika Kaul, and Jürgen Wilke, 55–81. New York: Hampton Press, 2011.

Wirth, Max. *Geschichte der Handelskrisen*. Several eds. Frankfurt am Main: J. D. Sauerländer, 1858/1874/1890.

——. *Die Reform der Umlaufsmittel im Deutschen Reiche: Ein Nachtrag zur 'Geschichte der Handelskrisen'*. Frankfurt am Main: J. D. Sauerländer, 1875.

Witte, Andreas. "Zum Golde drängte alles? Die Genese des klassischen Goldstandards, diskretionäre Notenbankpolitik und das Klischee von Mythos versus Realität." *Bankhistorisches Archiv* 37 (2011): 1–61.

Wladika, Michael. *Hitlers Vätergeneration: Die Ursprünge des Nationalsozialismus in der k.u.k. Monarchie*. Vienna: Böhlau, 2005.

Wright, Robert E. *Corporation Nation*. Philadelphia: University of Pennsylvania Press, 2014.

——. "Capitalism and the Rise of the Corporation Nation." In *Capitalism Takes Command: The Social Transformation of Nineteenth-Century America*, ed. Michael Zakim and Gary J. Kornblith, 145–168. Chicago: University of Chicago Press, 2012.

Wuttke, Heinrich. *Die deutschen Zeitschriften und die Entstehung der öffentlichen Meinung: Ein Beitrag zur Geschichte des Zeitungswesens.* 2nd ed. Leipzig: Krüger, 1875.

Yeager, Leland B. "Fluctuating Exchange Rates in the Nineteenth Century: The Experience of Austria and Russia." In *Monetary Problems of the International Economy,* ed. Robert A. Mundell and Alexander K. Swoboda, 61–89. Chicago: University of Chicago Press: 1969.

Zimmerman, Andrew. *Alabama in Africa: Booker T. Washington, the German Empire, and the Globalization of the New South.* Princeton: Princeton University Press, 2010.

Zimmerman, David A. *Panic! Markets, Crises, and Crowds in American Fiction.* Chapel Hill: University of North Carolina Press, 2006.

Zucker, Stanley. *Ludwig Bamberger: German Liberal Politician and Social Critic, 1823–1899.* Pittsburgh: University of Pittsburgh Press, 1975.

INDEX

Adams, Charles F., Jr., 119
Adams, Henry, 119
Africa, 150
African Americans, 46, 106
agriculture, 3, 63, 102
Aktionär, Der, 20, 27, 40, 41, 42, 44, 47, 56, 59
Alsace, 72
American Railroad Journal. See *Railroad Journal*
Ames, Oakes, 120
Annapolis & Elk Ridge Railroad, 75
anti-Semitism, 20, 95, 102, 114–116, 119, 123–124
Appleton, Wisconsin, 76
aristocracy, 122, 186n97
Asia, xvi, 150
Associated Press, 9, 26
asymmetric information, 32, 38, 167n86
Austria: American perceptions of, 61–62; and anti-Semitism, 119; culture of, 96; and corruption, 116–119; currency, 62, 83–85, 91, 149; economic depression, 73–74, 102–103; economic development of, xvi, 2–3; government of, 101–102, 136–137; international trade, 149; savings banks, 107; state investment, 73, 80.

See also panic(s) of 1873: in Vienna; railroads, Austrian; Vienna
Austrian National Bank, 58
Austria: Tagblatt für Handel, Gewerbe und Communicationsmittel, 27
A. W. Sprague, 76

Bagehot, Walter, xii, 151
Bamberger, Ludwig, 85, 87
Bancroft, George, 69, 92
bank act (Austria), 58, 73
Bankers' Magazine, 11, 17, 27, 48, 64, 95, 96
bank notes, 86–87
Bank of California, 64
Bank of England, xi, 60, 62, 70, 82, 173n99, 178n41
bankruptcy, 80, 101, 110, 139, 181
banks, bankers: after the panics, 101; banks of issue, 86–87; buying and selling securities, ix, 8, 40; criticism of banking power, 151–152; and currency reform, 81; during the panics of 1873, 58, 64, 68, 173n86; failures, 64, 68; financial capitalism, 152; as investment advisers, 35–36; investment banks, 4, 142, 152, 193n72; investment in, 36; networks of, 36–37, 39, 66; newspapers, 29; in New